CONTENTS

ILLUSTRATIONS

INTRODUCTION

"I HAD the pleasure of seeing him but once, when he called on me . . . at Elmwood," wrote James Russell Lowell, "but the image of his shining presence is among the friendliest in my memory."[1] Those who knew him, almost without exception, have testified to the nobility of his character and the charm of his personality; but this tribute by a comparative stranger is the happiest phrase ever used of Sidney Lanier and aptly symbolizes the figure that emerges from the following pages. There are many standards for measuring the value of letters, but on one point there seems to be general agreement, namely, that they should reflect the writer. In his correspondence Lanier revealed himself with unusual candor. Only on the rarest occasions was he formal; with his friends, even those he had never met in the flesh, he was ingenuously confidential; from his wife, to whom nearly half of his surviving letters were addressed, he withheld nothing. The autobiographical record that follows, therefore, is a remarkably full one, especially on the human side—the life of the emotions and the spirit so essential to the understanding of a musician and lyric poet.

The external narrative is not so full, however, for Lanier seems by temperament to have preferred the elaboration of a passing mood or a fanciful sentiment to a sober transcript of facts. Early in his career he was sharply arraigned by his father for this tendency: "Letters however graceful which consist of mere emanations *from* the mind are never so interesting as those which are made up of *actualities*. . . . In other words, in writing to your friends put in plenty of facts, circumstances, & things pertaining to actual life as you see them or as they affect you";[2] but this sound advice was followed less by son than by father. Lanier himself for the most part clung to the *mélange* of his early favorite, the romantic Jean Paul, with whimsical digressions and evocations of mood, and always the "extra-leaf" of sentiment—especially in writing to his wife. Just what his letters lost in effectiveness thereby is demonstrated by the vivid accounts he sometimes rendered when a

---

[1] Letter to D. C. Gilman, Jan. 29, 1888, printed in *The Forty-Sixth Birthday of Sidney Lanier* (Baltimore, 1888), p. 25.

[2] See letters of May 7 and 12, 1863. Robert S. Lanier's letters are among the most interesting in the surviving collections, filled with crisp detail, terse observation, and witty comment in the best Augustan manner. See also Gertrude Lanier's letter about her brother to J. A. Fisher, Oct., 1883: "His letters to family and friends were gems of thought. One of us would say: 'he never writes us anything about himself!' His letters were full of flowery descriptions and beautiful imaginings." All letters referred to in this Introduction are printed or listed in vols. VII-X, unless otherwise indicated.

strikingly new scene or experience caught his imagination and held his pen closer to the actual, as in his descriptions of western immigrants and a stagecoach journey across the plains of Texas or in the account of his first meeting with the New York *literati* at the Century Club.[3] Fortunately there are enough of these to give the requisite bone and sinew to his total correspondence; and, even in the other vein, he rarely sank to the level of mere rhetoric, though his adoption of Elizabethan archaisms in writing to his family and intimate friends is a distinct handicap to the modern reader's enjoyment.[4] Ideally for posterity, the letters of a lyric poet should contain a just proportion of concrete factual narrative and of imaginative insight into the life of the emotions; and though one may wish that both were more abundant in Lanier's epistolary record, one feels that he wrote much as he talked, that his letters faithfully reflect his personality.

His intellectual life is not adequately represented here, however, and the purpose of this study is to fill in the musical, literary, and scholarly background that is missing in the letters, without attempting a full-length biographical sketch. All of the newly discovered material pertaining to his early life has been put in the notes and appendices. A separate volume on his war years and the writings growing out of them is now in preparation. And, in all likelihood, little new evidence will be turned up for the period of his law practice, 1868-1873, for during more than half of these five years he was prostrated with illness, and there was not much literary and musical activity at that time in small towns like Macon—or, with few exceptions, anywhere in America save in or near the large centers of population.[5] For these reasons the present inquiry will be limited to the last eight years of Lanier's life, when for the first time he gave himself wholeheartedly to a career

---

[3] Letters of Nov. 22, 23, 1872, and Oct. 4, 1875.

[4] See for example the complaint of E. G. Parker, agent of a literary bureau that was trying to place *Tiger-Lilies*, that Lanier used " antique " affectation of speech in his novel (letter of July 12, 1867). Lanier himself confessed to " redundancy " and a " tendency to a profusion of metaphors " in his letters as well as in his prose style (letter of Sept. 12, 1867).

[5] The appendices (vol. X) contain reminiscences by family and friends and all the known facts about his imprisonment at Point Lookout, 1864-1865. Garland Greever, editor of vol. V of the present edition, has been working for years on a book about Sidney and Clifford Lanier to be called " Troubadours in Grey." The files of the Montgomery *Advertiser* have been searched from 1866 to 1872; those of the Macon *Daily Telegraph* and the *Telegraph and Messenger* from 1860 to 1873, though none have been discovered for the period of Jan., 1867-July, 1871. Lanier's cultural life during these years consisted chiefly of participation in amateur musicales, companionship with his brother and literary lawyers like his father and uncle, and correspondence with Paul Hayne. All of this is fully represented in the letters and the notes thereto. Vol. VIII (1869-1873) can be thumbed lightly by the student of literature.

in art and literature. A sample of what his cultural life in Baltimore was like can be gained from the diary of a week's activities coaxed from him by his wife, February 26, 1875. But lacking many such ideal letters, the record must now be supplemented from outside sources.

When in September, 1873, Lanier set forth for the North, "armed only with a silver Boehm flute, and some dozen of steel pens," [6] his plans for a career wavered between music and poetry, and even his destination was somewhat vague. The best conjecture seems to be that his "true labor" was to be in the field of authorship, and that he hoped to support himself by playing the flute in Theodore Thomas's Orchestra.[7] New York was certainly the logical choice, for by the 1870's, with its publishing houses, magazines, and orchestras, it offered the best opportunities in America to both poet and musician. It was here that Lanier had found a market for his novel and his first poetry; it was here he had had his first experience of good music, especially at Thomas's concerts in the Central Park Garden, which drew from him the ecstasy of the novitiate.[8]

After the serious breakdown in his health and the long months of meditation in San Antonio during the winter of 1872-1873, when he determined to abandon Macon and the law, he turned to the composition of poems and music and to practicing on his newly acquired flute. Driven into the world of art by "an impulse, simply irresistible," as he declared, it was only natural that the Mecca of this world for him should be New York. Devoting himself at first to music, his hope for earning a living, he planned to take a few lessons from a Mr. Eben " to polish off one or two little faults in my amateur style"; won the plaudits of Frederick Schwaab, music critic of the *Times,* of A. G. Badger, flute-manufacturer, and of "the very best players" in the city; and received enthusiastic notices in the newspapers for what they called his "début" with the Symphonia Quartette Club at a concert in Brooklyn.[9] But after two months of skirmishing, he had found nothing more substantial in New York than praise. His real disappointment is revealed in two letters to his wife. On October 10, he wrote: " It *was* my hope to get an engagement as concert-soloist with Theodore Thomas: but he left town before I could find him." On November 16,

[6] Letter to Hayne, May 23, 1874. The phrase, though applied to a second trip to New York, summer 1874, equally fits the circumstances of the previous year.

[7] Letters of May 24, 26, 27, July 21, and Oct. 10, 1873. The statements of his plans vary with his moods and his correspondents.

[8] *Tiger-Lilies* was published by Hurd & Houghton in 1867 and a dozen poems in the *Round Table*, 1866-1868. For music see letters of Aug. 7, 13, 15, 1870.

[9] See letters to his wife, Sept. 23 (omitted); Oct. 6, 8, 10, 26; Nov. 16, 1873, and note 123.

making light of his performance in Brooklyn, he added: "When I am ready to come out, . . . I shall make my début under the auspices of the Philharmonic, or of Theodore Thomas,—or not at all." For three more years Lanier cherished the ambition of associating himself with Thomas, clearly the leading figure in the American orchestra of that day.[10] But this ambition was not to materialize, and New York was not to become the scene of his career in the world of art.

Instead, Lanier had to fall back on a second best. On the way to New York, probably realizing the difficulties of an unknown artist in the metropolis, he had stopped off in Baltimore, September 18-23, to see what possibilities might offer through his acquaintances there. For several years he had known Lawrence Turnbull and William Hand Browne, contributing occasionally to a magazine they edited, and quite recently Henry Clay Wysham, an amateur flutist.[11] Though the first two were later to aid him in many ways, it was Wysham who offered a helping hand at this juncture. Taking quite a fancy to Lanier, he introduced him to a large number of musical friends culminating with Asger Hamerik, director of the conservatory of the Peabody Institute, who was invited to Wysham's house to hear Lanier play. The audition was so successful that Hamerik made him a tentative offer of $120 a month to play first flute in the Peabody Orchestra, provided the trustees granted the necessary funds for its expansion; and Wysham promised enough pupils to bring this up to $200.[12] The warmth of Lanier's reception here undoubtedly did much to encourage him to pursue music as a career and, when his New York prospects failed, to begin it in Baltimore.

Hamerik was well aware he could not compete with such an orchestra as that of Theodore Thomas, but he held that organization up to his trustees as a model. When he went to New York in the autumn of 1873 to engage three new players peremptorily needed, he found that first-rate musicians wanted sixty dollars a week and none less than thirty, which was more than he could pay. But he finally located an oboe for twenty dollars and a bassoon for twelve—the salary paid to

[10] Theodore Thomas (1835-1905) did more than probably anyone else to develop the symphony orchestra in America. He was the conductor of his own orchestra from 1862, of the New York Philharmonic from 1877, and of the Chicago Symphony from 1891 until his death. (See John T. Howard, *Our American Music*, New York, 1939, pp. 294-305; and Charles E. Russell, *The American Orchestra and Theodore Thomas*, New York, 1927.)

[11] Turnbull, editor of the *New Eclectic*, 1868-1870, he had met in Macon (letter of Mar. 4, 1870, and note 16); Browne, editor of its successor, the *Southern Magazine*, he had not met but had corresponded with since 1871; Wysham he had apparently corresponded with and had bought through him his new flute (see notes 7 and 69, Letters of 1873).

[12] Letters to his wife and his father, Sept. 24, 1873.

the Baltimore players. On November 19 he made his last addition to
the orchestra, as he reported to the trustees: " I have engaged the first
Flute at a salary of $240 for the sixteen weeks. Mr. Lanier, from
Georgia, is a perfect gentlemen, and wanted to come to Baltimore for
his health's sake." [13] These new players, together with the twenty-six
local ones and additional brass instruments and harp on occasions,
constituted the orchestra that Lanier joined at the end of November,
1873, at half the salary he had been originally promised. It was not
Theodore Thomas's Orchestra, but it was a good beginning.

Baltimore, engrossed in commercial prosperity, had for years lagged
behind other cities of the eastern seaboard in cultural activities. But
during the 1870's three newly organized institutions, with all of which
Lanier became intimately connected, did much to improve this state of
affairs. The first of these was the Peabody Institute, endowed by a
successful merchant with a million and a half dollars. It embraced
several departments, two of which flourished and played a large part in
developing the city with which the rest of Lanier's life was to be identified, the Library and the Conservatory of Music.[14] An annual series
of concerts had been given for seven years (orchestral since 1868),
though at first they do not seem to have been taken very seriously.[15]

[13] See Hamerik's " Reports to the ' Committee on Music,' " Nov. 11, 21, 1873
(MSS, Peabody Library, Baltimore). Thomas's sixty players were paid $48,000
for the season, he pointed out; his own orchestra, of half that size, had cost a
little less than $6,000. See also Lanier's letters of Nov. 21, Dec. 16, 1873.

[14] The Gallery of Art never developed to any extent and was finally abandoned.
The School of Lectures was considerably more important. For Lanier's connection with this and with the Library, see pp. liv-lvii, below. The building,
dedicated in 1866, consisted of a large concert and lecture hall with the library
on the second floor. (See IX, 490, facing illustration; and the anonymous
pamphlet, The Peabody Institute. . . . Founder's Letters and Papers Relating to
its Dedication and History, Baltimore, 1868.)

[15] During the directorship of Southard (1868-1871), the provost advised the
trustees that the success of the concerts "should not divert attention from the
more important objects of the Institute, nor lead to lavish expenditures on
what borders so closely on mere amusement." (Second Annual Report of the
Provost to the Trustees of the Peabody Institute, Baltimore, 1869, pp. 25 ff.
See also the Third Annual Report, p. 29; Fourth, p. 24; Fifth, p. 20; and the
summary in the Tenth, pp. 20-22.) The concerts improved somewhat during
Southard's last two years, as indicated in the provost's estimate at the time of his
resignation: "There are, in this country, but four trained orchestras, which
undertake the regular production of the best musical compositions. The Peabody
orchestra, though by general consent not the first, can fairly claim an honorable
position among these organizations." Two of these he named as Thomas's
Orchestra (founded in 1862) and the Harvard Musical Association (orchestral
concerts since 1865) ; the third was the New York Philharmonic (1842), the
oldest in the country. Many orchestral organizations of one sort or another had
existed in America prior to this time, but in 1871 these four seem to have
been the only important permanent ones in the East. The Peabody was never to

Under a new director, however, the Peabody Orchestra began a promising period of development. Asger Hamerik, Danish composer and pupil of Gade, von Bülow, and Berlioz, arrived in Baltimore in 1871 with considerable prestige for one so young.[16] Energetic and resourceful, he turned his attention at first to problems of quality rather than quantity, and by the time Lanier joined the orchestra most of his goals had been achieved.[17] His strenuous appeals to the trustees had finally produced an appropriation that had enabled him to assemble a better though smaller band of musicians. Now he made his appeal to the public by offering weekly concerts throughout the season, eight with the " best soloists available," seven with student soloists— all with full orchestra based upon frequent rehearsals. The season opened auspiciously.[18]

For Lanier also it was a new and promising beginning. His delight in his new life in the world of music is amply testified to in his letters, but his own contribution to the orchestra and his reception in Baltimore must be filled in from other sources. His engagement had been heralded somewhat extravagantly in the local papers even before he arrived. He

take rank as a leading orchestra, but it deserves more attention than historians of music have accorded it. See N. H. Morison, *Management and Objects of the Peabody Institute*, Baltimore, 1871, pp. 32-37. See also Howard, *Our American Music*, New York, 1939, *passim*, who does not even mention the Peabody Orchestra, and who refers to Lanier merely as " the poet-musician who deserves a place in our music history " (p. 350).

[16] Grove's *Dictionary of Music and Musicians* (New York, 1934), II, 502, gives an account of intimate and privileged relationships with Berlioz which are not entirely borne out in the biography of that great master. However this may be, Hamerik (1843-1923) was later to win some distinction as the composer of a number of orchestral works, including six symphonies, several of which were performed by the Peabody during Lanier's membership and at least one had its première under Theodore Thomas.

[17] He had reorganized the Academy in order to make it a " University for Musical Art, and not a mere school for small girls." He had spent $6,000 on his musical library, so that it now included an excellent set of instruments, 255 volumes of scores, and 199 of parts for symphony music. (See the *Fifth Annual Report*, pp. 39-41; *Sixth*, pp. 18-20, 34-36.) To amalgamate the work of the conservatory and the orchestra, he instituted a series of " Musical Soirées " in 1871-1872 in which the professors and orchestral players performed exclusively for the benefit of the pupils. (See the etching reproduced in the present edition, VIII, facing 382. The performers listed on the programs of these Soirées indicate that this is a composite caricature. The six musicians here represented, all of whom became Lanier's friends, are authoritatively identified on the copy at the Maryland Historical Society in the handwriting of Wysham.) The next year these were replaced by fourteen concerts in which the students played with the orchestra.

[18] *Seventh Annual Report* (1874), pp. 22-24. The rehearsals had been stepped up from one or two to four a week. Hamerik reported only 29 in the orchestra on Nov. 21, 1875; but Lanier gave the figure as 35 in his letter of Dec. 9 (see also his letter of Jan. 8, 1874).

was described as a "masterly" performer on the Boehm flute who
"has made quite a sensation in New York, and . . . will, beyond
doubt, be a great ornament to the orchestra." A later notice reprinted
the eulogy on Lanier's performance in Brooklyn from the New York
Times, which had called him "a remarkably accomplished flautist, and
a performer of fine taste and culture," particularly praising his original
composition, "Blackbirds." [19] And it was with this piece—the one
he had played for Hamerik at their first meeting in September—that he
made his bow to Baltimore. A description of Lanier as he looked at
about this time has survived:

His eye, of bluish gray, was more spiritual than dreamy—except when
he was suddenly aroused, and then it assumed a hawk-like fierceness.
The transparent delicacy of his skin and complexion pleased the eye,
and his fine-textured hair, which was soft and almost straight and of a
light brown color, was combed behind the ear in Southern style. His
long beard, which was waving and pointed, had even at an early age
begun to show signs of turning gray. His nose was acquiline, his bearing was distinguished, and his manners were stamped with a high
breeding that befitted the "Cavalier" lineage. His hands were delicate
and white, by no means thin, and the fingers tapering. His gestures
were not many, but swift, graceful and expressive; the tone of his voice
was low; his figure was willowy and lithe; and in stature he seemed
tall, but in reality he was a little below six feet—withal there was a
native knightly grace which marked his every movement.[20]

Written by Henry Wysham, who played the flute beside him in the
Peabody Orchestra, this gives a fair picture of how Lanier appeared
when he was introduced to his Baltimore audience on December 6,
1873. For this initial concert Hamerik had skillfully constructed a
program to launch his bid for public support of his reorganized
orchestra. In addition to the announced numbers, moreover, he gave the
"overflowing and enthusiastic audience" a special treat by introducing
his new acquisitions, who responded with short pieces in solo. The
critic in the Baltimore *Gazette* declared that they "came fully up to the
reputation which had preceded them," and said specifically of Lanier
that his tone seemed particularly fitted for expressing the theme of his
decidedly original "Black-birds": "His performance was all that could
be desired for excellence and finish, and was warmly received." He

[19] Two unidentified clippings (Charles D. Lanier Collection), probably from
the Baltimore *Gazette*, whose music critic was Innes Randolph, an old friend
of Lanier's (see p. xxxiii, below).

[20] H. C. Wysham, "Sidney Lanier," *Independent*, XLIX, 1489-1490 (Nov.
18, 1897). This description has not been previously reprinted; compare the
photograph taken in the winter of 1874 and reproduced in the present edition
(IX, frontispiece).

concluded that this was "one of the very finest concerts ever given in this city" and congratulated Hamerik and the orchestra upon their "brilliant opening." [21]

Lanier's own comment on his performance was modest enough, as he wrote to his wife (Dec. 11): "[I] failed not,—though half dead with cold, and though called on unexpectedly." Two days before he said: "Hamerik is greatly pleased with my Orchestral playing." Lanier's success as first flute in the Peabody Orchestra is somewhat astonishing in view of his statements that he was "a raw player and a provincial withal, without practice, and guiltless of instruction," and that when he first took his place he did not even know the value of a dotted note and was "unacquainted even with the meaning of a Conductor's motions." [22] Though these comments are somewhat colored by Lanier's self-depreciation and his natural apprehensiveness over his lack of experience, they are more or less true. He was entirely self taught, and though he had been playing the flute all his life, he had always been strictly an amateur, unconnected with any but local music groups that were impermanent in nature and composed of players inferior to him in talent if not in training. However, set against his further statement that he was now playing in company "with old musicians most of whom have been playing ever since they were children and doing nothing else," with the implication that they were first-class professionals, the total impression is misleading.[23]

Actually, the personnel of the Peabody Orchestra in 1873 was largely made up of local talent, ranging all the way from the instructors in the Academy to semi-professional teachers and out-and-out amateurs, like Wysham, the Baltimore lawyer whose musical career was perhaps parallel to Lanier's. Few if any of them had had more than a limited experience in orchestral work. Only two or three were professionals brought in from the outside, and even these (see page x, above), could not be chosen from the top because of lack of funds. Lanier was not being pitted against the best musicians in America by long odds. Ac-

[21] Innes Randolph in the *Gazette*, Dec. 8, 1873. A program, preserved in the Lanier Room, Johns Hopkins University, shows that the concert began with Beethoven's *Fifth Symphony* and concluded with Hamerik's own *Nordische Suite*; the numbers in between featured the guest soloists, Miss Jenny Busk and Mme. Nanette Auerbach. Lanier's original musical compositions and estimates of him as a flutist are given below, pp. xx-xxi.

[22] Jan. 4 (to his brother) and May 23, 1874. See also the account by his close friend and admirer, Isabel L. Dobbin, "Lanier at the Peabody," *Peabody Bulletin*, pp. 4-5, Apr.-May, 1911.

[23] The quotation is from Lanier to his brother, Jan. 4, 1874. The best summary of the previously known facts in his musical career, both before and after 1873 (together with some legends and a few errors here corrected), is by A. H. Starke, "Sidney Lanier as a Musician," *Musical Quarterly*, XX, 384-400 (Oct., 1934).

cording to Isabel Dobbin, at that time one of the advanced pupils at the Academy who attended the rehearsals and played in the student concerts:

Our orchestra was composed chiefly of rather dingy old hack players, though some were of much better quality; and when Mr. Lanier, with his refined countenance and noble presence, took his place among them you felt that the level had been distinctly raised.

The truth probably lies somewhere between this extreme and Lanier's own account. His native talent and aptitude went far to make up for his lack of training, and much of the charm of his playing undoubtedly came from his felicitous improvisations and the poetic tone of his interpretations, as she and others have testified.[24] But he was also a conscientious musician, according to Wysham, the second flute:

His mere executive work in the Peabody Orchestra, where the writer sat beside him for several years, was done with a carefulness and precision worthy of a veteran of the band; and his sole aim, regardless of the temptation to express one's self, was to discover and aid in the interpretation of the composer's meaning; this done, he merged his individuality and became a part of the marvellous machinery of orchestration.[25]

[24] Dobbin, *op. cit.*, " Lanier's wonderful trills and roulades and soulful melodies completely captivated his audiences." See also Wysham, *op. cit.*, p. 1489: " His facile improvisations . . . were often a continuous flow of strange, fascinating arpeggios and trills, which it is quite certain the instrument could never voice in other hands "; and speaking of Lanier's performance of " Black-birds " at the opening concert: " [He played it] with tone of surpassing brilliancy and beauty, and . . . without accompaniment (or rather with an accompaniment of his devising by a roll of deep arpeggios in the lower octave)." A third tribute to his native skill was paid by his friend Ronald McDonald, critic of the New York *Times*: " Mr. Lanier's peculiarities in flute-playing are his cultivation of the low tones, . . . and of the *cantabile* style. Besides this, he is a thorough master of florid styles, executing the most brilliant passages with the utmost ease and grace. His facility in reading elaborate compositions at first sight is a marvel to all who have heard him." (Quoted in Earl Marble, " Sidney Lanier," *Cottage Hearth*, IV, 141, June, 1877.)

[25] Wysham, *loc. cit.* Louis J. Doetsch is said to have played second flute at the time Lanier joined the Peabody, but even then Wysham was apparently a member of the orchestra. When he left for California in 1879, he was succeeded by Frederick H. Gottlieb, whose reminiscences add an interesting note on Lanier's serious concern with orchestral music and his desire to spread its culture: " He had intended associating himself with a nonette club, consisting of himself, for flute; oboe, clarinet, basoon and french horn, and a string quartette, for the purpose of travelling throughout cities [of from three to twenty thousand inhabitants], performing original compositions for this combination as well as excerpts from the greater symphonic orchestral works, and thus educating the masses to an understanding of orchestral tone, and the relations, in an analytical form, which the wood wind instruments bore to the string family. . . . [And] it was his purpose, after each movement of a composition,

So Lanier took his place as an integral member of the orchestra, and as the winter progressed he broadened his acquaintance and his activities. As Miss Dobbin has recalled: " He was speedily in demand as soloist at all the musical organizations of the city."

This was true. Lanier had hoped to augment his meager salary by teaching and solo work. He decided against taking pupils, for reasons that are not entirely clear.[26] But, besides the occasional solos with the Peabody Orchestra for which he received extra compensation, the letters of 1874 are filled with references to his engagements to play at churches and with various orchestras and the German singing societies throughout the city, his solo parts in which are indicated in surviving programs. He kept his wife posted on his musical progress (Feb. 7): " How much I have learned in the last two months! I am not yet an artist, on the flute . . . and I would not call myself a virtuoso within a year." But he added (Feb. 12): " I have conquered myself a place, here, as an orchestral player," listing six of his recent outside engagements. He even joined the union on March 21, 1874, thus establishing himself as a professional musician; and after the Peabody season was over he went on a concert tour to West Virginia and Ohio as one of several instrumentalists accompanying Miss Jenny Busk.[27] How much he was paid for all this is not known, but it was probably a pittance. The middle western tour was a financial failure; and as early as Feb. 20 he was complaining to his wife that playing in local orchestras did not pay and, besides, was taking up too much of his time. It will be remembered that Lanier came to Baltimore as much to be an author as a musician, and as literary success came the following year the references to outside engagements became fewer. The next winter, he wrote: " As for the little side-playing I used to do, there is now none to be done." [28] But

to lecture on the same." (MS, written in 1904, Edwin Mims Collection, Johns Hopkins University. His published reminiscences in the Macon, Ga., *Telegraph*, Feb. 3, 1929, are much less significant and less reliable.) Gottlieb, who for two years not only played beside him in the Peabody Orchestra, but at his home in flute trios with Carl Wehner, Edward Heindel, and other artists visiting Baltimore, regarded Lanier as " one of the most finished flute virtuosos of his time."

[26] Letter of Jan. 20, 1874. There is only one piece of evidence that he taught the flute in Baltimore, and this is in a vague and unreliable reminiscence (see Eleanor Young, " The Trail of a Silver Flute," *Christian Science Monitor*, Sept. 12, 1931). He was never connected with the instructional staff of the Academy (letter to Price, Jan. 8, 1874).

[27] The last Peabody concert was on Mar. 28, the tour with Miss Busk Apr. 14-26. The programs of this tour and Lanier's union card are preserved in the Lanier Room. For an account of the various orchestras, theatres, singing societies, etc., of this period, see the articles by Otto Ortmann published under the title of " Musical Baltimore in the Seventies," Baltimore *Evening Sun*, July 8, 16, 1935, and *Peabody Bulletin*, pp. 42-43, Dec., 1937.

[28] Letter to his wife, Jan. 22, 1876. One of his last outside engagements was

during his first season in Baltimore, music was almost the whole of his life.

As concert succeeded concert at Peabody Hall, Lanier's enthusiasm mounted, and so apparently did that of the audience. The average attendance was three times what it had been the previous year, and on several occasions the hall was filled to capacity. Hamerik used every resource at his command to stimulate the public interest. Realizing that the chief of these was the soloists, he secured for the next year the continued services of the best of them, Mme. Auerbach, by making her professor of instrumental music. In June 1874 he changed the name of the Academy to the Conservatory of Music, " a name which better describes its actual functions." [29] Of the concerts he said that music of a higher grade had been performed and the execution had been somewhat better than in former years, but added: " Of course our renderings, with but few exceptions, have never been perfect, and the errors are yet far too many." He called for daily rehearsals in the future and concluded with an appeal to the trustees to increase the appropriation, pointing out that " concerts of the high order of excellence which we desire to give " could not be maintained without a substantial subsidy.

Such an energetic director was bound to succeed, and he seems to have won the support of the orchestra as well as the public. Lanier's own relations with Hamerik, a man of about his own age, progressed from mutual admiration to genuine friendship. At first he was a little apprehensive that the maestro, in spite of his technical abilities, lacked " culture of the soul " and a " broad and liberal spirit "; and he never exulted over his conducting as he did over that of Theodore Thomas, who brought his orchestra to Baltimore every winter for a series of concerts. But a musician who in his routine annual reports could find place between statistics for such poetic flights as: " True Music, having its origin in the religious or highest elements of human nature, becomes at once an interpreter of divinity and a tongue of the ideal," [30] was a man after Lanier's own heart. As the years passed on he became one of Hamerik's staunchest supporters and particularly admired him as a composer, writing to his wife after an evening of music and talk (Jan. 20, 1875): " The fellow is a rare genius! his music is the most poetic

during the week of Dec. 6-11, 1875, when the entire Peabody Orchestra played a series of concerts with Hans von Bülow, one of Hamerik's former teachers (program in the Lanier Room).

[29] Another reason for this change was possibly to avoid confusion with the Academy of Music on Howard St., a deluxe theatre then under construction and opened Jan. 5, 1875. (See J. T. Scharf, *History of Baltimore City and County*, Philadelphia, 1881, pp. 697-698.) The other facts in this paragraph are taken from the *Seventh Annual Report* (1874), pp. 22-24, 41-45. The cost of the orchestra had exceeded Hamerik's estimate, $9,000 instead of $6,000.

[30] *Fifth Annual Report*, p. 40. See Lanier's letters of Jan. 10, 22, 1874.

subtlety of tone-combination that could be imagined." This admiration was returned, in kind. Hamerik's often repeated eulogy of Lanier, written to his wife several years after his death, was as much an impression of the man as of the musician:

In his hands the flute no longer remained a material instrument, but something that sets heavenly harmonies into melodious vibration. The tones were not only true and pure, but poetic. . . .

His conception of music was not reached by an analytic study of note by note, but was intuitive and spontaneous. . . .

His playing appealed alike to the musically learned and to the unlearned; but the artist felt in his performance the superiority of the momentary living inspiration to all the rules and shifts of mere technical scholarship.[31]

At the end of the orchestral season of 1873-1874, Lanier left for Georgia to spend the rest of the spring and summer with his family, enthusiastic over his baptism into the world of art and filled with plans for the future. A misconception has persisted about his residence in Baltimore that should be cleared up at this point. Though it was technically his home from 1873 until his death in 1881, he did not really establish himself with any degree of permanence before the autumn of 1877, when he finally brought his wife and children with him. During the first four years, in fact, he spent a little less than twelve months there. Taking a room by himself in a private home on Centre Street, just a block from the Peabody Institute, for three or four months he would plunge into his musical life, which as the years went on was more and more encroached upon by his literary activities, and then after the last concert he would leave for the South to join his family. Furthermore, he seems at first to have considered his residence in Baltimore as only tentative.

The evidence on this point that is scattered through the letters becomes significant when gathered together. When he went to New York at the end of the summer of 1874, he was definitely seeking a better and more profitable career as an artist.[32] His letter to his wife (Aug. 26) suggests the nature of his principal hope and its disappointment. He had gone immediately to a concert by Thomas's Orchestra, where during the intermission he had met his friend Stovasser, first oboe of the Peabody during the past season and now employed by Thomas, though in second place. But Stovasser introduced him to Carl Wehner,

---

[31] Hamerik to Mary Day Lanier, undated MS letter in the Charles D. Lanier Collection. A second letter has survived, dated Sept. 29, 1884, which is another version of the same description. These tributes were originally written for the " Memorial " introducing the first collected edition of Lanier's *Poems* (New York, 1884) ; the text there printed, pp. xxxi-xxxii, is a composite of the two.

[32] See, for example, his letter to Hayne, May 23, 1874.

just brought over from St. Petersburg to take the post of first flute in the same orchestra. Whatever chances Lanier thought he had to play under the baton of his idol were dashed, at least for the present. He had other plans, however, and he now set about forwarding them, all without success. He had composed some poems and some music which he tried to get published with profit to himself, but in vain. He experimented at Badger's with the invention of a long flute, but the money he invested never brought any returns. He planned to organize a group to give " Soft-tone Concerts," but it never materialized. He talked of taking lessons from Leopold Damrosch, whom he described somewhat unconvincingly as now " at the head of fine music in New York "; but though Lanier finally played for him and received some words of encouragement, nothing came of this meeting.[33] He also played with and for other musicians, but after three months of frustrated effort he realized again that New York had only good words to offer him. Then came Hamerik's letter begging him to take his old place in the Peabody Orchestra, and after a visit to Macon, where he gave an unsuccessful concert, he returned to Baltimore at the end of the year.[34]

In spite of Lanier's disappointments he must have plucked up heart soon, for the situation there had improved. The success of the previous season had induced the trustees to increase the subsidy: a new concert master had been brought from Berlin, the orchestra increased to forty-four members, and Lanier's salary raised from fifteen to twenty dollars a month—though the shorter season made his total earnings the same. But into these weeks were crowded more concerts than ever before, eight with full orchestra, four chamber, and twelve in which the students participated. Though bad weather cut the attendance, the Peabody's star continued in the ascendancy, and the provost reported in June: " The Symphony Concerts were conducted on the same liberal scale as during last year, and were undoubtedly the best musical performances ever given at the Institute." [35] The programs do not list

[33] See letters of Sept. 3, 8, 13, 25, 1874. On Oct. 29 he wrote to his wife of the audition when he played his original composition " Wind-Song " for Damrosch, who " said it was done like an artist." He then closed the door on his next pupil and talked with Lanier for half an hour on the sacrifices to be made in pursuing a musical career. The acquaintance seems to have ended there. Just what he hoped Damrosch could do for him is not clear. A few years later, as conductor of the Philharmonic (for one season) and then of the New York Symphony Society, he could have placed Lanier in a leading orchestra had he been so minded; but in 1874, though the leader of several singing societies and other musical organizations, he was hardly in a position to give him better employment than he already had.

[34] Hamerik's letter has not been found, but see Lanier's letters of Oct. 28 and Nov. 3.

[35] *Eighth Annual Report* (1875), p. 20; see also pp. 17-23. For the other facts above, see Lanier's letters of Nov. 6, 1874, and Jan. 3, 1875.

Lanier for any special parts, but he had occasional solo work that elicited praise from the newspapers and from his fellow-musicians. On one occasion, he reported that his playing won " many compliments from the stolid Germans of the Orchestra "; on another, for his part in a symphony by Svendsen, he was feasted with praise at a champagne and oyster supper given by Knabe, the piano manufacturer, to Hamerik, Seifert, Lanier, and others.[36] Failing in outside engagements to supplement his income, he cheered himself for a while with the prospect of getting a chair of the " physics and metaphysics of music " at the Peabody Conservatory, and planned a lecture tour through the South using some acoustical apparatus owned at the Institute; but these projects, like many others evolved in his fertile imagination, fell through.[37]

At about this time, also, Lanier seems to have abandoned his ambition to become a composer of original music. He had been toying with composition for a number of years, most actively between 1872 and 1874, but his efforts in this field are too fragmentary to indicate anything more than a hint of his direction.[38] Some of them throw light on his devotion to the inter-relations of the two arts of music and poetry, as in the settings for his own and Tennyson's poems, and the suggestive fragments: " Beowulf's March " and " On Keats' Ode to a Nightingale." But his most interesting experiments are those in the allied field of program music that flourished in America during this period. " Lanier's marked preference for descriptive music," writes a recent commentator, " suggests that he sought to turn his music into poetry exactly as he tried to make his verse into music." [39] Had he persisted, it is possible that he might have won a place as a pioneer in the history of American music.

Indeed, he was given extravagant encouragement in that direction by

[36] Letters of Jan. 24, Feb. 7, 1875. See also the Baltimore *Gazette*, Jan. 25, Feb. 8.

[37] Letters of Jan. 6 and Mar. 17, 1875. He later tried to get a similar chair in New York (letter to Peacock, July 31, 1875).

[38] All of his known musical compositions are listed in the Bibliography, I, E (see vol. VI). The earliest recorded date is 1863, the latest 1874. Only one piece was published during his lifetime, a ballad, immature both in words and music; two others have been published posthumously, an arrangement from *Il Trovatore* and a setting for words by Tennyson. Seven other compositions have survived in MS, two of them likewise settings for Tennyson's poems and two others conventional songs without words. It is from the remaining three, together with some sixty-odd fragments and the titles of a few lost pieces, that the principal conclusions will have to be drawn. This material is available in the Lanier Room, Johns Hopkins University, awaiting the study of a qualified musicographer.

[39] Philip Graham, " A Note on Lanier's Music," University of Texas *Studies in English*, XVII, 107n. (1937). For an account of descriptive music in America at the end of the nineteenth century, see Howard, *op. cit.*, pp. 367-461.

Alice Fletcher, herself a pioneer writer on Indian music. After he played his " Black-birds " and " Swamp-Robin " for her in the autumn of 1873, she wrote him (Nov. 14) : " Your flute gave me that for which I had ceased to hope, true American Music." And Lanier reported excitedly to his wife two days later:

Miss Fletcher declared that nothing like it existed out of Wagner: that I was not only the founder of a School of music but the founder of American music: that hitherto all American compositions had been only German music done over, but that these were at once American, un-German . . . : that I belonged to the Advance-Guard, which must expect to struggle but which could not fail to succeed.

Miss Fletcher, however, was an ethnologist, not a musician. He might have been spurred to serious and sustained efforts as a composer had he received such praise from one really qualified to judge. But the best musicians who heard his pieces, though complimentary, were non-committal. After hearing this same " Black-birds," Hamerik had " declared the composition to be that of an Artist "; a year later, Damrosch said of Lanier's rendering of his own " Wind-Song " that " in view of my education . . . he was greatly astonished and pleased with the poetry of the piece." [40] If he ever played for Theodore Thomas or Dudley Buck, no record of it or of their estimates has been preserved. These were the highest musical authorities with whom Lanier had any acquaintance.

It is true that his compositions continued to receive praise, here and there, from friends, musical amateurs, and newspaper critics. The fullest and perhaps the best of these was written by his friend Ronald McDonald of the New York *Times,* who said:

His taste in music leads him to study the works of the classic composers, and his own compositions, while modeled on purely classical methods, are full of the sweetness and freshness of nature. . . . The " Black-birds " and the " Swamp Robin " are compositions in which the notes of these birds are woven into melodies full of the coolness and freshness of the woods. The " Midge Dance " suggests the fantastic swirlings, minglings and sudden and unaccountable subsidings of a swarm of midges dancing in a cool spot in the woods, and in its light and brilliant structure rivals the famed " Queen Mab " scherzo of Berlioz.[41]

This seems to be a representative description of Lanier's tone-poems as they sounded to the sympathetic contemporary. And it emphasizes a point that impresses the layman today, deprived as he is of the

[40] See Lanier's letters to his wife, Sept. 24, 1873, and Oct. 29, 1874.

[41] Quoted in Marble, *op. cit.*, p. 141. See also the newspaper comments quoted in note 123, Letters of 1873.

composer's own renditions: whatever originality they have is more in idea and intention than in musical execution.

Lanier himself did not set a high value upon his own compositions, and the matter is best concluded in his own words. His conception of the function of the flute itself, for which most of his music was composed, is significant. As early as 1867 he had written:

The flute seems to me to be peculiarly the woods-instrument; it speaks the gloss of green leaves or the pathos of bare branches; it calls up the strange mosses that are under dead leaves; it breathes of wild plants that hide and oak-fragrances that vanish; it expresses to me the natural magic in music.[42]

This conception he seems to have retained to the end. In the midst of his most active period of composing he wrote to his brother (Sept. 27, 1873): "The 'natural magic' of my compositions . . . is all that I now pretend to as distinguishing them from others." This would be interesting enough in itself, and one only wishes there were more than the three surviving experiments in nature music in which to look for this magic. Several of the fragments are also suggestive. One would like to know, for example, what he intended to do with his " Plantation Symphony " and his " Southern Suite: The Corn-Shucking. The Break-down "; but these are mere musical notations, and most of what he left is fragmentary. Lanier, by his own confession, began the study of composition for the first time in the winter of 1874 (letter of Jan. 28). His lack of training was apparently too great a handicap, as implied in a letter written over a year later (Apr. 1, 1875):

Things come to me mostly in one or two forms,—the poetic or the musical. I express myself with most freedom in the former *modus*: with most passionate delight in the latter. Indeed I ought to say that . . . music is, in my present stage of growth, rather a passion than a faculty: I am not its master, it is mine.

By the time this was written there were sufficient inducements to turn his creative energy exclusively to the former art.

The success of two long poems, " Corn " and " The Symphony," published in *Lippincott's* during the winter and late spring, won him something of a national reputation. And from April 13, 1875, when he left for the South at the end of the Peabody season, he may be said to have been fairly launched on his career as an author, with music gradually taking second place. The next six months were spent in writing a travel-book called *Florida*, a pot-boiler. Seeing it through the press kept him for many weeks in New York, where for the first time he met successful literary men and began his friendship with Bayard Taylor.

---

[42] *Tiger-Lilies*, V, 27, of the present edition.

Encouragement from these high places made him hope for sufficient employment with his pen to support himself there, and he lingered throughout the autumn. Meanwhile Hamerik sent out his annual plea (Oct. 23, 1875): " Our Peabody Concerts commence the 4 of December. . . . Come, take your old place, with Wysham as your second. You can writ [sic] your beautiful poetry as well in Balt° as any place else." And since nothing substantial had materialized in the literary line, Lanier went. To his wife he wrote (Dec. 2) of his old delight in the orchestra, saying, " I have wonderfully improved in tone: which is strange since I have had no practice." Apparently the flute had been idle while the pen was busy.

Lanier's third season with the Peabody Orchestra was again a successful one. At the end of the year Hamerik boasted: " The Peabody Concerts have made their name; they are known throughout the Country, and are spoken of in the highest terms by accomplished critics. The secret of their superiority lies in the regular and tenacious training of the orchestra." [43] But Lanier's national recognition was keeping pace with Hamerik's, and he was still looking elsewhere for wider opportunities. For a time an old ambition was revived. His appointment by the Commission for the Centennial Exhibition brought him into correspondence with Dudley Buck, Theodore Thomas's assistant conductor, who was to write the music for his Cantata. On January 12, 1876, he met Thomas himself in Baltimore, showed him the text and discussed with him the musical problems involved.[44] His orchestra was to play all the music for the exhibition, and Lanier's heart must have leaped when the great conductor promised to hire him as an additional flute if his membership should be enlarged. This unexpected offer had come upon the " voluntary recommendation " of Carl Wehner, Thomas's first flute, with whom he had played duos and had begun a friendship that was to last the rest of his life.[45] The prospect of assisting in the performance of his own Cantata, with the added possibility of a permanent post in the leading orchestra of the country, aroused Lanier to unwonted efforts. He exchanged his silver Boehm flute for two wooden ones, as better suited to orchestral work, and wrote his wife that he was now refusing all social invitations so as

[43] *Ninth Annual Report* (1876), pp. 54-56. Only eight symphony concerts were given however, because of a smaller appropriation ($6,500); and the provost appealed for gifts to form an endowment for the music department (pp. 32-34).

[44] Letter of Jan. 22, 1876. Lanier apparently had met him before, probably as early as 1874 (see Taylor's letter, Dec. 28, 1875: " Thomas remembers you well ").

[45] Letter to Peacock, Jan. 25, 1876. Two autographed photographs of Wehner have been preserved in the Charles D. Lanier Collection, Johns Hopkins University.

to have uninterrupted practice in order to acquire the technical proficiency needed for such a post.[46]

Thomas's Orchestra was to return to Baltimore for another concert at the end of March, and until this brought him final word he kept his plans for the future in the air, clinging to the hope that he would be able to bring his family north the next year and establish a permanent home. But the now familiar bad news was not long in coming. On April 4 he wrote to his father: "Thomas will not be enabled to enlarge his orchestra as he expected, and . . . my prospect of that engagement is swept away." Thomas was having his own troubles.[47] But the scales were even more heavily weighted against Lanier during 1876. Though he heard his Cantata successfully performed in May and got considerable literary notice out of the controversy it engendered, the months that followed brought a succession of disasters ending in the complete collapse of his health. In the autumn (Nov. 1) Hamerik as usual urged him to return to the Peabody Orchestra, saying: "You know how much your playing is appreciated by every body and all, and how glad I shall be to find the commander of the wind in his wont place." But Lanier, too ill for any work, had been ordered to Florida for the winter. Hamerik sent his condolences in a letter (Dec. 2) that indicates what a blow he felt this to be: "What shall we do, and how get along without you? Indeed I am afraid to direct, without both seeing, hearing and feeling your flute."

When Lanier did return at last, in October, 1877, he brought his family with him, content now to make Baltimore his permanent home. As he resumed his old position at the Peabody after an absence of eighteen months, he found the orchestra suffering under considerable financial handicap. The trustees had decided that the funds of the Institute would not permit such large appropriations as in former years, so a city-wide campaign was put on to make the concerts more nearly self-supporting. Five hundred subscriptions were sold, and the season was carried through with more "general satisfaction to the public" than in any previous one. But Hamerik did not share this satisfaction. In his annual report he declared: "The Peabody Concerts given this season were only eight in number, with an entirely too inefficient orchestra. . . . [They] have not been an artistic success."[48] The

---

[46] Letter of Jan. 22, 1876. See also his letter to Buck, Feb. 14, and to his brother, Mar. 11.

[47] See Russell, *op. cit.*, pp. 97-102.

[48] The first comment is in the report of the provost, who said that the expenses had been cut to $4,000 (*Eleventh Annual Report*, 1878, pp. 17-20). Hamerik's report was filled with complaints, not only of the orchestra but of the Conservatory and of the general failure in America to treat the study of music as a profession: "Art, as now practised in music, is an importation, or a

orchestra had not only been reduced in size, particularly the string section, but part of the salaries had been made dependent on the sale of tickets at the door. This was a crisis for the players, and for no one more so then for Lanier. Yet he was apparently the one who came to the rescue. A note from Hamerik has survived, asking him to drop by the Conservatory for a conference, with the cryptic conclusion: "You, and *but* you can act in this matter, as to ensure us a perfect success, it is even *necessary* that nobody knows of our arrangements." The explanation for this is found in a newspaper comment the following spring: "Mr. Lanier's flute . . . actually held the orchestra together and made the current series of concerts possible. He was the first member of the orchestra, when they were promised only a contingent pay last fall, to come forward and volunteer, and his example inspired the rest." [49] The notice, headed "A Merited Compliment," announced that the Peabody season would end in a benefit concert for Baltimore's "distinguished poet." "Such was his popularity with the orchestra," wrote the originator of the idea, that when the members were asked to assist "they consented in enthusiastic unison." The beneficiary, characteristically, offered to give them a dinner out of the proceeds.[50]

Lanier was by this time the most indispensable member of the Peabody Orchestra. Though this was partly attributable to his character and personality, it was also partly because of his musicianship. On the announcement for the season of 1877-1878 his name is printed at the top along with the professors of the Conservatory and the guest artists, the only regular member of the orchestra so listed. At the seventh concert, March 2, 1878, he was assigned by Hamerik a full solo, Emil Hartmann's *G Minor Concerto*, Lanier playing the violin part on his flute. The critic in the *Gazette*, after commenting on the technical difficulties of this piece that was far superior to the average flute music, congratulated him on his admirable execution and declared that "the performance showed not only a mastery of the instrument, but a refined and cultivated musical intelligence." The concerto brought down the house and won him a basket of flowers and the applause of players and conductor as well.[51]

When the complimentary concert was given a month later, Lanier repeated this number as his contribution to the program. Miss Elisa

weak imitation of Europe, and not a plant which has any permanent root in American soil" (*ibid.*, pp. 44-46).

[49] Hamerik's note, dated merely "Monday," has been assigned to Nov. 12, 1877, from external evidence. The notice in the Baltimore *Evening Bulletin*, Apr. 1, 1878, is preserved in a clipping (Charles D. Lanier Collection), no file being discovered.

[50] Dobbin, *op. cit.*, p. 5.

[51] Baltimore *Gazette*, Mar. 4, 1878. See also Lanier's letter to his brother, Mar. 3.

Baraldi sang selections from two of Hamerik's operas, Mme. Auerbach played a Mendelssohn concerto, and the orchestra Beethoven's *Eighth Symphony*. Besides bringing a modest purse to the hard pressed poet-musician, the occasion was a love-feast all round, as his wife described it:

I cannot imagine an evening more musically perfect and the audience was as choice, as harmonious, as happy as the music. I say "happy" advisedly, for Mr. Hamerik, with a delicate sentiment that evoked my gratitude, had declared in making up the programme that the music must be joyous, and had vetoed everything sad: the one necessary exception being in the thrilling minor strains of Sidney's *Hartmann Concerto*, first and second movements only; the last movement being composed *and played* in a brilliant "blaze of glory." [52]

And she was not the only one who spoke of it in extravagant terms. Mme. Auerbach pronounced it the performance of a consummate artist. Hamerik's eulogy, heightened by retrospect and the circumstances under which it was written, was unrestrained:

I will never forget the impression he made on me. . . . His handsome, tall and manly figure, his flute breathing noble sorrows, noble joys, the orchestra softly responding! You could have heard a pin drop, the audience was spell bound. Such distinction, such refinement! He was the master, the genius. [53]

This was the nearest Lanier ever came to making a formal début as a virtuoso on the flute, at its best a limited instrument for solo work. Although his reputation as a musician remained to the end largely local, he had scored a genuine triumph in Baltimore circles. But it is ironical that just as he reached the high point of his musical career he should be turning his energies irrevocably in another direction. Because of his literary successes of the past two years, culminating in the Lippincott volume in 1877 and the sheaf of poems with which he bombarded the magazines from Florida, he had come to think of himself primarily as a poet. [54] And though music remained a major interest until his death, it was from now on not so much a career as a means of support, and

[52] Letter to R. S. Lanier, Apr. 15, 1878. In a letter to his brother, Apr. 21, Lanier said that the concert, which was given at Lehman's Hall on Apr. 6, had netted him $164. A program is preserved in the Lanier Room, Johns Hopkins University.

[53] Hamerik to Mary Day Lanier, Sept. 29, 1884, written for the "Memorial" to *Poems*, 1884 (see note 31, above). For Mme. Auerbach's tribute see Dobbin, *op. cit.*, p. 5. Lanier's reciprocal praise is recorded in his sonnet "To Nannette Falk-Auerbach" (I, 117), written just prior to the concert, and in his account of her playing at the "Maryland Musical Festival" (II, 316) the following month. This was a grand finale to the season, staged at the new Academy of Music building from May 28 to 30, in which all of musical Baltimore participated, including a large chorus, the Peabody Orchestra expanded by local instrumentalists to 150, and Mme. Auerbach heading the list of soloists.

[54] Out of 71 poems published during his lifetime, 32 fall in the years 1876-1878.

even in this category it was finally to take second place. Already he was looking about for other employment to supplement his meager salary as flutist, principally with an eye to the newly established Johns Hopkins University. As he took his bow at the complimentary concert on April 6, 1878, he was midway in his first series of lectures in English literature. In the next annual report of the Peabody Institute Lanier appeared in the new rôle of lecturer, and this in turn led to his Hopkins appointment. He played in the orchestra for two more seasons, but the success of his academic venture was such that during the last year of his life, what with the pressure of his teaching duties, his publications, and his failing health, music was crowded out altogether.[55]

As a sort of grace-note to Lanier's career as a musician in Baltimore, this is a fitting place to record his relations with the " Wednesday Club," a brilliant association of amateurs in music and dramatics that for more than a decade played a leading part in the cultural life of the city, reaching its hey-day in the late 1870's with monthly " Soirées " performed in its own club house and theatre on Charles Street. For the last five years of his life he was a member of this club and joined in its activities, though the extent of his actual participation is a matter of some conjecture.

As Lanier settled into the groove of his life in Baltimore, his acquaintance widened to include most of the musicians of the city. The names of scores of these are scattered through his letters, but not all of them became his close friends. He was opposed to Bohemianism and spoke out strongly against it, though this opposition sprang more from his idealization of art than from moral prudishness, for he relished conviviality, within limits, and was more of a *bon vivant* than has been previously realized. With most of the regular musicians, especially certain of the German element that he described on occasion

[55] The season of 1878-1879 was another bad one financially. Only eight concerts were given, with a reduced orchestra and contingent pay, and results that were unsatisfactory to both public and players. (See *Twelfth Annual Report*, 1879, p. 24. Hamerik made no separate report this year.) But that of 1879-1880 was much better, with the orchestra increased to its old size. " The result was a musical but not a financial success," expenses far exceeding receipts. Hamerik, however, was pleased. The student concerts were revived, sixteen of them in addition to eight symphony concerts, and this was declared to be artistically " one of the most successful seasons " in the history of the Institute. (See *Thirteenth Annual Report*, 1880, pp. 15-16, 35-37. Hamerik said he was inclosing a list of the orchestra members, but none has survived earlier than the one for 1891-1892.) Thus Lanier's connection with the Peabody Orchestra terminated on a high note. All of his writings on the subject of music are collected in vol. II of the present edition. For a detailed account of his lectures at Mrs. Bird's, at the Peabody, and at Hopkins, see the Introductions to vols. III and IV. (I am indebted to Lubov Keefer of the Peabody Conservatory and Clifton Furness of the New England Conservatory for a critical reading of this section of the Introduction.)

as " beery " and "heathenish," he seems to have maintained pleasant but largely professional relationships. As one who knew him well has put it: " Although Mr. Lanier seemed always to have been on excellent terms with his musical confreres, his associations seemed to be with the circle of his old Georgia friends—and to extend outward from that centre, rather than to have been with his fellow workers in the orchestra." [56] Though Lanier's friends included many intellectual and artistic ones in addition to the more social group here alluded to, this account is in general borne out by the evidence of the letters. Of those connected with the Peabody only Hamerik, Wysham, Mme. Auerbach, and Isabel Dobbin seem to have become his intimates. These, together with several families such as the Rabillons and the Sutros, made up the inner circle of his musical friends.[57] Moreover, it was through them, and especially the last named, that he formed perhaps the pleasantest of all his Baltimore connections.

For Otto Sutro, proprietor of the principal local music house, was the founder and leading spirit of the Wednesday Club. Growing out of gatherings at his bachelor quarters, it enjoyed an informal history for more than a decade. At these meetings the city's best amateurs would get together for evenings equally divided between frolic and serious devotion to art: " Native creators of music and verse were especially sponsored, their works performed and received enthusiastically." With Sutro's marriage in 1869, the group formed themselves into a permanent club, the purpose being a continuation of the Wednesday reunions supplemented by monthly Soirées which were to consist of elaborate musical and dramatic programs. After one successful season they decided to amalgamate with the Allston Association, a group originally organized for " the promotion of art." The union, though not a happy one, rocked along for several years, and such it was when Lanier first visited Baltimore and was taken by his friend Wysham to the club rooms on St. Paul Street for a whiskey and soda. Two guest cards, extending him the privileges of the Allston for thirty-day periods, have survived; [58] but it is doubtful that he had any further connection with it at this stage of its history. Finally, realizing that the association was drifting into a purely social one with no adequate facilities for dramas and musicales, in 1875 the Wednesday Club withdrew. The

[56] Reminiscences of Sophie Bledsoe Herrick, daughter of Dr. A. J. Bledsoe, editor of the *Southern Review*, apparently written in 1904 (typescript in the Edwin Mims Collection, Johns Hopkins University). The Georgia friends referred to were Mrs. Edgeworth Bird, Mrs. Arthur Machen, and R. M. Johnston.

[57] See, for example, Frederick Kelly, " Sidney Lanier at the Peabody Institute," *Peabody Bulletin*, Dec., 1939, pp. 35-38.

[58] They are dated Sept. 18 and Dec. 24, 1873 (Lanier Room, Johns Hopkins University). In a letter to his wife, Sept. 19, 1873, he described it as " an Art Club."

next year, reorganizing with most of their original membership, they "enthusiastically launched their long cherished plans." [59] The decision was a wise one, for its significant years date from this separation.

Early in 1876 Lanier received an invitation to join the Wednesday Club. It was signed by the Board of Governors, at least half of whom are known to have been his personal friends: George W. Dobbin (President), Henry Wysham, Otto Sutro, Fred W. Colston, James Gibson, and Dr. J. J. Chisholm. The program of the newly reorganized group was stated succinctly: "The primary object of the Club is the cultivation, performance and enjoyment of music. Its secondary object, the promotion of rational amusement by any literary or artistic means. The first general meeting of the Club will be on Wednesday Evening, February 16th, at its rooms, No. 42 North Charles Street." [60] Lanier was invited to become a "complimentary member," and he is said to have been the first person taken into the club under this category.[61] The nature of this new type of membership is hinted at in an acknowledgment by the Board of Governors several years later: "We owe to them ALL the entertainments we have to offer at our Soirées." [62] This would seem to be something of an exaggeration, since many of the regular members were leading participants in the musical and dramatic performances, but it indicates that numerous people of talent in the city who could not afford membership in this rather expensive club were generously invited to become "complimentary members."

Lanier's invitation extended to him the "hospitalities" of the Wednesday Club for the ensuing year, and he quite possibly took part in one of the early performances in the spring of 1876. But his relations with this pleasant group were broken off temporarily by ill health, and he left Baltimore in April, not to return until the autumn of 1877. Meantime, during the eighteen months of his absence, the young club prospered. Its "fame spread . . . with each succeeding soirée," and the membership soon increased to two hundred. With the need for

---

[59] The facts in the early history of the club are taken, with the author's permission, from "The Wednesday Club: A Brief Sketch from Authentic Sources," *Maryland Historical Magazine*, XXXVIII, 60-64 (Mar., 1943), by Miss Ottilie Sutro, who is now engaged in writing a history of the club. A somewhat different version of the origins of these two clubs has been preserved in a sketch entitled "Allston & Wednesday Club" (MS, 7 pp. foolscap, Johns Hopkins University), written by J. T. Scharf and apparently originally intended for inclusion in his *History of Baltimore City* (1881).

[60] Printed invitation, dated Feb. 7, 1876, preserved in the Lanier Room.

[61] Information by courtesy of Miss Ottilie Sutro.

[62] See printed pamphlet entitled *Wednesday Club*, n. p., n. d., unpaged—copy in the Enoch Pratt Free Library, Baltimore. According to Miss Sutro, a more accurate appraisal is contained in a pamphlet in her possession, unavailable to me but from which I am permitted to quote: "[the complimentary members] to whose coöperation the club is largely indebted in the past and for its future success."

larger space the Monumental Assembly Rooms, corner of Centre and St. Paul Streets, were leased and it was here that the performances were given during the highly successful season of 1877-1878.[63]

That Lanier's membership was renewed upon his return to Baltimore, and that he participated in the activities of the Wednesday Club during the following winter, is attested by the survival of two clever pen drawings made in 1878 by Dr. Adalbert J. Volck, one of the most versatile of the group. The first of these is an imaginative sketch, showing all the prominent performers at the Soirées as they would have looked had they passed before the footlights in review. This " Parade," reproduced in the present edition,[64] preserves for posterity the spirit as well as the varied activities of the Wednesday Club in its prime. Three groups are shown: Music, Drama, and Art (including culinary!), with the members attired to suit their parts and a running script beneath reflecting the gayety of the occasion. Lanier is represented in the first group, a fair likeness, flute under arm and dressed in the uniform of a military band. Among the other thirty-six, the reader of his letters will recognize many familiar names. The second is an illustrated invitation entitled " Recollections of Old, February 18th, 1878, at 8 P. M. Please Reply," decorated with numerous scenes and an amusing account in verse describing a typical Wednesday evening at Sutro's. Lanier's copy has been preserved but his reply has been lost, which is unfortunate, for he is said to have answered all such with appropriate poems.[65] There is but a single reference in Lanier's letters to his attending one of these regular meetings, but it is casual enough to indicate that he probably went with some frequency.[66] It is certainly not difficult to picture him joining whole-heartedly in such innocent frolic.

This, of course, represents the lighter side of the Wednesday Club's activities. But even in their serious undertakings, the monthly Soirées, entertainment was one of the purposes, as indicated by the list of musical and dramatic performances given during this same season of 1878.[67] In February William B. Rhodes's operetta *Bombastes Furioso*

[63] Sutro, *op. cit.*, p. 64. See also the anonymous article, " The Wednesday Club," in the Baltimore *Sunday News*, Dec. 2, 1894.

[64] Vol. X, frontispiece. The original, 8" x 39", is owned by Philip G. Straus of Baltimore and reproduced by his permission.

[65] The invitation, to a stag party given by Sutro, is in the Lanier Room, Johns Hopkins University. Miss Ottilie Sutro is authority for the statement about Lanier's clever verse replies, carefully treasured by her father but lost after his death along with his other personal papers.

[66] Letter to D. C. Gilman, July 28, 1878: " I happened to meet Mr. Gildersleeve at the Wednesday Club a short time before he left town." Gildersleeve, the distinguished Greek scholar, was a member; Gilman, President of the Johns Hopkins University, was a stockholder (according to Scharf's MS, see note 59, above).

[67] Being a private club, its activities were not often written up in the news-

was put on with Lanier's friend Innes Randolph in a leading rôle. Then followed three plays in the spring: Victorien Sardou's *A Scrap of Paper*, with ladies in the cast; Henry J. Byron's *Our Boys*, one of the club's greatest hits that was repeated in later years; and Charles S. Cheltnam's *A Lesson in Love*.[68] In June came another operetta with chorus and orchestra, Mendelssohn's *Son and Stranger*, in which another of Lanier's friends, Léonce Rabillon, Jr., took part. Apparently there were no Soirées during the hot months. *Son and Stranger* proved such a favorite it was given again in October; in November there was a double bill, S. Theyre-Smith's *Cut Off With a Shilling* and *A Happy Pair*; and the year closed with W. S. Gilbert's *Sweethearts*. Lanier is not listed in any of the casts of characters, and it is extremely doubtful that he played even a minor rôle in any of the club's dramatic performances, there being no evidence throughout his life of any skill in this line. The talent that he furnished was as a musician, and he certainly played in the orchestra for the operettas and for the chorals, chamber concerts, and other musical performances that were given from time to time.[69]

These were unquestionably the finest amateur theatricals and musicales that had ever been given in Baltimore. In spite of occasional distinguished guests and quite a few professional soloists, the spirit of the performances was strictly amateur.[70] The house was packed with fashionable audiences, and outsiders clamored for tickets. The Wednesday Club was now an established success, and with an increasing flood of applications for membership a movement was set afoot to

papers (the files of the Baltimore *Sun* have been searched without result); and I have not been able to see any programs of the Soirées for 1878. But the fortunate survival of drawings by Dr. A. J. Volck for seven of the performances given during this year, showing scenes and giving dates and casts, makes it possible to picture a sample season. All of these (four originals and three copies) are in the Otto Sutro—Wednesday Club Room, equipped and presented to the Maryland Historical Society by the Misses Rose and Ottilie Sutro and are described here with their permission. Approximately eight to ten Soirées were given each year.

[68] The last named is dated merely 1878, and may have been given in January or May, the only other seasonal months of this year not accounted for. A program of *Our Boys* dated Nov. 25, 1880, survives in the Charles D. Lanier Collection, Johns Hopkins University.

[69] Sutro, *op. cit.*, p. 66, lists among the chief musical works performed by the Wednesday Club: Handel's *Alexander's Feast*, Schumann's *Paradise and Peri*, Mendelssohn's *Elijah*, and Bruch's *Lay of the Bell*; and a number of Gilbert and Sullivan's comic operas, including *Pirates of Penzance* and *Iolanthe*—all of which were given after the club moved into its own building on Charles St. in the winter of 1879-1880. She adds that Wysham and Sutro had charge of the musical programs and (together with James Gibson and John McKim, in charge of dramas) the operettas.

[70] Sutro, *op. cit.*, p. 66. One of the best amateur actresses was Lanier's friend Isabel Dobbin, the first woman to take part in a Wednesday Club play.

erect their own club house and theatre. The result was a handsome new building, erected on Charles Street in 1879.[71] The editor of the local *Gazette* took this occasion to congratulate the Wednesday Club for its work in elevating the taste of the city and giving direction and purpose to its artistic impulses:

Baltimore has suffered for a long time under the reproach of being indifferent to the work of her artists and literary men; and the Wednesday Club promises to do much toward removing this stigma from us, by securing the prompt recognition and encouragement of native talent. At the reunions of the club, all who have any special aptitude or taste for art, music, the drama or literature, meet on common ground and share in enjoyments toward which all contribute. . . . Indeed it would be hard to overestimate the importance of the work which the Wednesday Club has done and is doing. . . . [It] should be regarded as a public benefactor and, as such, we extend to it our best wishes for a long and prosperous career.[72]

Thus was inaugurated the golden period of the club's history. At the gala opening on December 30, 1879, there was a performance of Gade's *Erl-King's Daughter*, and the next month Gilbert and Sullivan's *Trial by Jury*, in both of which Lanier was scheduled to play in the orchestra.[73] Thus the Wednesday Club went on from success to success during the seven remaining years of its existence. Lanier continued to be a member at least until the end of 1880,[74] and possibly until his death. But increasingly frequent periods of illness, such as that which confined him to his bed at the time of the opening of the new club house, and the exhausting work of lecturing and writing which occupied the last two years of his life, make one suspect that the season of 1877-1878 marked the high point of his activity. Meager as the evidence of his participation is, his affiliation with Baltimore's Wednesday Club was one of the brightest spots in a life that needs relief from the somber colors in which it is usually painted.

Several of Lanier's intimates in this group were enthusiastic amateurs in many fields. Two of them, in addition to being prominent actors in the Soirées, did some very creditable work in sculpture.[75] Léonce

[71] According to the pamphlet quoted in note 62, above, the cost of the building was $29,180, the lot $11,000, the furniture and stage equipment $5,850. According to Miss Sutro the cost of the building was only $26,000.

[72] Baltimore *Gazette*, Dec. 30, 1879.

[73] Information supplied by Miss Sutro who has kindly read this section of the Introduction. See also the Baltimore *Sun*, Dec. 31, 1879, and the anonymous " The Wednesday Club " in the Baltimore *Sunday News*, Dec. 2, 1894.

[74] Indicated by the survival of a program inclosing a " Member's Ticket " with Lanier's name thereon and a lady's ticket, all dated Nov. 25, 1880 (Charles D. Lanier Collection).

[75] See the tribute to the work of Randolph and Rabillon in Ephraim Keyser's " Baltimore the Monumental City," *Art and Archaeology*, XIX, 230 (June,

Rabillon, the French Consul, also had ties with Lanier through his interest in music and literature, later becoming a fellow lecturer at the Peabody and Johns Hopkins. The other, Innes Randolph, was an old friend he had known before coming to Baltimore, and there is evidence that they frequently spent evenings together in musical and literary discussions.[76] Among his many outside interests, this young lawyer from Virginia wrote dramatic and music criticisms for the *Gazette* and tried his hand at light verse, his humorous narratives of antebellum plantation life being still readable today. His parody of Poe's " Bells " entitled " That Amateur Flute " must have amused Lanier, and even more so his burlesque of Italian opera, *The Grasshopper: A Tragic Cantata*, dedicated in 1878 to the members of the Wednesday Club.[77]

The artist who illustrated this pamphlet, Dr. Adalbert J. Volck, was equally versatile and considerably more talented. He illustrated books, painted in oil and water color, did *repoussé* work in silver and copper, and carved a massive walnut mantelpiece for the Wednesday Club building in 1879—all as a pastime while he practiced his profession of dentistry. But he is chiefly remembered in Baltimore for his pen and ink sketches of the club's activities; and his inclusion of Lanier in at least one of them (see p. xxx, above) is sufficient evidence of a pleasant acquaintance.[78] Lanier knew two other local artists, both professionals, with one of whom he became intimate, John R. Tait the landscape and cattle painter. During a vacation in the Virginia mountains he is said to have given the poet some instruction in sketching, and Lanier in turn helped him put one of his poems into shape; but this exchange was not taken too seriously by either one.[79] It was Tait,

1925). In 1875 their marble busts of William Pinkney and John Pendleton Kennedy were presented to the Peabody Art Gallery (*Eighth Annual Report*, p. 24). See Lanier's letter of Feb. 26, 1875, for his first acquaintance with Rabillon, a man nearly twice Lanier's age.

[76] Randolph (1838-1887) is first mentioned in Lanier's letter of Jan. 22, 1874. An account of a debate between them on poetry is recorded by Isabel Dobbin (MS Reminiscences, Henry W. Lanier Collection, Johns Hopkins University).

[77] A copy of this is preserved in the Charles D. Lanier Collection. See also the posthumously published *Poems by Innes Randolph* (Baltimore, 1898), with a preface by his son, who says that Randolph was also a skillful 'cellist.

[78] He is not mentioned in Lanier's letters, however. The varied activities of Volck (1828-1912) are listed in the *Dictionary of American Biography*. His reputation was extended beyond local boundaries by his series of caricatures of Lincoln and the Union cause, published as *Confederate War Etchings* and *Sketches from the Civil War in America*.

[79] See John W. Wayland, *Sidney Lanier at Rockingham Springs* (Dayton, Va., 1912). (Ephraim Keyser, see the following note, says of this same vacation merely that Lanier and Tait had long walks and talks together.) See also Tait's " The Story of a Stanza," *Lippincott's*, XL, 723-725 (Nov., 1887), which refers to Lanier as his " dear friend, . . . gentle, warm-hearted, large-brained," and which links Professor Sylvester of Hopkins in this same poetic puzzle; and Mor-

finally, who took him to the studio of Ephraim Keyser in May, 1880, and initiated the brief acquaintance resulting in the bronze bust that has preserved the only likeness of Lanier in his last years.[80] All of this was pleasant enough, especially Lanier's relations with the amateurs of Baltimore, but it was far from satisfying for a man who had dedicated his life seriously, and professionally, to art—the art of poetry. It is necessary now to examine what Baltimore had to offer him in his career as a creative author.

A pivotal figure among Lanier's literary associations in the city of his adoption was William Hand Browne, who had corresponded with him since 1870, who sponsored him as an author, served as a pall-bearer at his funeral, and helped to edit his literary remains.[81] Though not himself a creative writer, Browne's whole life was centered around literature. For nearly a decade he devoted himself to providing Baltimore and the South with a magazine, first the *Southern Review* with Alfred T. Bledsoe (1867-1869) and then as co-editor with Lawrence Turnbull of the *New Eclectic*, succeeded in 1871 by the *Southern Magazine*, a regular monthly of original matter which continued under his sole charge for five more years. The purpose of this latter was specifically announced as "to develop the nascent literature of the South," [82] and it was here quite fittingly that Lanier found one of the

gan Callaway, Jr., ed., *Select Poems of Sidney Lanier* (1895), p. 79, who says that Lanier discussed the source of his own "Revenge of Hamish" with Tait, winter of 1878. Most of Tait's poems had come early in his career and were collected in *Dolce Far Niente* (1859). His later writing was chiefly art criticism for the magazines, the most interesting of which for the present study is "Art in Baltimore," *Lippincott's*, XXXII, 531-534 (Nov., 1883). He was born in Cincinnati in 1834, moved to Baltimore in 1876, and died there in 1909 (see sketch in the *Dictionary of American Biography*).

[80] Information through the courtesy of John S. Mayfield, Washington, D. C., who had a conversation with Keyser in 1935 and has preserved a stenographic report of it in typescript, entitled "A Poet and a Sculptor." See also Lanier's letters to Keyser, summer of 1880, and note 52. (The bronze—see vol. II, frontispiece—was not cast from the original clay model until 1888.)

[81] See the Introduction to *The English Novel*, vol. IV of the present edition, and note 55, Letters of 1881. Browne (1828-1912) seems to have been definitely responsible for Lanier's introduction to Edward Spencer, R. M. Johnston, and other literary figures. Twenty-six of Browne's letters to Lanier (Mar. 29, 1870-Aug. 8, 1881) survive, filled with discussion of musical, literary, and scholarly matters, but none of Lanier's letters to him have been found. (See note 18, Letters of 1871.)

[82] *New Eclectic*, VII, 768 (Dec. 1870), editorial by Lawrence Turnbull announcing his unavoidable withdrawal from what he had hoped would be his life work, and giving the changed title and prospectus of the new magazine. That Browne continued this policy in the *Southern Magazine* is indicated by his biographer, who says that during Reconstruction he directed all his efforts to restoring cultural conditions in the South (see sketch in the *Dictionary of American Biography*), and by thumbing through the list of contributors in the

first vehicles for extending his reputation beyond his native state. Among the contributors were the best of the Southern authors of the period, including his friend Paul Hayne and the group of Maryland writers he came to know shortly after he turned to the arts for his profession in the winter of 1873-1874.

As Henry Wysham had introduced him to the musical circle centering around the Peabody Conservatory, so Hand Browne brought Lanier into friendly relationship with Baltimore's men of letters. Almost without exception they were, like Browne himself, cultivated gentlemen with a taste for literature which they indulged as a side-line in the spirit of amateurs. Typical of these was Severn Teackle Wallis, for half a century leader of the Maryland Bar but with a local reputation as *literateur* that is somewhat hard to understand today. A trustee or sponsor of all the cultural institutions of the city and an eloquent speaker at local celebrations, he was also a prolific writer, leaving behind verses, addresses, and essays on political and historical subjects that were collected after his death by loving friends in a memorial edition.[83] The poems were all of the sort admired in that day—or more properly in the eighteenth century—as polished and elegant; and so they are, metrically smooth but imitative and utterly lacking in distinction. Though Lanier knew Wallis, as evidenced by occasional references in his letters,[84] men of such tenuous connections with literature as an art could have meant but little to him except in the way of social friendship.

More fruitful were his relations with Edward Spencer, a journalist with considerable literary ambition and some talent, especially as a playwright. A particular friend of Browne, through whom he had heard much of Lanier, Spencer initiated the acquaintance with a hearty letter of congratulation upon the publication of "Corn" in *Lippincott's*, February, 1875, adding: "I do not feel as if we were strangers to each other, but only members of the same coterie, kept from familiar intercourse by the accidents of space and time."[85] Lanier replied warmly, and after another exchange of letters—in which Spencer complained of the scattering of his own artistic efforts and Lanier that most of his friends in the past had been business men—they apparently

files of the magazine. Three of Lanier's poems and five prose pieces were published here between 1870 and 1875; the only other periodical with more than a local circulation which printed his early writings was the *Round Table* of New York, 1866-1868 (see vol. VI, Bibliography, I, B and C).

[83] *Writings of Severn Teackle Wallis* (Baltimore, 1896), 4 vols., edited by Wm. H. Browne. Vol. I contains the poems and other semi-literary writings, II the essays (mostly on politics), III-IV his writings on Spain growing out of two visits to that country.

[84] The earliest mention is in a letter to his wife, Feb. 26, 1875. Wallis (1816-1894) was a generation older than Lanier.

[85] Spencer to Lanier, Feb. 22, 1875.

met.[86] But the intimate tone of the letters is not matched by evidence of very frequent meetings, for "space and time" remained barriers. Spencer lived several miles out in the county at Randallstown, and the journalistic work that kept him on the rack called him to New York as often as to Baltimore. But he probably met on occasions with Lanier and Browne for evenings of literary discussion, and at least a symbol of this three-way friendship is preserved in Lanier's inscribed copy of Spencer's *Maternus*, a blank verse tragedy published in Baltimore, 1876, and dedicated to Browne.[87] This, his most serious effort, which is said to have won the approval of Booth, was a closest-drama. But he also had aspirations as an active playwright and composed several comedies, at least one of which, *Kit, the Arkansas Traveller* (written in collaboration with T. H. DeWalden) was produced.[88] Their continuing friendship is indicated in his engagement by Lanier as one of the supplementary lecturers in his Shakspere Course at the Peabody, winter of 1878-1879. Spencer is certainly not to be reckoned as an important influence in the career of a professional poet, but he helped to fill a gap in a somewhat lonely literary life.

The two most important authors whom Lanier counted among his friends in Baltimore were John Banister Tabb and Richard Malcolm

[86] Spencer's second and only other surviving letter was written on Mar. 31, 1875. Lanier's letters, dated Feb. 26, Apr. 1, 1875, and Aug. 15, 1876, were first discovered and published by E. P. Kuhl, "Sidney Lanier and Edward Spencer," *Studies in Philology*, XXVII, 462-476 (July, 1930); they are reprinted in the present edition along with two further ones—Nov. 1, 1878, and Jan. 5 (?), 1879—which he failed to discover. Kuhl says that Lanier had known Spencer for about a year before the first letter (Feb. 22, 1875) but furnishes no evidence; the letters themselves seem clearly the beginning of the friendship.

[87] In the Charles D. Lanier Collection, Johns Hopkins University. Kuhl, *op. cit.*, p. 476, is authority for the statement that they "met often," but he cites no evidence beyond the mention of a number of surviving letters from Browne to Spencer, which I have not seen. According to Kuhl, Spencer (1834-1883) was by 1875 a regular contributor to the New York *World* and the Baltimore *Evening Bulletin*; after 1878 chief editorial writer of the Baltimore *Sun*.

[88] Kuhl, *op. cit.*, pp. 467-470, implies that this and the following were all performed: *Electric Light: An American Comic Opera, Pork, Three Days After Death, Across the Continent*, and *Counting Chickens*—but he cites no evidence for his statement. The only one listed by A. H. Quinn (*The American Drama Since the Civil War*, New York, 1936, II, 286) is *Kit*, which had its première at the Boston Theatre on Feb. 4, 1870; but it is credited to DeWalden with Spencer, who is not otherwise mentioned, merely as collaborator. According to Kuhl, Spencer also wrote a biography of Senator Bayard of Delaware (1880), a history of Baltimore manufacturing, and, as editor, the *Memorial volume . . . of the Settlement of Baltimore* (1881). Besides poems published in *Putnam's Monthly* and the *Southern Magazine*, he is said to have left two volumes of verse in MS.

Johnston. Both of these friendships are well known, and it is only necessary here to indicate in broad outline their scope and significance in order to complete the picture. Father Tabb he had known as a fellow prisoner at Point Lookout in 1864-1865, but untoward circumstances prevented their reunion until the autumn of 1877. At this time he was teaching at St. Charles College, near Ellicott City, Maryland, and reading theology preparatory to his final studies for the priesthood.[89] Although engrossed in the religion to which he was a recent convert, he discovered Lanier's whereabouts with delight and made a trip to nearby Baltimore to see him shortly after his return from Florida.[90] Other meetings followed, but Tabb's circumstances prevented them from being many; according to Mary Day Lanier: "He was not much with us. When he was, poetry, music, the children, his friend . . . were his themes." [91] The depth of their attachment is a matter of record—in Lanier's letters, in the numerous poems addressed to him by Tabb, and in the dedication of his first important collection, *Poems,* 1894. This friendship bore tangible fruit in the form of criticism of Tabb's poems and aid in getting them published, as well as in a perceptible influence on his style.[92] But the stream flowed mostly one way, for he did not come into his own as a poet until the end of the century and at best had little to offer Lanier besides his devotion.

Pretty much the same situation holds for Richard Malcolm Johnston, though their friendship covered more years and involved many more meetings. Through the good offices of Hand Browne, Lanier met him shortly after his arrival in Baltimore in the winter of 1873-1874, and they soon became intimate.[93] Both were transplanted Georgians, both

[89] See Lanier's letter to Tabb, Jan. 20, 1867, and note 5, for the account of an abortive attempt at reunion. After the war Tabb had taught at St. Paul's School in Baltimore until 1870, studying music and also studying for the episcopal ministry. Then his conversion to Catholicism two years later took him to St. Charles College where he was graduated in 1875. For three years he taught at St. Peters School in Richmond, returning to St. Charles in 1877. Here he remained until he began his theological studies at St. Mary's Seminary, Baltimore, Sept. 14, 1881, being ordained in 1884 (F. A. Litz, *Father Tabb,* Baltimore, 1923, pp. 33-34). Thus, ironically, he lived in Baltimore almost up until the time of Lanier's arrival, and returned there one week after his death.

[90] Tabb's first letter has not been discovered, but Lanier's reply of Aug. 25, 1877, has. This and ten other letters by Lanier (all in 1877-1878, except one in 1881), long thought to be lost, have been recently published by Gordon Blair, *Father Tabb* (Richmond, Va., 1940), and are reprinted in the present edition. For an account of their first meeting see note 106, Letters of 1877. Only two of Tabb's letters have survived, Oct. 4, 1877, and Mar. 26, 1878.

[91] Quoted in Jennie M. Tabb, *Father Tabb, His Life and Work* (Boston, 1921), p. 66.

[92] Litz, *op. cit.,* pp. 56, 140-141, 164-168; he also quotes Tabb as saying that Lanier first encouraged him to poetic effort (p. 99). For Lanier's aid, see his letters of Aug. 25 and Dec. 19, 1877.

[93] See Lanier's letters of Dec. 12, 1873, and Feb. 3, 1874, and accompanying

were fond of music and literature—though these were avocations with one, vocations with the other. Johnston, it is true, had published an anonymous volume of *Georgia Sketches* in 1864 before coming to Maryland. In his new home he had taken up fiction writing again, encouraged by the Turnbull brothers, Baltimore publishers, through whose presses he issued his best known volume, *Dukesborough Tales*.[94] But this was the pastime of " Philemon Perch." At the time of his meeting with Lanier and throughout the years of their friendship, his serious business was as headmaster of his Pen Lucy School. Indeed, it was with a hope of securing employment as a part time teacher that Lanier made his first visit to Johnston in surburban Waverly; and, though it was four years before this particular desire was consummated, friendly relations were established from the first.[95] Their intimacy seems to have reached its highest point during 1877-1878, when Lanier was living on Denmead Street, just beyond the northern city limits and not far from Johnston's country home. From this time, apparently, date the " years of intimate literary association," recalled by Johnston's daughter, the frequent visits at Pen Lucy, the long afternoons of talk and writing under the great chestnut trees, where the poet read to the local colorist his " Marshes of Glynn," part of which is said to have been composed on the schoolhouse steps.[96] Just what benefit Lanier derived in the way

notes. Of course it is possible that they may have known each other in Georgia, but this is doubtful; for at the time Johnston left there for Maryland, 1867, he was forty-five years old as compared with Lanier's twenty-five, and they had always lived one hundred miles or more apart.

[94] The first collection, 1871, was privately printed; an enlarged edition was issued in 1874 (see F. T. Long, " The Life of Richard Malcolm Johnston in Maryland, 1867-1898," *Maryland Historical Magazine*, XXXIV, 314, Dec., 1939). Johnston's pen-name for his fiction was " Philemon Perch." Under his own name, and in collaboration with W. H. Browne, he wrote a text-book, *English Literature*, in 1872 (a copy of which Lanier took with him to Texas that year), and a *Life of Alexander Hamilton Stephens*, 1878.

[95] See Lanier's letters of Feb. 3, 1874, and Feb. 24, 1878. The latter makes it clear that Lanier taught at Pen Lucy in the winter of 1878, but his letter of June 12, 1879, implies that he did not teach there the following year. E. L. White, a pupil of the school in 1877-1878 and 1879-1880, said that during the latter year Lanier taught at Johnston's school after it had been moved inside the city limits, corner North and Maryland Avenues, and pays a tribute to his ability as a teacher (" Reminiscences of Sidney Lanier," *Johns Hopkins Alumni Magazine*, XVII, 329-331, June, 1929—partly quoted in note 27, Letters of 1878) ; but White's dates must be taken with caution since he says positively that Lanier did not teach in the session of 1877-1878. By way of reciprocation, Johnston served as a supplementary lecturer in Lanier's Shakspere Course at the Peabody, 1878-1879.

[96] See the reminiscences of Miss Ruth Johnston (who in 1878 was fourteen years old), quoted in Long, *op. cit.*, pp. 314-315, and the Baltimore *Sun*, Jan. 16, 1943, p. 14. Johnston is frequently mentioned in Lanier's letters from 1874 to 1877, but the fullest record of their friendship comes from the surviving

of criticism of his poems is not known, but it was certainly worth something to have a sympathetic listener, if only an amateur writer of fiction, and this fleeting glimpse of actual literary comraderie is one of the pleasantest that has come down to us. That Johnston himself profited from it is amply testified to. The earliest surviving letter to him is a detailed criticism of " Mr. Neelus Peeler's Conditions," which Lanier then proceeded to sell to *Scribner's*, forwarding to the author the first check he had ever received for any of his stories. *Old Mark Langston*, Johnston's first novel, undertaken at Lanier's prompting, was the concern of a letter from the deathbed of the poet-friend whose encouragement and sympathetic criticism started him on his real literary career. As his biographer says: " Lanier's guidance seems to have been the most important single friendly force in aiding Johnston to learn the craft of writing." [97] The other side of the debt, one suspects, was paid mostly in the warmth generated by gratitude and deep personal attachment.

Such was the Baltimore literary scene in the 1870's. There was no real group of practicing authors, and of the few Lanier was the only one who looked upon creative writing as a profession to which all else was subordinate. Most of the benefits that come from literary companionship went from him to others; and the two most important recipients, Johnston and Tabb, even at their best in the two decades following, were but minor figures in the national picture—one the author of a few first-rate examples of the local color story, the other of a handful of intense religious lyrics. At the beginning of his career Lanier had complained to Bayard Taylor (Aug. 7, 1875): " I could never describe to you what a mere drought and famine my life has been, as regards that multitude of matters which I fancy one absorbs when one is in an atmosphere of art, or when one is in conversational relation with men of letters." With little exception he might have made this same complaint at the end of his life. He was to get an occasional glimpse of the world he hungered for, chiefly through Taylor in New York; but in Baltimore he was never among his peers as a man of letters.[98]

correspondence between them, which falls in the last four years of Lanier's life, one letter by Johnston and eight to him. Most of the latter were first discovered by Long and published by him (*op. cit.*, pp. 315-323), reprinted in the present edition.

[97] Long, *op. cit.*, p. 323; see also p. 316, and Lanier's letters of Nov. 6, 1877, and July 5, 1881. The novel appeared in 1883, the story was collected the same year in the comprehensive edition of the *Dukesborough Tales*, and a dozen more volumes followed before Johnston's death in 1898.

[98] Baltimore's two other principal authors had departed from the scene before Lanier's arrival: Poe had been dead for a quarter-century; John Pendleton Kennedy had died at Newport, R. I., in 1870. Some light can be shed on the local state of literature at the time of Lanier's death by the efforts of George E.

It is somewhat ironical that a creative artist whose real talent was in poetry should find his most rewarding companionship in the academic field, but so it was with Lanier. Years before coming to Baltimore he had written from the deep South in Reconstruction times (June 11, 1866) : " There's not enough attrition of mind on mind, here, to bring out any sparks from a man." This to Milton Northrup, with whom he hád once planned to study at Heidelberg, in preparation for the career of a scholar and teacher. This dream, long dead, was revived in a new shape with the founding of the Johns Hopkins University. The early history of this institution is already well known and needs to be sketched here only in relation to Lanier.[99] In the very month of his arrival in Baltimore, public announcement was made of the will of the founder which provided the unprecedented amount of three and a half million dollars for the establishment of a university. Lanier was alert to the possibilities from the beginning. Two months after the first business meeting of the trustees, when the corporation still existed only on paper, he wrote to his wife (Apr. 3, 1874) : " Now, the present aim of my heart is to get the Chair of Metaphysics in the great Johns

Dorsey to establish a magazine. The prospectus (a copy of which survives in the Charles D. Lanier Collection, Johns Hopkins University) laments that Baltimore's literary progress has not kept pace with that in industry, commerce, and society, " But happily there are now some signs of a literary renaissance." As a trial balloon, he proposed a *Christmas Magazine* to be issued in December, 1880, with contributions from " our best local literati," to be paid for if possible. When it appeared, the editor made a plea to Baltimore for support, saying: " The time has come, we think, when a national magazine can be established at this point, to derive its mental and material sustenance mainly from the South," but warning that the need was not sectional literature but " more Laniers and Cables." (Copy in the Lanier Room, Johns Hopkins.) Lanier was a contributor, as were his friends Wallis, Spencer, Browne, and Johnston, though there is no evidence that they received any pay. Dorsey's venture was stillborn, however, whether killed by apathy or lack of talent is not known.

[99] There is no single adequate history, but of those in print the most compact is W. Carson Ryan's " The Johns Hopkins: University Pioneer," prepared for the Carnegie Foundation for the Advancement of Teaching, Bulletin No. 30 (*Studies in Early Graduate Education*, New York, 1939, pp. 15-46). A convenient factual summary of the operations of the university during its first four years may be found in Lanier's own previously unknown article written for Appleton's *American Cyclopaedia* in 1880 and reprinted in the present edition (III, 411-419). A comprehensive history is now in preparation by John C. French, Librarian Emeritus of the Johns Hopkins, who has kindly read the present account. The purpose here being chiefly to recreate the atmosphere of the early years, no effort has been made to go beyond the standard printed sources, except in a few matters pertaining specifically to Lanier. In the following pages facts and figures are used without further citation from the official university publications—the *Annual Reports* (1876-1881), the *Register* (1876-1879), the *Circulars* (1879-1882)—and from the sketches of the first faculty in the *Dictionary of American Biography*.

Hopkins University, wh. is soon to be built." But it was two more years before its doors were opened, and five before Lanier's ambitions and talents could be adjusted to the university's needs.

The three steps that started this pioneer institution on its remarkable experiment were: the generous endowment by Hopkins which was largely free of strings, the selection by the trustees of a president to whom they gave a free hand, and the passing on of this freedom to his faculty by Daniel Coit Gilman. All deserve credit for this simple but wise (and unique) program, but the present concern must be entirely with the shaping personalities and policies. From the outset Gilman seized upon the idea of a true university, as distinguished from a college, there being at that time no institution in America primarily devoted to advanced studies.[100] In selecting his staff and formulating his plans, he spent nearly two years traveling all over this country and Europe. His principles, as announced at his inaugural on February 22, 1876, and later put into practice, were few in number but revolutionary in character: (1) the university was to be free from ecclesiastical, political, or other partisan influence; (2.) the emphasis was to be not on buildings or equipment but on teachers and students, and even there the aim was quality and not quantity; (3.) the faculty—selected for their eminence as specialists, their capacity for original research, and their enthusiasm for teaching—would be few in number, with high salaries, small teaching loads, and ample opportunities for publication; (4.) to attract a small but select body of students, with emphasis on doctoral candidates, a large number of fellowships was set up and for the most promising graduates temporary appointments as associates with promise of promotion; (5.) the curriculum, while giving due attention to the traditional humanities, would offer full encouragement in the new departments of scientific research, the chief aim being to extend the boundaries of knowledge rather than merely to preserve the heritage of the past; (6.) though allowing virtual autonomy within departments, the methods of study would be modelled on those of the German universities: personal guidance in laboratory and seminar, with a modification of the English tutorial system for the undergraduates and a compromise between free electives and intensive specialization; (7.) supplementary to the work of the permanent staff, following the tradition of the *Collège de France*, eminent scholars in all fields would be brought in from the outside for regular courses of lectures, open to the public as well as to the academic body; (8.) the administrative policy would be informal, flexible, and above all tentative.[101]

[100] For a summary of the opportunities for graduate work in the United States prior to 1876, see Ryan, *op. cit.*, pp. 1-14.

[101] See Ryan, *op. cit.*, pp. 15-46; Gilman, *The Launching of a University* (New York, 1906), pp. 4-85; and Fabian Franklin, *The Life of Daniel Coit*

To dream great dreams is one thing, to make them come true is another. But in addition to being an idealistic planner, Gilman was a resourceful administrator and a wise co-ordinator, with an uncanny knack for reading personality. According to Abraham Flexner he rose to the leadership in American educational administration because he knew the difference between significance and insignificance.[102] With his rare gift for spotting men of talent, Gilman picked some of the most distinguished scholars of the century for his first six professors, the most remarkable feature being that only one of them had already attained eminence. This was J. J. Sylvester, an eccentric London Jew, somewhat thwarted in his previous academic career, but with the reputation of being the leading mathematician in England; and though in his early sixties, he came to stand out above any of his colleagues as a source of intellectual enthusiasm.[103] The original plan had been to get similar men for the other departments, but with an infant university this proved impracticable, and Gilman turned to the even harder task of finding the young men of the future. In between came Basil Gildersleeve, a Ph. D. from Göttingen, whose abilities had been cramped for the past twenty years by routine classroom duties at the University of Virginia; and though he had already issued his series of Latin textbooks, it was not until he came to Hopkins that he began the career of research and publication that put him at the head of Greek scholarship in his day.[104] Thus the traditional classics and mathematics were taken care of. For the three new departments of science, extraordinarily young men were chosen, all under thirty. Ira Remsen, also with a doctor's degree from Göttingen, soon surrounded himself with a brilliant group of students, through whom and through his journal and textbooks he was to exert a profound influence on the development of chemistry.

Gilman (New York, 1910), pp. 182 ff. A summary of his inaugural address is given by Lanier, III, 412-413. According to Franklin (p. 192) on the day that Gilman formally accepted the presidency, Jan. 30, 1875, he set down a tentative scheme apportioning 25% of the endowment income for administration, Library, and apparatus, and the other 75% for instruction—with full professors' salaries at $6,000. Actually Sylvester was the only one who received that amount; Gildersleeve was paid $5,000, the others somewhat less. But these were high salaries for university professors in 1876. (Information by courtesy of Dr. French.)

[102] Quoted in Ryan, *op. cit.*, p. 26.

[103] See Franklin, *op. cit.*, p. 213. Gilman had been warned of his eccentricities, but after a conference decided these were infinitessimal in comparison with his brilliancy and renown; and in the end declared that his explorer's attitude had a stimulating effect on the entire university, and that at times he seemed "the youngest of the academic council, so exuberant was he in suggestion, so unexpected and emphatic in his counsels, so proud of his pupils, so irascible and so conciliatory" (*Launching*, pp. 51, 66).

[104] Gilman, *op. cit.*, pp. 53-54. Gildersleeve and Gilman were both forty-five in 1876.

Then came Newell Martin, fellow at Cambridge and assistant to Huxley (who recommended him), to set up the first biological laboratory in America. Finally, Henry Rowland, an obscure young instructor in a polytechnic institute and the author of a single but important article on electricity, attracted Gilman's attention and impressed him with his " rare intellectual powers and . . . uncommon aptitude for experimental science." Though cut down in his prime he became the leading physicist of the country and a scientist of international repute.[105] To assist the professors in instruction a dozen even younger men were engaged as associates, and for a corps of fellows twenty students were hand picked who, almost without exception, won distinction in later life. Thus the best evidences of President Gilman's ability lie in the actual careers of the men he chose for his first staff, and in their testimonials to his worth.[106]

Persuading the trustees to postpone the question of a campus until the scope of the university's development became more apparent, he purchased two private residences near the business district of the city, and by the autumn of 1876 he was ready to launch his experiment. Eighty-nine students reported for enrollment, about half of them undergraduates and " specials," the other half graduates working for the Ph. D. degree or engaging in post-doctoral study.[107] In September Thomas Henry Huxley, the eminent English biologist and champion of evolution, gave a public lecture, congratulating Baltimore for putting its money into men rather than brick and mortar and emphasizing the importance of increasing the stock of knowledge by original investigations. Thus the key-note of the " new education " was

[105] The sixth member of the original faculty, Charles Morris, was Collegiate professor of Latin and Greek, a teacher rather than a scholar. (See Gilman, op. cit., pp. 47-49, 51-53, 54, 70-75.) Rowland was the first member of the faculty actually engaged, but he was not officially appointed until after Gildersleeve and Sylvester; Remsen followed on Apr. 17, 1876, Martin and Morris in September.

[106] See, for example, those by Sylvester, Remsen, and Gildersleeve among the professors (quoted in Franklin, op. cit., pp. 230-231, 310-311, 359-360); and those by Charles Lanman, Josiah Royce, and Stanley Hall among the fellows (quoted in Ryan, op. cit., pp. 34-39). In addition to Lanman and Royce, who became professors of Sanskrit and philosophy at Harvard, this first brilliant group of fellows included Walter Hines Page and Herbert B. Adams, professor of history at Johns Hopkins. (For an account of their careers see Edwin D. Slosson, " Johns Hopkins University," Independent, LXVII, 1233-1234, Dec. 2, 1909.)

[107] Among the graduate students, twelve came from studies in Europe where they had already won the Ph. D. or M. D. degree. Even after ten years, for the growth was purposefully slow, there were only 184 graduates, 96 undergraduates, and 34 specials. (See Ryan, op. cit., pp. 24-33.) A view of the university buildings approximately as they looked at the time of Lanier's lectureship is given in the present edition, X, facing 129.

struck and the university began its important career, quietly and without pomp. The winter of 1876-1877 was one of great expectations, but the public was inquisitive and not a little skeptical. Huxley's speech itself, unaccompanied by invocation or benediction, created something of a storm. As one religious periodical observed in reporting the ceremonies, Huxley was bad enough, but Huxley without prayer was intolerable; and it was some time before Gilman's diplomacy quieted the local clergymen's fears of infidelity. Certain individuals and groups were indifferent for a while because of the failure of partisan influence to secure the appointment of their candidates. Others were disappointed that so much money had produced such a small show. But in academic circles, both in America and Europe, the university was a success from the outset, as Lanier declared in his ode: " So quick she bloomed, she seemed to bloom at birth." [108] Exilaration was in the very atmosphere, and all were conscious of the pioneer character of the venture. Faculty and students, despite the modest beginnings and inadequate quarters, worked together in harmony and enthusiasm. Gildersleeve, the professor of Greek, commented humorously that Gilman put him in an empty room and told him to " radiate." Rowland, the professor of physics, declared that all he wanted for his laboratory was one of the back kitchens, a solid pier built up from the ground, and the finest set of precision instruments available. Yet in a few years these and the other heads of departments had built up such a galaxy of brilliant pupils as resulted in the founding of scholarly journals to publish their researches and, according to President Eliot of Harvard, in raising the standards of graduate education throughout the country.[109]

What place was there in such a scheme of things for a poet, with a modest collegiate education and with no proven ability as a scholar to certify his ambition for research? To this question the answer was found by President Gilman, who seems to have been just as anxious to make a place for him in the university as he was. Two weeks before instruction in the first session began, Lanier wrote to him (Sept. 18,

[108] See Ryan, *op. cit.*, p. 25; Franklin, *op. cit.*, pp. 219-225; Gilman, *op. cit.*, pp. 20-23; Josiah Royce, " Present Ideals in American University Life," *Scribner's Magazine*, X, 383 (Sept., 1891).

[109] The Gildersleeve anecdote is quoted in *Dictionary of American Biography*, Rowland in Gilman, *op. cit.*, p. 71, and Eliot's tribute in Franklin, *op. cit.*, p. 389. The publications, with editors and dates of founding, are as follows: *American Journal of Mathematics* (Sylvester, assisted by Rowland, 1878), *American Chemical Journal* (Remsen, 1879), *Studies from the Biological Laboratory* (Martin, 1879), *American Journal of Philology* (Gildersleeve, 1880), *Studies in Historical and Political Science* (Adams, 1882), and *Modern Language Notes* (Elliott, 1886). To these—among the earliest learned journals published in the United States—should be added the *University Circulars*, begun in 1879, which reported the meetings of the six scholarly associations in the several fields with abstracts of the research papers read before them.

1876) asking for a prospectus, particularly with regard to the opportunities in science. He followed this up with a conference, the results
of which he reported to a friend:

I found that Mr. Gilman was familiar with all my poems, and he
told me that he had thought of inviting me to a position in the
University, last winter, but did not know whether I had ever pursued
any special studies. . . . It was finally agreed that a proposition should
be made to the Trustees to create for me a sort of nondescript chair of
" poetry and music." [110]

Another visit and letters followed but the prospect hung fire. Meantime
his health collapsed to the point where work of any sort was impossible,
but Gilman's interest had been definitely aroused. " I was anxious to
have him appointed to such a chair," he recalled in later years, " but
the trustees did not see their way to do so." [111] Considering the
scholarly qualifications of the half-dozen he had previously selected
for his " chairs," one is somewhat puzzled that Gilman should have
thought of Lanier for such a position. But the difficulty lies in the
word, for he obviously had in mind not a professorship but merely
" a connection . . . of some description " in which the " work and
salary would be small," as Lanier himself described it to his father
(Oct. 1, 1876). Even in this category, considering his lack of
training and his age, it would be hard enough to fit him into a regular
academic niche. But one must remember that though Gilman's first
emphasis was on eminence in research, his second was on personality,
and in all his many reminiscences of Lanier it is the man and not the
scholar that is stressed.[112] His recent rise to prominence as a poet had
been followed by Gilman with considerable interest, and remembering
his successful appointment of Edward Rowland Sill as professor of
English literature at the University of California (1874-1882), he

[110] Letter to Peacock, Oct. 4, 1876. See also Lanier's letters to his father,
Oct. 1 and 10, and to Gilman, Oct. 22, and his wife's letter to Clifford Lanier,
Nov. 8, 1876.
[111] " Sidney Lanier: Reminiscences and Letters," *South Atlantic Quarterly*, IV,
116-117 (Apr., 1905).
[112] In that cited in the note above he spoke of " his sweetness of disposition,
his cheerfulness, his courtesy," " his rare combination of gentleness and intellectual brightness," " that sunshiny and sympathetic smile which illuminated his
face . . . always brave, full of resources, confident of ultimate triumph "
(pp. 120-121). In his remarks at the memorial meeting in Hopkins Hall, Oct. 22,
1881, he referred to Lanier's " many endearing qualities " (see the undated
pamphlet entitled *Sidney Lanier*, p. 3). The next year, " a man of remarkable
personal qualities," " He made a strong impression on every one who met him.
They loved him for his enthusiasm toward all that was lofty and noble " (see
" Personal Recollections of Sidney Lanier," *Our Continent*, I, 130, Apr. 12,
1882). See also the extended comments in *The Launching of a University*
(New York, 1906), pp. 94-97.

probably thought that Lanier could somehow help to restore the balance at Hopkins, which at the beginning was overweighted on the side of science. But he had other plans for the professorship of English. He apparently offered the post to Francis J. Child, the Harvard balladist, in 1875; the next year Sylvester recommended Matthew Arnold, but there is no evidence that Gilman considered this seriously.[113] The tradition of the German universities was to study literature as a branch of linguistics, and this idea, imported into American graduate schools, was to flourish for half a century. Pending the discovery of the proper philologist, the matter was left in abeyance at Hopkins for several years.

On his return from Florida in 1877, Lanier made a second try by applying for a fellowship in science to pursue " research in the physics of musical tone," offering a conglomerate program of courses he wished to study, but he was turned down. Gilman's comment on this application explains why: fellowships were awarded only to those " who had already made a considerable degree of progress in special studies, and Lanier's attitude was that of a beginner in Physics, who had not even shown strong predilections for scientific study." [114] His undergraduate studies twenty years before under James Woodrow, pupil of Agassiz and Ph. D. from Heidelberg, had been stimulating and valuable in many ways, but unaccompanied by laboratory work and not followed up until his thirty-sixth year they could not open the doors of even so liberal an institution as Johns Hopkins. Gilman's resourcefulness was not exhausted, however, for there still remained the system of lecturers, one of the many examples of his alertness to seize upon excellence outside the customary routine; and it is barely possible that he is the one who suggested the idea of building up a reputation in this field that would impress the trustees.[115] Lanier also had the example of his friend Léonce Rabillon, whose lectures at the Peabody on French literature had brought about his appointment at Hopkins during the first session. At any rate, in the spring of 1878 through the generosity of another friend, Mrs. Edgeworth Bird, he began his career as a lecturer on English literature, with the result that he was asked to give a more extended series the next year at the Peabody. He had succeeded; Gilman's interest in this second course is demonstrated by his

[113] Franklin, *op. cit.*, pp. 235-236, 374-375.
[114] Gilman, " Reminiscences of Sidney Lanier," *Pathfinder*, I, 3 (Sept., 1906). Lanier's letter of application to Gilman was written on Sept. 26, 1877. See also his letter to his father, Oct. 26, 1877.
[115] In the reminiscences cited in the note above, immediately following the account of why Lanier failed to get a fellowship, is the statement that he then turned to the study of literature which resulted in the series of lectures at Mrs. Bird's, one of which Gilman attended.

helping Lanier to secure supplementary lecturers from the university staff—Gildersleeve, Remsen, and Herbert B. Adams, recently made Associate in history.[116]

Although a failure financially, these efforts achieved the desired result, for mid way in the Peabody course came the invitation that was at last to connect Lanier with the Johns Hopkins University, as lecturer in English literature during the academic year of 1879-1880.[117] Gilman's idea in making the appointment is revealed in a letter of July 16, 1879, in which after pointing out that the present language courses were chiefly linguistic he said:

Now we need among us someone like you, loving literature and poetry and treating it in such a way as to enlist and inspire many students. . . . We may wake up a few persons (such as Royce was) among the Fellows or Graduates, who will take up literature in a truly earnest and philosophical spirit.

But his emphasis was on the afternoon lectures, with the suggestion that later on a class course might be organized chiefly composed of undergraduates. Lanier, with his customary zeal, looked upon this as an entering wedge that would lead to a more substantial connection with the university proper. Though his public lectures proved to be a marked success, he had looked upon them from the first as accessory to his main efforts which he hoped would be with the students, both graduate and undergraduate, as a bona fide professor of literature.[118] But these hopes were doomed from the start. Co-eval with his appoint-

[116] See Lanier's letter of May 13, 1878. Earlier plans for the Peabody lectures had included Sylvester (professor of mathematics), Child (visiting lecturer in English), Brandt (Associate in German), and Royce (fellow in philosophy and literature). Lanier's literary friends Johnston and Spencer also participated. For a detailed account of Lanier's lectures at the Peabody and later at Johns Hopkins, see the Introductions to vols. III and IV of the present edition.

[117] See Gilman's letter of Feb. 4, 1879. The implication of his biographer as to his motivations is not borne out by the other evidence (see Franklin, *op. cit.*, p. 239: "Mr. Gilman's sympathetic insight effected a service in which his interest was perhaps equally divided between the question of promoting the University's work and that of helping to relieve the burdens of struggling genius and noble manhood").

[118] See his letter of July 13, 1879, outlining an ambitious scheme of courses and reiterating his desire for a "Chair of Poetry." Even as a lecturer he had his hands full living up to the precedent set by James Russell Lowell and Child, who had given lectures in literature in 1877-1878. But the average attendance at his lectures was higher than at any other series except that of Prof. Adams on the Italian Renaissance (see note 66, Letters of 1879). A mimeographed notice was sent out by the university on Oct. 25, 1879, saying: "Those who have not received tickets to Mr. Lanier's lectures are respectfully informed that there have already been 330 applications for less than 200 sittings in Hopkins Hall" (copy in Alumni Office, Johns Hopkins University).

ment as lecturer, a trained philologist, Albert S. Cook, was engaged as an Associate in English and began a regular program of courses in Anglo-Saxon, Chaucer, and Shakespeare. And at the end of the first year Lanier wrote to his father (June 19, 1880), announcing his reappointment as " Lecturer " and reporting somewhat dejectedly:

The prospect of a professorship is completely clouded by the fact that one of the Associates already has a department of English, and there is really not full work for two,—under the present system. I could soon *make* work enough for more than two, if I were in charge; but my ideas are all revolutionary.

So they were, and if he had lived to carry out his ambitions he might have been a pioneer in the introduction of literature, studied as such, in the graduate schools of America.[119]

Failing health and early death, however, limited his work among the students to two classes during the winter of 1880, and even these were in the nature of " specials " outside the curriculum.[120] Here, as always, Gilman was his personal sponsor. One of the graduates who took the course has recalled the first meeting and the words with which the president introduced Lanier, his poet-protegé: " Mr. Sylvester says the only way he can teach Mathematics is to show how he works at it. So the students of this class will see how a literary man works at Literature." [121] The group was small, and with some of them at least he developed literary friendships during walks and meals at his home to which they were invited. One remembered him as " a refined, culti-vated gentleman "; another said that his methods of teaching brought about " a subtle expansion of the power of appreciation and an unde-finable exaltation of the instincts of taste that I have since learned were more precious than any precise increments of knowledge "; a third emphasized his essential youthfulness of mind, his " startling keenness . . . that was not so much philosophical as intuitive," his " insatiable desire to know and understand." [122] He was well liked by the students,

[119] For his class courses as given and planned, see the Introduction to vol. III, xiii-xv, and note 28.

[120] The *Register* for 1879-1880 does not list them among the regular courses of instruction given during the year.

[121] Reminiscences of Dr. George F. Nicholassen, quoted in W. F. Melton, " Sidney Lanier in Baltimore," Griffin (Ga.) *Daily News*, June 20, 1935.

[122] See the note above; the unidentified student quoted in J. S. Short, " Sidney Lanier ' Familiar Citizen of the Town,'" *Maryland Historical Magazine*, XXXV, 137 (June, 1940) ; and the more extended reminiscences of Dr. Waldo S. Pratt, quoted in Starke, p. 375. While actually a student, however, Pratt had written to his parents, Nov. 16, 1879, that Lanier's public lecture course was " altogether too popular and transcendentally poetical . . . and the attendance of University men is constantly diminishing " (quoted in Starke, p. 363).

both for his poetic personality and for those native qualities which in time would have made him an excellent teacher. Gilman has summed the matter up:

With a poet's imagination, he made far-reaching plans for the instruction of the enrolled students. . . . Alas, these lofty aspirations were constantly handicapped by frequent attacks of illness.
Brief as was his academic career, it left a strong impression upon all who heard him. Many students of those days are perpetually grateful for his inspiration.[123]

Thus Lanier's position with the Johns Hopkins University was never really more than tangential, but he relished the substantial intellectual fare now set before him for the first time, as the letters abundantly show. Since they do not indicate very clearly his personal relations with this eminent group of scholars, it seems desirable to supplement them. Three members of the staff were old friends of his: Rabillon, like himself a lecturer; Philip R. Uhler, librarian of the Peabody and associate in natural history since 1876; and William Hand Browne, who was made librarian at Hopkins with the rank of associate in 1879. With others of the associates some degree of acquaintance can be assumed, such as Hermann Brandt in German and Herbert B. Adams in history, because of their connections with his Peabody course; with Cook, the associate in English, he is said to have conferred " on questions of Anglo-Saxon," and he may have been one of the small group of Baltimore teachers invited to a special course in " Early English " in the winter of 1880, but this was after Lanier had finished most of the work he was to do in these fields.[124] So with others of the lesser lights he was probably on friendly terms, but what of the stars in this galaxy?

With Martin, professor of biology, there is no evidence of any relationship. With the professor of chemistry, Ira Remsen, on the other

---

[123] " Reminiscences," *Pathfinder*, p. 4.

[124] None of these three are mentioned in Lanier's letters. (Charles Morris, collegiate professor of Latin, is mentioned twice.) For Adams and Brandt, see note 116, above. For Cook see Mims, p. 240, and III, 415, of the present edition. *The Science of English Verse* and Lanier's lectures collected as *Shakespere and his Forerunners*, his principal works dealing with medieval and renaissance literature, were completed by the autumn of 1879. Cook's regular courses in Old and Middle English had only one student, Bright, who was to succeed him in later years; his linguistic courses in Chaucer and Shakespeare, given at the same time as Lanier's classes in the same as literature, were attended by half-a-dozen, but Lanier's name is not included. It was W. H. Browne, as a matter of fact, who first drew Lanier's attention to the oldest English poetry. (See his letter to Henry W. Lanier, Feb. 19, 1903. After he became librarian Browne's interests shifted from literature to history, and by his death he had edited thirty-two volumes in the *Archives of Maryland*.)

hand, he apparently had much in common. The references are slight, merely to his participation in the Peabody course and to an engrossing conversation in the halls of the university between classes, but are suffi- cient to suggest a real intimacy. And knowing Remsen's interest in the historical significance of science and especially his concern in reconciling the supposed conflict between it and Christianity, one can even con- jecture the substance of this and other conversations between them.[125] Suggestive of a more specific relation between Lanier and one of the science departments is the statement of his first biographer: " On matters of scientific interest, such as he pursued in his investigation into the physics of sound, he sought advice from the scientists of the University, even taking courses with them." [126] This was not the great physicist Rowland, however, whose special interests were light and heat and who was distinctly not interested in the scientific study of sound, in spite of his recent year with Helmholtz, then in the midst of the very discoveries in acoustics that so excited Lanier.[127] Further, the official publications of Johns Hopkins reveal no course given there during Lanier's lifetime in the physics of sound, nor is Lanier listed in any of the class rolls of the department. But during the winter of 1878-1879, a series of public lectures was given by Charles Hastings, associate in physics, on the " Theory of Sound in its Relations to Music." [128] That Lanier attended these lectures one may be sure, but what influence they or his conferences with Hastings had upon the *Science of English Verse*, then in the process of formulation, must remain dark; for here the evidence ends.

Lanier's best friends on the Johns Hopkins faculty, one discovers without surprise, were the two professors who could be considered in 1879 its most distinguished members. For during those pace-setting first years, the younger men discussed above—with the possible excep- tion of Remsen—were engrossed in their work as scientific specialists, with their reputations largely ahead and little time at the moment for

---

[125] Remsen's Peabody lectures were on the place of science in Shakespeare's time. See Lanier's letter to Gilman, Feb. 17, 1880; see further the Introduction to vol. I, present edition.

[126] Mims, p. 240.

[127] See Rowland's letter to Gilman, July 26, 1876: " Acoustic instruments always seem to me more like playthings than anything else, but I suppose we must have some " (quoted in Franklin, *op. cit.*, p. 371). Rowland's great con- tributions to physics on which his fame rests were: (1.) determination of the mechanical equivalent of heat, (2.) accurate ascertainment of the value of the ohm, (3.) his spectrum analysis. He is not mentioned in Lanier's letters.

[128] *The Fourth Annual Report of the Johns Hopkins University* (Baltimore, 1879), p. 29, lists these in a summary of the lectures during the past three years, without a specific date. But since they are not listed in the two previous *Reports*, they can be safely assigned to 1878-1879.

the broader cultural interests that come with full maturity. Not that
Lanier sought out eminence, but it was natural that he should find the
greatest congeniality with those who in the flush of achievement allowed
their intellectual powers to expand in many directions. Another strong
attraction was the magnetism of personality, and though the others
caught up with them later in many ways, Basil Gildersleeve and James
Sylvester were, along with Gilman, the presiding geniuses in the early
history of the university.

Gildersleeve, a decade older than Lanier, was at this time in his early
prime. A man of imposing manner and physical presence, tall and well
proportioned, with Olympian head and dominating eyes, tradition has
attributed to him a Zeus-like personality. His academic record as a
classicist is well remembered even today; but with his range of knowledge, uncurbed satire, and fearless criticism, he was as famous among
his contemporaries for his ideas as for his philological talents. According to Gilman: " His love of literature and his acquaintance with the
best writers, ancient and modern, gave him great weight in all our
discussions in respect to letters and language." [129] One did not have to
be a specialist in the classics to find stimulation in Gildersleeve's society.
Like Lanier he was a southerner and a Confederate veteran. They
moved in the same social circles in Baltimore and had already established personal relations before they became professional colleagues.
They were fellow members of the Wednesday Club, and from Lanier's
mention of a conversation with him there, in the summer of 1878, one
assumes that they often met at the informal gatherings of this group.[130]
Again, Gildersleeve has left an amusing anecdote of a dinner party
given the following winter in the poet's honor when, arriving from a
lecture at the Peabody without time to put on his dress clothes, he was
so discomfited that he hardly roused himself even when the talk fell
on Blake. In the same reminiscence of Lanier, he has recorded the
more serious side of their friendships:

We never became intimate, and yet we were good friends and there was
much common ground. Our talks usually turned on matters of literary
form. He was eager, receptive, reaching out to all the knowable, trans-
muting all that he learned. He would have me read Greek poetry
aloud to him for the sake of the rhythm and the musical effect.[131]

[129] *Launching*, p. 54. His brilliant career as a teacher and his wide influence
on classical scholarship are matters of record that need not be detailed here.
In addition to his texts, his voluminous contribution of scholarly articles, and
his *magnum opus* (*Syntas of Classical Greek*, 2 v., 1900, 1911), he published a
large number of interpretative criticisms of classical literature collected in
1890 as *Essays and Studies*. As a young man he had even taken a fling at
creative authorship, writing a novel which, however, was never published.
[130] See note 66, above.
[131] A letter from Gildersleeve quoted by Mims, pp. 239, 302. (Gildersleeve

And more specifically, Gildersleeve adds that during the composition of the *Science of English Verse* they had many talks about classical prosody.

When Sylvester came to the Johns Hopkins University he was sixty-two years old. But far from basking idly in the golden glow of his international renown, in zeal and enthusiasm he was more like one just beginning his career. An inspired teacher, he gathered around him a group of brilliant students and, with his *Journal* and other publications, set new standards for mathematical research, so that upon the posthumous collection of his papers he was characterized as " perhaps the mind most exuberant in original ideas of pure mathematics of any since Gauss." [132] Much of this research was done during his seven years residence in Baltimore, which, he declared to Gilman upon accepting the Savilian Professorship of Geometry at Oxford (1883), had been the most quickening and prolific period of his life.[133] He was widely known and loved throughout the city, delighting in lively society and symphonic concerts, partly for themselves and partly because they stimulated him to abstract thinking. His mercurial temperament and eccentricities of conduct have left a host of legends behind him. But we do not have to depend on hearsay, for one of the quirks of his genius found its way into print, an experiment in nonsense verse constructed on mathematical principles, entitled *Spring's Debut. A Town Idyll, In Two Centuries of Continuous Rhyme.* A copy of this unique poem, " By J. J. Sylvester, F. R. S. . . . Printed for Private Circulation only," has survived,[134] with many amusing references to Baltimore life in 1880: to Johns Hopkins and Professor Gildersleeve, to the Wednesday Club, to the cattle pieces of John Tait, to Hamerik's violin. This goes on for two hundred lines of highly unreadable poetry that is chiefly remarkable for its fantastic rhymes and for the appended notes. Most pertinent to the present study is the line celebrating the " Marshes and wet sands of Glynn " with its accompanying footnote:

Glynn is a sort of Lido, on the coast of Georgia. Mr. Lanier, the author of *Corn* and the *Centennial Ode*, the apostle of " phonetic syzygy " and admittedly the finest flute player in the United States, has written a poem which has been much admired, called " The Marshes of Glynn," drawn from his impressions on the spot, where like Byron at Venice

gave two lectures in Lanier's Peabody Course, comparing Shakespeare with the Latin and Greek dramatists.)

[132] *Collected Mathematical Papers of J. J. Sylvester,* 4 vols., 1904-1912. The characterization is from the sketch in *Dictionary of American Biography.*

[133] Gilman, *Launching,* p. 51. See also pp. 68-69.

[134] Copy in the Johns Hopkins Library. The title-page is undated, but the final note, p. 28, is headed " Johns Hopkins University, January, 1880."

he was used to take long solitary rides, or accompanied only by his
Muse, up and down the beach.[135]

This, of course, was merely the offshoot of an exuberant mind
amusing itself. But Professor Sylvester, who was a good linguist and
an ardent student of literature, stoutly maintained that imagination has
as much to do with mathematics as with poetry, and after a long discussion with the astronomer Simon Newcomb made an absolute equa-
tion of the two. His most important correlation of these two fields of
interest is embodied in *The Laws of Verse*, published in 1870, where,
among much serious discussion lightened with witty notes, he
coined the term "phonetic syzygy" to describe the apt juncture of
syllables. "This definition," according to one of the students at
Hopkins during this period, "quite captivated the poet-musician, Sidney
Lanier." [136] Both in his *Science of English Verse* and in his Johns
Hopkins lectures Lanier cited this volume as an authority on English
prosody. And in his Ode to the university, read on Commemoration
Day, 1880, he singled out the author for special praise in his tribute
to the "sages" of the first faculty, "Led by the soaring-genius'd
Sylvester," returning the scholarly compliment by according him a
poetic footnote for his work in demonstrating and extending a theorem
of Newton's.[137] More indicative of personal attachment is the evidence
of a letter written to Ephraim Keyser the next autumn (Oct. 5, 1880)
asking what sum he would charge to make a bust of the great mathematician, so that Lanier could begin his subscription list at the university
without delay. That this admiration was reciprocated is proved by
Sylvester's eulogistic reference to Lanier as "this great poet"; and
though no further account of their friendship has survived it was
certainly as close and as profitable as that with Gildersleeve.[138]

[135] In connection with a similar effusion, "To Rosalind," occurs one of the
many anecdotes of his absentmindedness, on the authority of Gilman, who
declared that Sylvester was "possessed by a sort of monomania for rhyme."
Quoted from Gilman, without citation of source, by David C. Holly, "Baltimore
in American Literature," typescript, Johns Hopkins University, 1933, p. 86; see
also Franklin, *op. cit.*, p. 375, and Gilman, *Launching*, p. 67-68.
[136] Allen K. Bond, *When the Hopkins Came to Baltimore* (Baltimore, 1927),
p. 38. (Bond says that he saw Lanier only at his lectures.) See also Gilman,
Launching, p. 67.
[137] See the present edition: I, 133; II, 6, 12, 237; III, 315, 326.
[138] H. E. Shepherd, "Southern Poets," *Confederate Veteran*, XXVII, 450-
451 (Dec., 1919). I have found no trace of a bust of Sylvester actually made
by Keyser. Johns Hopkins as an institution has honored Lanier on many
occasions: the Commemoration Meeting on Oct. 22, 1881; the Memorial Fund
Meeting in 1883; the Forty-sixth Birthday in 1888, with the unveiling of the
bronze bust by Keyser; on down to the Centennial Celebration, Feb. 3, 1942,
when the Lanier Room was dedicated and the present edition formally announced.

Such an array of Lanier's friends and acquaintances in the cultural life of Baltimore is likely to be misleading unless qualified by the reminder that his constant ill health and his economic struggle, which saddled him with a heavy load of pen labor, prevented him from giving free reign to his naturally sociable disposition. His life was not nearly so isolated as has been thought; but as a devoted family man, he spent much of his time at home, and as a true poet and an ambitious scholar he spent many hours alone with his thoughts and his books. His poetic career is treated elsewhere, but a word must be said here in conclusion about the feverish reading he undertook in his last years to prepare himself for an academic life.[139] Of Lanier's book-hunger, starved for the first thirty years of his life, a pathetic testimonial has survived written on a slip of paper in his late autograph:

I have never read anything. I have seized several books with wolfish ravening and torn off bits and swallowed them. Do you remember Caliban's first draught of wine in [the] *Tempest?* He claws the bottle, gulps, and warmed by the generous liquid, cries to the author of it, " Be my God! " It is thus I have absorbed the few books I have ever had a chance to read. The passion of all this is not for words.[140]

Though expressed in poetic symbols, this is not too far from the truth.

One of his chief reasons for accepting the offer to play in the Peabody Orchestra in 1873 was that " I might dwell in the beautiful city, among the great libraries and . . . write my books." [141] At this period the combined libraries of Baltimore contained nearly two hundred thousand volumes, an impressive collection for that day.[142] A large number of these and by far the most important ones for Lanier's purposes were in the Peabody Library, and it was here that he did most of his reading. This unique institution was designed, as John Pendleton Kennedy declared in the opening address, " to establish a University adapted to the conditions indispensable to the cultivation of a taste for science and letters in the adult population of a large city . . . , to begin where the ordinary college known to our traditional system of education terminates its instruction." This purpose was elaborated by the provost: " We cannot create scholars or readers to use our library; but we can

[139] See the Introduction to vol. III, xv-xviii, for an estimate of his accomplishment as a scholar.

[140] MS, Charles D. Lanier Collection, Johns Hopkins University.

[141] Letter to his wife Sept. 24, 1873. To his father, the same day, he also emphasized this opportunity, " the deprivation of which I have so keenly felt heretofore."

[142] See the *Johns Hopkins University Circular*, No. 4, p. 42 (Apr., 1880). N. H. Morison estimated the combined holdings of the Harvard and Boston Public Libraries at less than 300,000 a decade earlier (*Management and Objects of the Peabody Institute*, Baltimore 1871, pp. 7-9).

make a collection of books which all scholars will appreciate, when
they shall appear among us, as they surely will do some day." [143] The
Johns Hopkins University, opening a few years later, was to take
advantage of this opportunity, relying upon the Peabody for research to
such an extent that its own library was at first confined largely to books
for class courses. Even earlier had come Lanier, only an amateur
scholar, but one who profited from this collection more than almost any
other reader during the 1870's. Deprived of the opportunity to pursue
advanced study in a regular academic institution, here he found a
substitute designed for his very needs.

Long before the building was opened to the public, the library committee, after consulting with leading specialists all over the country,
published a long list of books which it desired to purchase and with
this circularized dealers in America and Europe.[144] The program was
to buy the significant books in every department of learning (except
law and medicine), with special emphasis on science, literature, history,
and philosophy, with careful selection of rare and expensive volumes
" not ordinarily obtainable in the private libraries of the country," and
with no catering to popular tastes in the matter of fiction and other
pastime reading. Morison the provost, who superintended the selections
in the field of literature, declared: " I doubt whether there is a library
in the land in which the same pains have been taken to secure the
best, and to avoid useless books "; and this was amplified by Uhler
the librarian, who specialized in the field of science: " A great library
cannot be created in a day; but it must grow by slow accretions."
Adding that every aid would be given in purchasing books to facilitate
the researches of the Hopkins faculty, he contrasted the Peabody with

[143] See Morison, *op. cit.*, p. 12, and the anonymous *Peabody Institute . . .
Founder's Letters and Papers Relating to its Dedication and its History* (Baltimore, 1868), pp. 106-107. The library itself was supplemented by a School of
Lecturers, which brought to Baltimore during Lanier's residence there the leading
men of Europe and America in the fields covered by the special collections of
books. For example, during his first winter, there were among those of special
interest to Lanier: 4 lectures by Prof. Lounsbury of Yale on the English Language, 6 by Fields the Boston publisher on Tennyson and others, 2 by Prof. E. S.
Morse of Bowdoin on evolution. A lecture by Mayer on Sound in 1875 was
written up by Lanier in the Baltimore *Gazette* (see II, 329). The following two
winters there were lectures by his friend Bayard Taylor, and in 1878-1879 his
own course. The annual average was thirty general lectures by distinguished men
and ninety more specialized ones for smaller study classes, such as those given by
Lanier, Rabillon, and Johnston. (See the *Annual Reports of the Provost*, 1873-
1881, *passim.*)
[144] *Alphabetical Catalogue of Books Proposed to be Purchased for the Library
of the Peabody Institute* (Baltimore, 1861), consisting of more than 400 closely
printed pages. The copy in the Peabody Library has MS inter-leaves showing
the purchases actually made. When the library was first opened to the public in
the autumn of 1867, there were 24,000 volumes on the shelves.

the usual circulating library: " A reference library is vastly more important, because it is of more importance, in any community, that its best minds should be instructed, than that ordinary ones should be amused. . . . Its value is not to be measured so much by the number, as by the quality, of the persons who use it." [145]

By the time of Lanier's arrival, the collection had gradually been built up to over fifty thousand volumes; by the time of his death in 1881 it numbered nearly seventy-five thousand.[146] During his first year in Baltimore, 1873-1874, he was too engrossed with his new career as musician to devote much time to study, though he may have done some reading in French history by way of background for his medieval poem, " The Jacquerie." [147] The next winter he was studying books on the physics of music and examining the institute's newly arrived acoustical apparatus with an eye to the establishment of a " chair " in this field.[148] He was apparently going to the library with some regularity at this time, for in a letter to his wife (Feb. 28, 1875) he speaks of: " a delicious hour in the Peabody Library where I go twice or thrice a week." It was during the last four years of his life, however, that he made the largest use of this excellent collection, in preparation for his lectures in English literature. An interesting picture of Lanier at work in the Peabody has been recorded by John Parker, one of the reference staff at that time:

Perhaps the person who was most assiduous in coming to the Library and who derived the greatest benefit from its books was Sidney Lanier, who began here in the winter of 1877-78, his studies in English which ended only with his life. He usually came in the morning, occupying the same seat at the end of the table, where he worked until lunch time, so absorbed with his studies that he scarcely ever raised his eyes to notice anything around him. During the winters that he was a member of the Peabody Orchestra he came back in the afternoons when the rehearsals were held, bringing his flute with him, and continued his studies until it was time to go into the rehearsal.[149]

[145] See Morison, *op. cit.*, pp. 13, and 24-25; *Ninth Annual Report . . . to the Trustees* (Baltimore, 1876), pp. 9, 15-16.

[146] *Sixth Annual Report* (1873), p. 8; *Fourteenth* (1881), p. 7.

[147] See the Introduction to vol. I, present edition.

[148] Letter to his wife, Jan. 6, 1875. See Frederick Kelly, " Sidney Lanier at the Peabody Institute," *Peabody Bulletin*, pp. 35-38 (Dec., 1939), who notes that the large collection of scientific books in the library at this time included: H. Helmholtz, *Die Lehre von den Tonempfindungen*; A. J. Koch, *Neue Tonlehre*; Mathis Lussy, *Traité de l'expression musicale*; and D. D. Jameson, *Colour-Music*.

[149] " Reminiscences of fifty years in the Library of the Peabody Institute," dated Feb. 13, 1922 (typescript, Peabody Library, Baltimore). Parker's connection with the institute thus dates from 1872; he later became head librarian.

His most intensive period of reading came after the library had been moved into the new building (adjoining Peabody Hall where the concerts were held), erected at the cost of half a million dollars and opened to the public in September, 1878.[150] How completely Lanier gave himself over to scholarly studies at this time is indicated by the decline in his published poems from a peak of twenty-two in 1877-1878 to a single one in 1879. No specific records of his reading have been preserved, but references to the books that he used are scattered through his writings during the last years. And Parker has indicated the general trend of his interests: the publications of the Early English Text Society, the Chaucer Society, the Percy Society, works relating to Shakespeare, and especially the reprints of Elizabethan literature edited by Alexander Grossart and others, issued in small editions only to subscribers, of which the Peabody was one of the few in this country:

These were Mr. Lanier's particular delight, and he often expressed to me his pleasure and gratitude for the privilege of being able to consult reprints whose originals American scholars have rarely ever seen and English scholars have seldom handled. . . .

After [his] appointment as lecturer on English literature at the Johns Hopkins University in 1879 his investigations in the library naturally became more extended and included modern literature, as well as the old English which had heretofore occupied his attention. . . .

During the autumn and early winter of 1880 Mr. Lanier's visits to the library became less frequent, and then he would remain as long as his strength permitted him, as if to make up in this way for his inability to come as often as he wished. A little later on in the year his visits ceased, and one day I received a pathetic note from him stating he was confined to his room by illness, and asking me to supply him with some data he wished to use in the preparation of his lectures.[151]

Moreover, like any devoted student, Lanier cherished owning his favorite books, though this was a luxury he could not indulge to any

[150] See the often quoted passage in Lanier's letter to Taylor, Oct. 20, 1878, and his letter to Kirk, Aug. 24. See also *Twelfth Annual Report* (1879), pp. 7, 30-34, for a description of the new building, with illustrations. Until the summer of 1878 the library had been housed on the second floor of the old building (see illustration facing p. 490, vol. IX, of the present edition).

[151] John Parker, "Sidney Lanier. Some Interesting Recollections of Him by One Who Saw Him Often," Baltimore *American* (undated clipping in the Charles D. Lanier Collection, Johns Hopkins University). In his reminiscences cited in note 149, above, Parker adds that Lanier's wife frequently came to the library to do the copying for him. The librarian is also said to have relaxed the rule occasionally and allowed Lanier to take books to his home for study ("Reminiscences of Sophie Bledsoe Herrick," MS, Edwin Mims Collection, Johns Hopkins University). See also Philip Graham, "Lanier's Reading," University of Texas *Studies in English*, XI, 63-89 (1931), for a list compiled from his printed works.

great extent. But during his last years, with the necessity of doing at home much of the preparation for his lectures and other writings and with the ever present hope that financial security was near at hand, he began to collect a working library, some two hundred volumes of which have come down and are now available to the biographer.[152] Small as this collection is, it is not without significance. In the first place, it testifies to the wide range of Lanier's interests. As would be expected, a majority of the books are in the field of literature. Besides anthologies, literary history and criticism, and presentation copies from his friends—Calvert, Hayne, Sylvester, Taylor—there are the works of his favorite authors: Chaucer and Shakespeare, Emerson, Keats, Shelley, Swinburne, Tennyson, and Whitman; some of the great writers of other nations, Dante, Goethe, Homer, and a number in the original Greek and Latin—Aeschylus, Cicero, Juvenal, and Lucretius; and a few less expected ones, such as George Herbert, William Langland, and several of the Arber reprints. There are some of the usual volumes on history, biography, and travel, but more unusual ones on linguistics, versification, music, and religion. Most surprising are the comparatively large number of philosophical books—by Ascham, Bacon, and Burton, by Cousin and Hamilton, by Epictetus and Socrates, by Montaigne and Swedenborg; the numerous scientific works—on astronomy, botany, chemistry, geology, and physiology, on acoustics, climatology, and the philosophy of mathematics; and several of those that for the Victorians spanned the two fields, such as Asa Gray's efforts to reconcile religion and science, Darwin's *Origin of Species*, Huxley's *Crayfish*, and Spencer's *Principles of Psychology*. Of course many people have owned many books and have read them, but this is of importance only if they make something out of their reading. A glimpse of Lanier at work in his own library should prove revealing.

That he read his books assiduously is witnessed by his many markings. Though it is a hazardous matter to attempt an interpretation of underscorings and marginal checks, there is sufficient evidence of other sorts to show the purposes and results of his home reading. The cut pages and annotations in his copies of Froissart, Malory, Percy, and the

---

[152] 227 volumes are preserved in the Lanier Room, Johns Hopkins University. From the dates on title-pages, inscriptions on fly-leaves, and surviving statements from booksellers, it appears that most of them were purchased between 1878 and 1881. For example, a statement from the Turnbull Bros., Baltimore publishers and booksellers, covering the month of April, 1879, shows 27 volumes purchased at a cost of $45.91, with a balance of $72.50 owed as of March—an unusually heavy purchase following close upon the heels of his Hopkins appointment. It should be added that 11 of the books here listed have not survived. See also W. M. Lind ("A Dead Poet's Library. Sidney Lanier's Literary Treasures," Baltimore *Sunday News*, July 24, 1892), who examined a number of volumes in Lanier's library that have not survived.

Mabinogion show him editing and expurgating his books for boys. His marginalia in *The Leopold Shakespere* were for use in his Peabody and Hopkins lectures; the cross-references to the Knight's Tale in his copy of *A Midsummer-Night's Dream* indicate preparation for his class course in the winter of 1880 comparing Chaucer and Shakespeare; and the numerous passages marked throughout *Prometheus Unbound* point to the introduction of Shelley's treatment of personality in the so-called " English Novel " lectures of the following year.

Much more instructive than this evidence of the practical uses of his reading are the occasional notations that his responsive pencil jotted down as he read, only the most interesting of which can be cited here. In Skeat's edition of *Piers the Plowman*, where Langland reviles as a worthless set Jack the juggler, Janet of the stews, Daniel the dice-player, and Robin the tale-teller (p. 97), Lanier applied the moralizing of the thirteenth century to the nineteenth:

Now become Jack the adroit politician and convention-packer.
    "   "   Mlle. ———— the Bright Prima Donna of opera boufe.
    "   "   Daniel Drew or Vanderbilt, the gambler in stocks.
    "   "   Zola, or Ouida, or Whitman.

Naturally enough his serious reading in Old and Middle English stirred him to linguistic comments growing out of his interest in the speech of his native Georgia. Where Langland wrote, " What he lerned ȝow in lente " (p. 73), he added: " Evidently an old transitive use of ' learn '—in the sense of teach—still very common in the South." [153] Likewise, in the introduction to his Aldine Chaucer, opposite a passage on grammatical forms (I, 147), he wrote: " *Qu.* Is it possible that the barbaric Southern habit of dropping the g in the present participle may be a relic of the A.-S. participle in *ende* or *ande* with the *de* softened out." But his usual response was of course more literary, as where he wrote beside a passage in the Doctor's Tale in this same set (III, 77): " The strong dramatic bent of Chaucer's genius is here shown—as in many other places—by making Nature speak out of her own mouth, rather than giving a description from his." ·Beside this should be placed a similar remark at the end of the selection from *Beowulf* in Sweet's *Anglo-Saxon Reader* (p. 132):

This poem becomes very pathetic as revealing how Nature—which has become the poet's Mistress and the philosopher's Delight in modern times was to our hapless ancestors only a Mother of Grendel. . . . On how much sweeter terms we are with nature! It is a wonderful advance.

The largest number of annotations deal with matters of prosody and music, the only fields in which he considered himself an original

[153] Used by Lanier himself in an early letter, Oct. 8, 1860, p. 29, below.

investigator. Working notes for the *Science of English Verse* can be found in his musical notations for scansion of passages in Old English poems, in Langland, and in Chaucer. Sometimes the notes are fuller: " The logaœdic dactyls in Beowulf show very conclusively that the prevalence of the iambus in modern English poetry is *not* due to the fact that the iambus is the genius of our tongue." [154] He pursued the subject in correcting Richard Morris's theory of the versification of *Piers Plowman*, with a note: " This is a mistake. The metre is dactylic, and is a true survival of Anglo-Saxon rhythmic ideas." [155] And so into the Renaissance, supplementing Sir Philip Sidney's comment (*An Apologie for Poetrie*, p. 71) on the large number of " natural dactyls " in English with: " Which proves the commonness of the three-syllable pronunciation so often necessary to rhythmize Shakespere's verse." Again, where Sidney referred to the element of time in music (p. 25), he added, striking out the key-note of his own theory: " That is, in the temporal proportions which constitute rhythm." All of these matters are elaborated in his published volume. But some jottings in the fly-leaves of his well marked copy of Pietro Blaserna's *Theory of Sound in its Relation to Music* (New York, 1876) indicate that he had further investigations to make. One memorandum on music points out the relationship of a minor third to a major chord. Another calls attention to the instinct for parallelism in word and rhythm that was unconsciously responsible for the ludicrous error in a prayer: " O Lord, we pray that thou wouldst make the intemperate temperate, and all the industrious dustrious." [156]

By far the most significant hint for future research is a note in the same volume, combining several of his life-long interests:

Is not the first problem to be solved (in the acoustic construction of music halls) this: to save to the audience all that half of the sound which ordinarily goes to the rear of the performers, and to send back this rear-going wave, with a straightened front, towards the auditorium.

---

[154] See his copy of Henry Sweet's *An Anglo-Saxon Reader* (Oxford, 1876), p. 119. See also pp. 174-175 for his musical scansion of *Wanderer*, and the back fly-leaf for four bars of a fragmentary musical composition, " Beowulf's March."

[155] See the introduction to his copy of the Aldine Chaucer, I, 172. This set reveals better than any of Lanier's books the many interests that lay behind his reading. Besides those already mentioned, he corrected the editor a second time by commenting that Oberon had appeared in a play by Greene before Shakespere's *Midsummer-Night's Dream* (I, 200) ; he wrote a number of " Poem Outlines " on the flyleaves (see vol. I of the present edition) ; and the cut pages and numerous other annotations show that he was using this as " copy " for his projected textbook on Chaucer (see vol. IV, 255-256, 304).

[156] In the same volume there is a partial draft of his poem " To Beethoven " and other matters discussed in the Introduction to vol. I, present edition.

Thus: if the auditory be at *a* and the performers at *b* each tone made by the performers spreads naturally in a circle around him; now if all the rear semicircle *ced* be reflected from a suitably constructed wall in

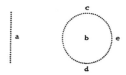

the performers rear so that it will return in a wave practically simultaneous with that which has already gone forward, then the effect of the tone is instantly doubled. I have observed the remarkable effect of playing the flute close up within the angle of a wall, and am inclined to believe—without yet having been at all able to experiment fully—that the orchestra should sit in front of a $>$ shaped wall. It is more than possible that this arrangement might necessitate a different disposition of the performers from that now in common use: but this will soon have to be done anyhow, if Prof. Mayer's experiments be correct.

He did not live to prosecute this investigation, but that he was abreast of the times if not something of a pioneer in acoustical ideas seems to be indicated by the fact that just about this same time (summer of 1877) Theodore Thomas was astonishing the engineers by constructing a similar sounding board for his orchestra.[157] Lanier had met A. F. Mayer, who on September 24, 1877, wrote to offer him the use of his laboratory apparatus. Two days later he applied to the Johns Hopkins for a fellowship to pursue researches in the " physics of musical tone." It is barely possible that the trustees missed an opportunity when they turned him down.

So Lanier read and worked and planned in a fever of excitement, even as fever of another sort was consuming him. When he went on his final pilgrimage to restore his waning health in North Carolina, May, 1881, he took with him among other newly acquired books, F. K. Beilstein's *Qualitative Chemical Analysis* and J. H. Collins's *Mineralogy*, and borrowed meteorological instruments from the physics department at Hopkins to study the " so-called no-frost belt on the side of Tryon Mountain " [158]—all for the purpose of writing another travelbook. In June, on his sickbed, he wrote the preface to his last two juveniles, the *Percy* and the *Mabinogion*, and jotted down notes for a new volume of poems to be called " Hymns of the Mountains." The next month he wrote to Gilman (July 1, 1881) accepting his reappoint-

[157] C. E. Russell, *The American Orchestra and Theodore Thomas* (New York, 1927), pp. 105-106.

[158] Statements from John B. Piet, Baltimore bookseller, May 7 and 9, 1881, list these and a dozen other volumes. See the letter to Gilman, June 5, 1881.

ment as lecturer and outlining for the coming winter his most ambitious program of courses. But there is a note of desperation in all this. The inevitable could not be staved off forever, and a month before the end Lanier knew that the battle had been lost. The final book that he purchased was a long cherished copy of Montaigne, on the title-page of which is written, " Lynn, N. C. August 1881." This he began reading on his deathbed. The final entry occurs on p. 76, where the great essayist expresses his dislike of physicians and his refusal to take their potions, concluding: " I let nature work." Opposite this page he quoted two lines from one of his favorite poems, Chaucer's Knight's Tale:

> And certéynly their nature will not wirche,
> Farewel phisik, go ber the man to chirche.

Life had come full circle. President Gilman was never more apt in reading character than when he inscribed on the memorial tablet erected at the Johns Hopkins University a motto for Sidney Lanier:

Aspiro dum expiro.

The Text

The aim has been a literal text. Editorial emendations, in brackets, have been kept to a minimum: to correct or complete the dates and to supply missing words or parts of words needed for clarity. All letters are printed entire from the original manuscripts, with the exception of a very few which have not survived or have come down in mutilated or fragmentary form. The footnotes are limited to explanatory matter and to citation of prior publication. A Calendar at the end of volume X lists all letters known to the present editor, with ascription of ownership and with indication of those previously and those now first published. Of the letters by Lanier that have been found, nearly three-fourths are printed in the present edition.[159] The basis of selection has been kept

---

[159] Of 1597 letters by Lanier, 1161 are here included. All of these were previously unpublished except 274, of which 152 are collected in *Letters* (New York, 1899) and the rest scattered in various books and periodicals. (No effort has been made to indicate the part so published, except by the word " excerpt " when it was very small.) All but 58 have survived in MS; 16 of these are reproduced from the most reliable printed sources, the rest from contemporary copies made before the originals disappeared. Of 1096 letters to Lanier, 29 are here included; of 372 letters concerning him, 25. The vast majority of the MSS are preserved in the Lanier Room, Johns Hopkins University; acknowledgement to the owners is made in the General Preface, vol. I.

Two rarely used marks of punctuation . . . and x x x have been changed to – – – to avoid confusion with the symbols used to indicate editorial omissions and *lacunæ* in the MSS. Drafts of Lanier's poems appearing in the letters have

as objective as possible: to give all letters necessary to the complete story of his inner and outer life. All previously published ones are included, regardless of this criterion, since many of the earlier texts are incomplete or inaccurate and some are difficult of access. The majority of those omitted duplicate information more fully given in those selected; the rest are concerned with the personal affairs of others, with domestic trivialities or matters that never materialized, or with expressions of sentiment to his wife amply represented elsewhere. Excerpts from these have been woven into the notes wherever they shed new light. The earliest letter dates from his entrance into college, shortly before his fifteenth birthday, the latest a few days before his death. On the whole the distribution is fairly even; after 1865 scarcely a month is unrepresented, and often the record is almost a daily one. In a few places gaps in the narrative are filled in with letters to or concerning him. The letters to all but three of his principal correspondents have been located: to his first important publisher, J. B. Lippincott & Co., and to two influential friends, Salem Dutcher and William Hand Browne.[160] Thus the four volumes in the Centennial Edition constitute virtually a complete collection of the letters of Sidney Lanier.

C. R. A.[161]

been omitted unless inextricably bound up with the contents. No other alterations have been made in the text. When no source is cited for minor information in the notes, it has been taken from standard reference works, from collateral correspondence in the Lanier Room, or from statements to the editor by members of the family.

[160] The letters to Lippincott were destroyed by fire, except a few to J. F. Kirk, editor of the magazine. Those to Browne and Dutcher (with one exception) were not preserved (see Lanier's letter to Spencer, Feb. 26, 1875, and his brother's letter to Mary Day Lanier, Feb. 23, 1899).

[161] The editing of the letters was originally undertaken by Aubrey H. Starke, but he was called into the armed services after preparing the Calendar, a preliminary selection of letters, and a first draft of notes. The task of completion then fell upon the general editor. I have made the final selection of letters, doubled the number and scope of the notes, written the introduction, and put the four volumes through the press.

LETTERS
1857—1868

CHRONOLOGY

1842	Feb. 3	Born, Macon, Ga.
1857	Jan. 6	Entered Sophomore Class, Oglethorpe University, at Midway, near Milledgeville, Ga.
1858	Summer	At Montvale Springs, Tenn. (also in 1859, 1860). Wrote earliest known poems. Withdrew from college end of Junior year; spent part of next year as clerk in Macon Post Office.
1859	Oct.	Re-entered Oglethorpe. Friendship with Prof. James Woodrow.
1860	July 18	Graduated with first honor.
	Oct.	Returned to Oglethorpe as tutor. Friendship with Milton Northrup. Planned to study at Heidelberg.
1861	May 15	First prose article published.
	July 10	Enlisted in Macon Volunteers, 2nd Battalion, Georgia Infantry, C. S. A. Stationed at Sewell's Point, near Norfolk, Va.
1862	Apr.	Furlough in Macon. Brother Clifford enlisted in Volunteers.
	Summer	Stationed in and near Petersburg, Va. Participated in first battles. Transferred to Signal Corps (July 21).
	Winter	Campaigns in North Carolina (Dec.-Feb.).
1863	Mar.	Furlough in Macon. Began friendship with Mary Day.
	May	Stationed at Fort Boykin, near Newport News. Began friendship with Virginia Hankins.
	Oct.	Furlough in Macon. Returned to Fort Boykin.
	Dec.	Began writing *Tiger-Lilies*, also poems.
1864	Winter	Campaign in North Carolina. Back at Fort Boykin in March.
	Summer	Detailed as Signal Officer on a blockade-runner out of Wilmington, N. C.
	Nov.	Captured aboard *Lucy* and imprisoned at Point Lookout, Md.
1865	Feb. 15	Released from prison. Reached Macon, *c*. Mar. 15, ill.
	July-Oct.	Tutor at the Fulton plantation, Scott's Mills, near Macon. Writing poems and novel.
	Oct.-Dec.	At Point Clear, Mobile Bay, Ala., for his health.
1866	Jan.	Took position as clerk in the Exchange Hotel, Montgomery, Ala., with his brother. Renewed literary activity.
	Autumn	Renewed correspondence with Mary Day. Began friendship with Salem Dutcher (Dec.).
1867	Mar.	Completed *Tiger-Lilies*. In New York seeking a publisher.
	Summer	In Macon. Engaged to Mary Day (Aug.). Moved to Prattville, Ala., as principal of Academy (Sept.).
	Nov.-Dec.	*Tiger-Lilies* published. Married (Dec. 19).
1868	Jan. 17	First hemorrhage and beginning of serious illness.
	Winter	Wrote poems and started novel dealing with Reconstruction.
	May	Closed Academy because of health and financial depression.
	Summer	At Fulton plantation, Scott's Mills, Ga. Began correspondence with Paul Hayne.
	Autumn	Residence in Vineville, suburb of Macon. First child born.
	Dec.	Began study of law in his father's office.

1857

Midway. Jan'y 6th, 1857.

Dear Father

Willie and I arrived here yesterday, all safe & sound, and spent the day in trying to find a room. As events have turned out, we find that we have arrived in the nick of time. The advantages of our situation are so many that I can hardly tell you all of them. As Uncle Clifford has perhaps told you, we concluded to put up at Mrs Tufts, with Ol'y Poe & John Nisbet, who we find are very studious boys. Every night as soon as Supper is over we come up to our room, where we find a good fire burning and *two* candles on the table, and we immediately sit down to study. Prof. Woodrow [2] rooms next to us, so that you may be satisfied on the point of rows, &C, though there would be no danger of that anyway, as none of the boys ever come up to our room except one or two very gentlemanly fellows. There are no other scholars that room in our boarding house, besides us, although there are about twenty who eat here. Our landlady, Mrs Tufts seems to be a very nice sort of a lady,

[1] Excerpt previously published, *Chautauquan*, XXI, 406 (July, 1895) ; Mims, p. 30. On Jan. 5, 1857, Sidney Lanier and William L. LeConte left Macon, Ga., to enter Oglethorpe University, at Midway, two miles from Milledgeville, then the capital of Georgia. Willie LeConte was the younger brother of Anna LeConte Anderson. Her husband Clifford Anderson was the law partner of Lanier's father, Robert S. Lanier, and the brother of his mother, Mary Jane Anderson Lanier. The other boys mentioned in this, Lanier's first letter home, were also from Macon and were sons of friends of the family. The boarding house was that of Mrs. Frank Tufts.

[2] James Woodrow, the young Professor of Chemistry, Natural Philosophy, Geology, and Botany at Oglethorpe. In a letter of Jan. 14, 1904, to Henry W. Lanier, Woodrow wrote that Lanier did not attract his attention during his first year in college: " his standing in his class was not high. But his health was not good; and it was to this cause that I attributed his failure to take a higher rank." Later, intimate friendship was to develop between them (see note 4, 1859).

and she keeps a splendid house, too, where everything is well cooked, & *plenty of it too.* The house is a new boarding-house; this is the first term that it has been opened. Our room is a fine, large, airy one, with a *good fireplace* and a closet where we put our dirty clothes, boots and shoes, and "fixins." The price of board is 18 Dollars per month, *washing & fuel included,* which I do not think too high. Willie & I stood our examination this morning, and came out very well: I did not miss any questions which were put to me, and I believe Will, did not. We were both admitted into our classes, I into Soph. Willie into Juniors. I have just done studying, to night, my first lesson, to wit: forty-five lines in Horace, which I " *did* " in about *fifteen minutes.* We had better luck than two other fellows, who came here to be examined for admission into the Soph. class, and had to travel back home, not being found fit even for the fresh! I have not time to write a long letter as it is now nearly nine, and I must despatch some sort of a note to Joe Welles " according to promise," & so I will close; kiss Ma & Sister, & Aunt Ella [8] for me, & believe me as ever

Your affectionate Son

S. C. Lanier.

To Robert S. Lanier

Oglethorpe University
April 21st "/57

Dear Father

I have been intending to write to you for a day or two, but have been delayed always by some unforeseen cause, and have only a little time now to write a few lines before the bell rings for recitation. Willie and Charley Williamson arrived over here yesterday — Willie says he would have gone down to tell you all " good-bye " but was so hurried that he did not have time — I have been studying quite hard since I came over,[4] and intend doing so all the Term as our lessons or rather our

---

[8] Probably Mrs. R. S. Lanier's younger sister, Ella (Eloise) Anderson.
[4] This letter was apparently written after a spring vacation spent in Macon. The Williamson brothers were Macon friends and fellow-students.

studies are a good deal harder than they were last Term. I think I shall try and get a " No 1 " Circular this time, although I had as good as any boy in College, last Term — By the way, I have enquired about Bojesen and find that there was *one* in the class who had 1 in his Circular and *only one*; the rest were generally 1 1/2 or 2 [5] — When does Mother intend going to the Springs? [6] I would like to know as I want to go home again before she starts — But the Bell is ringing and I must close — Love to all the home folks together with a large portion for yourself, from Your devoted son,

Sid —

P. S. Pa, I have need of about ten doll[ars.] Please send it to me as soon as you can —

S.

To Robert S. Lanier [7]

Oglethorpe University
April 26th "/57

Dear Father:

Mother's letter was received yesterday and was warmly welcomed as I had begun to think that you had all forgotten me — I intended answering it last night, but delayed writing, thinking that I might receive one from you to-day; not having received it I have concluded to waive formality and write again, as there is something, which if I do not tell you *quickly,* God knows, I fear it will break my heart — My Father, I have sinned! against your law of conduct which you laid down for my observance have I sinned! Yet without bad motive, without

[5] A surviving MS record of grades (Clifford A. Lanier Collection, Johns Hopkins University) shows that Lanier stood midway in his class during his first year at Oglethorpe.

The allusion to " Bojesen " is somewhat puzzling, but it may have been to a textbook: E. F. C. Bojesen, *A Manual of Grecian and Roman Antiquities*, published in an English translation by J. K. Arnold, New York, 1848.

[6] Montvale Springs, Tenn., a resort owned by her father-in-law, Sterling Lanier, near Knoxville, where numerous members of the Lanier family went every summer.

[7] Excerpts previously published by Mims, p. 31.

evil intent, without wrong feeling – But I shall not attempt to palliate my fault—although I might very plausibly –   O, with what intensity of thoughts, with what deep and earnest reflection have I contemplated this, lately –   But Father, bear with me, if possible while I tell you *all*: Often, last Term, when I would happen to be in need of some little affair, not having any money with me at the time, Willie, (who was my constant companion) would press it upon me, telling me that he did not need it, and that I could pay him back at any-time –   Thus, (cheating myself with the delusive hope that I would be able to pay him out of my own pocket-money, without having to call on you for it) I often accepted it, until now I owe him about $15.00! It is with heart throbbing with the intensity of its anguish that I write you this, but Father, Mother said that you thought *I did not love you enough to place confidence in you,* and I MUST clear myself of *that*—therefore do I tell you all this, for I think that I *love you* and *Mother* with *all the filial affection that mortal ever possessed* –   But I have not done yet –   however, I believe this is not in violation of any of your rules –   There is a *secret Literary* Society [8] here, an *old* and *time-honoured* one, existing with the high approval of the Faculty, composed only of the smartest members of the Senior and Junior Classes, (I am the only Soph. in it) which, in the middle of last Term elected me a member –   This being told me by one of my most intimate friends, and he promising me upon his word of honor that there were no boys there, except those with whom I had been in the habit of associating, I joined;—and father, I assure you that *I have derived more benefit from that,* than any one of my Collegiate studies –   We

---

[8] Lanier's membership in the Thalian Literary Society is treated in Leola Selman Beeson's *Sidney Lanier at Oglethorpe University* (Macon, Ga., 1936). The badge of the society appears on the left lapel of Lanier's coat in the 1857 ambrotype (see frontispiece).

Mrs. Beeson says that Lanier was also a member of Sigma Alpha Epsilon, giving as her authority a reminiscent letter by the roommate of his senior year, John A. Weems. There was a chapter of this fraternity at Oglethorpe, and Clifford Lanier was initiated into membership on Feb. 11, 1859; but the official records do not show Sidney Lanier as a member. (See the fraternity magazine, the *Record*, Dec., 1938, p. 390, and letter to the present editor, May 26, 1943, from Lauren Foreman, Eminent Supreme Recorder, Sigma Alpha Epsilon, Evanston, Ill.)

meet together in a nice room, read Compositions, declaim, and debate upon interesting subjects, being controlled by a strict Constitution and by-laws, which we have promised faithfully to observe upon our honor as gentlemen – This Society has concluded no longer to remain secret, and has sent on to have beautiful badges made for its members (we have twelve—it is limited to fifteen) and when these arrive we will all come out in them and thus it will be known – It was for *this* (*partly*) that I wrote to you for ten dollars: there are some other things which I need, such as Ink, writing-paper, a coat-brush, and a hair comb – I thought you understood why I did not mention these things as the bell for recitation was ringing and the Cars were whistling at the Depot, just as I finished the letter that far, and so I had to stop to get the letter on board in time to leave that day – The badge does not, by any means, cost near that amount, but as I wanted these other things I just wrote you for ten Dollars –

And now I have told you all – My Father, can you forgive me? If by hard study and good conduct I can in some measure atone for this, *God in Heaven knows* that I shall not be found wanting – This is what troubles me, Father – I know how hard you have to work to sustain the many burdens that are imposed upon you, and for me to be thus continually calling on you for money – O, Father you know not how *very much* it distresses me – I know you will be grieved at this: but if *you* are grieved at it, then what must be *my grief*, who am the cause of it all?

But I must close this letter. Father, please be certain and not breathe a word to any one about our Society as we are all pledged upon our honor not to divulge the existence of it, but I got permission to *tell you* – Give my love to all the folks at home, and rest assured that not a night passes but what the supplication, "God bless my Parents," ascends to the great mercy-seat, from the lips of their absent but loving son

Sidney.

Write soon –

From Mary J. A. Lanier

Macon Geo May 13th 1857

My dear Son

     We received your letter yesterday [9] & were glad to hear from you. I shall only write you a few lines this time, being very busy Your pa is very much engaged at the court house (this being the first week of court, so he wished me to write you for him as you wrote to him about going serenading,[10] he says that although he does not like for you to go out at night, he consents *this time provided* you do not abuse the privilege & says also do not stay out late or drink any wine should any be offered you, not that he thinks you will do so my son but because he loves you so much & feels it his duty to caution you. he says he will send you the money to pay for the clothes in a few days I hope my dear child that you will be careful of them and make them last you as long as possible. your pa seems to be pressed for money this spring & I want us all to try to spend as little as possible now for a while – I will try to have some spending money to give you when you come home again. Poor Julia Holt died last sunday & Grimes is now very sick, I attended Julia's funeral monday afternoon. Do my son be careful of your health I am constantly anxious about you. I am glad you got the box safely you did not say anything of

    [9] Lanier's letter mentioned by his mother (*c.* May 11, 1857) has not been found.
    [10] In a letter of Feb. 28, 1903, to Henry W. Lanier, reminiscent of their college serenading William L. LeConte wrote: "There was a magnatism about your father that was always irresistable, and hence every body loved him. I remember how rigid Dr. Sam Talmage – the President tried to be in the enforcement of the rules. Every student was required to be in his Dormitory by 9 oclk each night. I suspect that the frequency of our petitions were outragious, hence we always made Sid our 'envoy extraordinary,' relying on his persuasive eloquence to overcome the old Doctors severe adhesion to *rule* and let us go into Milledgeville to serenade. His reply would be, in effect, 'Well Sidney, you have been a good boy, and you seem to have chosen orderly young men for your companions. You may *go*—but dont stay out too late.' We never failed to give the old Dr. some *good music too*. I cannot now recall all the names of those composing our campus Orchestra. John Hill Lamar played the Violin and Tom Newell played the Cello, and I had the Guitar. We were all so music filled that we would follow Sid in his loftiest attempts at harmony. It was somewhat singular that he would often take a theme and launch out extemporising, and we knew his trend of feeling so well that we could easily accompany him, without discord."

the bundle of clothes which were tied on the box, but I presume you got them also, write to us as often as you can.   all well and join me in much love to you.   give my love to Willie

affectionately yr mother

M. J. Lanier –

To Robert S. Lanier

Oglethorpe University
May 26th "/57

Dear Father

I received your letter, or rather note, on last Saturday and immediately went in town, in order to settle up Sperling's Bill—which I did to that dutchman's *infinite satisfaction* –

We had quite a grand time last Thursday, seeing the review of three military Companies in Milledgeville, under the command of old Captain Rockwell, and listening to several complimentary effusions, on the " high-falutin " order (" soldier's welcome," " soldier's hearts," " gratitude everlasting " &c &c) which were elicited from the big-men of Milledgeville, upon the reception of our Floyd Rifles, and their Eatonton companions in arms, by the " Baldwin Blues " [11] –   It was really quite amusing to hear captain R. in his reception-speech upon the disembarcation of two companies from the Eatonton train, speaking of the good-will manifested towards them, as evinced by this vast concourse of citizens, (ragged little boys, negroes, &c) assembled to greet your coming into the Metropolis (!) of Georgia " –   Then, " Battalion-forward, – guides right – March," was thundered forth, and they passed in grand style to the Hotel, where being drawn up in line, they were formally received by a fulsome address of Miller Grieve's, which was responded to by Tom Hardeman, on the part of the Floyd Rifles and Capt. Branham of the Eatonton Rifles –   The Governor then, arm in arm with Capt. R. walked before and behind the ranks, amid the *plaudits* of the assembled *multitude,* and the clangor of horns and Base-drums –

[11] The Floyd Rifles was a Macon infantry company of militia that had seen service in the Mexican War. With a company from Eatonton, Ga., they were visiting the Milledgeville militia.

Willie received a letter from his Mother this afternoon, in which she mentioned that Mother said that I must not come home until Saturday — I think if you knew how the circumstances are you would change your opinion — This is the way that such an arrangement would work, Pa — By staying until Saturday, I only gain *one* recitation and lose a whole day and night's stay at home; — whereas by going home Friday morning, I can stay at home, three days 'and a half, only losing five recitations in all, and come back Tuesday — But it is getting my bed-time and I must close — Give my love to all the home-folks, and accept a large portion for yourself, from,

Your devoted son

Sid —

There is a great deal of sickness on the Campus; about a dozen cases of Dysentery, some of them aggravated forms of it, too—

Please send me two dollars to come home on, Pa, I've had to spend all that you sent me, (there was four dollars over) for half soling a pair of boots, pair of shoes, & a Surveying — — — Please write by Thursday so that I may know whether to come home on Friday or not —

TO ROBERT S. LANIER [12]

Oglethorpe University
October 8th "/57

Dear Father,

Having at length got our room in something like ship-shape, I have an opportunity to write to you —

We are having quite cold weather over here, and, to-night, are sitting comfortably over a fire — Old Boreas has been indulging himself to-day in a storm of wind and rain, and, with his gusts of the one, and torrents of the other, has made the

[12] Excerpt previously published by Mims, p. 31. It is probable that Lanier had spent some part of the summer of 1857 at his grandfather's mountain resort. (On Sept. 25, 1883, R. S. Lanier wrote to J. A. Fisher: " From the time [my son] was eight to fifteen years of age I was in the habit of taking my family to Montvale Springs . . . for part of the summer.") Now, in Oct., 1857, he had returned to college for his Junior year.

old Campus look as bleak, and cheerless as could well be imagined –

We will have, before the term ends, about one hundred and thirty students, and perhaps more, but I am almost certain there will be at least as many as that, – there are about ninety in attendance at present, forty of whom are new students; with others, both old and new arriving daily, by dozens –

On arriving here we found the place in a terrible state, with respect to board – Mr Fairleigh, who kept one boarding-house, and Mrs. Evans, who kept another, have both myster-iously vanished, during vacation, (by the way, they *owed a bill* of *three* or *four hundred* Dollars in Milledgeville) and this, together with the closing up of Mrs. Tucker's house, has left only two Boarding houses, for ninety boys!! There is a man here, however, who is erecting a large dining room, in connec-tion with the old Evans house, to accommodate a hundred and twenty; so that that difficulty will soon be abolished – In the mean time, some eating at old Charley's, others at Mr. Smith's, the boys have to get along as best they can – Willie and myself fortunately got our old places at Tufts', who, when Fairleigh left, very generously saved our places,– I say gener-ously because every other place had been written for and secured, and there were applicants for the places which he saved for us, which he refused, knowing what our situation was – As Frank wishes us to pay our first month's board in advance, please send me the money (14.00) in your next;– and also, Pa, send me enough to get the following Books: an Olmsteds Phi-losophy, Blair's Rhetoric,[18] Cicero de Oratore, and Analytical Geometry; all of which I can get, at second-hand, for about five or six Dollars – Our Greek text-book for this Term I have already –

Father please send over those shoes as quickly as possible, for I need them badly, having nothing to go through the mud with, except a pair of low-quarters –

I feel quite enthusiastic on the subject of studying, and intend going in for a regular No 1 Circular this Term – There is, after all, nothing like " *putting a man on his dignity,"* in fact

[18] Probably Denison Olmsted's *An Introduction to Natural Philosophy* and Hugh Blair's *Lectures on Rhetoric and Belles Lettres.*

the very name of " Junior " has something study-inspiring, and energy exciting, to me –

Write to me soon,–   Tell Buddy and Sister [14] I promise to answer their letters this time, if they will write to me, and present to all the very warmest love, of their,

Most affectionate Son and Brother,

Sid –

P. S.   Please send me a lot
of Postage Stamps –

---

[14] Lanier's younger brother Clifford and his sister Gertrude, usually referred to in the letters as " Sissa."

1858

To Anna L. Anderson [1]

Oglethorpe University
Feby 22nd '57 [1858?]

Had I not been very busy indeed, dear Auntie, in studying to catch up with my class, I should certainly have written you, sooner, for you do not know, Aunt Annie, what a great privilege I esteem it, to be able to pour out all the feelings of my heart of hearts, to you and to be conscious that they are not only safe in your keeping, but that they are also sympathized with, whether gay or sorrowful. — — — — Aunt Annie, it is *all over now* – No more can I listen to Willie's tales of his Gussie's [2] love for him, and feel that *I too* have one devoted heart bound to my own, in that sweetest of all earthly ties – No more can I look forward to the future, my heart bounding with joyful anticipations of the time when I shall again behold the graceful form of her, upon whom my soul's best affections have settled – Oh Aunt Annie, I can counterfeit gayety to the very life – One would think, seeing me in company with the boys, laughing and joking, that I was one of the happiest persons imaginable,

[1] Previously published in the Macon *Telegraph* (Sunday Magazine), Feb. 3, 1929, p. 1. This letter is apparently misdated and was actually written on Feb. 22, 1858; for the same unhappy love affair of which it treats is recorded in three passages dated Feb. 12, 14, and 20, 1858, in Lanier's College Notebook, his only surviving attempt at a diary (Clifford A. Lanier Collection, Johns Hopkins University). That the diary passages are themselves correctly dated is sufficiently proved by a fourth entry dated Dec. 13, 1858, stating that this " Journal " was begun " last February."

[2] Probably Augusta Lamar, long a close friend of Lanier. In his reminiscent letter to H. W. Lanier on Feb. 28, 1903, W. L. LeConte wrote: " at Oglethorpe University we soon discovered that we each had met his ' fidus Achates.' We were both quite sentimental. . . . It was our habit as often as possible to take long walks in the country where we could exchange confidences without interruption."

but could I be seen at night, when Willie and I have retired to our bed, my arms around his neck and my whole frame quivering with the very violence of conflicting emotions, then indeed would I be thought, on the contrary, one of the most *wretched* and *woe-begone* persons imaginable – And alas! Aunt Annie, *it is too true* –: that gayety and flow of spirits which once was mine, has flown far away, and I must be ever on guard in company, lest I relapse into that sad and pensive mood, which is truly befitting me in my situation – Excuse me, Aunt Annie, if, under the influence of these melancholy feelings I have grown sentimental but I feel sincerely every word that I have written – I have not told you about it –: A day or two ago, Willie received a letter from P.[3] in which, among other things, she told him, that she had analyzed her feelings very closely, and discovered that what she had taken to be real and true love was only a sort of sisterly regard which she had for me! – – The shock, when Willie told me this, although I had been for a long time dreading it, had almost been too much for me. – Aunt Annie, I am in an agony of doubts and perplexities, and do not know what to do or which way to turn – Willie has been telling me to turn my affections to some other more worthy and more constant object, for that Phelie is too fickle, but, my dear Aunt Annie, I do really love Phelie too much to think of doing this. *Please,* Aunt Annie, write me very soon, and tell me whether I must continue, hopelessly, to love P. or endeavor to eradicate love from my heart, for as to loving another I do not believe that it is possible – – – – – – But I am wearying you – Love to Lou: & tell her to write. Respects to all the family, and accept a *great* deal of love from your devoted nephew.

Sid.

Write soon – P. is still in love with Joe Wells,[4] I think.

[3] "Phelie" (Ophelia) LeConte, the sister of Lanier's roommate and of the aunt (only seven years Lanier's senior) to whom this letter was written. The only mention of her in any later letter is in that of Oct. 13, 1871, from Mary Day Lanier to Sidney Lanier: "Phelie came home well but has not continued well – has again her old cold and cough."

[4] Joe Wells (or Welles) was a Macon boy, mentioned in Lanier's first letter home and in later letters, 1861-1865. The fourth and final diary entry in Lanier's

From Mary J. A. and Robert S. Lanier

Macon Geo May 20th 1858

My beloved Son

Your most welcome letter was recieved yesterday [5] & read with pleasure, I had become quite anxious about you as you were not very well when you left, you must write often, I am always uneasy if I do not hear from you at least once a week.

Your pa has been speaking of writing to you for several days but has been so busy at the court house that he has not had time, he is engage there today in a case but I will leave room for him to add a P. S. in this.　　Your Uncle Sid & Mollie came over from Charleston [6] on Saturday & staid with us only two days as he was anxious to get home having only a short time to arrange their business to give up the House[?] he is looking very well indeed for him, the trip to Charleston has improved his health very much indeed, I had no idea of seeing him look so well, but he will have to be very cautious about attending too closely to business through the summer. Your Uncles William & Watt — did a very good business last week at the convention having taken in something over four thousand

College Notebook, dated Dec. 13, 1858, reads: "How this world of ours does change! I have just been looking over the beginning of the Journal which I started to keep last February — What changes since then! Ah! me — . . . Heaven helped me and I bore it — Nay I even saw her, talked with her, held her hand in mine — A little while and I saw it all — She loved J — — W. — — Loved him, till her whole soul was wrapped in him. Loved him, despite her knowledge of the fact that his heart was given, and his troth plighted to another — 'Pshaw, 'tis an old tale."

[5] Lanier's letter mentioned here (c. May 18, 1858) has not been found, nor any other letters by him during 1858. This letter from his parents is included for the light it throws on this period of his development, especially in religious matters.

[6] Lanier's uncle, Sidney C. Lanier, had married Mary Russell, whose father was a judge in New York. At this time he was apparently engaged in business in Montgomery, Ala., and associated with his father in the management of the resort hotel at Montvale Springs, Tenn. A sister, Wilhelmina, Mrs. T. D. Eason, lived in Charleston, S. C., where Mr. and Mrs. S. C. Lanier had been visiting. They are both mentioned frequently in later letters by Lanier.

dollars,[7] had a letter last night from your Grandpa, all well &
doing well at Montvale.

I entirely agree with you my son about the denominational
differences & feelings of competition in the churches & wish it
were otherwise, & the only remedy I see is for all who so think
to pray earnestly to God, who in his great wisdom & mercy can
so change the hearts of men as to reconcile all differences &
unite them all in one body, one loving brotherhood, a union
prayer meeting was commenced here on Monday morning at
eight oclock — I am told that they are well attended & all
seem to feel much interest, God grant that good may be done
in this place. You ask me my son, what your pa thinks of
religion or what his feelings are, I do not know, I am sure that
he has great reverence for God and religion but my great
trouble is that he does not come out before the world & accept
the offers of mercy, I often wish to talk with him on the subject
but feel so deeply my inability & am so sensible of my own
leanness & inconsistency as a christian that I shrink from the
attempt, but my constant prayer to God is that he will have
mercy & order all things aright, I thank God for his great mercy
to me & pray that I may be in some measure made worthy of
so many blessings.

I have been interrupted several times since I began to write
and am somewhat fatigued, so I'll close

Give our love to Willie tell him I am sorry for him, & hope
his letters will all come right, but he must remember the
" course of true love never did run smooth " all the family unite
in affectionate love to you — take care of yourself — May God
bless you my son —

> Your Mother.
>
> M. J. Lanier.

My dear son, Our court continues in session, I have not time to
write you a letter, & indeed on that account find it inconvenient
to attend to your request.

---

[7] Lanier's uncle, William B. Lanier, and Abram P. Watt (husband to his aunt,
Jane Lanier) operated the Exchange Hotel in Montgomery, Ala., which Sterling
Lanier owned at this time, and at which Sidney and Clifford Lanier clerked some
years later. As Montgomery was the capital of Alabama, meetings of the
legislature and party conventions contributed largely to the business of the hotel.

Try & get on as you are. We can't have every thing as we desire it. I will send you an umbrella in a few days, if I can find anyone to carry it to you; that will help out some. I hope you are earnestly engaged in your studies – – [8]

Most affectionately.

Your father—

---

[8] At the end of Lanier's Junior year, summer 1858, he was temporarily withdrawn from college, whether because of his youth, because his father wanted him to have a year of practical experience, or for other reasons is not known. A letter from his schoolmate William Ridd, Oct. 12, 1858, indicates that he spent the summer at Montvale Springs. At least part of the next twelve months he spent in Macon as a clerk in the Post Office, where he is said to have picked up his first interest in the Georgia "Cracker" (see Clifford Lanier, "Reminiscences of Sidney Lanier," *Chautauquan*, XXI, 405-406, July, 1895). The diary entry for Dec. 13, 1858, in his College Notebook, looking back to the previous year at Oglethorpe, records his own impressions of the value of this experience: "What hard knocks and bumps and bruises have I received from this old world since then! How many gradations of love has my heart passed through since then – –! How many noble friends have I made for myself since then! How many lessons in world-love have I learned since then! How many strange characters have I intuitively dissected since then! . . . How many strange, and wild, and beautiful scenes have I beheld since then! What glorious moments of genial, whole-souled friendship have I enjoyed since then! How have my musical proclivities been gratified since then! How have beautiful women smiled on me since then; not only smiled but kissed me! How have the faculties of my mind grown larger and more powerful and more generous since then!"

1859

To Iverson L. Harris

Macon,   Feby 25th ''/59

Col. Harris:
　　Dear Sir:
　　　　My Grand-Father, Sterling Lanier, was telling
me a few days ago, that you once promised to give him the
genealogy of the Lanier Family — Feeling considerable interest
in the subject, (especially since he hinted something about our
descent from the Washingtons, and our connection with your
own family,) I beg you will pardon the liberty which I take in
addressing you, and transfer the favor from my Grand-father
to me, by sending over said genealogy [1] to

Yours most respectfully,

Sidney Lanier

To Robert S. Lanier [2]

Oglethorpe University
Sep. [Oct. ?] 8th   1859

My Dear Pa;
　　　　I am here, safe and sound; and have already been
doing some hard studying, made harder by the rust that I have
to rub off —

---

[1] Lanier made use of Harris's genealogical notes years later in preparing a
family history for J. F. D. Lanier, July 6, 1877 (VI, 353). R. S. Lanier commented on this matter in a letter to his son Clifford, July 26, 1866: "Hon.
Iverson L. Harris, now a Judge of the Supreme Court of Ga. is here, & we have
talked of our ancestors, & he has brought out his book, & I have taken from it
the enclosed extracts — which may be of some interest to you. You have perhaps
seen a part of it in different form. His branch of the family has furnished many
distinguished & useful men to the country. So far our *name* has not. It is time
there was a beginning. I look to my boys for help. They are capable of doing
much."

[2] This letter marks Lanier's return to college for his third (Senior) year after

Went up and saw the Faculty, Thursday evening; they all expressed themselves delighted to see me back, and the old D^{r} [3] advised me, in emphatic terms, to " pitch in "; which expression caused Prof. Woodrow,[4] (who is a great stickler for purity of language) to look at the D^{r} with an air of the utmost consternation, as if he thought the presidential dignity ruined forever –

Sam Knox, one of my old class, who shared the Honor, has been elected Tutor in the College, and entered upon his duties at the beginning of this Term – He came in last night and I had a long talk with him – He says there is only one man in the present Senior class who is at all likely to bother me: and tells me he is certain that if I'll study, I can beat him for the 1st Honor, – easily – That is enough –

his experience in the postoffice clerkship. The date of the postscript, Oct. 8, is apparently that on which the letter was sent.

[3] The Rev. Samuel K. Talmadge, D. D., President of Oglethorpe and Professor of Ancient Languages and Belles Lettres.

[4] It was during this Lanier's Senior year at Oglethorpe that the influence of Professor James Woodrow became strong. Years later Lanier said " that he owed to Professor Woodrow the strongest and most valuable stimulus of his youth " (*Poems*, 1884, p. xiii). The greater part of his College Notebook consists of Lanier's notes on his science lectures; and scribbled over several blank pages at the back are repetitions on the theme: " Sidney C. Lanier Took notes in this book on Professor Woodrow's Lectures on Chemistry, commencing October 10th, 1859. Future ages read and ponder." (Other dates recorded are Oct. 31 and Nov. 10, 1859.)

In a letter of Mar. 7, 1904, Clifford Lanier wrote to Edwin Mims: " Concerning influence of Prof. Woodrow:–Sidney was about 16, reared in an atmosphere of Presbyterian strictness: his home was sweet indeed in its influences, Father liberal, tolerant, open-minded, genial-humored, etc. but Sunday School & Church airs were strict: there was some intolerance of broad scholarship (as was shown many years after against Prof. W) and so when Sidney met the high aspiration of Prof. W. in 1858-59, for knowledge of physical Sciences and all fact no matter if it did seem to militate against old ideas of the Bible, the effect was tonic and inspiriting."

Woodrow was born at Carlisle, England, graduated at Jefferson College (Pa.) in 1849, studied at Harvard with Agassiz in 1853, took his Ph. D. *summa cum laude* at Heidelberg in 1856, and came to Oglethorpe as Professor of Natural Science the year before Lanier entered college. In a reminiscent letter to H. W. Lanier, Jan. 14, 1904, he wrote: " At the beginning of [his Senior] year, he came back well, strong, wide-awake, and industrious,– a changed person. I saw a good deal of him, as his room was near mine; and I often asked him to take walks with me. He had become an eager enthusiastic student; and he very soon became the leader of his class. . . . After he graduated, I caused him to be appointed Tutor in the College." (For further details see Philip Graham, " James Woodrow, Calvinist and Evolutionist," *Sewanee Review*, XL, 307-315, July, 1932, and " Lanier and Science," *American Literature*, IV, 288-292, Nov., 1932; A. H. Starke, " Sidney Lanier: Man of Science in the Field of Letters," *American Scholar*, II, 398-408, Oct., 1933.)

Our Society met this morning, but we had no debate on account of the election of officers — I was solicited by a great many members to run for President, with a certainty of being elected — But declined to run, as I had rather turn my attention to the debates —

I am rooming with John Weems, of Columbus, a brother of Miss Mollie Weems — He is a very clever, steady, studious boy, and mingles very little with the other students — He has very generously offered to let me use his room for the three months between now and the First of January, when Cliff will be over, and then we can buy a room permanently —

Of the money you gave me, I have expended for

Books — $4.00
Railroad fare — 1.65
To the College for room rent — 3.00
"   "   Society   "   term fees — 1.00
———
$9.65
S. C. Lanier
Oct 8 —"/59

I need a little more to buy some candles, and to get a Chemistry which we will have to start next week — Please have my shoes made as quickly as possible, as this Midway gravel is rapidly wearing out the nice pair that I brought over — Suppose Murphy has got my suit done, by this time —

Ask Ma if she is certain that she put the hair brush and comb in my trunk? Am unable to find either —

Give to all the best love of your Son

Sid. Lanier —

To Clifford A. Lanier

Oglethorpe University
October 11 1859

My Dear Cliff,

My time is so fully occupied with hard study, and with wearing off the rust that a year's disuse has caused to accumulate on my mental machinery, that

I have very little time for letter-writing: but I drop you a short note, more for the sake of your answer to it, than for anything interesting I have to tell you in the shape of news –

I suppose that, before this, you have heard recounted each and every one of the incidents of that famous Camp – hunt, " cujus magna pars fui " –   Suffice it to say that I killed two deer, running, about as near as I could estimate, as fast as the buckshot flew–: that I was the hero of *that* hunt: (the which I did enjoy most marvellously and hugely)–: that I on *that* hunt, according to mathematical calculation, (which is as follows: *three* deer were killed: consequently *three* deer were eaten: and as I was unanimously conceded to have devoured at least one third more than any of the other three hunters, the demonstration proves very conclusively that I) did eat, in the course of ten days, *one whole venison*!!! [5]

I only stayed in Macon, one day; then came on over here – Heard as I came through, that Judge Powers was dead, that Thomas A. Napier had committed suicide and that Uncle Clifford had been elected to the House of Representatives – Consequently I'll have the pleasure of hearing the gentleman's lucubrations on matters of state in November during the Session.

Love to everybody –   Write to me soon, and believe me,

Your Bro,

Sid Lanier

To Robert S. Lanier

Oglethorpe University
November 14th 1859

My Dear Pa:

I should have written to you before this, but, aside from the fact that every moment of my time has had its necessary duty, I was looking for a letter from you every day, and thus refrained from writing –

[5] Before returning to college, Lanier had enjoyed his usual vacation at Montvale Springs. The deer hunt of 1859, described in this letter, was probably only one of several that inspired the account of the deer hunt in *Tiger-Lilies* (V, 15-20) and the reminiscences in Lanier's letter of Dec. 21, 1873, to his wife.

My hands are completely full; almost too much so — Prof. Smith has appointed me to open the Senior debate, which comes off in about two weeks hence — I shall make my opening speech at least a half-hour in length: my closing effort must not cease under an hour — The first I am now writing off; the last, will, of necessity, be extempore, as it will consist of defence against attacks made on me by opponents succeeding me, and what strictures I may see fit to put forth upon any arguments they may advance — The question is purely moral, connected with our present study of Paley: " is *one's own* happiness a *legitimate object of pursuit* "? [6] — I am on the affirmative: & can speak with the more advantage by reason of the fact that I believe in the doctrines that I shall be called upon to advocàte —

Before long, I will have to read my essay before the class — On it I base hopes of getting a high mark; but to substantiate my hopes I must think and read a great deal — I have chosen, as my subject " Government " — I shall try and trace its origin; set forth its uses and effects; discuss the duty of civil obedience; and investigate the authority of human Government, whence derived, how limited, & how enforced — At least, I *think* I shall treat it in that way; the subject only occurred to me last night, & I have not yet had time fully to determine on it — I would be very much obliged if you would send me, soon as possible, one or two of the profoundest writers on the subject that you may have in your library — I say " profoundest," not because I expect my essay to be of that character at all, but for the reason that the subject is one somewhat puzzling, and at the same time extremely interesting to me, wherefore I wish to get to the bottom of it — And any suggestions that you may happen to make with reference to that disposition of the subject which will enable me to embody most of its leading principle (for of course *all* can not be treated of –), will be appreciated —

---

* Among Lanier's unpublished college papers, two speeches on this topic survive, totalling 18 MS pages (Charles D. Lanier and Clifford A. Lanier Collections, Johns Hopkins University). The Rev. R. C. Smith, A. M., Professor of Moral and Mental Philosophy at Oglethorpe, who conducted the debate, used for his class textbooks those of the English theologian, William Paley (see Leola Beeson, *Sidney Lanier at Oglethorpe University*, Macon, Ga., 1936).

The essay on " Government " mentioned in the following paragraph is probably the surviving MS entitled " Democracy," dated Jan., 11, 1860 (Charles D. Lanier Collection, Johns Hopkins University).

I, under peculiar circumstances accepted on last Saturday a nomination for the presidency of the Thalian Society,[7] and was elected *unanimously* –:   I take my seat on the First of January of next year –   Our President who was to have taken his seat at that time, (they are always elected three months in advance–) has left College –   It being necessary then to elect another president, some of the members came to me with the request that I would run, stating that another man contemplated running, who was very distasteful to them and who could, being from Liberty County, carry all the Liberty vote, which is equivalent to an election, from their majority in the Society –   I consented: and accepted a nomination on Saturday morning, after which my opponent who had also been nominated, declined –   I was then unanimously elected President – I find that I can at any time, vacate the chair, and, substituting my vice-P–, debate on the questions –   Have I done right?

[7] The surviving records of the Thalian Society show that on Sat., Nov. 12, 1859, the constitution of the society was suspended after a single nomination had been made, and that Lanier was elected president *viva voce*; the regularly elected president, one Johnson, had left college and Lanier's election was to fill the vacancy. He took office on Dec. 10, 1859, and served until Feb. 22, 1860, at which time he was elected Senior Essayist (see Beeson, *op. cit.,* p. 9).   His speech accepting the presidency, an unpublished MS of 9 pages (Clifford A. Lanier Collection, Johns Hopkins University), contains an interesting comment on the impending conflict:

"Thalians, do you understand your times? do you comprehend your epoch? . . . A lonely student from his dormitory on this campus looked out yesterday upon his country's length and breadth— . . . He saw all along and through the northern half of his country, a restless mass of moving myriads, aye, a mass of demons, frenzied with fanatic rage and hatred and fury! He heard, and shuddered as he heard, a leader of those frenzied myriads, with murderous malignity, exclaiming 'War to the knife, and the knife to the hilt!' . . . Delegates of such men as these . . . must sit upon the floor of the legislative assembly of this country, such delegates must debate and decide questions and measures of vital interest to the perpetuity of this union, aye, to the rights, and not only to the rights, but the peace and the property, and the very lives of Southern men!—

"Thalians! it is with such men, that you and that I must in a few years be called upon to cope–: it is the sophisms of such men that you and I must expose; it is the measures of such men that you and I must defeat and overturn— . . .

"And if you prepare yourselves, do it here & now, or never do it! If you would have your souls in readiness for that terrible conflict, here, even here, within these walls, gird about you the invincible panoply of truth, of skill, of preparation!"

Several surviving speeches from this winter of 1859-1860, show that Lanier took his own advice literally and used the Thalian Society as an arena for debating the issues of the times.

Received the shoes and chess-men to-day: the former fit, the latter please! many thanks for both –

Had letter from Cliff, two days ago: wish very much he was with me –

I should be afraid I had bored you with these dry details of college-duties no doubt familiar to you, were I not conscious of the interest you take in all I say and do here – And in truth, the classic garb with which my imagination invests the scenes about me, I seeming in my long purple dressing-gown (I speak in it, in the Society!) to be an "old Roman" in all the dignity of the "virile toga," and my companions of the Society Conscripti Cates; I say my imagination makes the whole thing so delightful that I can scarcely keep from prating of it –

I want to see you all; Mother, Father, Sister, Brother, Cousin, all elements of home" – What say you to a flying visit on the 1st of December, only about two weeks hence, I believe?

Yours always
Sid. Lanier

Was invited to tea at Prof. Smith's a night or two ago; went and enjoyed myself hugely – He is a rare, old, ugly, good, and witty man, is Prof S. –

1860

To Robert S. Lanier

Oglethorpe University
Feb'y 3rd 1860

My Dear Pa:

I've been thinking a good deal upon the contents of your last letter; but have not as yet come to any very definite conclusion in regard to the matters spoken of – The reasons of which indecision you will see more clearly from the following statement of the case –:

I have for some time had in my eye, the *tutor's place* of *this* College, now occupied by my old class-mate, Knox – The place is to be vacated in July next; and I do not doubt but that I could get it –

Its advantages would be briefly these –

1st My association with Prof. Woodrow –; which would be of inestimable value –

2nd The large amount of time which I could devote to private reading: I being occupied with my classes only *three hours* per day –

3rd Instead of being occupied day after day with the drudgery of maintaining order amongst a crowd of unruly *city* school-boys; instead of having to slash and whip the rudiments in through the medium of the corporeal extremities, after the fashion of my friend Singleton; instead of these things I would teach young men who consider themselves gentlemen, and who generally behave as such in the class-room –

4th I have at my command the Libraries of the College and of the two Societies, and that of the *State* in Milledgeville – (which latter, by the way, I have but recently become aware of – It appears absolutely vast, in comparison with ours at the College) –

25

5th I am still further on, in that *line* of promotion, of which you have spoken –

The salary of the Tutor is Five-hundred and Fifty Dollars – I state these things, so that you may have the case plainly before you: and in order that you may make the decision – *I* am unable to decide which place would be best: there are so many advantages on both sides –

I have just seen Weems, and effected a compromise in the purchase of his room – Cliff [1] will pay him $18.00, and thus buy half his room – Besides that Cliff needs, now, $10.00, for his Society dues – We need also, for board, (to-day closes our month) $28.00 – We need, for washing $2.50: owe for wood $5.00 – Fluid $3.00 making in all $66.50 – If you can possibly raise it, I would like also, $6.00 – I need it, to pay Weems for my use of his room: for under the present arrangement (by which, you know, Cliff buys half the room, and *I* have paid nothing), I will have sponged on him, (Weems,) for a whole year, & occupied his room for that time without paying him a cent – It is an obligation that I do not like to be under –

By the way, *to-day* is the 3rd of February: it is one which I hope the histories will record at some future day, as being the birth-day of one S. C. Lanier – Methinks I hear the orator, the 3rd of February orator: " The day we celebrate: the birth-day of a man whose love was his fellow-man " – And the historian: " born 3rd of Feb'y, (of poor but honest parents,?) in the then flourishing town of Macon, Georgia " – – – – Apage Satanus!

Give a great deal of love to all—from Cliff, and

Your Son

Sidney Lanier –

---

[1] Clifford Lanier had entered Oglethorpe in Jan., 1860, apparently as a Freshman, since he later stated that he left college at " the end of the Sophomore year " (letter to J. A. Fisher, Sept. 27, 1883), and it is known that he was not at Oglethorpe after June, 1861. Before entering college he seems to have worked for a while in his father's law office. Now he took a room with his brother and followed him into the Thalian Society, being elected to membership at the meeting of Jan. 7, 1860 (see Beeson, *op. cit.*, p. 11).

To Robert S. Lanier

Oglethorpe University
May 7th   1860

My Dear Pa:

Please excuse my half-sheet: it is all I have got, – inasmuch as the money didn't last to buy more –

We have no news – weather is extremely warm –

Got your letter on Friday; and papers on Saturday – Haven't yet had time to read them –

Delivered a lecture in Metaphysics on Friday; haven't seen Mr Smith since then, to get his opinion of it – Am busy as a bee: our class has to review the whole college course, between now and the middle of June; when the Senior vacation commences – [2]

Cliff is coming on finely – Is taking his stand in the Society, as one of *the* debaters,– I make him speak at every meeting –

The Doctor was mightily pleased with our Pastor –: & has invited him over to preach our Baccalaureate Sermon –

I delivered the invitation to Mr Woodrow – He expressed himself very favorably to the project; says he has long wished to go there, and will assuredly do so, if his engagements will permit him –

Think probably my white suit at Baird's is done by this; – Cliff wants a pair of shoes, No 5 – And we need letter-paper; some small size, and the rest large – Please send all over soon as you can – Besides; our Board-day came on the 3rd of this

[2] No further letters during Lanier's Senior year have been found, but from various surviving documents the account of his graduation can be filled in. After spending the month of " Senior vacation " in Macon, he returned to Oglethorpe for the commencement exercises, July 18, 1860. Lanier (with an average grade of 9.63) shared the First Honor with E. F. Hoge of LaFayette, Ga., and of the rival Phi Delta Society (with an average of 9.58). Lanier delivered the valedictory " To the Community, Trustees, and Faculty; " Hoge delivered the valedictory " To the Class." Lanier and Hoge were two of a committee of ten in charge of the " Commencement Party." John B. Gordon was the commencement speaker. (Commencement programs, a card of invitation to the party, a MS record of the standing of all members of the class, and Lanier's speech in 12 MS pages are in the Clifford A. Lanier Collection; a second draft of the speech in 13 MS pages is in the Charles D. Lanier Collection, Johns Hopkins University.

month— Aunt Jane will send Cliff's board I suppose [3]— Please send over mine. $14.00   And for washing, room-cleaning,

$$\frac{11.50}{\$25.50}$$

blocking, lights shoes (which I had made in town) & sundries, no space to mention.

Love to all from both—

Your Son,

S. C. Lanier

To Samuel L. Knox [4]

[Montvale Springs, Tenn., Summer, 1860]

Dear S———: Write me a summary of your experiences condensed into aphorisms, that I may have a pocketful of them ready to profit by on all occasions. x x x I tremble when I think of tutorship (by the way, my rightful title of tutor here has, owing to my exhibition of talents as flutist, been corrupted into " tooter," it being considered that the last mentioned word euphoniously expresses whatever distinctive cognomen I ought to possess in the exercise of my two professions.) x x x I have just thought what an assemblage of facilities for enjoyment I have up here in the mountains. Kinsfolks, men-friends, women-friends, books, music, wine, hunting, fishing, billiards, ten-pins, chess, eating, mosquitoless sleeping, mountain scenery, and a month of idleness; shades of Apicius and Heliogabalus! [5] Not finding my delight in life increased, I am come to the con- clusion that the luxuries of this world are humbugs and the idea that they are essential to happiness a most magnificent absurdity.

---

[3] Apparently Clifford's expenses were borne in part by R. S. Lanier's sister Jane, Mrs. Abram P. Watt.

[4] Previously published with omissions, *Chautauquan*, XXI, 406 (July, 1895), from which the present text is taken (MS not found). Name of addressee and conjectural dating from internal evidence.

[5] Commencement over, Lanier spent his vacation, as usual, at Montvale Springs. An idealized account of the experiences of this summer of 1860 is given in the opening chapters of *Tiger-Lilies*, written in the same mood as this letter to the college friend whose place as tutor at Oglethorpe Lanier was to fill in the autumn.

To Robert S. Lanier

Talmage,[6] Ga
October 8th ″ /60

My Dear Pa:

I should have written you last week but was very busy, and did not have time –; and have snatched a half hour from sleeping-time to drop you this note –

We got your letter to-day, containing $11.00 – Am glad that you are so comfortably fixed up: but you did not write how *Ma* was pleased with the plan –

If there is one man under the sun infected with the *cocoethes* DISSENDI, it is your humble servant – What between yourself, Mr Woodrow, Mrs Talmage & the D^r, and my own ambition, (the latter strangely aroused since my collegiate success – why, I really think some learning *must* come out of it – Have been studying with might and main all the week: find the madness growing on me – Mr Woodrow is to learn me French & German:[7] I commence them to-morrow – He also superintends my private classical studies –

---

[6] On Oct. 1, 1860, Clifford Lanier wrote to his father from Midway (which seems about this time to have been renamed Talmadge) that they had arrived safely; and on Oct. 7, he added: "Bro^t Sid has got fairly started in his doctorial duties, but I have not heard him express the result of his week's experiense."

[7] The plan that had formed itself in Lanier's mind at this time, as he assumed his tutorial duties at Oglethorpe, was to study in a German University (following the pilgrimage of Woodrow, and of such young southerners as Basil Gildersleeve and Thos. R. Price), as preliminary to a professorship in an American college. But that he was still undecided as to his life work appears from a passage in a lost diary, apparently of this date: "The point which I wish to settle is merely by what method shall I ascertain what I am fit for as preliminary to ascertaining God's will with reference to me; or what my inclinations are, as preliminary to ascertaining what my capacities are—that is, what I am fit for. I am more than all perplexed by this fact: that the prime inclination—that is, natural bent (which I have checked, though) of my nature is to music, and for that I have the greatest talent; indeed, not boasting, for God gave it me, I have an extraordinary musical talent, and feel it within me plainly that I could rise as high as any composer. But I cannot bring myself to believe that I was intended for a musician, because it seems so small a business in comparison with other things which, it seems to me, I might do. Question here: 'What is the province of music in the economy of the world?'" (quoted by Mims, pp. 38-39). During the ensuing year a third interest manifested itself—creative authorship. And between these three Lanier's later career was divided.

I have a private pupil in Greek, who will bring me in some $25.00 per term –

Cliff is well: he recites finely: is a head-and-shoulders in advance of his class –

PLEASE SEND ME YOUR DAILY NEWSPAPERS, AFTER *you read them as soon as possible* – My brethren (Fathers?) of the Faculty have to tell me all the news – Also, please inquire who is the best plasterer in Macon, and write me by return mail – We, (the Thalian Society) have a large plastering job to let out, and want to correspond in reference to cost &c – [8]

Love to Ma & Sister, & Aunt Eliza, & the children generally, & Beaumont, the Fletcher-less –.

Sid Lanier [9]

To Robert S. Lanier [10]

Talmage, Georgia
Decb^r 6th 1860

My Dear Pa:

Having learnt an immense deal, and been otherwise a very good boy, during the week, I have concluded to give myself an hour's holiday to-night, wherein I may have a small

---

[8] The part played by the Thalian Society in building Thalian Hall (which still stands) is told by Leola Beeson in *Sidney Lanier at Oglethorpe University* (Macon, Ga., 1936).

[9] On October 21, 1860, Clifford Lanier wrote to his mother: " Bro^t Sid is boarding at the Hotel kept by Sherman a very clever man who has I believe ignored Yankeeism. I board at Mrs. Tucker's." (Clifford was now rooming with a student named Goetchius, undoubtedly the brother of Sidney's classmate J. M. Goetchius of Columbus, Ga.).

It was at Ike Sherman's boarding house that Lanier met Milton Harlow Northrup (1841-1906), a native of New York state and a graduate of Hamilton College, who was principal of an academy for younger boys at Midway during 1860-1861. Some of the best of Lanier's later letters were written to him. A rough pencil sketch labelled " Squire Northrup " bears the note, verso: " The sketch hastily drawn on the reverse of this scrap was made by Sidney Lanier in the winter of [1860-]1861. Milledgeville, Ga. M. H. N." (Northrup Collection, Johns Hopkins University.)

[10] This long letter by Lanier to his father is typical of the letters he was to write throughout the war, even to Mary Day and other young women with whom he fancied himself in love. His sister Gertrude (Mrs. J. C. Gibson) wrote in a letter of October, 1883, to J. A. Fisher: " His letters to family and friends were

sort of Politico-philosophical talk with you — What ideas I
have to advance are crude, for I haven't had time to develop
them:— At any rate, however, I console myself with the assur-
ance, that I shall not fall below the Standard instituted by that
Englishman, who, in criticising some youngling's speech in
Parliament, remarked: " Some things were *good,* and some were
original: but the *good* things were not *original,* nor were the
original things *good*! "

Do you remember the long discussion that we had, going
down the other side of Chilhowee,[11] on our fishing-frolic to
Abram's Creek? — and the theory that I then put forth in
regard to the education of the *Emotions,* as contradistinguished
from the education of the *Intellect*? It is with a view to the
practical application of that theory to the present condition of
the Country that I wish to talk to you — For fear you have
forgotten it, I will briefly explain it again —

Convey yourself, in thought, back to that period in the
world's history, which immediately preceded the inauguration
of educational institutions of any sort whatsoever — Suppose
that you and I in the progress of things, have conceived the
idea of *educating,* (that is, literally of *drawing out,* with the
implied idea of drawing out so as to *work rightly*) — The first
question that occurs to us, as we sit down to talk over it and to
mediate upon it is, what are we going to educate? " Man,"
we answer ourself immediately, and think we are getting on
swimmingly — But almost simultaneously with the answer,
pops up another question, for, What is man? The first consequence of which is the discovery that we *don't* get on
swimmingly, nay verily we don't, for some time, get on *at all* —
Supposing, however, that you and I are very acute and far-
seeing philosophers, after a laborious process of, first, analysis,
and, secondly, generalization, and, thirdly, of exclusion of all
such definitions of man as " a two-legged animal without
feathers " &c, we reduce him to these primary ingredients: a
body, an *intellect,* and an *emotional faculty* — So that here

gems of thought. One of us would say: ' he never writes us anything about
himself '! His letters were full of flowery descriptions and beautiful imaginings." R. S. Lanier complained frequently that his son gave too few facts in
his letters, and indulged too much in literary composition.

[11] A mountain in Tennessee, near Montvale Springs, frequently mentioned in
Tiger Lilies.

we have arrived at a full and satisfactory answer to the question, what are we going to educate?

But there is again a most important consideration which here presses upon us — Shall we educate both body, and intellect, and emotion? Or, to save trouble, shall we only educate some one or two of them: and if so, which one or two?

Now, here, we will remember that in our investigation of man, which led us to the resolution of him into those three elements, we were frequently astonished at the wonderful way in which they act and react among themselves — That too, in spite of the fact that they are essentially distinct from each other, not only in mode of operation but also in *kind* — Our remembrance of these facts will, at *least*, dispose us to be very careful how we educate *one* of the elements in preference to any other — While we are still meditating, in doubt, upon this phase of the question, we happen to think of a fact which has repeatedly presented itself to our admiration, in our career as philosophers; that is, " *Harmony*, is the great Law of the Universe " — We will say to ourselves, *by all means* let us not *violate* this *great* law in disposing of the *highest* being in the Universe — Therefore, let us not educate man *in*harmoniously: therefore, let us not educate *one* of the elements which compose man, to the exclusion of the *rest* —

Thus we will have settled the question: and if we be practical men we will proceed to inaugurate the *harmonious* education of man —

Thus we, two *heathen* philosophers, have been irresistibly led to the conclusion that the *whole* of a man, his intellect, his emotions, his body, must be educated: and that to educate him otherwise is to violate the great law of his Structure, (which is, the action and reaction of intellect on emotion, of emotion on intellect &c), and also to violate the great law of the Universe, (which is, harmony) — And, I say we two HEATHEN philosophers: because every fact entering into our investigation is discoverable by the light of *reason* alone — But suppose we had had the Bible! And with it, the metaphysical knowledge of the Nineteenth Century!

It would have been wonderful, if, even as Heathen Philosophers we had arrived at any other conclusion than that the *whole* of a man should be educated – Does it not pass beyond wonderful, that not only Heathen Philosophers, but men who have the Bible, men of the Nineteenth century, should, year after year, and century after century, have continued to sanction and originate institutions having in view the mere education of the *Intellect* of man, to the utter exclusion of the remaining parts of him?

So much for what seems to me to be a true and comprehensive theory of education – By deducing it, as we did, in the character of heathen philosophers, I have saved space, only adducing proofs enough to demonstrate its truth, and no more – Yet, a volume might be written, pursuing the same train of thought, upon *collateral* proofs –

I come now to speak of the theory, in connection with the present condition of the country – In doing so, there are two facts which it is necessary to keep in view continually: 1st. A man must always *feel* rightly, (that is, his *emotion* must operate rightly,) before he can *think* rightly, (that is, before his *intellect* can operate rightly) – This is the principle practically recognised by the newspaper-editors who every day exhort their readers, during the present crisis, to "Keep cool: suppress passion" &c – : & just so when the public speaker asks, in prelude, for your calm judgment &c – It arises in part from the (:) 2nd fact, (that we must keep in view) that the *initial step of every plan* and *every action,* is *an emotion* –

Now let us see how important, in view of these facts, it is, that *especially* in a *Republican* Government, the emotions should be educated into a right and healthy operation – It is a fundamental principle, that, in a Republic, *Public Opinion* is the *reigning power* – Now Public Opinion governing, it is necessary that Public Opinion should be right and sound – But if the operation of the intellect, by which opinion is formed, be dependent for soundness upon the right operation of the *emotion*; then, Public Opinion, depends for soundness upon *Public Emotion* – How if Public emotion be itself unsound, that is, uncontrolled, that is, uneducated? – I remember on my last visit home, reading you an article in a newspaper, in which the writer maintained that a Republican form of Government did not suit, and could not be maintained by, an *educated*

people – And *you,* in view of the present conditions of the country; half coincided with that theory – But do you not agree with me, now, in thinking that the trouble is *not* in the education of the people, but *rather in the education of their intellect to the exclusion of their* EMOTIONS? That is, the difficulty lies *not* in *education,* but in *unharmonious* education – Suppose, however, we go a little into details – And What a Spectacle! I firmly believe, Sir, that our sacred memories of the revolution have been violated: our national Commerce has been suspended: our people thrown into distress: our brotherly love for the North been turned into deadly hatred: our fifteen Southern states been compelled to secede: *all,* by the *un*educated *emotion* of a single man, together with his *educated intellect* –: *that man,* the founder of the Black-Republican party –, (remembering while you think of it, that an *emotion* is the initial step of every plan or action) – Is it not so? – – – – – –
I have not time or space to talk about that branch any longer – I could write it seems to me, a great volume on that one instance of the non-observance of the theory of harmonious education – –

I am a full-blooded secessionist [12] – I think it the merest folly to attempt to bring the Black-Republican party to terms, by any system of reprisal, in any shape –: reprisal either in the form of money; or in the form of mortification, by repealing Personal liberty bills &c, – (which might be called a moral reprisal) – My reason for thinking so is this: all fanaticism is a mixture of *pure* doctrine with bad: perhaps better, a *bad application* of *pure* doctrine – The fanaticism of the Crusaders had a right foundation – principle: namely, the spread of the Gospel –. But the Crusaders adopted the wrong ways and means to do that good work – The fanaticism of the French Revolution had a right-foundation-principle: namely, the attainments of liberty: but those Revolutionists looked with blind eyes upon the *ways* and *means* – just so, the fanaticism of the Black-Republican party has a right foundation-principle; namely, that when the laws of *God* clash with the laws of *man,*

---

[12] A month before, Nov. 6(?), Clifford Lanier had written to his mother: " I hear of nothing but disunion and see only blue cockades fluttering in the wind. My politics are practicable and honorable Union—beyond that dissolution." The secession of Georgia from the Federal Union was voted by the state legislature at Milledgeville on Jan. 19, 1861.

God must be obeyed rather than *man,* for He is Higher —   But what an application of that principle! Now, this being so; fanaticism being the monstrous offspring of a *forced* union between pure doctrine and the depravity of man: it is traceable to this fact, I say, that *sacrifice* is the food of fanaticism: martyrdom is its glorious gate of Heaven — Every fanatic killed is apotheosized by his party into another god who will incite them to fresh endeavor — By oppressing it, we feed it: by threatening death to it, we hold open the doors of its Heaven — A strange way, truly, to conquer it! —

I had intended to say something in reply to your strictures on Mʳ Stephens' speech: [18] *not* because I *agree* with *him,* but because I understood him very differently from what you did — But I have not time to write more — Pardon a letter dashed off in great haste —: On reading it over I am ashamed at what I *have* said, when I compare it with what I *wanted* to say —

Give a great deal of love to all, from

Your Son,

Sid. Lanier —

[18] Alexander Hamilton Stephens, though later to become Vice-President of the Confederacy, remained an advocate of settling the controversy within the Union until the very last. The speech here referred to was delivered by invitation before the legislature of Georgia on Nov. 14, 1860—after Lincoln's election; as a substitute for the immediate secession advocated by Thos. R. R. Cobb and Robt. Toombs on Nov. 12 and 13, Stephens urged a conference of all southern states and a policy of watchful waiting to prevent Lincoln and Congress from violating the Constitution and invading southern rights. (See A. H. Stephens, *A Constitutional View of the Late War Between the States,* Chicago, 1868-1870, II, 299.)

1861

To an Editor [1]

Talmage, Georgia.
February 5th 1861

Dear Sir:

Will you have the kindness to insert, in your March Number of the " Monthly," (Somewhere in the first part of it: after the *first article,* for instance) the enclosed *short* piece –

If you do not think it worthy, why – *burn* both letter and piece, and say nothing about it – If, on the other hand, you conclude to insert it, Please affix to it the name of

(Your much obliged)

S. C. *Lanier*

To Robert S. Lanier

Talmage, Ga
Feb'y 12th "/61 –

My Dear Pa:

I told Cliff, yesterday, to write you and acknowledge receipt of the money which you sent him; but he forgot to do so – Wherefore I drop you this short note, to perform that duty for him –

Cliff is very well – I have a severe sty on my eye, which gives me immense annoyance –; and is a perfect veto on all such things as *poetic inspiration,* (unless one wanted to compose another " *Inferno* "!) – Alas, what an immortal Poem that

---

[1] This letter to an unidentified editor, the first one containing evidence of Lanier's interest in authorship, is possibly a draft retained by Lanier; or perhaps the letter was never sent. For the poem attached to the letter, " On Reading of One Who Drowned Herself," apparently hitherto unpublished, see I, 5.

wretched, infinitesimal, material, puny ill has probably cut the world out of!

I enclose a short note, apologising to Uncle C for my unceremonious departure – Love to all –

Your aff. Son,

Sid Lanier –

FROM ROBERT S. LANIER [2]

Macon Feby. 21, 1861 –

Dear Son,

Your letter enclosing the verses came some days ago – & would have been answered before but for Inferior Court engagements &C.

I sent your brother two papers yesterday & you two or three with this, – among them the N. Y. Observer with Dr Thornwell's article on the "State of the Country." Your Uncle C. wrote the Editor, Mr Prime, to publish it; but received a reply that he was then doing so. It is the ablest paper I have seen on the subject: and is attracting attention as it deserves to do, as I see by the Papers. You & Clifford must read it & read carefully to get the full benefit of it.

I had intended to write you somewhat at length in relation to the verses, versification &C: but do not feel exactly in the spirit of it this evening – as I have on my *business* rather than a *critical* mood. Let it be enough to say that so far as I have seen of your efforts in this line you have quick poetical sympathies, a rich fund of imagery, inexhaustable conceit, & a clever knack of versification. The first however, may be due to youth, & may in some measure pass away with it. The second & third "come by nature" & are likely to remain. And the fourth is the result of culture. (I mean by the word, "conceit," rather, subtlety of thought, in connection with the old *English* acceptation – than the more modern acceptation.)

---

[2] This is an answer to a lost letter by Lanier. The verses referred to have not been identified (but see I, 220). Like so many of R. S. Lanier's letters to his sons, it reveals the father as sympathetic and appreciative, but cautiously practical in his encouragement of their literary ambitions.

As to the verses themselves, they show more of promise in the author than present worth in themselves. No. 1 is unsuited to excite sympathy or poetical ideas. No. 2, is very handsomely done. As a setting in some Eastern story it would look well. The description of sunset &C. is natural & striking. No. 3 jumped so well with Gertrudes humor that she recorded it in her memory at once & has repeated to me since. It came out of the " conceit " fund & is very sprightly – & happily expressed. Perhaps this is as much as I ought to say on this subject now. I have however to add that I am glad you are exercising yourself *in every way* – as the young " wrestler " does to develop & test his powers. But dont forget the archaeology. I wish to see your mind stored with that classic wealth which gives such a lustre to every study & topic & to half of life. I will advert to this again when the occasion for writing & thinking is better suited.

Your mother has improved greatly – & has resumed her prandial journeys up & down stairs. The rest of us are well. Your mother says you & bro. do not write often enough. Push him up a little in that respect & set him a good example!

Much love to both of you. Have had my watch put in good order & will probably send it to you in a day or so.

I have quit smoking altogether – & beg you to do likewise. You will never attain what you now aspire to if you do not. You are like me – you cannot smoke without doing so in excess. Some people can. Many cannot. You & I belong to the latter class. If you wish to be strong, hearty, active, full of vigor – *always ready* – in mind & body – quit tobacco. I was so conscious of this truth that I felt it sinful to persist in the opposite course.[3]

Your father,

R. S. LANIER.

---

[3] As Lanier's own later letters reveal, he very much enjoyed the use of tobacco, especially the smoking of cigars. Notes in the Charles D. Lanier Collection in the handwriting of Mary Day Lanier, but probably taken down from the recollections of Clifford Lanier, indicate that Lanier began the use of tobacco during his first year at college.

To Robert S. Lanier

Talmage, Ga
March 1st – "/61 –

My Dear Pa:

I got your letter, (with Ma's) to day; as also the paper –

What a *disgusting* scene was the Lincoln *hand-shaking* affair –! I think the disgrace of the United States had its fit culmination therein: the scene ought to go into History under the title of " The Great Apotheosis of the Great Hog: " [4] –

My passage-at-arms with the cigars still goes on: but the enemy is growing perceptibly fainter, while I increase in vigor; and remain certain of victory –   I stopped smoking last Sunday night: this is Friday night, and I have not smoked yet –   Verily it does take an exertion of will that is very unusual for *me*; for it was *so glorious* to smoke and dream, with inspiration, as if from Helicon, in every puff – –   Yet, after one has accomplished the thing, and has *stopped*; he is so far repaid by the glorious consciousness of *heroism,* that, after all, it amounts to a vulgar quid pro quo affair! *Almost!*

Cliff's Company [5] was invited by the three military companies of Milledgeville to take part with them in the ceremony of a banner-presentation, to-day –   We gave them holiday: and they went, making, I thought, the best show of the crowd –   After the speeches &c, Adjutant General Wayne drilled the battalion for some time: they then separated, and the boys drilled separately, firing salutes &c, until late in the afternoon, when they

[4] The reference is apparently to some event during Lincoln's journey from Springfield, Ill., to Washington, Feb. 12-23, 1861.

[5] By the time this letter was written, an Oglethorpe military company had been organized, and Clifford Lanier had become a member. Sidney Lanier had as yet taken no steps toward military service, but of his state of mind at this time his friend Northrup wrote (*Lippincott's*, LXXV, 305, Mar., 1905): " As to the future of the new Confederacy he had some fond illusions, which at this distance we may smile at while we pity. While the new Confederacy was to enter upon an era of prosperity such as no other nation, ancient or modern, had ever enjoyed, the city of Macon, his birthplace and home, was to become a great art centre. Its streets were to be lined with marble statues, like unto Athens of old. Once in after years I was cruel enough to recall to his memory this glowing vision. The only response was, ' What fools we were! What fools we were! ' "

marched back to the Campus –   When they broke ranks, Cliff's face looked like a full-blown rose, as he " dragged his slow length along " [6] towards his room –   " Tired, Cliff? " says I – " Tired "!!! he answered; I would you could have heard the utter sublimity of derision that he threw into the tone of his voice: derision at the superfluousness of the question –   The poor fellow was completely broken down –: and was unable to write you, to-night, as he had intended –

Love to Sister: and tell her I'll try to write her soon –   In default of which, she can, in the meantime, appropriate whatever letters are written to the other members of the family –

Love to Ma –   Was much surprised to hear of Pink Towns choice; had thought she would look higher –

Love to Uncle C. & family: and believe me your aff. Son,

Sid Lanier

From Robert S. Lanier

Sunday evening
[Macon, Ga., April 21, 1861?]

Dear son,

You have probably heard that the Macon Volunteers & Floyd Rifles left here last night for Norfolk, V[a] on very short notice. Your Uncle Clifford, having been absent for some time at court, & just returned the day before the Co[s] left could not get off with them – but goes tomorrow night & takes Annie, the baby & nurse. George Ross & W[m] Ross's wives also go there husbands being now with the Rifles. I supposed they will be stationed some time at Norfolk, but cannot tell. I should have preferred to go myself – but your Uncle C. said as he was an " active member " he could not decline to go, & so I remain.

It was a solemn sight to see these Citizens, armed & equipped as soldiers – marching off to a distant state – perhaps to battle & to death. It was an impressive scene – We all felt it.

Troops are going over the Road daily – some to V[a] & some to our own sea-coast.

I send you an Extra.

[6] Alexander Pope, " Essay on Criticism."

Your mother not very well – nor I. Gertrude is the exception.
Not time to write more –   Love to you both.

Your father

R. S. L.

Will write Clifford tomorrow – [7]

FROM ROBERT S. LANIER

Macon Geo.   May 16/61.

My dear son:

Your mother and grandma came last night – both
improved. Your grandma left this morning for Montvale.
Your mother had a good time at Charleston – riding out frequently & visiting the forts in the harbor –: brought back quite
a variety of souvenirs presented to & gathered by her at fort
Sumter. She will probably write to you tomorrow.

I sent you paper yesterday: –   one containing the account of
the " flag presentation." [8] The Editor this morning remarked
that it was " quite sprightly."   I like it pretty well – *especially*
the *first* paragraph – in fact all except the " nom de plume."
CACOETHES Scrib always reminds me of the classical claptrap of
One Dr D'Amour – and therefore you may set it down to pre-

---

[7] Conjectural dating from the fact that the militia companies left Macon on
Apr. 20, 1861. On Apr. 26, 1861, R. S. Lanier wrote to his son Clifford,
urging him to continue his studies until the issue of the war was settled, and
reminding him that the young men of the South had an obligation to educate
themselves for the better service of their country: " If the war continues, they
will be needed then worse than now: if it does not, the more will be the pity
the exercises [of the college] were suspended. . . .

" Let your brother read this letter. I presume he will communicate the substance of it to the Faculty & you can, also, to the students—as occasion offers."

In spite of the threat of war, Mrs. R. S. Lanier was planning to accompany
her mother-in-law, Mrs. Sterling Lanier, to Charleston, S. C., to visit her sister-
in-law, Mrs. T. D. Eason.

R. S. Lanier concluded his letter: " Your Uncle C. telegraphed us yesterday
that he had arrived safe –   had good quarters for his family at Portsmouth &
that he was over at Norfolk."

[8] The " Flag Presentation at Oglethorpe University," published in the Macon
Daily Telegraph, May 15, 1861, and hitherto uncollected, is apparently Lanier's
first venture into print (V, 197). He had adopted the same pseudonym, *Cacoethes
Scrib.*, to which his father objected, for several essays and poems in the College
Notebook, begun in 1858.

judice if you will. At all events you can get a better. Record your thoughts as often as you can.

I will send you tomorrow a copy of the report of the committee on Federal relations made in our congress & just published – I wish you to read it carefully, & study it carefully: because it is the most able, thorough & satisfactory exposition of *our* view of the sectional controversy emanating from any source. The facts and argument must produce a profound impression every where.

I am in fair health again.
Love to the boy Clifford.

Your aff father,

R. S. Lanier.

To Clifford A. Lanier [9]

[Macon, Ga., July, 1861?]

My dear Cliff:

I enclose a letter which please stamp and mail immediately.

Am just about to start to the scene of hostilities. On to the Field of Glory!

Sid

[9] At the end of the college year, Lanier enlisted with the Macon Volunteers, a militia company that had gone to the front, Norfolk, Va., on April 20. The extant data on his first two months of service are somewhat confusing. The official records of the U. S. War Department show that on July 10, 1861, he became a member of Company D (subsequently Company B), 2nd Battalion, Georgia Infantry, C. S. A., at Sewell's Point, Va. But the Order Book of the Second Georgia Battalion, kept by Maj. Thos. Hardeman, Jr. (MS, Mrs. Frank Jones, Clinton, Gray, Ga.) contains the following entry: "Sidney C. Lanier, enlisted Macon, Ga., July 10, 1861; mustered into service August 31, 1861 at Sewell's Point by Major Hardeman." It seems clear, therefore, that the enlistment on July 10 took place in Macon. But the last half of the Order Book entry does not square with the rest of the available evidence, unless the statement "mustered into service August 31, 1861" refers to a purely formal ceremony. For Lanier apparently went on to Virginia immediately after enlistment, as the following letters witness: (1) On July 14, 1861, Gertrude Lanier wrote to Sidney from Montvale that she had received his recent letter, and that she hoped he had already arrived at Sewell's Point. (2) On Aug. 24, 1861, Capt. R. A. Smith, Commanding Macon Volunteers (2nd Georgia Battalion), Sewell's Point, Va., wrote to Gen. Withers: "Private Lanier . . . has relatives at Montvale Springs

FROM ROBERT S. LANIER [10]

Macon Ga. Sept[r]. 23[d], 1861.

My dear Son:

I had the pleasure of getting your letter last saturday & would have answered it immediately but saw Basil Wise, who said he was going back tomorrow; and would

---

in Tennessee for whom he feels a deep solicitude inasmuch as that region of Tennessee is full of traitors—and he desires a Furlough of ten days to assure himself of their safety. I cheerfully recommend him to receive a Furlough for the time stated as his father, mother, grandfather & grandmother are all at Montvale." (3) On Sept. 9, 1861, Capt. R. A. Smith wrote to Private S. C. Lanier (from the Army Hospital, near Norfolk, Va.), that his furlough was extended to Sept. 18.

Thus Lanier's farewell message to his brother here printed (probably a note delivered by hand rather than a posted letter) was written on the day of his departure from Macon for Virginia, on or about July 10. And after some six weeks of service there—the exact dates are not known—he returned to Georgia and Tennessee on a furlough of about three weeks. Thereafter, he was at Sewell's Point, Va., until the spring of 1862, principally engaged in picket duty on the beach. Maj. Thos. Hardeman has recorded these uneventful months succinctly (*Floyd Rifles. Presentation of Gettysburg Medal*, Macon, Ga., 1879, p. 9): " They were ordered to Sewell's Point, in sight of Fortress Monroe, and within reach of its guns. This camp was indeed a military school, where strict military discipline was enforced, and where the command was perfected in the drill which gave them a reputation throughout the army of Virginia. The summer was spent here without any military movements of note. In the fall they moved in the vicinity of Norfolk and went into winter quarters." (For many of the details of Lanier's war experiences during 1861-1862 I am indebted to the researches of Mrs. Frank Jones of Lowther Hall, Clinton, Gray, Ga.)

[10] This is apparently an answer to Lanier's first letter (now lost) after returning to Virginia from his furlough. None of his letters during the first five months of war service have been found.

When, some years after her husband's death, Mary Day Lanier sought to collect the letters that Sidney Lanier had written to his parents during the war, she was able to find but a few. She herself suspected that they might have been stolen from her father's papers, or destroyed by mistake. Only the score that she discovered have come down. These, however, are supplemented by a few surviving letters written by Sidney Lanier to other relatives, and to friends, and— after April, 1863—to Mary Day, to whom he was married in Dec., 1867. Letters by Clifford Lanier to their parents, written during this period, are numerous, however, and since from 1862 the brothers were almost constantly together until the fall of 1864, letters written by Clifford probably tell the story of their military experiences quite as well as, and somewhat more factually than, the lost letters of Lanier. A few letters from their parents have been included to fill in gaps. (This letter has a small tear on p. 3 of the MS; restorations, in brackets, are conjectural.)

therefore take the letter & papers I send you quite as quick & more surely.

I met John Hill Lamar [11] to-day, who told me you were well. By the by if you will correspond with him from time to time I feel quite sure he can & will aid your advancement. I should be sure therefore to do so. I should be very glad to get you on the coast (Ga) this winter – so that we could see more of you. In relation to Knox's proposal, my impression is he never received my answer to his. I regret you did not write him also on receiving the letter I sent you from him. Yours might have had better luck.

Last saturday Mr Gresham spoke to me about your returning to the College this fall. Said you would be wanted – that the College exercises would go on provided there were twenty students: but he said there would be no money to pay your salary. Under the circumstances, he added, that as for himself he wished your *place* kept *open* for you for say six months, & then for you to return &C. I stated to him that was my view about it & hoped he would so arrange the matter. I have no doubt he will do so.

I rejoice that you have so far escaped disease so well. How much is due to your own attention in that behalf I do not know; but I trust you will in no wise neglect those precautionary measures which contribute so greatly to health. Open your tent so that it can ventilate well. If it have no *ventilator* invent one. Four or five men sleeping in a close room or tent will create a *local cause* for disease in the healthiest region – in winter or summer.

How uneasy should I have been had I known you were sick in Petersburg! I should have probably gone to you.

We are still forming Companies here in Macon. Some four are now in process of organization. There is one from the Warrier[?], C. A. Thorpe, Captain, to start this week. We take up a subscription for each, & the people pay out liberally.

Mrs Weed, Miss Mary & Phebe came home friday night. I went to see them yesterday. Miss Mary has improved aston-

---

[11] John Hill Lamar was the brother of Lanier's close friend Augusta Lamar, and like the Laniers a Thalian at Oglethorpe.

ishishingly.   Your Uncle Melville & son [12] are at Dr Fitz^d.
I took a long walk (to the Cemetery) with the former yesterday.
He is " pitchin in " at E M Winships' – & is as " bearded as the
pard."

Say to your Uncle C[lifford] that Alex Menard (or rather
his wife) is keeping a good boarding house at the old Marshall
house, on Walnut Street.   I have just come from there & find
everything very neat; & that I can get board & lodging for
Melville & son there for $25 per m. (very moderate) & Mary
& myself for $50 — & that I have about determined to try it
for the winter.   Gertrude will be in Montgy. till after Christmas.
Melville gets at present $50^{00} per month – so that he can save
money.   Mary can look after his little boy, & it will be close to
my business & Melville's.   We shall all be quite comfortable &
can thus save money despite the war.   My object is to make
both ends meet during the war & afterwards shall ask no odds.
I rent our house for $425 –

Several days ago the weather was hot enough, but since the
copious rains it h[as] turned cool & pleasant reminding us of
[the] fall – now coming.   Judge Nisbet is ru[n]ning for Govr
with some prospect I th[ink] of being elected.   I do hope he
may defe[at] this disgusting Brown.   Read his last *prononce*
in the Telegraph I send you, & feel as I feel —phaugh! –

Tell your Uncle C. I fear I shall fail to rent his house to
Hiram Roberts; but will do my best to get him a good tenant.

I would advise you to devote more or less of your leisure to
advancing yourself in military knowledge.   We know not how
long the war may last & you will not fail to be promoted when
you show your fitness for it.   It seems that a formidable naval
expedition is getting up to be launched on some point or points
south: – do you all apprehend danger at Norfolk.   Are you
prepared – or are you confident?   Suppose 25,000 troops were
sent against Norfolk.   Could you hold it?   I trust our officers
are providing against such an emergency.

Had a letter from your Ma saturday.   She wrote in good
spirits.   Love to Uncle Cl.

>   Your aff. father,   R. S. L

[12] Melville Anderson's wife, a native of Philadelphia, had died five years after
her marriage, leaving an only child, Henry.

To Clifford A. Lanier [13]

In Barracks. Near Norfolk, Va
December 4th "/61

You would not think, my dear Cliff, that I was a soldier,
enduring the frowns of " grim-visaged war," if you could see
me, with slippers and smoking-cap on, pipe in mouth, writing
to you on a real pine table, surrounded by ten noisy boys, in a
room with ten sleeping-bunks built against its walls, and a
" great and glorious " fire blazing in the fire-place – I can hardly
realize that I am in a *house,* but find myself continually asking
myself if it is not some delightful dream: it is impossible for
you to imagine with what delight I hail a real, bona-fide *room,*
as a habitation for the winter, unless you had, as I have, shivered
in cold tents, for the last few months, which the rains beat
through and the winds blew down at every available opportunity (and oh pluvial Gods! with what astonishing frequency
the said availables *did* occur!) : unless you had become accustomed, 1st, to going to sleep with the expectation that your tent
would blow down, and the rains wet you to the skin before you
could get your clothes on, and 2nd to having the said expectations *realized* in the most satisfactory manner; unless you had
been in the habit of eating in a drenching rain which diluted
your coffee, (without any sugar) before you could drink it, and
made mush of your biscuit before you could eat it: unless you
had customarily made your ablutions in a mud-puddle, (which
you had previously caused a swine to vacate, for that purpose;) :
unless you had, in short, been as horribly uncomfortable as it
is possible for a man to be – –   The room, which so excites my
delight, is the one which my mess occupies in our winter-quarters, which we have been actively engaged in building for two
weeks past—; and, by the way, you ought to have seen me car-
pentering: I have hammered, sawed, filed, planed, toted bricks

[13] Clifford had not yet returned to Oglethorpe because of his health, but was
at Montvale Springs with his uncle, William Lanier, and his aunt Lucy, Mrs.
William Lanier. Sterling Lanier and his wife had gone for the winter to
Pensacola, Fla. Towards the end of the month Clifford went to Montgomery to
clerk in the Lanier owned Exchange Hotel. (See R. S. Lanier to Sidney, Dec.
28, 1861.)

and mortar in a hod, (real Irish style) built partitions, bunks, and gun-racks, shingled roofs, and done various and sundry feats in the house-carpentering line –

We had snow night before last, which is yet on the ground: and the rest of the night was occupied with a terrible storm of wind and sleet, which had nearly blown down our winter-quarters: had we been in tents we would have suffered severely –

Uncle Clifford returned, day before yesterday from Macon, where he has been on furlough for the past two weeks – He brought me your last letter to Pa: and I cannot tell you how much pleasure the reading thereof gave me – The bold, nervous energy of the style, the flowing, Ciceronian diction, and the nobleness of the sentiments expressed, led me off into an affectionate revery, which swelled into a glorious vision of your future: but that very affection which attended the vision, contributed to lessen its brightness, by magnifying my fears for your safe passage through those evils which attack all men just at your age; evils which I have gone through, very recently, by no means unscathed, and from whose horrors I am too fresh, not to look with fear and trembling upon *your* journey through their midst – You have not mixed with promiscuous society near as much as I have: and you will therefore have, as yet, but a faint idea of those evils of which I speak – Do not, however, delude yourself with the thought that they are merely romantic, or imaginary, evils; ah, Cliff, I grow earnest and solemn, while I tell you that they are " *real* as grief," real as life, real as the hard earth on which you tread, real as your own existence, and indissolubly connected with it –

I have not time to enumerate all of these evils, nor the tenth part of them: but at the risk of being prosy, and boring you, I am going to talk about one, which has caused *me* more unhappiness, than I could ever express, and which I more particularly select because *you* are, as I was, peculiarly liable to its wretched effects—I mean, *sensitiveness to the opinions of others*— When expressed in that way, I confess, it doesn't look terrible enough to justify my seriousness in speaking of it: but when you have suffered from it a thousand acute pangs in a thousand different ways; and when it has driven you, disgusted, into the opposite extreme of utter indifference to the thoughts and opinions of others; and when this has degenerated into a

selfish, egotistical misanthropy, which drives you into a dreaming, wretched solitude, " a weary, wormy darkness, spurred i'
the flank with flame," in which you wrap yourself up from all
free communion with men, and are blind to the good that is
in the world, seeing only the great, hideous *Bad,* and preying
upon *that,* gloomily and greedily, like a vulture on a carcass;
when, in your listless isolation, you feel that *your* life is an
insult to all other life, when your talents and acquirements are
only burdens, when instead of aspirations you have only regrets,
instead of hopes, only suspicions, and instead of joys, only
weariness, when you are ready to swear that there is no God
but only a Devil, when you read Job's black curses on the day of
his birth and doat on them as the language of your inmost soul;
then, my dear Cliff, you will feel, with me, the terrors conveyed
in those simple words – I do not write so gloomily, from any
depression of spirits, nor with any intention to discourage you,
on the contrary, I was never in better humor in my life; and I
wish to forearm you, by forewarning you – I was reading some
days ago, Eugene Sue's " Matilda," and was peculiarly charmed
with a character named M. de Rochequne; a more brave, noble,
generous, talented, utterly despising the *foolish* portion of
society's conventionalities, and continually flying in their face;
while, at the same time, reverencing, with high veneration, those
formulas and customs which have the sanction of age and a
foundation in reason; perfectly independent of the hasty opinions or unreasonable desires of others, yet delicately attentive
to all the real wants of his fellow-men, and a paragon of polite-
ness – I thought, while I contemplated the great character, of
you: and will send the book to you, if I can get it –

'Tell Uncle William that I took the breech-loading Carbine,
which he gave me, to a Gunsmith, in Norfolk; who hummed
and hawed about it, until he made me mad, when I took the
gun back to my tent, and after three days of incessant work, got
the breech-chamber open! It then took me about a week to
clean it out: it was the rustiest affair I have ever seen – I succeeded, however, at length, in getting it in order: and made
some very good shots with it, at a quarter of a mile's distance –

It is rumored in camp that our Battalion may possibly be
discharged in January: tho' I am not disposed to attach much
importance to the rumor –

A steamboat came up to Norfolk from Fortress Monroe, yesterday, under a flag of truce; amongst other items, she brought news that England has formally demanded of the Federal Government a full apology, or a fight, on account of the Mason and Slidell affair, — [14]   If the news be true, I think it extremely probable that we will have peace in the Spring —

Do write me soon, Cliff — I have not written you, often, before, because of the great inconvenience of writing while I was living under tents — Now, however, I am much better prepared to carry on a correspondence: and hope I shall have many of your letters to reply to —

Give a great deal of love to all at Montvale: Kiss Aunt Lucy for me, and the babies — I long to be with you, up there in the grand old Mountains, to hunt and fish —

Very affectionately your Bro,

Sid Lanier

[14] The United States and England were brought to the brink of war when on Nov. 8, 1861, J. M. Mason and John Slidell, commissioners from the Confederate government to London and Paris, were arrested by a Federal warship while aboard a British merchantman, en route to their posts. But the matter was adjusted before the end of the year, and war averted.

1862

Georgia Barracks –
January 18th ″/62 –

My Dear Cliff;

You don't deserve the slightest consideration from me in the epistolary line, after the contempt with which you've treated my last lengthy epistle: perhaps, however, its very length won for it the aforsaid contempt: perhaps you refrain to write, for fear you should provoke an answer of equally boring capacity –

I wish you'd write, tho': inasmuch as I don't know anything whatever of your movements – The last I heard about you, was, when Grand Pa wrote me, that you were about setting off on a journey from Montvale to Montgomery in the convoy of two horses and three mules, or some such magnificent retinue— Of a verity, you do travel in state, in high and mighty state – The first-honor man and poet of Oglethorpe University [1] turned Mule-driver! Well; Ulysses himself did once tend Swine: nay; was not Phoebus Apollo at one time a Cow-herd? So that you have consolation, in making the third of a brilliant trio of God-like graziers –

I suppose you have Tennyson's Idylls of the King with you – If so, I wish you'd copy for me the little song which I have admired so much in " Elaine, the lily Maid of Astolot ": I think the song commences so:

" If Love be sweet, then bitter Death must be;
If Death is bitter, Sweet is Love to me:
I know not which is sweeter, no, not I;

I follow, I follow, let me die," &c &c, or something of that

---

[1] The reference is obviously to a prospective honor only, as Clifford Lanier had not yet been graduated.

50

sort — Copy them off and send them to me, as early as possible — I'm going to try and set them to music — [2]

I think the Montgomery folks must have forgotten me entirely; or else they cannot have received my letters — Tell 'em, that I'm not dead yet: " I still live "; and still have the feelings of a Soldier, away from home, and mournful and lonely because his dear ones think too little of him even to bestow a passing half-hour upon a letter to him —

Do write me soon, Cliff; and stir up the rest; and kiss for me everybody that I love, there; and believe me,

Your Aff. Brother
Sid Lanier —

To Robert S. Lanier

Georgia Barracks.
Feby 19th "/62

My Dear Pa:

I wrote you, a day or two ago, requesting your opinions on the reenlistment question, especially with reference to my own action — For fear you should not receive that letter, I write again: I am particularly anxious to hear from [you] on the subject, as the question is being extensively agitated in camp now, and I do not wish to commit myself before consulting you: indeed, I do not know what to do about it, and want advice — I was in Capt Smith's room, some night's ago; he attempted, then, to get me to sign a re-enlistment paper which he has prepared, but I refused to do so, on the ground that I had not considered the subject, and was unprepared to commit myself — He, you know, is raising a regiment, and is, of course, anxious that the Macon Volunteers should reenlist, expecting that they will join his regiment — He gave me quite a talk: " was anxious," he said, " to *bag* me; and to provide a *good bag* for me: " all of which, of course, I understood as mere blarney, as I have neither the money nor the influence to bring men enough into his regiment to secure me a position in it — I think the

---

[2] This musical composition has survived (photo, Henry W. Lanier Collection, Johns Hopkins University); but apparently Lanier did not complete it until over three years later (see p. 199, n. 27, below).

Capt. will have a great deal of difficulty in raising his regiment: and Lieut. Jones, with whom I was talking is confident that he (Capt. S), will not be able to raise it – [3]

You have, of course, heard, before this, of the capture of Fort Donelson,[4] and our forces there – It is a terrible blow upon us: I have had the blues all day, in consequence of it – –. I have very little doubt that Norfolk will shortly be attacked: how soon, of course, no one can tell – And I write so, because I think " honesty is the best policy," – and that you will be less anxious, knowing the exact condition of things, than when you are held in suspense by the thousand reports and rumors, which I hear of, are reaching you daily – I believe that we will whip them here: we have good fortifications, splendid batteries, plenty of ammunition, a body of the finest troops in the service, a wrath which has been nursed for ten long months, and, confidence in our ability to defeat the enemy – So, *please* do not be anxious about me: if I thought you were so, I should be very unhappy – I shall keep you honestly advised of our conditions here –

I went over to Gosport Navy-yard yesterday: and went down to see the *Merrimac,* which was lying at one of the Navy-yard wharves, receiving her last guns – She is the ugliest-looking Monster imaginable –: and will sail, certainly, in a few days – the rumor about her *failure,* was a mere *hoodwink,* to deceive the enemy: I laughed heartily at the article in the Telegraph, on that subject! Clisby [5] was effectually fooled by the Day-Book's hoodwinking article – I also went to see Cousin Sallie,

---

[3] The first enlistments in the 2nd Georgia Battalion were for one year only, expiring on Apr. 20, 1862. For details of the return to Macon and the re-organization, see notes 10-11, below.

At some time during the spring, Capt. R. A. Smith was commissioned colonel of the 44th Georgia Regiment. On Mar. 19, Maj. Thos. Hardeman, commanding 2nd Georgia Battalion, was commissioned colonel of the 45th Georgia Regiment (see MS Order Book, p. 231, owned by Mrs. Frank Jones, Clinton, Gray, Ga.). A month earlier he had made an announcement of his intention to raise a regiment, stating: " Arms, uniforms and $50 bounty will be furnished to all who enlist " (letter dated Georgia Barracks, Norfolk, Va., Feb. 18, 1862, and published in the Macon *Daily Telegraph*, Mar. 15, 1862).

[4] Fort Donelson on the Cumberland River, defending Nashville, Tenn., fell on Feb. 16, 1862.

[5] Joseph Clisby, editor of the Macon *Daily Telegraph*, is mentioned several times in the Lanier letters; he also figures, under his own name, in Lanier's dialect poem, " Jones's Private Argument," written in 1870 (I, 24).

M^rs. *Daniells* (of Athens, you know): she afforded a most agreeable contrast to that *ugly* monster: she is the perfect image of Grandma: I never in my life have seen so striking a resemblance — She was very glad to see me: and I enjoyed it hugely — 'Twas like getting back to Montvale — Kiss Mother for me — Had a letter from Cliff yesterday — all well —

Your Son,

Sid Lanier

Do be *very* particular to say nothing about what I have written you: either of the Merrimac, or Capt. Smith &c.

From Mary J. A. Lanier

Macon Geo Mch 9th 1862

My dear Son

I got your letter two days ago and have read it again & again for it does me so much good to read it. I am glad that you got to see your Aunt Annie before she left even if you did " run the b'ckade to do so, she tells me that you are looking very well, how I do long to see you, we have just heard to day that the Battery at Sewells Point has been attacked by the Federals & that the Merrimac sunk one of their vessels & run one ashore, we are anxious to hear more about it but to day is sunday & we never can get much news only enough to make us anxious for more — I am all the time expecting to hear of an attack on Norfolk itself & think this is the beginning of it I suppose they want to try the strength of your Batteries. Have you confidence in Gen. Huger?[6] it seems to me that every thing depends on the commander & we hear so many opinions, some of the boys write to their friends that Huger is not the man for the place — & many seem to think that Hardeman will show the white feather himself & that he insinuates that his Battalion will not fight Several of us were made quite angry the other day by hearing that Mrs Hardeman said that her husband wrote her word that Norfolk was as good as taken

---

[6] Maj.-Gen. Benjamin Huger, commanding all Confederate troops and defences around Norfolk. The rumors in Lanier's mother's letter about him and Maj. Thos. Hardeman seem to have been ill-founded gossip.

now for the men would not fight – that he knew not a man in his Battalion would, now I think if he talks that way he is doing much harm, and if he does not feel like fighting himself – he should come home & work for those that can & will fight. I am glad that martial law has been proclaimed & now I think the next thing that ought to be done is to send the women & children out of the place, for there are always plenty of women who make a fuss & besiege the Genl with petitions to surrender & they had all better be out of the way, I heard that some ladies in Norfolk said that as soon as they heard of the approach of the enemy they would petition Huger to surrender to save the women and children – but we hear so many things that we never know what to believe. We have rather discouraging accounts from Tenn – lately, many union men from around the springs leaving to join the Lincolnites.[7] Your Grandpa was in Montgomery when on getting an exciting letter from your Uncle William he left for Montvale to see what is best to be done about bringing Lucy & family & the negroes to Montgomery – he left (we suppose) two days ago – we are anxious to hear from him – These are times that I never expected to live to see I can but hope that our own dear Southern land will soon be free from the invader I cannot believe that a Merciful God will permit our insolent foes to triumph over us, let us put our trust in God O May he bring us safely out of this struggle.

Your pa wrote to you two or three days ago by some one going on, he will try to get the position for you that you spoke of in your letter. Monday morning I wrote this letter yesterday but did not finish it & this morning we are much cheered by the news of the battle & victory of the Merrimac – or Virginia as she is now called – & hope she will do a great deal more yet.[8]

[7] The desertion from the Confederate Army of a Tennessee mountaineer, Gorm Smallin, forms one of the most effective episodes in *Tiger-Lilies* (V, 113-124).

[8] The reference is to the victory of the *Merrimac* (*Virginia*) over the *Monitor*, Hampton Roads, Mar. 9, 1862. On Mar. 10, R. S. Lanier wrote to his son Clifford: " I expect Sidney saw the grand Naval fight, & was no doubt full of excitement. He could see it, I am informed by walking about ¾ mile from his camp, which of course he did unless tied or guarded! "

That Lanier and the rest of the 2nd Georgia Battalion did see it there is no doubt. In a letter to the Macon *Daily Telegraph*, Mar. 11, 1862, one of the soldiers reported witnessing the battle from Lambert's Point. And an interesting sequel is recorded in a letter dated Camp Hardeman, near Goldsboro, N. C., Mar.

Have a letter from your brother this morning   he is almost crazy to go into the army.   I think it will be impossible to keep him out much longer [9] – your pa will write to him to day – give love for us to your Uncle C. & tell him to write & do you write my son as often as you can – excuse my paper it was the last I had in the house & it being sunday – I could not send for more   take care of yourself – my child for your Mothers sake & pray to God to take care of you –   May he bless & keep you in safety is the prayer of your mother

M. J. Lanier.[10]

31, 1862: " As we, members of the 2d Georgia Battalion have witnessed with entire satisfaction the recent naval victory gained by the Virginia in Hampton Roads near Norfolk, Virginia, and as the good citizens of our noble state are taking an interest and freely contributing to the immediate construction of a number of these ironclad monsters [the women of Macon were raising money for one]. . . . Therefore, we the undersigned, Georgia volunteers, do freely contribute the amounts annexed opposite our names." (Published, belatedly, in the Macon *Daily Telegraph*, Apr. 21, 1862.) The entire contribution of the battalion was $1431. Opposite the name of S. C. Lanier was $5.00. This is the only time Lanier's name was mentioned in the dispatches to the Macon *Daily Telegraph*.

[9] In his letter of Mar. 10, 1862, to his son Clifford, R. S. Lanier wrote: " I am going up to Griffin tomorrow – where there will be several regiments to see what I can do for each of us. If I could get a commissary appointment I would take you with me. There are so many regiments to be organized & now organizing that I trust we may secure some satisfactory position in some of them. I will not keep you out of the service much longer, & agree with you that we must all do our duty."

[10] Since no letters by Lanier between Feb. 19 and May, 1862, have survived, the record of these months must be filled in from other sources.

The entries in Maj. Thos. Hardeman's Order Book (see note 3, above) continue through Mar. 19, and then (p. 231) is recorded the following, in the handwriting of his wife, Jane L. Hardeman: " Received marching orders for Goldsboro, N. C., March 19th, and on reaching this place Major Hardeman learned of his election to the command of the 45th Reg. and here his connection with the celebrated 2d Geo. Battn. ceased."

Dispatches in the Macon *Daily Telegraph* tell the story for the next two months. The battalion arrived in Goldsboro on Mar. 21 and went into camp on the New Bern road, in high spirits, anticipating immediate action from the Federal troops under Gen. Burnside, who had just captured New Bern; but no engagement with the enemy occurred. Original orders to muster the battalion out of service at Goldsboro were cancelled, and after nearly a month's stay they left for Macon on April 15, arriving on Apr. 17.

Parades and banquets marked the celebration that day, at one of which Lanier's uncle answered the address of welcome: " Lieut. Clifford Anderson, upon call, handsomely expressed the thanks of the military guests, also for the constant attention of the Macon ladies to the comfort and welfare of the corps during the

To Augusta Lamar

[Wilmington, N. C., May? 1862?] [11]

We have been stopped, dear Gussie, at Wilmington, and are now encamped about two miles from the city, behind a series of batteries extending for a mile or two near Cape Fear River – I don't think we will stay here long; but have no idea where we will next be ordered.

Our camp is on a hill of white sand, upon which a few scraggy pines maintain a scanty subsistence – reminding one of a bald head, with two or three gray hairs on it!

As I sit here, everybody asleep *but* myself, the bare desolate hill, the wind wailing through the pines, the bleak, cold rain dripping on my tent, and the murky glare of a pine torch (by which I write) : all accord well with the feelings of my desolation which this black cloud of unexpected separation has snowed upon my heart –   It is with a fierce earnestness Gussie, that I

year's service. ' The 2nd Georgia Battalion which has never yet had the fortune to meet the foe in actual field conflict has done much in valuable service to illustrate Georgia.' "

Orders were received from the commanding general not to muster out the battalion, but to reorganize and report for duty on May 1. On Apr. 23, the Macon Volunteers (Lanier's company) celebrated their 37th anniversary with a dress parade. The next day was Clifford Lanier's eighteenth birthday; a week later he celebrated by enlisting in his brother's company. (Official records of the U. S. War Department.) On April 29, the Amateur Club of the city of Macon joined with that of the 2nd Georgia Battalion (of which Sidney Lanier was certainly a member) in a musical concert at Ralston Hall. Finally, after two weeks in Macon, on leave of absence, the battalion left on Apr. 30 " for the seat of war, having their full complement of men. A large concourse of friends and relatives assembled to witness their departure and many a heart-felt prayer went up for their safety. . . . They are a brave and gallant band." Their destination was Camp French, Wilmington, N C., where they spent the month of May. (See the Macon *Daily Telegraph*, Mar. 22, 28, 31; Apr. 17, 18, 19, 21, 23, 28, 29; May 1, 1862.)

[11] This letter to Lanier's musical friend in Macon is undated, but internal evidence seems to place it beyond doubt during the period when Lanier was stationed, with the rest of the 2nd Georgia Battalion, at Wilmington. Here the reorganization was completed: the new " rifled Enfield musket " was distributed to the men, new officers were elected (George W. Ross of Macon taking the place vacated by Maj. Thos. Hardeman), and the battalion is said by tradition to have helped in the building of Fort Fisher. On May 29 they left for Petersburg, after nearly a month's encampment. (See the Macon *Daily Telegraph*, May 9, 10, 16, 30, 1862.)

shake off the chilly winding sheet, and seize my pencil to say
to you, with *it* some little of all that brimming soul-full which
my sealed tongue, for some inscrutable reason, *could* not utter
whilst I was with you – – "Oh, the Glory," (exclaims Ike
Marvel) "the Passion and the Freedom, of a Letter!" And
so exclaim I – I have never described to you (*because* I *could*
not) the blackness which once enveloped my life; "a weary,
wormy darkness spurred i' the flank with flame," in which my
soul lived, like a hermit in a horrible cave, with the snakes –
If you knew *that*, you could better appreciate my otherwise in-
excusable and foolish passion for my pen –: tho' I am conscious
that your *Friendship*, if not your judgment will pardon *seeming*
exaggerations –.

My visit home, dear Gussie, was like the rising of a Sun upon
[me?]: and it stood, and shone upon my heart and soul genially
for ten days – *Now*, its setting-time is come: and while some
faint, warm rose-glow of that sun-set yet lingers on the Home-
Heaven in the West, all my recollections and good pure emotions of that visit come out above, like sweet, pale Stars, one by
one, at dusk, and shine down through the night which is come
over me – Says Jean Paul, "Every sentiment and every emotion
is *mad,* and exacts and builds its own world" – If, with all
my emotions stirred up in this way: with each one's separate
"World" already brought into existence and whirling in a
primal Chaos through my brain: with the unforgotten, wild
music of La Melancholie, and Gottschalk's Serenade and Il
Corsoro "rising and falling swaying and swelling, in golden
calls and response" through that immeasurable temple in
which I seem to wander now: if, I say, with all these things *so,*
you get a mad, passionate letter from me, – – – – what wonder?

That dear glorious You
must know, when &c! I first,
heard Miss Day [12] play it, I said to myself, how beautiful! and
yet, what a strange misnomer, to call that strange, wild, half-

[12] Presumably Mary Day, who was later to become Lanier's wife. The reference is not entirely clear, but all available evidence indicates that Lanier did
not make her acquaintance until his furlough the next year, April, 1863 (see note
4, 1863). He was probably here speaking of hearing her play at the musical
concert of the combined Amateur Clubs on Apr. 29, 1862 (see note 10, above),
which seems to be the subject of this letter.

sombre, half-glad piece, a "Serenade"! But, gradually I entered into the Spirit of the glorious thing; and as I did so, my soul expanded and took larger views – True, in it you do not hear a single sign of

> " The love-lorn serenaders' light guitar
> Tinkling adown the vale " – – –

It is no common, light love of a mortal which breathes itself forth in *such* a serenade But then there might occur to the Poetic mind other serenaders besides Troubadours, et id omne genus – Gottschalk's Serenade, out of the white throats and red lips of the enamored Angels, (in Byron's "Heaven and Earth ") might well have thrilled through the glorious Eastern Night, to the ears of Anah, and Aholibamah the beautiful –: nay, without waking them from earthy sleep, might have pierced in to their dreaming Souls, and moulded their dreams into visions of that wondrous Other Land, from which the Lovers had just descended –

And so Lucifer, in "Festus," could he really have loved Helen, might have serenaded her with Gottschalk's piece – Ah, Gussie, if I could only describe to you the vision which passed before me, as I stood by you and listened to Miss D's perform-ance of that piece – I thought I saw one of those nights which Bailey so thrillingly describes, filled with glittering stars and flowers and perfumes, and still whisperings amongst the happy leaves – I saw Lucifer step forth from the Forest surrounding Helen's garden and bower in all the dignity of those noble and majestic qualities with which Milton has invested him in that Magnificent portrayal, of Paradise Lost –. And I could see that the immeasurable sadness of his one great Sin clouded the grand glitter of Lucifer's eyes like a film over two stars – It seemed that the beauty of the night, and the calming influences of sweet Love and Music had deprived even the Arch-Demon of his cunning and malice and hate, and left him only an infinitely sorrowful, half-repentant immortal Spirit – I thought his hand trembled, as he swept from some unearthly instrument the first simple notes of the "Serenade ": but as Music, Beauty, Love, and recollections of his old, high joys when he was near God in Heaven, warmed his soul, the chords grew wild and troublous and troublous and passionate, till I thought all the

stars and the trees and the flowers and the waters and Helen
stood still in a trance and bent towards the Kingly Serenader
and — — —

Ah God, Gussie, will God make us lunatic with these emotions which we cannot utter, raised by Music which agonizes
while it fascinates us?

Gottschalk is to me, a Miracle — There is, in his compositions,
an indefinable feeling of a phantom-like Presence, like that
which one has in solitary summer twilights — His Music produces in me a supernatural thrill, as if I saw a ghost, that too,
not a frightful ghost, but the spirit of a dear friend as it were,
come in some beautiful shape, like the false lady Geraldine,
which I, like Christabel, could draw lovingly and tenderly into
my bosom, — Beethoven is wild: but Gottschalk's wildness is
more etherial, more spirituelle — Gottschalk is to Beethoven
what Tennyson is to Byron, what the Christian Religion is to the
Grecian Mythology — Beethoven sorrows like the sea, moaning
through caverns on a desolate shore —: Gottschalk grieves like
some wild-eyed Angel, flitting to and fro in eternal restlessness
through the Universe — The one is a materialist, tho' as
spiritual as his philosophy will allow him to be: the latter is a
pure Idealist — His Music lifts me out of myself, until I almost
lose consciousness of my own individuality: whilst all other
German Music, (La Melancholie, for instance) makes me intensely selfish, in making me *love*: I do not mean to say *makes*
me love, but irresistibly compels me to demonstrate that love,
which under any other circumstances, and by whatever terrible
struggles I am strong enough to conceal —

And what shall I say of La Melancholie. I thought your soul
and mine stood before the Gates of Heaven and shivered with
the intense sadness of our vain desire to enter — Ah, of what
avail or beauty Pearl, when it forms an impassable barrier?

I *would* write you a long letter: I am too sad, (or mad?) to
do so, *now* —

By that last holy, blessed caress, which has made me pure
for life, I am

Your Friend

S [18]

[18] Lanier's movements during the summer of 1862 are not entirely clear, as no
letters by him between this one and that of Sept. 10 have been found. In a

To Robert S. Lanier

Petersburg Va. Sept 10th ″/62 –

My Dear Pa:

I got your letter, written at Knoxville, yesterday – I am astonished that you have not heard from us: for Cliff. and I have been writing and writing: impelled more especially to do so, not only from considerations of affection, but also by the fact that we are in pressing need of money –

We have each engaged a uniform suit of the Corps, consisting of gray double-breasted frock-coat, vest, and pants, for Thirty Dollars a piece: also a pair of shoes for Ten Dollars – The Suit is by far the cheapest one we could procure: we are confident it will be a good investment, as it is made of very thick gray cloth, which was purchased by one of our Lieutenants for the Corps, in the mountains of Virginia –: and is at least thirty Dollars cheaper than any other suit that could be obtained – The shoes are less than half what we would have to pay for them in Petersburg: they are to be made by one of the Corps who was at our station, and got detached to go to his home at Salem, (above Lynchburg) for the purpose of making shoes for the

reminiscent letter to M. H. Northrup after the war (see p. 226, below), Lanier wrote that he was sent from Wilmington to " Drury's [Drewry's] Bluff." This seems to tally with the information in note 11, above, for Drewry's Bluff is on the James River between Petersburg and Richmond. (In May there had been some fighting at this point, for the *Monitor* had advanced up the river and fired on the fort; but Lanier's company was presumably not stationed there until June, so that previous biographies seem to be in error when citing this as Lanier's baptism of fire.) From there, he continues, they were ordered to the Chicka-hominy and participated in the " famous Seven-days battles around Richmond "— June 26-July 2, 1862—a true baptism of fire, for this was warfare at its worst. Shortly afterwards, he adds, his regiment was sent on an expedition down the south bank of the James River, and " after a little gun-boat fight or two " they returned to Petersburg to rest. This is the only record that survives for these months, and it is not altogether reliable, as witness his statement to Northrup that before these experiences they had spent " two or three months " in Wil-mington, whereas he was actually there less than a month. Finally his reminiscent letter records that while at Petersburg he and his brother obtained a transfer to " Maj. Milligan's Signal Corps." This is verified by the official records of the U. S. War Department, which show that they were transferred to Capt. Nathaniel W. Small's Company, Signal Corps, C. S. A., on July 21, 1862. Petersburg remained his headquarters until the following spring.

Corps. So that, in the course of ten days, we shall need at least Forty Dollars apiece –

You cannot imagine, My dear Pa, with how much reluctance we call upon you for so much money – You would doubtless be amused if I could record for you the proceedings of the innumerable councils of War which Cliff and I have held on the subject: the investigations we have instituted as to prices, and the calculations we have made: with the thousand wild projects, successively named and abandoned, for *making* the money ourselves – We had to give it up, at last, however, in despair: and write you for the money – The only consoling reflection is, that after we are fitted out with winter clothes we will have no further occasion to call on you for a long time – We have been as economical in our selection as possible: as it is, I do not know what we shall do this winter, without overcoats: but Forty Dollars, which is the lowest price for which one can be obtained here, is out of the question –

Events have followed each other in such rapid succession, here, that I am dazzled, and, under the influence of exultant feelings, can hardly form a sober opinion in regard to the future [14] – Jackson, Longstreet, A. P. Hill, and D. H. Hill, with their respective corps, are across the Potomac, and are reported, in this morning's papers, at the Relay House – In the same report, Lee is said to occupy Arlington Heights – These are only well-founded rumors: but our brave fellows have accomplished such astonishing things lately, that unbounded credulity in regard to their rumored exploits seems to be, on the whole, about as safe a policy as the most captious skepticism – If the two reports which I have just mentioned be true, the fall of Washington is inevitable – And after the fall of Washington – ? Perhaps Peace! I somehow feel a presentiment of great events: at any rate, I had as lief utter, nowadays, the wildest and most visionary prophecy, as the most guarded speculation: for the former has at least the charm of *daring*, and is as likely of fulfillment as the latter –

[14] The successes enumerated in this paragraph were those following upon the Confederate victory at Second Manassas, Aug. 29-30, 1862. Lee penetrated as far as Frederick, Md. (Sept. 7), but was at last forced to retire across the Potomac after Antietam (Sept. 17), a bloody battle which was defined as " a defeat for both armies."

Apropos of the fall of Washington I managed to rig out two guitars, the other day, one for Cliff, and the other for Hopson: [15] for three days I kept them steadily thrumming, " from Morn till dewy Eve," and at the end of that time I had them tolerably proficient in the accompaniments to several tunes – In the meantime I wrote off some Second parts for Charlie Emmell, who had just received his flute, and who singuarly enough is utterly unable to play the simplest tune without the notes before him – All preliminaries being arranged, accompanied by Lieut. Cannon, we sallied out, night before last, armed with instruments, and the Station Lantern (which we lit up, at every house, for Charlie to see his notes by) – Amongst other places, we serenaded Capt. Milligan [16] – At the third tune, the burly Chief appeared, in night-shirt and slippers: " Walk in, Boys! " Loud enough, and cordially enough, for us to have been his children, and all deaf – We " walked in " both the house, and the Decanter to which he conducted us, on the piano in the parlor – We then chatted: he told us, amongst other characteristic remarks that he was expecting shortly to establish a Signal Station on the dome of the Capital at Washington: " but," said he, " them damned ten-inch Shells from the gunboats in the Potomac! *That's* the devil of it! Tho' I'll swear," (with a most comical earnestness) " I'd risk about Six of 'em to wave a message from that position! "

He's a singular Chap – Profane to an alarming extent: keeps open house: yet never touches a drop of liquor in any shape – He was elevated the other day, by the Secretary of War to the position of Chief of the Signal Bureau: and now commands all the Signal Corps of the Confederate States –

Our Serenade, by the way, was a magnificent Success – In the narrow streets of Petersburg, brick-built and rock-paved, the Music, which was intrinsically fine, sounded ravishingly: and

---

[15] Lanier's Macon friend, William Allis Hopson. The other member of the serenading group, mentioned in the following sentence, was C K. Emmell of Macon, a cousin of C. E. Campbell, another member of Lanier's company. He was the friend, three years older than Lanier, who (according to tradition) gave Lanier his first flute lessons at the age of eleven. All of these young Georgians were transferred to the Signal Corps together. (Some music transcribed by Lanier for this group is preserved at Wesleyan College, Macon, Ga.)

[16] James Milligan, in command of Milligan's Independent Signal Corps. He was obviously the original of the " Major M–––" in *Tiger-Lilies* (V, 130).

our first tune, every time, would be followed by a simultaneous hoisting of windows and protruding of night-Caps, on both sides of the Street, as far as we could see by the moonlight; insomuch that we came nigh to waking up by far the greatest part of the good City's inhabitants — We came back to our quarters laden with bouquets: we were invited in at several places: and, to crown the whole, we received yesterday afternoon, a nice note from Miss Dimitry (a splendid-looking woman, daughter of the Spanish Consul: has travelled, and heard fine Music, and sings gloriously) highly complimentary, especially to the " solo flutist " — I regret that for want of some clothes I can't " follow-up " that last " success " —

The extension of the Conscription Bill has passed the Senate: and will doubtless pass the House — What are you going to do? I think, by far, your best course will be to join our Corps immediately — Write us, as soon as possible what are your plans —

Have you yet received our letter, telling you what to send us, from home? If not will write you again —

Give a great deal of love to all the Family — I long to see them — Tell dear Grandpa he owes me a letter — Cliff wrote Uncle William several days ago —

Kiss Ma and Sister for us: and accept much love for yourself,

from Your Son,

Sid. Lanier

To Robert S. Lanier

Petersburg, October 5th "/62 —

My Dear Pa:

I got, yesterday, your letter written from Knox-ville: but our trunk has not yet arrived — These Expressmen are wretchedly slow: monopolizing all transportation facilities, and being amenable to nobody, they manage to make a pretty high-handed thing out of it —

We have no War-news: the only triumphs occurring, now, are those which " the Four Georgians " have been achieving, recently, not only over the affections of the Women of this

Good City, but also those of the burly Chief of the Signal Bureau, in addition (to cap the climax) to those of the General commanding this Department together with his whole Staff!

The interpretation whereof is as follows: – Capt. Milligan sent us a message, a few days ago, requesting us to come in and go with him to serenade Gen¹ French [17] – Of course, we went: met Capt. M. at our Head-Quarters: and, about Eleven O'clock, sallied forth, led by the Chief, and attended by Capt. Small, Lieut Cannon, our Orderly Sergeant Benson, and Commissary Jenkins – Our old Chief fairly lit up the route with witty, coruscations: I have never seen him so brilliant and so good-humored – Arrived at the Gen'l's house, we played some select pieces: shortly appeared one of his Staff, who flung wide the doors and conducted us into a finely-furnished parlor, the centre-table, whereof groaned under various good things –, and then the General and the rest of the Staff made their appearance – Capt. M. introduced us individually to the Gen: I, however, had met the Gen. as well as some of his Staff, (in Wilmington) before: after the handshaking, which I thought would be interminable, we all " proceeded to business " – I, like the wine, " circulated freely " amongst the company, trying to find out the best man in it: which, accordingly, I did, in the person of one Capt. Baker, of North Carolina – He was the finest-looking man I ever saw: a perfect Antinous, very tall, and muscular, and looked as if he were about to step into the Olympic Arena, indifferent whether to wrestle physically or mentally – I found he had travelled in Greece, and other countries: and so I had a good time with him— To cut a long story short –: we stayed there about an hour and a half: and when we left, we carried General and Staff with us, until we had finished serenading – A brave party of Troubadours, wasn't it? One General, Six Captains, one Lieutenant, and four privates!

---

[17] Gen. S. G. French in his autobiography, *Two Wars* (Nashville, Tenn., 1901), p. 157, says: " Often [Lanier] and a friend would come to my quarters and pass the evening with us, where the ' alarums of war ' were lost in the soft notes of their flutes." Another anecdote of Lanier appears on the same page, apparently belonging to this period: " One day the provost marshall arrested a blockade runner for not obeying his instructions. His goods were placed in a rented store, and J. A. Shingleur, of Columbus, Ga., and Sidney Lanier, of my signal corps, were detailed to sell them. . . . I have often wondered if that quiet, gentle soldier-poet remembered his experience as a merchant in Petersburg? "

The whole affair constitutes one of the most brilliant successes of the war— Captain Milligan has officially announced that the four Georgians are to be retained at this post, to constitute his field-Staff: so that unless he is ordered to the field, we will winter in Petersburg –   You cannot imagine how proud he is of us: he boasts of us as the Roman Matron did of her children: " these are my Jewels! " –

I had a dispatch the other day from Uncle Sid and Washburn in relation to his (W's) joining our Corps –   I immediately went in and saw Capt. M. about it: he said he could not possibly receive another man, *now*, as the Corps was completely crammed, and he had a long list of applications for membership which he was unable to grant –   He has, however, made an application to the Sec'y of War for permission to increase the Corps by twenty-five men, which is not decided yet –   If Washburn wishes me to try and get him in, in case of the Success of Capt. M.'s application, I think I may succeed –   Tell this to Uncle Sid: I telegraphed Washburn the other day –

Cliff. is applying for a detail to the Telegraph Office at Montgomery Ala to fill a situation which Roche has offered him there, as Book-keeper, at One thousand a year –   He has not heard from his application – [18]

Tell Ma, I can't imagine what has become of all the letters we have written to her and the other members of the family at M[ontvale]. We have been very faithful Correspondents since we were here –   And ask her to send on the Jeans as quick as she gets it, so that we can have pants made here –   I'll send a pattern for the leggings as soon as I can get one –

I was sick for about a week after you left, but have entirely recovered now –

Give a great deal of love to them all –   I long to see and embrace them –   Kiss Grandma for me –: and tell Grandpa I should like to bespeak a place on his plantation as a farm-hand: for I don't know what I shall do for a living when the

[18] Clifford Lanier had written to his mother from Petersburg, Sept. 24, the details of Roche's offer, adding: " I shall regret exceedingly having to leave Bro. Sid but he has generously advised me to go . . . Bro. Sid has been a little unwell but I think will soon be entirely well.   I continue in splendid health."   In a letter to his father, Oct. 19, 1862, Clifford Lanier reported that Roche's proposition had fallen through.

war is over: I've forgot all my Greek and Latin, and will probably have to descend from the Professor's Chair to the Cornfield –

Kiss Ma for me –   And accept a great deal of love from

Your Son

Sid Lanier [19]

To ANNA L. ANDERSON [20]

Petersburg, Va. Dec. 15th /62.

My Dear Auntie:

I drop a hurried note to let you know that we have been ordered off, to attend Gen'l. French, down to Kinston, N. C. I think it probable we will have a brush there, and do not know when we will return –

Excuse a very hurried note: I'm run to death getting ready to leave –

Have heard nothing from the Battalion –   Will write you from Goldsboro –

Most Affectionately, Your Nephew,

Sid. Lanier –.

[19] No letters written by Sidney Lanier between Oct. 5 and Dec. 15, 1862, have been found. However, some details can be supplied from his brother's correspondence. In his letter of Oct. 19, 1862, asking his father for $100.00 to buy a new uniform, Clifford wrote: " It required our combined resources to get Bro. Sid's uniform which is of magnificent dark-grey English cloth, very thick. We will hardly need overcoats if furnished with that." And on Oct. 31 he wrote to his mother that the post at Blanford, where they had been stationed, had been abandoned that day, and that he and his brother would henceforth be stationed " at the big customhouse in Petersburg." The postscript to the letter reads: " Do not knit any more socks for us, those you have already knit together with what we have got in our trunk will be enough."

In a letter of Nov. 29 Clifford admonished his mother to have no uneasiness about her sons so long as they were in Petersburg. They were well clothed, and well quartered over the custom-house, where they had " gas, water conveniences & coal fires." They drilled on horses every day, and Hopson had bought his own. Clifford wrote: " Bro. Sid has written to Pa about buying horses & has no doubt explained all the circumstances."

[20] Mrs. Clifford Anderson, who was still in Virginia in Dec., 1862 (see next letter).

From Clifford A. Lanier to Robert S. Lanier

Petersburg Dec. 30th 1862

My dear Pa

After another short campaign in North Carolina, about Goldsboro, Kingston [21] &c, we are again safely back at Petersburg. Returning, we came on horseback, there being want of transporation by Rail Road, and had a delightful trip, traveling about 35 miles a day & living on country fare, butter, eggs, turkeys &c. The distance is about a hundred & sixty miles which we made in a little more than five days. You have seen the papers & I suppose have all the information to be obtained concerning the raid of Foster, burning the Goldsboro bridge & tearing up the track. The damage was slight & will be repaired in two or three weeks.

We did not get fairly into any of the engagements, getting only close enough to hear a few bombs, one of which fell very close to one of our squad. Establishing our line from the headquarters of Genl Smith (Gustavus) to Genl French, we were of considerable service to them dispatching several important communications.

Brother Sidney & myself were on the outpost & our tent was within a few yards of that of Genl Evans, about half a mile from the Battle field. Having some very fine sweet potatoes, I presented Genl E a mess of them & was invited to eat dinner with him.

His aid de camp spoke of Uncle Tom Eason & of the regret with which they all gave him up. The Genl's invitation I did not accept but had several conversations with members of his staff.

I begin to be almost vain, associating with Generals & regard a major General with not half the reverence I used to bear to a Captain.

Last night I danced, at a little sociable, in company with General French.

I have just heard that Uncle Clifford is out at Mrs. Jones, with Aunt Annie. I have no doubt he is on his way home.

[21] The correct spelling is Kinston, as in the previous letter. For an account of the campaign see S. G. French, *Two Wars*, pp. 152-154.

Brother Sid & I will go out at once to see him – Pa! cant you spare me about 350$ to buy a horse? Several of the boys have got good horses & my old Government steed is very nearly used up.

Bro Sid got yesterday a check from Uncle Sid to pay for the horse he has brought.

Nothing would suit me better than to borrow it, if you have'nt it at hand, from the folks who are flush at this time in bona fide, business style, giving my note for the amount. The twelve dollars a month which I receive from the Government as hire coupled with the real value, will outbalance what I pay for him. I will be cautious in buying, being careful to get a horse capable of enduring hardship & severe service.

Discuss the matter, I will cheerfully coincide with any decision you may come to.

Our military prospects appear to me brighter than they have ever been since the first battle of Mannassas. God grant us an early peace! – Give much love to all, I do not know who is at Montvale they are all moving so much. Kiss dear Mother, Grandma & Aunt Mina.[22]

Your devoted Son

C. A. Lanier

---

[22] Aunt Mina was Wilhelmina Lanier, Mrs. T. D. Eason.

1863

To Robert S. Lanier

Petersburg, Feb'y 26th "/63

My Dear Pa:

Cliff and I have just arrived here after a long and toilsome ride, having made the journey from Goldsboro [1] to this place, a distance of nearly two hundred miles, on horseback – It had been raining for several days before we started, and all the creeks and rivers were swollen inordinately – added to which, on the second day of our journey, snow commenced falling early in the morning, and then rain fell on the snow, and the whole concern froze over hard: altogether creating the most indescribable compound of snow, ice, water, mud, and slush imaginable – We frequently had to cross swollen creeks and rivers by making long detours of miles out of our way: all day last Sunday I rode with my feet encased in a pair of ice-stockings, the water having frozen *inside* my boots – Through it all, however, we rode, indomitable as Napoleon in his retreat from Moscow: which celebrated evolution I appreciate more highly than I ever did before –

I ought to explain to you, that your failure to receive regular letters from us must be attributed to no neglect on our part – We have been absent from Petersburg on our last expedition about six weeks: during which time we have travelled, on horseback, considerably over four hundred miles, which would leave us you see but little time for stopping at any place – Wherever we *did* stop, we wrote you punctually, every time; tho' it seems you have not even received *those* letters – Joe Wells [2] is a clerk in Gen¹ French's office, always travels on the Railroad with the General, and has, consequently, many more opportunities for writing than we do –

[1] This was a second expedition to North Carolina, lasting from Jan. 5 to Feb. 23, 1863 (see S. G. French, *Two Wars*, p. 154).

[2] This is the Macon friend who had won the affections of Ophelia LeConte from Lanier in 1858.

69

Gen¹. Longstreet, with a part of his Corps, arrived here a few days ago, and has established his Headquarters here –: so that what with *his* Staff, and that of Gen¹ French together with their numerous retinue of gold-laced non-commissioned hangers-on, our streets fairly flash and glisten in the rays of the morning sun – He brought Picketts Division with him; Anderson's, the other Division of his Corps is to follow in a few days – I understand, by the way, that our old Battalion, with its usual luck, has been transferred to Anderson's Division recently; so that we expect to see it here shortly –

I saw, at Goldsboro, Capt. Ells Company of Artillery – Capt. E had been at Richmond on sick furlough; told me he saw Uncle Clifford there – Where is Aunt Annie?

Cliff and I will probably get a twenty day furlough, in a week or two – Do not look for us, however, *until* we *arrive*; as it may be a longer time than that before we can leave here – I suppose we had better go to Macon first, as I see by your letter of the 14ᵗʰ, which I have just received, that you and Ma will be there in a few days – We may have a chance of coming back here by way of Montvale, and so seeing all who are at that place –

Hopson has gone to Macon on furlough – Do endeavor to see him and treat him well – He is a devoted friend to me, and has done me many signal favors – Charlie Emmell is here – The rest of our field-squad has not yet been recalled: two are still stationed at Weldon, and two are with Gen¹ Pryor on the Blackwater – Things, in a military way, are quiet about here – We have been shivering under a most horrible visitation of snow cold rain &c – We have had the deepest snow I ever saw: it has been lying on the ground for five or six days, and has only just begun to thaw – I long for the Spring weather which you speak of in your letter –

Kiss Ma for us; and give much love to all that we love – Believe me, always,

> Your most affectionate son,

> > > Sid. Lanier [3]

[3] The official records of the U. S. War Department show that Sidney and Clifford Lanier were transferred to the 2nd Company, Milligan's Independent Signal Corps, on Mar. 1, 1863. On Mar. 4 Clifford Lanier wrote to his mother, from Petersburg: " Bro. Sid has a very severe cold confining him to bed caused

To Mary Day [4]

[Macon, Ga.,] March 30th ″/63

Certainly, Miss Day, Truth, and Honor, and Sincerity, and Friendship have not yet utterly died out of our World –
The unusual request which this note will bear to you must find its only apology, (if it need any) in an appeal to your faith in the existence of those qualities –.

My furlough has nearly expired; at the stern call of duty, I leave here, tomorrow, to rejoin my comrades in Virginia –. I shall probably not meet you again for years; *possibly,* never –. I am indebted to you for many pleasant hours; and I wish to make you my friend –.

Under which circumstances, you will surely acquit me, *at least* of presumption and of silly sentimentality, when I ask you to allow me to write you, sometimes –

I need not ask *you* to pardon me if I speak earnestly –

Dear Miss Day, the journey of my life, so far, has been little more than a rugged wandering, alone, over unknown mountains, in a stormy night –. But there have been *some* rifts in that gloom; and the few stars that have shone fitfully through them are the friends which the Mysterious God has, ever and

---

by exposure, traveling through the rain & snow. I assume he is well taken care of, for his female friends crowd his table with delicacies & flowers." Within a few days the Laniers were granted furloughs, and left Virginia for Macon, where they spent most of the month of March.

[4] In a surviving album kept by Mary Day (Charles D. Lanier Collection, Johns Hopkins University) there are three staves of music entitled "From Sidney Lanier's 'Number One.'" A note by M. D. L., dated June 30, 1908, reads: "From the first flute improvisation played for me by Sidney Lanier, March 23rd, 1863, in the home of our dear Gussie Lamar. He said that this passage meant to him myself, as I came into his life that day." (See the allusion to "No. 1" at the end of Lanier's letter to Mary Day, Apr. 6, 1863, below.) Two dates immediately below the music—Oct. 22, 1863, and Jan. 2, 1864— probably refer to a second rendition during Lanier's furlough the following autumn (see note 41, below) and to the date when these staves were transcribed.

Mary Day, who was two years younger than Lanier, had been born in Macon, but from her sixth to her sixteenth year had lived in the North, returning South at the outbreak of the war. Though Lanier apparently felt attracted to her at the time of their meeting, and though she seems to have been equally interested in him, it should be remembered that Mary Day was at this time engaged to Capt. Fred Andrews, and that Lanier himself was soon to develope an ardent affection for Virginia Hankins.

anon, given to me – I have indulged, perhaps foolishly, the idea that *you* might become my friend: must I, because inevitable necessity compels my absence, give up so delightful a hope? –

I cannot reconcile myself to it: and so, again, with all manly respect, I ask you to write me –

It will be only a proof of my candor, if I tell you that, should you be kind enough to grant my request, *gossip* may *possibly* follow –. But, (if you will accept the result of an experience only twenty-one years long, but unusually varied) believe me, Miss Day, *gossip will* seize upon *all* our actions, be they good or bad; as a dog will bark indiscriminately at honest men and thieves –. *As* a dog, then, let us treat it! – If we will gaze fearlessly in *Its* eye, It will slink away in terror; if we tremble and fly, we will certainly be overtaken and bitten! – –

But I fear I weary you; this note is already longer than I intended –

Let me beseech you, have no delicacy, in stating any objections which you may have to my request; or in withhholding them and giving a plain refusal, if it so please you –

I am, and shall always be,

Your Friend,

Sidney C. Lanier

TO VIRGINIA C. AND CELESTE CLAY [5]

Petersburg, Va.
April 6th [1863]

Have you ever, my Two Good Friends, wandered, in an all-night's dream, through exquisite flowery mazes, through labyrinthine grottoes " full of all sparkling and sparry loveliness,"

[5] On their return from Macon to Virginia, Sidney and Clifford Lanier accompanied Virginia C. Clay (wife of C. C. Clay the former U. S. senator but at the time Confederate States senator from Alabama) and her sister-in-law, Celeste (Mrs. Hugh L.) Clay, who had been in Macon visiting the father of the latter—Major Anderson Comer. Virginia Clay's account of the journey is found in *A Belle of the Fifties*, ed. Ada Sterling (New York, 1905), pp. 197-199. Lanier's letter is published in part on pp. 200-201. The MS has been damaged. Some of the lacunae have been filled here by reference to the printed copy; others, in brackets, by conjecture. The MS breaks off in the middle of the last sentence.

over mountains of unknown height, by abysses of unfathomable depth, all beneath skies of an infinite brightness caused by no Sun; strangest of all, wandered without wonder, as if you had lived an eternity in the familiar contemplation of such things? And when, at morning, you have waked from such a dream and gone about your commonplace round of life, have you never stopped suddenly to gaze at the Sun, and exclaimed to yourself "What a singular thing it is up there: and these houses, bless me, what funny institutions, not at all like my grottoes and bowers in which I have lived for all eternity; and those men and women walking about, there, uttering strange gibberish and cramming horrid masses of stuff into their mouths, what dear, odd creatures: what does it all mean, anyhow, and who did it, and how is one to act, under the circumstances?" And so, have you not wildly tossed up your hand to your he[ad] like a maniac to whom a gli[mmer] of reason appears, and reeled and sunk into a blessed oblivion, which, you feel, (when you have recovered) saved you from death?

If you have dreamed, thought, and felt *so*: you can realize the imbecile stare with which I gaze on all this busy life that goes on around me here. Macon was my Two-weeks dream: I wake from *that* into Petersburg, an indefinitely-long real life. Ah, (if you will have pity enough upon mine infirmities to allow me to grow poetic) [is] not Friendship the One-Flower of our l[ife]? And Love, a Mountain with its [base] on Earth and its top in Heaven? And Music an abyss which has only darkness for a bottom? I, for two weeks, with a rare fullness, have inhaled the intoxicating odor of Friendship: I have "perched and sat" upon the very ever-lighted Top of Love: I have [dived?] into the depths of Music and seen strange things. Precipitated from all *that* to *this*: I am overwhelmed with a sense of puzzled bewilderment which would be very amusing if it did not, sometimes, when at its greatest intensity, warn me to seek [so]me short oblivion, or die – – –

Under all [w]hich circumstances is it not natural that I should hesitate to write you? Ought I not be ashamed to show to you that even a short two-weeks flight in the Upper Regions disables the weak wings of my soul?

And may I not sum up all this rigmarole, and at the same

time prove my returning consciousness, by telling you that I
could with much greater propriety sign " Fool," than

Sid. Lanier?

P. S. I nearly forgot (what it was the principle purpose of this
le[tter to] state) to say that we rejoice to inform you we will
be here on Saturday and Sunday, Deo and Genl. French volente;
and will meet you then, with the greatest pleasure imaginable.
'Tis a shame for you [to] come twenty miles to see two men
who are in so woful a plight as Cliff. and I: yet if you can cut
off so large a slice of your Happiness (Beef, you know, especially *that*

x   x   x   x   x   x   x

To Mary Day [6]

Petersburg Va.
April 6th "/63

I can scarcely restrain myself long enough to say to you that
perhaps, having gained consent to write you upon the plea of
friendship, I ought to write *merely* as a friend –. I *will* do so;
but not *this* time –. For in a day or two we leave here for the
Blackwater: all things are being prepared for a speedy contest
with the enemy there: I shall be in the thick of it; there is a
possibility that I may not ever write you another letter, either
of love or friendship –. Oh, Mary Day, Child, Lily which the
deepest waters of my soul bear upon their bosom so proudly
and so lovingly, Best-Beloved, indulge me this once, *just* this
once: afterwards, if *you,* so will it, (as you will tell me in the
letter which *must* come quickly from you) I will write you only
the most unexceptionable, friendly epistles –. *Now,* I *cannot*
do it: my heart will burst and my brain will fail, if I do not
tell you, in such poor way as English words will let me, that
I love you — —

[6] This letter exists in two copies. The one actually sent to Mary Day is
followed here. The other is a first draft for this letter, and is dated Apr. 3.
Corrections made on it and followed on the final copy, indicate that Lanier
labored carefully over this, his second letter to Mary Day.

Child; tho' " unseen hands are hanging the night around me fast," the West yet glows like an Altar: a blush-colored incense-cloud is rising from it: three white-stoled, Vestal Stars, as ministering attendants, are standing out meekly and mutely in front of the great Star-congregation: and Our Lady Abbess, the Moon, is just entering the Temple, nor forgets She (knowing me for an old lover of hers) to utter a radiant " Benedicite " upon my head, which I bare and bow to receive that silver blessing –. Oh Shame! Moon and Stars, Abbess and Nuns in the Monastery of Heaven, have forgot their Holy Catholic Church, have turned Ghebers, and with their Roman Rites, are worshipping the Fire-God! And as the wind breathes across my guitar there in the window, I seem to faintly hear the far-off hymning of an unearthly Choir –. Nature is at her devotions; *I* will to *mine!* – For God (in reverence!) be my witness, I am nearest to *Him* when I am nearest to *you* –. –. – (Thou blessed Pen, (exclaims my heart) that, in these weary, hard hours of separation, canst bring at least my soul near to my Beloved!).

In this holy moment, a wild, solemn, half-Maenadic, half-Angelic " Io Triumphe " is echoing through all the Chambers of my soul; and those bare walls, which have so long been but desolate Sepulchres containing only the wan faces and uncere-mented corpses of young dead-Hopes, now catch the Sound joyfully and echo it lovingly back and forth, like a troop of girls tossing roses to and fro; and my Hopes wake into their old rosy life; and my Soul is full as Princess Ida's College [7] of beautiful faces and fair forms –. Would you know the Gabriel's-blast of this, my resurrection? O, it was light and faint, for it stole like a moonbeam into my heart; it was Soft and sweet, for an Angel whispered it: " She will forget, and smile again, and love again and still more sweetly " – –

Can you not call to mind some pieces of music where the Composer, in his introduction, brings in disconnected snatches of the Théme transposed to some minor key; which serve to keep the imagination in suspense, (like the " half-glimpse " of the Landscape-gardener) and make you long and yearn, 'till the grand Théme bursts upon you with such sweet, full satisfaction that you smile through your tears just wept? Believe, Child,

[7] In Tennyson's " The Princess."

that God has not composed the Music of your life *all* in the Minor; believe that like those composers of whom I spoke, He has but placed a transposed mournful strain of your life-théme in His introduction to your life; presently, (nay, is it not already begun?) the veritable, beautiful Théme will come stealing and swelling so sweetly and so grandly, that you will realize how His mournful Introduction has but served to heighten the effect, the blissful, glorious, satisfying effect, of the Piece –

But then, One Soul, alone, (like my poor Flute) especially *your* Soul, can only utter, at best, a faint life-melody; no grand harmony, no thrilling modulations can come from those weak single-notes –. Dear Mamie, " dear and dearly-honored," join your life to mine; Ah, be " Heart, mine own, and eyes, mine too "; and we two will enchant the dull ear of the World with so sweet a life-tune, that even Its dullness shall recognize God as the only possible Composer of such thrilling harmony – – –

In *that* Twilight, with that low voice whose unearthly, pleading sweetness thrilled me then and thrills me now, you said " I am lonely " –. Can I tell you how those words have haunted me? How they sing themselves monotonously through me all the day? How they call to me at night and wake me out of sleep which has itself been troublous with their echoings? Or how fierce I grow when I reflect that my utmost power is limited to the poor vain entreaty " be not, now or ever, lonely? " Oh, let me fold up your pale loneliness warmly in my love, as one white petal is sometimes found cored in a red rosebud; so that, when the Bud of our Love has opened into the perfect Flower, your white-petalled loneliness shall become a red, exquisite petal of soul-intimacy – – –

But my soul turns away, and mourns over these poor, cold words which I am writing; and so, I'll write no more of them – Do you remember " No 1 "? What I would say to you is *there,* far more fully and plainly than *here* –

Send me quickly, one word to sing a Clarion-Song in my soul in the day of battle –

Let me call *you my* Next-to-God; and *myself Your*

S —.

To Harriet B. Freeman [8]

Petersburg, Va.
April 10th, "/63

My dear Mrs. Freeman:
                    I have been consoling my sadness, until
within the last few days, by felicitating myself upon the prospect of remaining here, living with my books, or rather losing
myself *in* them ("for," says somebody, "books are *not* companions, but rather *solitudes*"): and of writing long, soul-full
letters to the dear friends whom I have left behind me. But
how often, in this life, do we have to remind ourselves of that
old French proverb which contrasts the abilities of "L'homme"
and "Dieu"! For when we first arrived here, we received
orders to prepare to move immediately. Just as we *got* prepared,
the orders were countermanded, and we were told that Petersburg would be our Headquarters for the summer. No sooner
have we gotten ourselves complacently settled into the delightful lap of such an idea, than presto, change! Here come sudden
orders to go to the Blackwater: and so we are all in a pretty
"mess" of confusion thrice confounded,—again. I wish that
the sultry dog-days of *Life* would come, and the "Dogs of
War" would get *Hydrophobish,* so that the Police of the Universe might receive orders to *shoot* those accursed canines! —
    You cannot know how often and how lovingly I think of
you,—"O thou," (exclaims Jean Paul Richter) "who hast still
a Father and a Mother, thank God for it on the day when thy
soul is full of glad tears and needs a bosom wherein to shed
them!" [9]— How, then, ought *I* to consider myself blessed, who
have not only a father and a mother, but, in addition to these,
a dear, well-beloved, and much-loving Second Mother! — True,
there are no *glad* tears in my soul: but only sad ones, aye, these

    [8] The widow of Robert Freeman, who had died in 1856. On Aug. 16, 1864, she
married Thos. W. Fulton. In the summer of 1865 Lanier served as tutor to her
children. (See p. 190, below.) For many of the facts concerning Mrs. Freeman
(Fulton), I am indebted to Mrs. Frank Jones, Clinton, Gray, Ga.
    The reference at the end of the letter is undoubtedly to Mary Day—the pale
flower whom Mrs. Freeman is to revive.
    [9] *Quintus Fixlein.* Lanier's source is apparently Carlyle's translation of the
passage in his essay, "Jean Paul Friedrich Richter."

in plenty: yet they need, far more than the others, a mother's bosom wherein to shed themselves.

On the other hand, am I not *un*blessed, nay wretchedly forsaken of Heaven, in that seven hundred miles intervene between my longing heart and your loving one? —

You have a flower, there, with you, which is too much shaded, I fear, and grows pale for need of some sunlight. Take her out to your sunny home there, and into your sunnier Love. She will be revived, I think. — Believe anything else but that I am meddling with what does not concern me. —

My companions await me: we leave in a few moments. You will forgive a letter dashed off in a hurry: and prove your forgiveness, by replying to it soon.

Know, dear, good Mother-friend, that there is no faithfuller love for you in any one's heart than in

Sid. Lanier's.

To Mary Day [10]

Camp in the Woods [Near Suffolk, Va.]
April 21st 1863

Dear Mary Day:

I wrote you, immediately on my arrival in Petersburg: but have had no word from *you* —. " How weak to say " (*simply*) " I'm Sorry "!

---

[10] This letter to Mary Day, while essentially another literary composition, begins with an account—unusual in Lanier's letters from Virginia—of military activity. An introduction to the action which he describes is found in Clifford Lanier's letter of Apr. 17 to Virginia and Celeste Clay (previously published, *A Belle of the Fifties*, pp. 198-199):

" The huge shell, that has just shrieked across the intervening distance, from the enemy's trenches to our pickets, and, exploding, is not yet done reverberating, reminds me, that as the last one of the ' disjecta membra ' (forgive that pedantry) composing this letter, I might tell you a little of our situation here. The reticence of our Genl forbids all knowledge of his plans and ultimate design. I can only say, that our army, embracing three divisions, closely invests Suffolk on three sides, its water and rail-road communication with Norfolk, being still complete, except that Genl French, having possession of one bank of the river, is working hard to get, in position, guns of sufficient calibre, to destroy their gun-boats. That in the meantime large foraging parties and immense [wa]gon trains have been sent out for provisions. So that this of forage, may be the grand design after all, and, instead of living that we may fight, we are fighting, that we may

In truth, I'm only writing to you this morning because *that* is next-best to what, at this moment, I most desire, of all things in the world: which is that *you* would write to *me* — For I'm as dull, to-day, and stupid, as "Sternhold and Hopkins": having waked, just an hour or two ago, from a fifteen-hour's dead sleep — Don't imagine, I entreat you, O Mamie! that I sleep *so* much *every* day —: the fact being that all of night before last and nearly all yesterday I was in the saddle, dashing about amongst shot and shell from Yankee gunboats —

Verily, the Yanks (to give the Devil his due) have just done a dashing and handsome thing —: which, (for you won't hear it true through the newspapers) I'll relate to you —.

We have been engaged, (*we* means Gen!. French and *me, you* know) for several nights, in locating batteries upon the west bank of the Nansemond River, to destroy the "pestiferous" gunboats which infest that stream — *One* of these (Five brass Twenty-four pounders and Forty men) was situated on a point of land which stretches out into a bend of the river and is nearly surrounded by the water —. Intervening between the battery's position and the woods was a bare space, in full view of the enemy, of about two hundred yards —. About Seven O'clock on the night of the 19th, (day before yesterday) the enemy stationed gunboats above and below this battery; which, together with their land-batteries and sharp-shooters on the opposite bank, swept the space between the battery and the woods with such a hail storm of lead and iron as to render it impossible for our poor boys to move an inch —. They (the enemy) then landed a few hundred men above our battery, who marched down the bank, and, without firing a gun, gobbled up guns, men, and all, and carried the whole posse to their boats: finishing the whole performance with a tantalizing impudent cheer through their whole fleet —

(And that's more space than ever I devoted to mere news, in any letter of mine, before —. Appreciate it; *three* fair, good

live, the latter, being a very desperate situation, but the more laudable endeavor of the two, perilling our lives, not only for the vitality of our principles, as patriots, but for the very sustenance of our lives, as men, seeking corn and bacon, as well as the ' bubble reputation, at the cannon's mouth.' "

"Sternhold and Hopkins," mentioned in the second paragraph, were joint versifiers of *The Whole Book of Psalms* (1562), ridiculed by Dryden in "Absalom and Achitophel."

pages of letter-paper! Enough to write an immortal poem on!). — — — — —

I never like to pull flowers, especially wild ones that grow in the woods —. But these — — — : you should have heard me beg, good Faun or Hamadryad (said I): sweet Nymph or Naiad: O good and sweet whoever doth preside o'er these woods and waters, — — — give me these flowers —. The Genius Loci (as I might have expected!) made no answer: and so I, taking silence for consent, plucked, and send them to you —. This violet was to me, this day, a passionate Morning-Prayer, such as one breathes sometimes in one's heart, as if fearing that to utter it in words would be sacrilegiously weak —, A violet alway seemed to me, a Prayer: I go to one to pray for me with nigh as much emotion as I ask you to play for me *our* Dähler's (or Mendelsohn's? I'm unpardonably forgetful) Nocturne, which you said was a prayer —. Nay, is it not Jean Paul, says, flowers are embodiments of music? Then this violet *is* Dähler's Nocturne —. And the Fern, here, has all its leaves, like arms, flung up towards Heaven, in a despairing gesture: it bears nor fruit nor flower: it grew by the brink of a black pool —: and so, I say it symbols Despair, and call it Gottschalk's " Last Hope " —. This little wild-briar bloom, has its petals closely folded around the sweet, strange Pistil; why so, Mamie, a man's soul will fold itself about some wild and joyful " *Day* that is no more ": [11] and so I call it " Tears, idle Tears " —   Tell Gussie if she'll get a bloom like this, that's not crushed, it will remind her, immediately, somehow, of Basvecchi's beautiful piece —. Last, (and least!) this Heart-leaf, is *all* Heart, you see: it is bound to Earth, its birth-place, by the very slenderest of stalks: it has on its *under* side (if you'll look) many veins branching off into all strange, irregular directions: wherefore I call it my " No 1 "; and that's *me*!

April 23rd —.

So far, dear Mamie, had I written, day before yesterday, when I was interrupted —. At Ten O'clock, night before last, I received orders from the General to conduct a detachment of scouts and pickets to the river, ten miles from here —. Circumstances required me to remain there: and I have just

---

[11] This quotation and the one following are from Tennyson, " The Princess."

returned, having been absent two nights and nearly two days, in all which time I've only slept about three hours: even *which* little, was troubled by *other* things besides the noise of bursting Shells –. For I've received your letters! (just an hour before I started on my expedition) and I think, I will never sleep peacefully 'till I have written you –

About Nine, night before last, I was standing, aloof from my camp-fire, and the noisy laughers round it, shivering before the beauty of the evening-star, then low in the west: yearning, as intensely as a man *can* yearn without dying, for you to be at my side with your sympathy: and (knowing the other impossible) longing for some friendly word from you, – when my friend Capt. Small rode up, just from Petersburg –. I stood, silently, and trembling, fearful he might say " no," if I asked for letters –. With diabolical slowness, (he *certainly* knew my eagerness!) he dismounted, walked to the campfire, unbuttoned his over- and under-coats as if each button was inextricably tangled i' the loop, and after, what seemed to me, at least several cycles of ages, extracted a bundle of letters –. One for me, two for me (both from you, I saw in a moment) another (from Gussie), and yet another, (from Mother)!

Need I tell you how first I plunged into yours, as into the sea, and found there whole caves-full of gems and treasures, more than the Sea holds? – I long for Briareus' hundred hands that I might but write you the half of what your letters make me wish to say to you: and *you* — had need to wish for Briareus' hundred eyes, before you read the half of what I wrote –

How I beat about: fire at long range: advance: and fall back: like skirmishers, before the main battle: as if I feared to begin! – I must begin, tho',: and so, in medias res, charge!

" Business before pleasure," however: and here are the " details," that you ask for –. *I* am vulgarly " robustious ": in fact, so unpoetically obese, that I think seriously of resorting to vinegar, chalk, and slate-pencils, as daily diet, in order to get up that paleness which is said to be a sine qua non with the craftsmen of my (prospective) guild –. Cliff, – is fat too: but, poor fellow, in a different way –: for, riding all day in the cold rain, his old boil (which you *must* have seen) inflamed; and he came home late last night with a " fearful and wonderful "

face –. The accompanying engraving ☙🐑🐾 (" gotten up
expressly for this work, by a Southern 🐛😀🐿 artist, with
Southern materials: encourage Southern talent!!! " &c &c) will
give you a better idea of his " front view," than any description –. His mouth is twisted into the perfect semblance of an
interrogation-mark: as if with the continual inquiry, how much
bigger *will It* get? – –. " Where we are? " – In four miles of
Suffolk, a strongly-fortified town now occupied by Fifteen
Thousand Yankees: for " what length of time," I cannot say
certainly, but think for about Six or Eight weeks at least: very
" comfortably situated," comparatively speaking –. Our " daily
occupations," may be thus averaged: we rise at daylight, look to
our horses, & eat our breakfast, consisting of corn-bread, bacon,
and Sassafras-tea without milk or sugar, (in which beverage
however *I* never indulge): we then saddle up, and fare forth to
the Front with the Gen., assisting him to transmit such orders as
the ever-changing necessities of the Front require: late in the
evening we return home, (home means Headqr's) eat our
supper, which is a painfully-perfect repetition of our breakfast,
light our pipe, and discuss matters of State around our Camp-
fire: after which we " retire," (!) a euphemism for saying that
we immerse ourself in our shawl, like a mummy or an Indian
papoose –. All of which is, of course, a mere average: it is frequently varied in such ways as I have told you in the first part of
this letter –. All day and night we hear the unceasing musket-
rattle of the opposing pickets, with the more unfrequent roar of
cannon and shell –. We do not think that while we are smiling
at some jest a bullet is crashing through some poor fellow's
brain or a shell is blotting him out bodily from the earth –.
Ah, we cannot *allow* ourselves to think of these things: one's
soul, in a day, would grow more " grey in poring o'er " this
" human ill " than Romney Leigh's [12] in Ten years –. And so
we go about our commonplace round of life, and smile, and
talk our commonplace talk: and so we build our little, quivering,
Alpine Reed-Bridge over the Splendors and the Burning Terrors
and the Eternities under us, and keep our feet from being
scorched! Blessed, my beloved friend, is he who hath eyes to

[12] The hero of E. B. Browning's narrative poem, *Aurora Leigh,* to which there
are numerous references in Lanier's letters, of this period and later.

see the infinite Chasms, and know they are *there*: thrice-blessed
he who waits, with good hope, for the Wings, the Salamand –
Wings that will not scorch even in a blaze of Hell, the Angel-
Wings that will him bravely bear across all such Abysses!
– – – – – The only books I brought, were Aurora Leigh, Festus,[13]
and *your* little present, with a Bible: these I smuggled, our
"transportation facilities" being none of the largest –. Apropos
of books, Cliff placed your Robert Browning in my valise by
mistake: and "answers for himself" in the pencilled sheet
which I enclose –. I shall write to Petersburg and have your
book sent you by Express –.– As for the "Magician's Wand"–:
Ah, poor Zauberflöte (your "attempt" was perfect.)! I had
no heart to bring him, and so left him in Petersburg –. All my
improvisations since I left you have been *farewells,* of the
saddest sort: and, in the last one I played, on the night before
I left P. I think Zauberflöte mingled notes of his own, as taking
farewell of *me*: I, indeed, was talking to *you* –. 'Tis the only
inanimate thing, Mamie, I could ever make friends with: in
some rare moments I have thought that stars and trees and hills
returned the love which I lavished on them: but only seldom –.
This piece of Rosewood, this dear Zauberflöte, is surely, and
forever, my friend: seven years he has borne my sorrows, and is
now nigh worn out with such a Job's-life, under such a Christian's-Pack –. When the War is over so that I can get another,
I shall lay him up, in stately ease, and only appeal to his friendship on extra occasions –. I heard no Music in Petersburg; save
one wild night with the Trios at Dr Robinson's –.[14] I did not
think my soul could stand so tense a straining as it underwent,
that night –. – We had the most delightful journey imaginable,
with the M^rs C . s –. M^rs. Lawson is so beautiful, I could have
sat, in silence, and gazed at her, all the way –. Mrs C. C. is,
I think, my very good friend: & I am hers –. I've written her:
but have heard nothing yet –. I'm curious to know what she
said of me: you *can't* make me vain, so write and tell me –.
Of course they both loved Cliff: and we all loved each other:
and a more perfect Mutual Admiration Society was never

[13] *Festus,* a narrative poem by James Bailey.
[14] Dr. R. Emmet Robinson was a physician of Petersburg, with whose family
Lanier was on terms of intimacy throughout 1863 and 1864.

organized –. Mʳˢ C. C. and I had many talks about *you*: she loves you, and *nearly* understands you – . –

How like a Gossip's tongue my garrulous pen doth wag! Kind Heaven! Sixteen pages of " details ": and I have but gotten the ship cleared for action! And I so burn, Mamie, to talk to you about yourself, and about these doctrines of Sidney, and Alex. Smith, and Goethe –. Child, dearest and best of all my dear and good friends, know you not there are many sayings, we meet i' this life, which sound so good and so noble that we unhesitatingly accept them, without waiting to ask whether they be true, and whether there are not *other* sayings *better* and *nobler* and *higher* yet? Of Such sort are these things you quote from great, brave Sir Philip, and from striving, half-blind Alexander Smith: as for that *fiendish* Göthe, he is a liar, I believe, in the sight of God! You will smile at my impudence: but wait: to-morrow I'll write again, and prove that these are wrong, and I right –.

Meantime, present to your Father and Brother my warm regards, (I know not whether to beg you thank them for the pleasure which I, at this moment, enjoy): as also to Ogden (whom I wrote, from Petersburg), Andrews, & Fulton –. As for Mother, Gussie, Mʳˢ Freeman, Ginnie, Mʳˢ Lamar,[15] et id omne genus, – – – you may kiss them, individually and collectively, for me: and tell them to bless kind Heaven for so sweet a proxy, better than the original kissor –

For yourself, Child, I do not know anything which is sweeter or better for me to say than that I am

Your Friend

Sid. Lanier –

My chirography, dear, is notoriously unsystematic and irregular: but it is usually better than *this* specimen – Your Friendship would easier pardon this illegible scrawling, if you knew the circumstances under which this letter is written –. Verily, as I

---

[15] Lanier refers to Charles and Harry Day; to James Monroe Ogden, who in Sept., 1865, married Augusta Lamar; to Fred Andrews of Washington, Ga., to whom Mary Day was at this time engaged; and to Thos. W. Fulton, who married Mrs. Harriet Freeman on Aug. 16, 1864. Ginnie (Virginia) was a cousin of Augusta Lamar; Mrs. Lamar was probably the mother of the latter.

look over this, the crawling of an intoxicated spider, with inky legs, is steel-engraving to *my* fearful handiwork –.

S.

To Mary Day [16]

[Camp in the Woods, Near Suffolk, Va.]
April 23rd [1863]

I take my cue from Jean Paul Richter; and write this " Extra-leaf," which you may burn and so utterly forget and forgive –.

Child, I'm glad you read me right –. Nigh infinite as is my love for you, nigh infinite as is my yearning for *your* love; I yet would not take from you, anything less than *all* your love and *all* your heart –. I love you so unselfishly, that I had far rather see you *wholly* happy with *him,* than *half-happy* (you could, *could* not be wholly *un*happy!) with me –.

You will not think it strange that sometimes I write and speak as if I cherished a hope that you loved me –. I cherish *none*: but *all* loves, you know, will, sometimes when they are careering high in the Heaven of the Soul, imagine themselves *Moons,* that can beget their own image in whatsoever fair sheet of water they shine upon –. 'Tis a tendency of Love to rely, egotistically, on its own Magic to recreate itself: such, of mine, you will pardon –.

And so, Mamie, do not distress yourself for *my* sake: or ever again " entreat me to forget you "–. If I chose to do *that,* I *could* not: if I *could,* I *would* not –. Believe that I am happier, (happy's not the word, tho!) even after all's done, in having seen, and known, and loved, and still loving you –. A man cannot stretch forth his hand, and pluck the Evening-star –. Because *I* could not do it, O my One Silver-Star, shall I therefore cease to gaze? Am I not higher and purer and better for loving my star, even unpossessed?. I thank you, with thanks I cannot at all express, that you have given me such Friendship, as, I think, comes nigher filling the place of love than any friendship I ever knew before –. Think of me, therefore, (with-

[16] This letter was meant as a postscript to the preceding one, and was possibly mailed with it.

out sorrow,) as a man, sad indeed (Ah, God!), but far nobler
than he would have ever been, but for *your* influence –. In the
long years which God may spare you and me, (I thought, once,
I would go and die: *that* were *easy*, but *cowardly* and *wrong*:
so, I live on.) you mayhap will sometime need a Friend with a
lover's heart cored in his friend's-heart to make him *very*
zealous –. When that time comes, *you know* –!

All's said –. To My Friend Mamie I say, all hail: I accept
you: I welcome you as I never welcomed friend before: I shall
long *for* your letters, *filled,* (I PRAY YOU!) like these two, *with*
YOURSELF, as I never longed before –.

And to Mary Day! – – – Child, with the mystery in thine eyes
which *I* may not read; Lily of Heaven which God would not let
grow in *my* waters: Silver-star, which I could not wear on *my*
forehead, to be Israfel: thou Beloved-through-Eternity: thou
dear thrice-blessed Next-to-God: forever and forever, farewell! –.

To Mary Day

> Near Suffolk, Va
> April 24th   ″/63

Child, *you* taught *me Heaven*: 'tis a poor response that I, in
return, teach *you* a little of *Earth* –. It is my *all,* however: and
freely given: – accept *it, so* –

Let me, lay my hand upon your head: while I tell you (to
begin my lesson!) that your exquisite sensibility to nobleness
and virtue has led you into error: by making you accept, too
unhesitatingly, the words of men whom you knew to be good
and noble: and by making you start too quickly at the bare
semblance of ill in yourself –.

Verily, the road to Truth *is* rocky: and I think *Falsehood,*
for this very reason, has recently laid out rocky roads to *her*
domain, to beguile more victims: who (she argued) would
think they walked towards truth, merely because the road in
which they found themselves *was* rocky –. Poor Sir Philip!

Think you, with him, that the only object of human love is to
make us love God more, after it is dead? 'Tis a doctrine vir-
tuous enough to be worthy of even good Sir Philip: 'tis a road

rocky enough to lead to truth –. But, dear, it is *not* true; there's a doctrine higher and nobler yet; and true, to boot –. " Love's an END in *itself* ": (truer thing never said our friend Mrs Browning) : nor does that fact prevent us from glorifying God in our human love –. I entreat you do me so much justice as to believe that I had far rather take that last sentence for a text, and write you a dozen sermon-letters upon it: I *will* not mutilate what I would wish to say, by confining it to *this* letter, where I must speak of other things: and so I'll just beg you take that text, and think on it: and, as if I had your ear instead of your eyes, and used my tongue instead of my pen, I'll repeat it. " Love's an *end* in *itself* ": nor does that fact prevent us from glorifying God (the " chief end of man ") in our love –. Mary Day, we *cannot* take our love-for-man, and add it to our love-for-God, so to increase the pile! Our God's-love does *not* sit, like an Eagle, and fatten upon the mangled Lamb's-carcass of our human love! Never –.. There's *One* on the earth that *I* love: I also, in some poor measure, love God: I find that these two loves proceed pari passu mutually increasing, purifying, and exalting each other, in a glorious reaction –. Sir Philip Sidney's two loves proceeded in inverse ratio, one increasing as the other diminished – – – –. Do the Angels crush their love for each other, in order to love God more? – Whose doctrine is higher mine or Sir Philip's? Not " higher," either; but whose is *true*? – For we will do well to take heed that we search for real actual *Truth*, and *not Nobleness*: also that Truth (the Poets to the contrary notwithstanding!) lies as often in sunny Valleys (however rocky the *way* to it), as on snow-covered heights!

You see how *impudent Youth* gets; when it speaks of Love and such things –. I blush that I, who " only stammer where " *Sidney* " sang," dare to place my thoughts beside his –. But Novalis says, " the *Child* is the only true Seer ": and *I*, Mamie, (counting by *years*) am not so far from Childhood, but that I retain enough of its Prophet-sight to make me bold, speaking the *truth*, even against this great Sir Philip Sidney: whom, indeed, I *love*, and admire, full as much as *you* do –. It is my bright dream to write you, when I have left this nomadic tent-life and returned to civilization, many letters on this same question –. I've but mooted it here, and made a beginning:

I'm *certain* I can convert you to *my* side –. Not now, tho': and
so I come on to Alexander Smith –.

He says rightly,
                        " The truly Great *Need* not the confirmation
of the World " –: but *all* after that, he's wrong –; and *before*
it, too –. The greatest heart will always bear the greatest love
for *man, and the greatest craving* for Man's love: one necessi-
tates the other: love cries for love –. The " truly Great " will
always seek " the confirmation of the World ": for, gaining it,
they and the World are great together! Oh Heaven, I get fierce
with a Poet who draws such bad lessons from such good
sources! –. . Why did the greatest man, the God-Man, suffer
and die? Was it not to gain, at length, the " confirmation of
the World "? . . .– What if a " Cataract " *does* wear its rain-
bow-crown alone? Did ever any *man* (since Robinson Crusoe!)
or *woman* wear *any* crown, of rainbows, thorns, or roses, – –
alone? 'Tis just the difference betwixt a *cataract,* and a *man!.*
Or if he *will* have his Metaphor, I turn it against him: and ask,
is not a Cataract *such,* simply from the fact that it leaps a height
in its *hurry* to *get rid* of *loneliness,* in its violent fierce longing
for the Companionship of *all* the *other waters,* in the Sea? –.
And Oh Alexander Smith, draw not a Metaphor to prove a
theory, from that inconsistent, wavering Sea! Its old cavernous
Heart is full of dead men's bones; and gems! Shiny things are
born of it: but they crawl on the floors of dazzling palaces!
To-day it will waft our friend to us from afar: to-morrow it
will suck him down to death, out of our embrace, forever! –
Does the Sea, for sooth, impartially erase praise and libel
written on its Sands? Why so did Christ, loving John and *Peter*
also, John praising and Peter libelling: but *Christ* erased this
praise and libel, not, like the Sea, with a scornful, *indifferent*
Wave, but, like *Himself* only, with *Love* and CRAVING for
Love! – – – –

Child, you're hard upon yourself –. You must have been
" very unhappy to be so cruel," to yourself –. Wretchedness *will,*
however, do so: avenging itself upon *itself,* wanting other
victims –. We chain our lunatic Grief in a cell, in our heart:
and when our feelings, like visitors, walk before its door, it
will pour a maniac's indiscriminate curses upon *all* their heads,
innocent or guilty! Friend of mine, are you not doing a Catholic

penance upon your soul's self, with a steel-thonged Whip? Is
not *that* heretic, for a Protestant? You are about to be *confirmed* in the Protestant Faith; remember — — At which I *rejoice,*
truly, in my heart; knowing not why you " feared it would *pain*
me " —. My God, Mamie, is the same with yours: if I am for
Heaven, I shall meet *you,* there: 'tis only on points, *minor* in *my*
view, that we differ —.[17]

Friend of mine, never read Goethe to *believe* him —. Goethe
is either a God or a Devil: he is not *our* God, but very different:
there is only one God (a Poet's chain of logic!): and so Goethe
is a Devil, therefore, a Liar —.

" No Artist responds with tears "!? When *you* do, Mamie,
instead of bewailing that you are no artist, get upon your knee,
and thank God for this special benediction, whereby he preserves to you your artists's reason, nay your life! And pity and
pray for, those of us who cannot *so* " rain our skies blue " — . — —
Think you, you are " touched, never penetrated " by Beauty –?
Oh I have seen you quiver through all your pulses, as a tree
through all its leaves, stricken by the Lightning-beauty of the
Stars: I have seen you so full of Music's divine dissatisfaction,
that I think one drop more would have overbrimmed and
drowned out your reason,—and my best wish for you was, that
you might but weep: aye, I've seen you prone, a very, trans-
figured Danae to Music's golden love-rain! — —.

You, no Artist! Listen: and let God listen: with you and Him
for audience, I think I should speak Truth! — — — It is *beneath*
your province to write a word-poem, or a music-poem! You are
all Love: it is *your* high Artistic province to create a *life-Poem,*
higher than words or music or both: and so we little Poets look
up to you!

Child, you are so tense, and delicate: you mind me of a Lily's
Pistil, that startles us unaware: you're a petal of a Jessamine,
filled with Lightning: you're a white Flame, which, tho' a breath
would blow it out, can burn Platinum! – Platinum? You'd burn
the Earth: and when all was consumed to ashes save the uncon-

---

[17] Mary Day was confirmed in the Episcopal Church on May 3, 1863 (Christ
Church, Macon), by Bishop Elliott, and she remained through life a devoted
member of the church. Sidney Lanier, though reared by his mother as a Presbyterian, was affiliated with no church in his later life and made vigorous protest,
in prose and verse, against orthodoxy in religion. Thus the difference between
them here referred to persisted to the end.

sumable Asbestos-essence, you might melt *that,* like Cleopatra her pearl, in your wine [18]: and be another Aurora Leigh, as she "– – – – held

> The whole Creation in her little Cup,
> And smiled with thirsty lips, before she drank,
> Good Health to you and me, sweet Neighbor mine,
> And all these peoples' "! ——

The habit grows daily dearer to me of calling myself,

Your Friend,

Sidney Lanier –.

Forty pages in two days: and the *beginning* is not yet made! I fear your father's wrath (to whom, & yr bro.[19] my regards): and will not hereafter be so garrulous in my *beginnings* –. What a world of things we'll have to talk about tho', when we *do* meet! – – – I send the flowers, for which there was not room in the letters I wrote yesterday: except the *Fern,* which somebody appropriated –. Hopson and I have been in the woods two hours, looking for another: but cannot find one!

S. C. L.

From Clifford A. Lanier to Robert S. Lanier

Near Franklin Va
May 5th 1863

My dear Pa

Day before yesterday I received yours & Ma's letters sent by Cottingham. We were then around Suffolk – that night, obeying an order from the War-Department to fall back towards Richmond and effect a junction with Genl Lee, Genl Longstreet withdrew his whole force, and, the three divisions marching by as many roads, we were twenty miles away, before the Yankees, who had boasted that we should never return, had

---

[18] This figure, of the pearl dissolved in wine, was such a favorite with Lanier that its appearance here should be noted. His finest use of it occurs in " Evening Song " (I, 88).

[19] Mary Day's brother Harry was serving in the Confederate Army in eastern Tennessee.

guessed our departure. Genl Hoods division crossed the Blackwater at Franklin and is now far on the way to Petersburg.
Arriving at the lower bridge at South Quay, Genl French drew
up his divisions, in line of battle, posted artillery to sweep the
road and remained so untill the last man of Pickets division
had crossed in safety. Then posting one regiment to protect the
bridge and throwing out skirmishers, ours, the last division,
passed over 'midst " the sweet discourse of music," the clash
of cymbals and the shouts of the brave fellows who, though
they had marched, since dark the preceding evening, yet straightened up and walked more proudly, caught the step & flung hats
in air at the news of a victory on the Rappahannock.[20] So, the
enemy not having summoned courage enough to pursue, blood-
lessly but very dustily the march was continued to the bivouac
several miles this side of the river. As we had been in the saddle
twenty four hours, you can guess with what delight we dismounted at last. The other two divisions are marching as
rapidly as possible towards Richmond. We will either remain
here on the Blackwater or go to Petersburg.

I suppose the mail has not been kinder to you than to us,
and several of our letters have never reached you. We have
had but two from you, untill the arrival of these, sent by
Cottingham. We have had a letter from Mrs Clay at Richmond,
filled with the kindest expressions of regard, affection and
grateful remembrance. The legislative labors of her husband
having ceased, she goes to Macon & then to her beautiful
residence, in North Alabama, on the mountains near Huntsville,
provided Genl Bragg will keep Rosencranz at a safe distance.
Knowing that if you heard of the retreat from Suffolk, you
would be very anxious untill you heard from us, I have just
telegraphed to you and I hope the telegraph will be prompter
than the mail – Tell Ma I have written both to Uncle Sid and
to Grandpa, one from Petersburg, the other from the advanced
position near Suffolk. Never was there a better conducted or
more successful retreat. I doubt if a man was left behind.
I know there was none in French's division, since an officer of
the rear guard so stated. We hear that Genl Lee is again

[20] The battle of Chancellorsville, May 1-5, 1863. Though a Confederate victory,
it brought a tragic aftermath in the accidental death of Stonewall Jackson on
May 10, commemorated in verse by Lanier (see I, 156).

triumphant. I hope that the Georgia battallion acted well.
I also heard that Uncle C had obtained a permanent position
on the staff of Genl Wright as Major and inspector-Genl. of
brigade. I hope it is true.

    We are well but very dirty – Expect to bathe in the Nottaway
river this evening tell Ma. Love to her – to you both

I am Your affte son

C. A. Lanier [21]

TO MARY DAY

Franklin. Va
May 5th "/63

Dear, Sick Bettine, whose Goethe *I* will never be:

    You are to me a very Hebe without the roses in her
cheeks: and the Golden Bowl, which you fill for me with
Ambrosia, is a Letter: and, as we drink to a Bride and then
break our wine-glass that no meaner Toast may ever dishonor
it, so *you* change the rich Beaker at every divine drinking –.
Think you, O Sweet, pale Hebe, Cup-bearer to a *man*: who yet,
in being *your* friend, is half a *God*: think you, that, as he feels
this generous Heaven's-vintage of your friendship leap along all
his Soul's veins, his moist lips do not utter blessings, and his
eyes grow dim with their yearning to gaze a benison into *your*

---

[21] On May 12, 1863, R. S. Lanier wrote to his son Clifford: "It is a hard
school you are in surely: but a very manly one, & a useful if one will only
profit by its advantages. I believe you & Sid do & will. By the by, if you
have time, take notes of many things you see or hear of— whether historical,
philosophical, dramatic or comic — to be preserved for future use. What
stories this war furnishes the materials for! For a century how many pens will
be employed in writing its annals & episodes! Who shall be the master spirits
in this work? Can you not emulate Irving? Cannot Sidney, Bancroft? At
all events you can store away facts & incidents to be used hereafter as the
muse of history or song may favor. . . . Miss Gussie [Lamar] . . . speaks in
very high terms & I hope, deserved, of Sid's letters. Indeed I have a fair opinion
of the fellow myself in that department, though he has much to do before he
gets out of my *critical* clutches, & when he does he may hope to be ready to
write the history of the wars of the Southern Confederacy! I should think it a
good trade to swap my critical skill for his creative talent." (This advice may
have been the starting point for the war novels begun shortly thereafter by
Sidney and Clifford Lanier: *Tiger-Lilies* and *Thorn-Fruit*.)

eyes? — — — — — —   Yesterday afternoon at Six O'clock, after
having been in the saddle for thirty hours, I rode up to Gen.
French's H'dqr's, and delivered to him information, from the
Gen. commanding the rear-guard, that the last man of our
army had crossed the Blackwater: and all was safe –. Turning
my horse's head I started for our tent, three miles distant, and
had just begun to abandon myself to pleasing anticipations of
food, rest, and sleep, when I heard Cliff, from far across the
field, shouting a perfect Io Paean: and, looking up, saw him
shaking two letters at me –. Of course I " had an interview "
with him, immediately: and found a letter to *both* of us from
our glorious Mrs Clay, and one to me from you –. I can't thank
you in any way which would not seem to me a perfect burlesque:
and so I'm dumb –.

You're sick: and to write " one short page," fatigues you
greatly –. And yet you've written *me* Twenty-four *long* ones:
and I am so wretchedly selfish that I will not say to you, write
me less –. Friend, I CANNOT say it: my hand would tremble,
as if I wrote my own death-warrant –. Verily — — — — — !

I rejoice that I am able to dissipate *one,* at least, of your
griefs: and that's your sorrow at the supposed loss of y^r first
two letters –. They came, late, but safe: ten days before we
retreated from Suffolk –. I hope you'll be able to return to me
this good office: for, for your Eighteen pages I sent you Forty,
two days after –. Have they reached you? – I'm particularly
anxious about them: for there were some things there which
my soul spoke in high earnest: they concerned *you* –. So much
so, that if you've not rec^d them, write me and I'll try to
duplicate at least the ideas for you –. They were dashed off
hurriedly so that I of course could not remember the words:
which would be of no importance, anyhow –. You can write
me at Petersburg, always, without fear that your letters will be
lost: as I manage, by hook and crook, to keep in constant,
trusty communication with my friends there –.

You cannot know how grieved I am at your continued illness –. And *I* – – –, I cannot alleviate a single pain: and the
only wall I can erect around the dear, frail shape and the gray
eyes (which dwell ever with me) is the thin mist of my own
sadness, my sympathy: *so thin,* it will not even keep off rough
winds! It is maddening –.

And yet I think I know what you need: if you only *could* adopt the remedy: or would not consider it worse than the disease! – All souls, my Bettine, when they catch a glimpse of blue sky and green trees through the flesh-bars, beat against these with wing and beak, and, according to their strength, wear away the cage –. *You need,* now, to act, as a fountain plays –. You-ve shot up, in a single jet, with all your strength, towards Love's Blue: having got to the height where *his* actions (I know not what they were), like Gravitation, stopped you, do *not* (the *fountain* does not!) return upon yourself, in the same stream, (for so the waters collecting will burst the pipes): but break, there, into a spray of *little loves,* friendship-drops, and fall a thousand ways into the quiet, clear Lake of Content below –. The spray, my Friend, is not so strong, or so great, as the streaming Jet: yet, Spray makes Rainbows! — — You are too much concentred, as yet: you need for a time, *diffusion* –. These " waves after waves " of emotion, which burst upon you, *ought* as yet to strike you only with their *spray*: so, they will but dash into your face, (and cold water on the cheeks refreshes, you know!): otherwise they will overwhelm you, who are yet but learning how to swim! O, a thousand images come to me to tell you what I mean: but no one is better than the other: you'll understand, I think –, without my accumulating more of them –.

Do you bewail your inability to express your feelings? It is what we all must do, Mamie: from Goethe, down to Dickens' " Poor Tom," [22] all, high and low, must ever mourn that the very feelings which most *desire* expressions are precisely those which cannot *be* expressed –. Surely I should speak, with a Connoisseur's authority, of *that* Sorrow-wine: for I've drunk it, to the dregs, all my life –. There's no help for it: the only consolation is, they who drink so deeply must turn their faces *upward* i' the act: and *that* reminds them, there's a God in Heaven! – Accept the sympathy of one who knows the feeling in its most agonized intensity–.

Your " pen," my Friend, might " travel with your *thoughts* ": it will *never* travel with your *emotions* –. Emotion flies through the Universe on a Hippogriff: *Thought* is a weary foot-traveller, to *it!* Have you ever thought of the connection between these

---

[22] Probably Tom Pinch in Dickens, *Martin Chuzzlewit.*

two? – It is about the same as that between this habitable green
Earth which is so beautiful at this May-moment, and the molten,
shapeless, embryo Earth, when, according to the Geologists,
she was first whirled off from the Sun –. The Earth, at first a
glowing, invisible, dazzling chaos, cools to a crust, *outside*,
her great Heart being still all a-fire: only *then*, do men and
trees appear, to admire and adorn her! *So*, Emotion, *cools* to
Thought –: Emotion *is potential* Thought –. To make a
Thought out of a Feeling, that is, to *show*, or express, a Feeling,
we cool it 'till a crust forms on the outside: *in*side, it is still a
molten mass –. There are emotions that are always at white-
heat, and cannot be *cooled*: these must remain unutterable –.
Hence too, you find (as on that " divine day " when you wrote
your last letter at Mrs F[reeman]'s) that you are never able to
describe your emotions satisfactorily *whilst under the immediate
influence of their causes* –. We write best " under the still influences of recollection," when the emotions have had time to cool
to thoughts –.

Do you know Laplace's " Nebular Theory " of the Cos-
mogony? If not, I suppose the most convenient place where
you'll find it, is in Edgar Poe's " Eureka," 3rd Vol., if I mistake
not, of the common edition of Poe's prose works –. If you
cannot find *that*, write me, and I'll endeavor to tell you the
Theory – You would be charmed with it, especially the beautiful extension of it which you'll find in Poe's Eureka –. I have
often thought it (what Laplace of course never intended it) a
beautiful description of the way a Soul gets filled with thoughts
and feelings –. We are all little Gods, Mamie: given a Chaos,
each, with his weak-omnipotent finger, stars the space of his
mind with world-thoughts that shine there forever –. We are
LITTLE, Gods, simply because our Chaos has to be furnished us
by the Great One! –

Why do I not hear from Mrs Freeman? I wrote her before
I left Petersburg –. Tell her so, between two kisses, for me –.

Zauberflöte is with me: I could bear it no longer, and so sent
for him –. Since his arrival I've had small chance to talk to him:
but I improved *that*, with all I could remember of your Chopin,
and Dähler, and Mendelsohn –. I dared Gottschalk: but got
frightened at the minor strain of the Serenade and stopped: it
is too thrilling –.

Your little snatches from the Two Serenades (Schubert's & Gottschalk's) half-tempt me to desert, and go back to you –. Thou magic Serenader, who, standing seven-hundred miles off, canst still tinkle sweet notes in my ear, faint notes, as if I heard them in my sleep! How wish I that my arm were long enough to fling thee this Bouquet of Wood-flowers!

If it will not trouble you, I shall be perfectly delighted with the extracts which you propose to send me –: delighted all the more, since I've learnt Aurora Leigh by heart: and Festus, nearly –.

Cottingham brought me a letter from Ogden: and a note from Andrews, whom he met in Petersburg – Do me the favor to express my obligations, and present my regards to those two gentlemen –: with your Father and Brother, and all our friends there –. Loving kisses to Mother and Gussie: will write them soon –.

I cannot refrain from again entreating you to pardon these hurried scrawls which I send you: and to believe that they are mere apologies for what I intend to do, when I again have leisure and writing-facilities –. I would write more to-day: but wish to relieve your anxiety about the fate of your two letters, and to have *mine* similarly relieved –.

We write, to-day, to Mrs Clay –. Do give her our warmest love –. Cliff. sends *his* to *you* –. You " doubt," forsooth, whether our correspondence " is a mutual pleasure "! And you " feared lest your reply to my letter from Petersburg had wounded me, or indisposed me to write again "! Child, after what has passed between *us,* how *dare* you say such words to me?

Dear, dear, Sick, Bettine –. I say it to myself a thousand times an hour – The words recur between my every thought, like the " Toll Slowly " refrain, in Mrs B.'s Linteged –. Child, your letters make me bold to say that, being beloved by you, I am, so far, at least, the equal, mayhap the Superior, of great

Goethe –.

From Robert S. Lanier

Macon Ga. May 7, 1863.

My dear boys:

We wrote you by Cottingham last. Hope you
have our letters. Clifford's dispatch of the 5th came to us yesterday & you may well imagine how much relief it gave us. We
heard that Genl. Longstreet had gone up to Fredericksburg &
suppose the forces have been withdrawn from around Suffolk,
& that your active duties have been more or less suspended for
the present. Hope you have left the Yankees no provisions
between the Blackwater & Suffolk. We had Clifford's letter a
few days ago speaking of his narrow escapes. How grateful
to Him who *so* orders events ought we to be ! –

Your mother has been quite sick for some ten days past with
Erysipelas. The worst is over & she is now recovering. She
suffered very much. Although quite unwell myself most of the
time – from the effects of cold – I nursed her closely. She
promises to be up again in a day or two. Mary Day was up to
see her yesterday & made her visit doubly agreeable by talking
of you, as she did, showing her your letters, referring to what
Mrs Clay said in her letters to her respecting you & of her
flattering comments on Sid's letter to her (Mrs Clay,) &C.
&C. I met Mrs Freeman the other day who said she had a
delicious (or some such word) letter from " her pet " & was
going to answer it, made me give his address, & piled it on so
strongly about you both – in the presence of others – that I tore
myself away as soon as I decently could. Well, I am rejoiced
that you write good letters to the ladies & that they are so well
received.

I believe you both to be excellent letter writers; but without
knowing *what* you write to the ladies let me caution you against
too high colorings, exaggerations, false or perverted views of
life's realities & the like. In the *chiaro oscuro* of false lights
there may be a brilliant semblance of what is true – but the
mind though admiring is still in doubt. But exhibit clearly the
true light – the light of truth & nature & the mind is satisfied.
Writers who have the accuracy of perception to do this, no
matter in what department of composition, make the most

lasting impressions. For example: compare Walter Scott's novels to most others – Bulwer's say. The former will live & become classic when the others have perished. And it is because of their superior *veri*-semblance to truth and nature. Bulwer is certainly the more powerful writer, but he may not survive the changes in taste as Scott will. The *common* mind has an intuitive power of detecting the true from the false, – not in a day certainly but in process of time. But I have gone beyond the idea I wished to express – which was about this: that as the " prep " must mind his " P's & Q's " in spelling so the ingenious " Soph " must mind his *tonings down* in writing. And this is only suggested *by* your correspondence *epistolaire*, not applicable *to* it, so far as I know.

Allow me to add one other word just here. Letters however graceful which consist of mere emanations *from* the mind are never so interesting as those which are made up mainly of *actualities*. The former may be compared to a level prarie of flowers of which one can remember nothing but a pleased sense of the beautiful, the latter, to a bolder landscape of mountain and valley of which there are prominent points to engage the mind and fix the memory. I do not state this as a correct abstract proposition – but only in the concrete as applicable to your own relations & surroundings. In other words, in writing to your friends, put in plenty of facts, circumstances, & things pertaining to actual life as you see them or as they affect you. The sentiments can then come in as *chinkings* & if rightly put in are then jewels.

But I am like to violate my own teachings! – So the " 2d Ga. Batn " has been in battle at last! We have news this morning of one killed in the Spalding Greys & some wounded, & several wounded in both the Macon Cos Sam Johnson (of Clinton) slightly, Boss (Salsbery's nephew) severely, Hafer & Vanvalkenberg also, – I believe are all we have heard of. Although the battle has been fought four days we have hardly any details yet, only the general official report of a victory.

Forrest [23] has been doing some brilliant things lately. We have 1700 prisoners in Atlanta he took with less than 600 men near Rome Ga. They were trying to get to the State R. Ro.–

[23] Maj.-Gen. Nathan B. Forrest, who conducted brilliant cavalry raids in Tennessee throughout the spring of 1863.

Everything seems to be working pretty well – except they are having tough times in Missi – but we are sending help there, & may break Grant to pieces in the end.

Prices are falling & things look more favorable than when you were here. The big wheat crop will be ready for the sickle in ten days.

I had a letter from Gertrude this morning. She will be here in a few days. Bro. William is now there – & will come by with Gertrude & Sallie.[24] He takes Sallie to Montvale. I am very anxious to hear from your Uncle C. I think he is safe as we hear nothing from him.

Well, I hope you find better quarters *this side* than beyond the *Black Waters.*

We send you, all we can get to you now, – our love and blessing.

Your father,

R. S. Lanier.

To Robert S. Lanier

Petersburg   Va
May 12th "/63

My Dear Pa:

I came up here yesterday, from Ivor, (a station on the Norfolk & Petersb'g R. R. forty miles from here) with despatches from Gen¹ French: and found your letter of the 7th, which arrived the same day –. I return on the train tomorrow –

Left Cliff. and the boys well –. The Gen. has his H'dq'rs temporarily at Ivor: I think he will move in a few days, probably back to Petersburg –. The disturbances in this Dep't are probably over, for a time at least: and we are doing nothing now except fortifying the upper bridges of the Blackwater, which does not require the presence of the Gen –.[25]

[24] Gertrude Lanier was visiting relatives in Montgomery, where she and her cousin Sallie, daughter of William Lanier, had recently given a concert as a charitable benefit.

[25] In a letter to his mother, May 10, 1863, Clifford Lanier had added that with only two brigades left on the Blackwater, they were to act only on the defensive: "Our camp, that of Genl French and retinue, is beautifully located here, . . . a sweet relief to the bombing, the bursting and shrieking of shells, and picket-firing we have had so incessantly for two weeks."

I had intended, day before yesterday, to devote the day to a long letter to you: which should convey to you a resumé of our Suffolk campaign and its results, together with a generally – discursive lucubration on matters and things –. But man *pro*poses, Gen. French *dis*poses! – Early in the morning, the *Dis*poser called for one of the Sig. Corps to ride with to the Broadwater Bridge: and I was detailed for the duty –. We had a pleasant ride: but I was disappointed in not having my téte-a-téte with you:　I *will* have it, soon as I get time –.

I am over head and ears in executing the thousand and one little commissions with which I am charged: and so have not time to join issue with you, in your remarks on letter-writing –. Indeed, I should not have said " join issue ": for I perfectly agree with you, *as far as you go* –: But then, did you say all? Can we lay down any general rule about letters, any more than about conversation? Ought not one's Correspon*dence* to vary as much as one's Correspon*dents*?

To Mary Day, I write precisely as I think and feel –. I do not know if I've ever told you, that there is between her nature and my own a more perfect *congeniality*, than I ever dreamed of before I met her –. When I tell you that I have a thousand times been startled, when in conversation with her, to hear her speak not only the very *idea*, but the identical *words*, which I was just on the point of uttering: you will accuse me of diving into *Mesmerism!* – To which I would reply, as Carlyle once; arguing, his friend suddenly broke in with, " but, my dear Carlyle, that is *flat Pan*theism " ! And, replied old Fiery-words; " what if it were *round Pot*-theism; so it be *true* " ? [26]

I wish that you would cultivate Miss D., even to intimacy: not only, for *my* sake, (for she is my *friend,* in a nobler higher degree than I ever knew before) but, more especially for your own –. You will find her possessing the most exquisitely delicate and sensitive organization, both physically and mentally –: yet perfectly free from the slightest tendency towards lackadaisical " exaggerations " –. So spirituelle, that you catch yourself wondering why she don't spread the Wings which *must* certainly (you think) be hid there under the boddice, she yet, over her father's Socks which she darns so deftly, will chat you all day

---

[26] The anecdote is told of a discussion between Carlyle and John Sterling on the occasion of their first meeting.

on domestic matters, if you choose: or rise with you to any
height –. Whether you fly in the Empyrean, or walk the level
of common every day life, she always proves a delightful,
sympathising companion –. *You,* my dear Pa, in the toil of life:
in the hard contact with meanness and littleness which is peculiarly incident to your profession: are apt to forget *some
things* –. So far, you have *not* done so: but have preserved
your fine natural love for the True and Beautiful, in a far com-
pleter degree than many I could name: in an astonishing degree,
indeed, considering the difficulties you've had to contend with –.
My friend Mary Day will *diminish* those difficulties for you:
she'll teach you the magic art of running the Aesthetic and the
commonplace into *one,* so that neither *strains,* but both pull
together the same way –, in a delightful intertwining –. Take
her, and make a friend of her, and love her –. You'll come,
in time, to look upon her as a sort of special revelation, that
Heaven has sent down here, to let men know that " God is
certainly " *not* " abolished ": that purity and fine Roman simplicity and dignity, of character, are still possibilities: and that
our passionate Love for Art, may, instead of *withering* as most
do, grow and flourish greenly in the overshadowing of a deep
Piety towards God –.

How garrulously my pen wags! I started to scratch off one
page to you: and here are six before I could catch my breath –.
I'm brimfull of talk for you: and in a day or two, you may hold
out your cup!

Had a letter from Sister this morning –. I've written Mary
Day *four* long letters: has she got them all? Love to her and
Gussie, and all our friends there –.

A hundred kisses for our dear Sick Mother: and another
hundred for you   from

Your Son,   Sid. Lanier –.

I hear no word from Uncle C: or any of Wright's Brigade –.
They fought finely – If you should hear anything, and it should
be necessary, telegraph me: as I might be of assistance to Aunt
Annie, if Uncle C. were wounded –.[27]

S. C. L.

[27] Mrs. Anderson was staying in Nottoway County, Va., with William Archer
Robertson, the maternal uncle of her husband and of Mrs. R. S. Lanier. Lieut.
Clifford Anderson received a slight wound, but it was probably at the Battle of
Gettysburg, in July. The following November, he was elected to the Confederate
Congress. (Information from his daughter, Mrs. John McKay.)

To Mary Day

Petersburg, Va.
May 19th "/63

There are so many things, My Friend, that I wish to say to you, which *cannot* be written, on paper that has to travel Seven hundred miles! – I've half a mind to make a spasmodic attempt to get another furlough. How long will it be, before you make the visit, of which you spoke, to Savannah and Wayneville? [28]

I didn't know whether or not you were ironical when you called my letter " *unique* as a floral dictionary –." Did I call a Stamen (you'll *never* make that out; so, *Stamen!*) a Pistil? And mix up Calyx and Corolla? And mistake Endogen and Exogen? And tangle up " Cryptogamous " and " leguminous," vascular and cellular tissues &c &c? – Well: it's quite likely: in the six years since I studied it, I've forgot my Botany –. Apropos of flowers, who is the kind lady who is so " charmed into a floral message," by a beginning and a finale, and a *length,* of a letter? And would she not have sent me a kiss outright, if, beginning and finale being moderately good, the " length " had been a *hundred* pages instead of twenty? And oh, wouldn't she, for a royal octavo volume in manuscript, give herself up, heart, body, and soul, to the writer thereof? Shade of Mary Montague! Wouldn't I write without ceasing from now 'till Christmas, to buy a sweetheart who comes recommended as " a valued and quite intimate friend " of yours! – Do express to her my very sincere thanks for the flowers: and oh kind, good Mamie! Sweet, dear Mamie!! most rare and exquisite Mamie!!! – tell me what's her name!!!! — As for the *emblems,* bless you, child, I didn't have the slightest idea what they were –. But I asked Mrs Clay, and she told me; – if I haven't clean forgot 'em again, tho', – – may my mustache wither and my beard grow henceforth Sandy! Indeed if I could remember the emblems, I'd say something pretty about them, for you to tell her –.

Somehow, I'm getting very forgetful of *names,* lately: a little of which is philosophy, and a great part of it – – – – – the

---

[28] Mary Day was at this time planning to visit her friends the William Duncans in Savannah and Lilla Hazlehurst in Waynesville.

imbecility of old age, I suppose –. The little philosophy-part
arises from the fact that people name things as they *see* 'em;
and few people see *things* as they really are –. Which reminds
me of a very pat illustration which I saw sometime ago, in
Harper's Punch –. Adolphus, walking on the sea-shore, at a
watering-place, suddenly discovers a party of ladies looking
at him through the window-pane of a neighboring hotel –.
He straightens himself up, adjusts his immaculate collar and
cravat; and *thinks* that he presents an appearance like this:
(it's devoutly to be hoped he *didn't*, tho!) It unfortunately happens however that the pane of glass, thro'
which the ladies are looking, has a *crack* in it: and the appearance which Adolphus *really* presents, is more like this:

More people, than one would imagine, have cracked window-
panes for eyes –. – – – You see what " afflictive dispensations "
your compliments (totally undeserved, I assure you! you should
see how I blush!) to my artistic genius are bringing upon
you! – . –
And so you think your " feminine way " of writing, " dull,"
and fear lest your " commonplace details " bore me?
Why – – – let me quote our friend Sir Philip Sidney:

" I would know whether She sit or walke,
How *cloathed*, how waited on, sighed she or smiled,
Whereof, with whom, how often did she talke? " [29]

– – And what saith Shakespear's Cleopatra?

" – – Oh Charmian,
Where thinks't thou he is now? Stands he or sits he?
Or does he walk? or is he on his horse? "

So, Friend, all *lovers* like, nay *must have*, " details " of the
Beloved: and *friends* do too! –. I like *yours*: and would *not*
" alter them " for a world –. On *me*, a pretty sentence, or an
eloquent paragraph (in a *letter*) is totally lost, if it be but pre-

[29] *Astrophel to Stella*, Sonnet XCII, a favorite of Lanier's and used by him
fifteen years later in his Peabody Lectures.

fixed by or ended with, a " dear," or " good friend," or " beloved," or other such caressing epithet: to one who looks for
love and friendship in his letter, *these* symbolic caresses, these
written kisses and hand-pressures, are worth all the labored
eloquence in the world: his eye will linger on these in utter
forgetfulness of the pretty words –. *You* give me all this:
wherefore I like and *love* your letters just as they are; and the
only possible objection I could have to them is, – not enough
of 'em! – . –.

I wrote Gussie and Mrs Clay in the last three days: and sent
all my messages to our friends –. So, I won't burden *you* with
any: save to kiss everybody, specially Mrs Clay: and present
my regards to Messrs Day, Sr. & Jr.–. What shall I say for
you? – Can I say more than that I am your friend forever, Sid.
Lanier?

You force me to write too many " extra-leaves," my Friend –.

Read again, what you wrote me –. " I am some times wor-
ried, lest I am erring in permitting selfishly so great a pleasure
to me as our correspondence –. You know the reason for this
fear: – what I dread it may, it must strengthen –, what it is my
own most painful, friendly duty *not* to strengthen –, in that or
any other way –. I think I could overcome my own feelings
alone, but it is hard to give you present pain for the mere hope
of future good –. Therefore I wish it might be *your* decision
that it were unwise " –.

Well –. I would not tell you, if I could, the struggle, whose
ground-swell, after the storm, yet heaves within me –.

You do not know: you do not know –. God, and the lonesome,
weary days and nights of many years, (*many,* being part of
Twenty-one): *these* only, know with what utterness, my Life
is in this Love, and *is* this Love –. So, if the Love be " unwise,"
the Life is unwise, too –. I've been very bitterly tempted to cut
off, with one word, from those who have been good enough to
speak kind words to me, on this life-journey: and to let despair
work its will: and to betake my foolish self, with the unwise
life and love, to Him who gave both, and tell Him that the
World cast off a servant who is too foolish to keep his place
or learn his business –.

This correspondence does *not* strengthen my love –. I am
sorry (how hard I am struggling to keep down hot words) that,

from the men you've seen in your life, you have conceived so light an idea of a man's love –. I am sorry that *mine* should ever have caused you any pangs or fears –. I am certain that I would have died very cheerfully to have averted from you any one, even the lightest, of those pangs –. I have no hope of your love –. In such hopelessness, I almost cease to long for it –. I still love you –. I shall always do so, each moment more purely, and more deeply –.

O my Beloved, I had wrapped you in a mantle of friendship, to keep my too-passionate arms from the dear form which it was forbidden them to clasp –. That mantle was sacred enough, to me, to have protected you forever –. So wrapped, and looking at you with friendly eyes, I still thought you altogether more beautiful than any I ever knew –. I far preferred seeing you *so,* than shrouded in the White of that Death which, otherwise you must inevitably have died, to *me* –.

I cannot restrain the words that are in me –. Hear me: it is surely the last time –.

In *that* first glance of your gray eyes, I knew the Dawn –. The Evening which had preceded it was very lurid: and, saith the Proverb:

> " Evening red and Morning gray
> Shall set the Traveller on his way –."

You, Pale, Gray Dawn, filled, for *me,* with holy Dew, the Flower-Cup of the Universe, which had grown shrivelled in the Night –. Making the sign of the Cross on my forehead with that Holy-Water, I would have faced and conquered all the thousand Devils that ever beset life's Travellers –.

I seemed, in that moment, to survey, from an immeasurable height, the vast Valley of General Life –. The Smoke from old burnt Universes overspread, but did not overgloom, all space –. The light which shone was the Light of Love, which is the Light of God –. The Veil which lay over the Fore-world, the Present-world, and the After-world, seemed to grow thinner, and thinner: and I shivered with the expectation of beholding, each moment, those mysterious countries –. Before, Human Life alway seemed to me only a mournful Sigh of God: but now arose through the mourning a faint note of infinite divine Delight, as a violet might grow amongst dead leaves – . – . – –

With you, I felt within me the half-infinite power of a complete man – . – – – –

Without you! Without you, – Oh God, the fascinating monotony in that Dirge of two words and one tone –, without you, – I am but a Tragedy so badly played that it is become a Farce, at which good Angels hiss and bad ones laugh – . – —

Must I then, in one short month or so, bid farewell to the only beloved, and the only friend, I ever knew, in all my life? –. Well –. I may look for one more letter from you, after this is received?

I have said farewell to you, already, once –. I like not the word well enough to say it a second time: and so you will consider *this* as but a lingering gaze of the eye, as it were: a last, reluctant pressure of hands which, alas, – and my soul like a light is gone out in the storm-wind of this last alas, – of hands, which shall be *so* pressed again, – nevermore –.

Cliff. sends you a great deal of love: and anxiously awaits yʳ promised reply to his note – –. I suppose Sister is at home, by this –. Dear Mamie, *do* love her, and take care of her, and teach her some of *your* simple, noble womanhood: she has been away so long, that she *may* have learned many bad things, and false views –. For *my* sake, train her, as much as you can: and kiss her for me –. I wrote you about a week ago: and got yʳ letter of the 1st May –.

S. C. L.

To Virginia Hankins [30]

[Bacon's Castle, Surry County, Va., May 30? 1863]
Porch, Saturday morning, 1 o'clock.

Did *all* that mortal men *could* to serenade you – failure owing entirely to " inclemency of the weather."

Field Corps.

[30] Virginia Hankins (facing) was the daughter of Gen. John Hankins, whose home, historic Bacon's Castle (so called because it had been held and fortified by the rebel Nathaniel Bacon in 1676), was near Fort Boykin—at the mouth of the James River opposite Newport News—where the Laniers and a detachment of the Signal Corps were stationed from June, 1863, to August, 1864.

The MS of this note has not been found. It is here reprinted from **Virginia Hankins**, " Some Memories of Lanier," *Southern Bivouac,* II, 760 (May, 1887),

VIRGINIA HANKINS IN THE 1860's

Courtesy of James DeWitt Hankins, Richmond, Virginia

FROM CLIFFORD A. LANIER TO ROBERT S. LANIER

Near Smithfield Va
June 4th 1863

My dear Pa

Since writing you so briefly from Bacon's Castle, we have moved twelve miles down the River to this point which is called Day's Neck and have established a signal post, the terminus of a very extensive line, proceeding partially by telegraph but mostly by signal to Petersburg.

We live – little like soldiers & no more in tents but as boarders of a family, in the residence of Genl Boykin deceased, – occupying neat rooms and porticoes, shadowed and cool as alcoves. Near us is Fort Boykin, built to protect the rear of Norfolk but now dismantled & in ruins, containing nothing but heaps of cannon balls, burnt gun-carriages and several heavy pieces, dismounted & half-buried in sand. The James is at one point four, at another seven miles wide and the shore receding, forms a magnificent bay. The whole resembles less a river than an ocean and looking across to the dim, misty outline of the opposite shore, with the waves coming in on the white beach, swelling and ebbing, you have the same emotions as one standing on the sea-shore. This country has never been permanently occupied by troops and presents none of the desolation and waste to which we had become accustomed & of which we were weary. Beyond Smithfield are a few cavalry pickets while a part of our squad does picket duty on the beach. We are all armed with sabres and carbines and keep a sharp watch lest a dash of the enemy from Suffolk or a boats-crew from the other side of the river should attempt to break us up. Looking on the map, you can easily locate us and see how near we are to Norfolk, so close that we can hear the drums at Newport's News. We are at Burwells Bay, ten miles from the mouth of Nansemond River.

where she stated: " His letter of introduction to us was a torn piece of coarse Confederate paper tied by a guitar string to our door-knob." That introduction of the Laniers to the Hankins family followed promptly is indicated from the next letter. The friendship between Sidney Lanier and Virginia Hankins soon ripened to intimacy, at one time apparently approached marriage, and lasted throughout his life. (Conjectural dating of the present letter from the fact that May 30 was the first Saturday preceding June 4.)

As I said before, our mail facilities are of the most difficult kind and you must make a margin for that if you fail to hear from us regularly. It, the mail, comes now every other day but a change is expected when we will get it but once a week. The fruit trees here are loaded with the young pendants and strawberries grow spontaneously. Our general expression of congratulations is – " too good to last."

A *pe-ert,* blithe damsel of eighteen daughter of " mine host " presides over everything, from the chickens up through the horses to the tea-table and our neighbors are of the true Virginia stamp, full of fun and hospitality. One, – Genl Hankins, proprietor of that ancient structure, " the Castle," –allthough white-haired and fifty years of age, rode five miles with us, the other night, on a serenading frolic.

With all these pleasantnesses of situation, My dear Pa, *my* enjoyment is tempered with the *absence from home,* for which nothing can entirely compensate. We have had no letter since one from you dated May 12th. We feel confident you have written but your letters have not reached us. We have had intelligence of you, through one of our female correspondents as late as May 21st, nothing from anybody since.

Enclosed is a Savannah shinplaster, not current here. Please exchange it for me. Can you get some Georgia bank bills? If so send me twenty five or thirty dollars or any convenient amount. We will probably have opportunities of purchasing things from the Yankee lines and can use such funds. A pair of cavalry boots, for instance can be bought for six & a half dollars, greenbacks or about twelve dollars state money. Let me state another comfort we enjoy – *no mosquitoes.* Love to dear Ma & Sister & tell them to remember us affectionately to Mrs Clays, Mrs Freeman, Miss Day, Miss Gussie, – Mary Lou – and Ginnie Lamar.[31]

Direct your letters allways to Petersburg, care Milligan. When you write, send our love to Montvale and Montgomery. They do not answer my letters.

Very afflty

Your Son

Clifford A. Lanier

[31] Mary Lou Lamar was Augusta Lamar's sister, Virginia Lamar their cousin.

To Mary Day [32]

Boykin's Bluff, Va.
June 13th 1863

Mamie; for whom I find no epithet that is half tender enough: –
Your
(doubly) *last* letter was received some days ago –. I did not
know that you would expect me to answer it, until I read,
yesterday, your note which was to have been enclosed in Mrs

x   x   x   x   x   x   x

Your " come, come, – to your Child," – – nigh broke my
heart –. For I *cannot* come –. *I* had based my hopes of a furlough upon the friendship of Genl French, and the confidence
which I know he reposes in me –. In my absence from Petersburg, however, Gen. F. has been ordered to assume command
of a Division at Vicksburg; and has been succeeded here by
Gen. D. H. Hill, a tyrannical old Curmudgeon

x   x   x   x   x   x   x

Surely, Child, you knew that the " tender words " from me
were yours before you asked them. As for " forgiveness," I
have no forgiveness for *you*: but I have honors and blessings
such as my heart guards, trusting them not to the tongue for
fear of sacrilege in the utterance: I have trust, love, and Worship, for you, in such degree, that my idea of expressing them
ends only in a bitter smile –. You, with your intense sympathy
which you almost mistake for love, find it hard, I see, to write
composedly about these things: how then shall *I,* with far less
self-control than you, write calmly? And I can not speak tenderly,
without speaking *too* tenderly, too passionately –; is not silence
better? And, dear, " Unkindness," is a word that, as between
you and me, has *no* meaning, forever –. If I know that I live,

---

[32] The MS of this letter has been mutilated by four excisions (indicated by
x x x), made probably by Mary Day Lanier. A few unrelated words have been
omitted from the surviving fragments for the sake of clearness, as well as a
fragmentary paragraph that seems to refer to a marriage of convenience about to
take place.

On the envelope of this letter, in Mary Day's handwriting, are some unidentified verses begining: " Many years ago, far too long to tell."

I know also, with the same faith, that *you* could *never* be unkind to *me*: – think you *I* could ever be so to *you*?

Ah, how that last question starts again the bitter reproaches with which I overwhelm myself each day –. You suffer: I am the cause of it! –. Hard, Child, hard is my punishment for the indiscretion which led me, in that twilight, with full conviction of hopelessness, to tell you that which has brought all this upon you –. I force myself to call it indiscretion: it was rather weakness – I *could* not have done otherwise –. Thou Unknown God! So strange, so maddening, that I, with my own hand which I *cannot* control, wound my one only Beloved, that I stand and see her quiver with the pain, that I *cannot* (this!) heal the wound, nor even alleviate a single pang, that I cannot command the cool grace of even one tear, nor my own heart bleed freely, wounded worse than hers

Thou well-beloved Mamie, in whom, for the years during which time and silence and distance must be between us, I yet trust with free, and full and never-failing faith: to me, all high eloquence of loving wishes, of wild regret that has a tone of hope within it, of true and passionate love — is centred in these simple words, God be wi' ye, which in later days, we shorten to, Good-bye –.

L.

To Robert S. Lanier [33]

Boykin's Bluff
July 9th "/63

My Dear Pa:

I was greatly rejoiced at getting, this morning, your letter announcing your partial success in Richmond –.

[33] A letter from R. S. Lanier to his sons written from Jarrett's Hotel, Petersburg, Va., June 25, 1863, is mostly illegible. Lanier's letter of July 9 to his father, addressed to Montvale Springs, makes it clear that R. S. Lanier had been to Virginia, probably in an effort to secure a commission or a civil appointment, and had visited his sons in the vicinity of Petersburg. Six months later he was appointed adjutant to a Maj. Rowland at Camp Cooper, on the outskirts of Macon (see R. S. Lanier to his son Clifford, Jan. 20, 1864).

Nottoway County, Va.—mentioned at the beginning of this letter—had been Mrs. R. S. Lanier's home until her marriage. Numerous relatives still lived there.

I think you had better close with the offer of the D^r who wished you to take his place –; and hope, earnestly, that you will bring Ma and Sister on to Richmond, or rather Nottoway, immediately –. Of course, this would only be with reference to a permanent position in some of the Departments –. I do not know the chances for such; wish I could see you and learn all that you did and heard, on your trip – . –. I have heard you speak, sometimes, of seeking a Quartermaster's place –. This, I am certain, after having seen a good deal of the business under all its forms, wouldn't suit you –. Whether you were Q'rmaster of a Post, (the preferable position) or attached to a Regiment in active service, you would find a thousand disagreeable duties incident to the position, which would be peculiarly repugnant to one of your temperament –. The place in Richmond combines a thousand advantages –. With your knowledge of the Law, & your general business abilities, you would be certain to rise –. Perhaps, in time, you might realize the dream I have often indulged for you, of getting appointed to some of the European Consulates –. If you had a permanent position in Richmond, you could easily find time from your duties to make yourself a good French Scholar: which is the only qualification you lack –.

At any rate, I do not see how you could possibly injure yourself, in view of all the circumstances, by devoting six weeks of the time now at your disposal to the endeavor to get an appointment in some of the Bureaus –. Richmond is the best place in the Southern Confederacy to *see* everybody; so that, even if you were seeking *other* positions than that mentioned, you would find more opportunities there than at any other one place – . –. So, bring Ma & Sister to Nottoway: Cliff and I will probably be able, during the summer, to get a short furlough, and visit them –

Tell Sister and Aunt Jane I have rec^d their good letters; and will answer them as soon as our sick boys all come in –. Which they are, happily, beginning to do very rapidly –. Charley Emmell & Cottingham arrived today; and Cliff is hearty as a buck, and is coming back to-night –.

Give lots of love to all and singular the dear ones at Montvale –

Write me your plans immediately; I am very anxious to see you secure from the further ravages of this dreadful war –.

Very Lovingly, Y'r Son,

Sid. Lanier

Pardon a very hurried note –. I have dashed it off to send to Wakefield for tomorrow's mail –.

To Virginia Hankins

[Boykin's Bluff, Va., July, 1863?] [34]

If my Little One has longed for me, half as often as have I for her, in the days since I saw her, – – – she will certainly have no difficulty in pardoning this greeting of pure and deep Friend's-Love, which my heart irresistibly insists on sending her this morning.

You know, darling Friend, Liebchen, Thou dear Violet whom I have found growing amid the cold Alpine Summits of cold human-hearts, (even my pen, you see, caresses you!) – – you know, it is my theory that there is no extravagance of pure love which is not *sweet,* and *pardonable* –. And so, my fingers are eager to write down for you the passionate love-letters that are crowding in my soul at this moment, the genuine, free forth-gushings of a friendship which will contentedly allow itself to be characterized by no other word except this – – – – *Infinite* –.

But my messenger, inexorable as Fate, hurries me, and I have no time to write; believe only, the love-letters are here in my heart; and, you know, *that* writing-desk is always open to *you!* – –

I've been spending some days with Father in Richmond: and have been quite unwell since I got back – Was up all last night watching the diabolical Yanks, who, I certainly expected, would attack us –: Two Gunboats with barges lay at our wharf all night, and have gone up the bay this morning –.

I'll see you tomorrow, the weather and the Yanks per-

---

[34] Conjectural dating from the reference to visiting his father in Richmond (see note 33, above).

mitting – Love, (for Cliff also) to Miss Spires – Cliff kisses your hand –.

What shall I say? What shall I say? I linger, as if I were pressing your hand for a final farewell, – instead of merely signing myself

Your Unchanging Friend,

Sid

Employ this long dreary day in writing to me!

FROM CLIFFORD A. LANIER TO ROBERT S. LANIER

Mantura Surry Co Va

Augst 3ᵈ 1863

My dear Pa

You will be very anxious untill you hear further from me and you left directions with Bro. Sid to write you, I think, at Petersburg. He may not see me in time to write by this mail, so I anticipate his report & write you myself that I am well. No ill effect followed the carriage ride and – thanks to all the kind influences that environ " Harp Hall " [35] – I feel as well as before my slight attack. The fair daughter of the Castle visited us yesterday *professionally* & decided on leaving that there would be no occasion for another visit in the same capacity – ending with an injunction, remarkable for a physician but conformable to her character natural & to the general kindness, of which you have had instances, of these good people – namely – that we " must not get well too *fast*."

I wish continually for your success in Richmond – leaving that however, as we should rightly leave everything – to the wise ordering of the *infinite God* – the proper means, with energy, having been employed.

With no new & wild impulse, in no spirit of Arcadian dreaming but with very settled – real convictions I have looked on & still regard Life as a gift possessing its pains but having

---

[35] This letter is written from the home of Mrs. M. P. Wilson, in which Clifford Lanier was apparently convalescing from a slight illness. Mrs. Wilson was a friend of Virginia Hankins, who is referred to in this letter as " the fair daughter of the Castle."

the glorious amenities of Love to God, Love to man – faith and duty – which will inevitably bring nobility of living, & of manner and a full capacity for the enjoyment of innocent pleasures. In this consists the great happiness I have in the contemplation of a fine Sunset – in the blowing of a pretty rose – in all natural beauty whatsoever.

These few lines of feeling have flowed from my pencil, my dear Pa, because they formed, just then, the pleasant smooth surface of my thought & because I believe they will not be unpleasant to you who have always sympathized with our feelings, ideas and aims.

I contrast hot, unpleasant Richmond with this tolerably cool grove & feel for you.

God bless you –

Your Son

Clifford A Lanier

To Virginia Hankins

[Mantura, Va., August 5, 1863]

Sanatary Report

12 – Ock – M

      Invalid quiescent – stillness profound – some apprehension that the late removal from the Castle may prove detrimental.

1 – P.-M. Alarming symptoms – – Patient has been heard to mutter incoherently and the words caught – " rain-storms," " Organ," " Monterey," " Greenwood " & " Crump."

Tis thought, some sad memory or bitter disappointment oppresses him – – a mental incubus. A straight-jacket seems inevitable.

2 – P.-M. Favorable evidences – – 1 Julep – 2 glasses of cordial – 1 huge slice of watermelon – 2 pieces of ham – 3 potatoes – an avidity equal to the spirit of " Friar Tuck " in attacking a chicken pastry. corn (several nubbins) – tomatoes proportionably. milk & pastry according &c.

3 – P-M. He has opened his mouth, *like Balaams ass of old,* evidently with the intention of speaking.

5 minutes after 3. P.M. Patient has spoken evincing remembrance – consciousness of the present & hope for the future – a remarkable sentence, including between its beginning & period the three grand subjects – War – Mather & Crump – being no other than this – " I wonder how the inhabitants of Greenwod endure the horrors of this civil war & are affected by the heated severity of the Summer "?

3-30- P-M- Patient sleeps – His mind relieved, confidence may be entertained in his speedy recovery – A ride prescribed for this evening.

M^{r.} – – – Surgeon & & c

Mantura Augst 5th 1863 –

To William A. Hopson [36]

[Fort Boykin, September 15, 1863]

I should have answered your kind letter long ago, but I have been indulging so liberally in chills and fever that I have had little leisure to devote to anything else. Your touching allusion to your own experiences in the chill line affected me almost to tears: I sympathized with you. Friend, when *thou* shookedst, *I* trembled; when *thou* wast feverish, *I* also burnt; and when *thou* perspiredst, *I,* in that selfsame moment (mine generally came about 11 A. M.) did sweat like the d – – – l. Verily, I have an idea of handing down to late posterity some fine dishes of juicy soul-meat, upon a poem for a dumb-waiter, the top shelf of which should be constructed " thus ":

> Oh, Life's a Fever and Death's a *chill*!
> 'Tis a disease of which all men are ill;
> Earth for a Hospital surely was given—
> Hell's an eternal relapse: Health is Heaven!!.

[36] Previously published by G. H. Clarke, *Independent,* LXI, 1095-1096 (Nov. 8, 1906) ; *Some Reminiscences and Early Letters of Sidney Lanier* (Macon, Ga., 1907), pp. 19-20. It is reprinted here from the second source (MS not found), which omits the beginning and the end and one passage in the middle, but supplies the date. Hopson was associated with Lanier throughout the war.

etc., etc., etc. And I *would* do it, by the Nine! only it looks menial and low to be shoving dumb-waiters up and down; even for Posterity, who, for all they say he's going to be so rich and lordly and refined, and all that, may, after all, turn out but a scurvy fellow that eats with his fingers; no better, if the truth was told, than we poor cooks and waiters of the present century.

How the Sublime and Ridiculous do nudge each other! They remind me of recruits trying to march in file; whichever one goes in front, the hindmost is certain to step on his heels; and one knows not whether to weep for the wounds received thereby, or to laugh at the awkwardness that caused them.

x   x   x   x   x   x   x

Ginna H. and I have become firm Soul-friends. She is a noble creature, and has the best-cultivated mind I've seen in a long time. I've initiated her into the beauties of Mrs. Browning and Robert B., together with Carlyle and Novalis; whereat she is in a perfect blaze of enthusiasm. She desires me to remember her very warmly to you, and to express to you her gratification that your only friend in Franklin of the female persuasion is cross-eyed and otherwise personally deficient; since so (she added) you will have less temptation to forget your friends in Surrey. Five young ladies visit the castle shortly, to remain some time; among them, Miss Alexander,[37] the intimate of Ginna, reputed a perfect paragon of all that is lovely, etc. We anticipate a good time, and wish that you were here, very much, to make it better.

To Virginia Hankins

Mantura
Sept. 18th ″/63

Petite;

I ran up here to get some medicines for Cliff; &, having succeeded, must hasten back to him —.

I'm very sorry I can't see you: — and *you* are sorry, too, I've no doubt —. So, to help you survive my absence, I send you

---

[37] Mary Rebecca Alexander of Mecklenberg County, Va. (See Lanier's letter to her, Jan.? 1864, below.)

Carlyle's Essays; and write this note as a sort of "Directions" accompanying the prescription –. Which said

Directions

are as follows; – read, *first,* the essay on Boswell's Life of Johnson (near the middle of the book): then the two essays on Jean Paul Friedrich Richter: – by which time I'll see you, and we'll talk further about it –. – –

Hastily,

S. C. Lanier

P. S. I saw Dr Crump this morning and told him we would not be able to come to his house to-day.

From Clifford A. Lanier to Robert S. Lanier

Boykins Bluff Va
Sept. 26th 1863

My dear Pa

Your two letters of the 15th & 19th came last night to relieve our anxiety which was becoming intense. Our joy at the complete escape of the Exiles [38] with so little damage or injury to all & especially our dear Mother needs no expression. We give thanks to God –

Honest Moses Martin has risen high in my opinion and I give him a blessing for his constancy, and the noble way in which he has shown his gratitude to our family.

We rejoice too at the first rate post you have obtained in Macon. You can no doubt live with that salary, and its other advantages are numerous.

I have been sick in concert with you but both of us are now perfectly well. Did you get two letters from me, written soon after you left Petersburg, one directed to Burkeville, the other to Macon? In them I asked you to send us a pair of blankets and the jeans cloth Ma had for our pants. I hope you will send them as soon as possible. Bro Sid has had a letter from Tip Harrison [39] who is well & who has seen lately Uncle Clifford.

---

[38] The reference is apparently to a forced and hasty departure from Montvale Springs, before the advance of Federal troops.

[39] Probably the son of Burwell Kendrick Harrison, who had married Eliza

Winter is fast coming on us, the bay this morning being tossed into a perfect swirl & boil, and the keen wind nearly taking my breath away.

Kiss and hug all for me at Montgomery – Love to dear Ma & Sister –

Your Affte Son

C. A. Lanier

I will direct this to Macon –

To Virginia Hankins

Boykin's
Oct. 1st ''/63

It is a mere form, Friend, for *me* to say good-bye to *you*; – for the best part of me, (which is my *Love*) goes with *you!*

S. – – – – –

To Mary Day

Boykin's Bluff –.
Oct. 1st ''/63

Sweetest: I, being in the dark, must needs think that all men grope!

So, how goes the night with *you?*

I write little: –   that you may have little to forgive –.

S.——————— 40

Woodson Robertson in a double ceremony with R. S. Lanier and Mary Jane Anderson (the slightly younger niece of Eliza Woodson Robertson). Although Tip Harrison does not otherwise figure in the Lanier letters, he was one of a very few people to whom R. S. Lanier sent an obituary notice of Sidney Lanier (see his letter of Sept. 13, 1881, to Clifford Lanier), and hence must have been a close friend.

⁴⁰ The ambiguity of this note is explained by a reference in the letter to Mrs. Freeman, which follows.

To Harriet B. Freeman

Boykin's Bluff, Va.
Oct 4th ″/63

Second-Mother;   This is a good and a kind and a loving letter, that you send me; I wish that my pen could thank you as my heart does –.

Friend, it seems *so* long since I was weak, or passionate, in the sight of any human being –. It seems *so* terribly long, that my soul, to all outward appearance, has sat still and straight, and held its feet under its dress, and spoke when it was spoken to, and been altogether a beautiful model of boarding-school propriety –

The " ordeal," of which you speak verily was " fiery " –. Ah, it *is* fiery: for I have not yet passed through it –. But there have lately been *other* fires that you wot not of; fires flaming from a Pit which ever yawns beneath the feet of a man; – through which I have had to pass, and whose kindlers I have had to fight –. Of *these*, however, the end is near –. I have passed, and fought –   I am the victor –. I am coming out not all unscathed, but with a far purer heart and a stronger soul than was mine before.

I am sorry that these friends, to whom I have given, once and irrevocably, the deepest loyalty of my nature, have allowed even my long silence to shake their faith in me –. Unintentionally, they do me bitter wrong –. Dear Mrs F. be kind for me: see each one of these, Gussie, and Mrs Clay, (and *yourself*: but *not* Mamie):   say to them that letters from me would have been nothing but mere inarticulate cries for help, and shouts of defiance to my Enemies, indistinct for breathlessness, half stifled with the dust of a fight –.   These were not worth sending: and so, I sent nothing –.   Tell them, there has not been an hour of any day since I left them, in which I have not arranged them over in my heart, as rare flowers in a vase, and breathed prayers, and blessings and love upon them –. Tell them I rejoice in having fought a victorious battle, single-handed: that I need no pity, having sought the conflict myself --; but that I ask from them a generous forbearance towards one whose sorrow has been full as much as he could bear –. Beg them finally, to love me: and, over and over again, to love me –.

I wrote Mamie a short note, some days before I received y^r letter –. *That* might explain why I have not written: – people do not write well " in the dark ": – and *I* had no light!

Write me: and tell Gussie and Mrs Clay to do so –. Mrs C. owes me a letter –. Mamie will certainly answer my note –. Two things *she cannot* doubt: God and my Love ! —

In a month or two, I may see you all –. I anticipate it with inexpressible eagerness.

Cliff is well, and sends a letter-full of love to all our dear ones –.

You *must* believe dear Mrs Freeman, that I am now as I have ever been,

Your faithful and loving Friend,

S. L.

This letter is far too full of " *I.*s ": but I could not help it – *You* will pardon it: (it has been said) " there is no egotism between friends "!

S. C. L.

Address me care " Signal Corps "   *Petersburg Va* "

To Virginia Hankins

Wakefield
Oct. 14th ″/63

My Dear Ginna:

I've just met Miss Joan [Douglass]; and feel so over-joyed that I must express my feelings &c &c –.

I wish, by the way, you'd tell Miss J. I'm a sight better-looking than I appear to-day; want of sleep has demoralized me –.

I know you are wondering what I really am scratching this note for: – – be Still, and hear! – – – – I'm afraid you'll give my segars away to somebody: & I want to charge you *not* to *do* it, by any means, under no possible circumstances, for no earthly consideration, at all at all!

Kiss M^rs W[ilson] for me: I'm going to write to her as soon as I get home –.

Good-bye, good-bye: , – isn't it strange that when *that* word is *most* painful, we then say it *oftenest?*

S. C. L.

To Mary Day

[Macon, Ga.?, Oct.? 1863] [41]

Come Child! My eyes clamor for *their* breakfast –
Your dear Eidolon, which I bear always with me, held my eyes open with its sweet splendid fingers all night – & so you'll see but a gaunt face this morning – But you'll pardon *that,* in your

S C L

From Clifford A. Lanier to Mary J. A. Lanier

Macon, 1st Nov. 1863

My dear Ma

Without accident or adventure, without even a fierce word shot back, Parthian-like at the " Powers that be," exceeding their authority & becoming impertinent – We got

[41] The furlough Lanier had hoped for in June was granted unexpectedly sometime between Oct. 14 and Oct. 22, 1863. Lanier and his brother Clifford not only visited Macon, but Montgomery, where his mother and sister were. Mary Day had by this time returned from her visits in Savannah and Waynesville, and may have been staying at Mrs. Freeman's plantation, Scott's Mills, near Macon. References to an October day in 1863, at Mrs. Freeman's, occur in several letters written long afterwards. In a letter of Oct. 17, 1872, Mary Day Lanier wrote to her husband: " The weather is fit for paradise: like that October day, nine years ago, when thou and I, with our Clifford, lay under the sweet autumn leaves of the hillside over Tobesaufkee and watched the building of the bridge."

In a letter of Oct. 19, 1874, Mary Day Lanier wrote to her husband: " Sweet memories of the autumn hill-sides at ' Mrs. Freeman's ' eleven years ago, when thou and I and our Clifford were happy together, have hovered around me during these two days past."

The note here printed, written on a scrap of paper and apparently delivered by hand, seems to date from the period of this October furlough (see also note **4, 1863**).

here Thursday night.[42] Did I say " without adventure "? I must retract. For he who attempts to kiss a pretty girl in the broad light of day starts on a very perilous venture indeed and his audacity, I suppose, is made excusable only by success. It is ten to one that a sudden squall will strike him " i' the ear " & overturn him, as an imp of Boreas treats the bold fishing smack, venturing in his jurisdiction.

Well! we visited, discoursed – lunched, drank & (" smoked "?) with Aunt Sallie and were sent on our way rejoicing, with a kiss from Milty. This glorious, bright Sunday is the last hour of our gala-day and we leave to night for Virginia. Equally & impartially, I think, we have divided our time with Pa & the girls & so, having got through the little happy dream, we wake up again to the business of the day – like freshened travellers, commence with light heart & vigorous step, the next days journey. Very grand & successful was the reception of the President [43] on Friday. The street before the Hotel was a mass of carriages, buggies wagons & eager, pressing men & women, all striving to get one look at the noble old fellow. With Mrs Clay, Mrs Freeman & Miss Day we stood on the balcony, heard the speech & enjoyed the busy scene. — I forgot to deliver your letter to Aunt Sallie & mailed it from here. Brother Sid left his knife on Aunt Jane's mantle. Please send it to him. Ask Sister to purchase for me at Mr Pfisters or White's book-store " Mrs Jamieson's Studies & stories " [44] & send it to me at Petersburg. Enclosed are (2$) two dollars, its price. She might send it by mail or, with the knife, by Express. Much love to all.

Your Affte Son

Clifford. A. Lanier

[42] Oct. 29.

[43] Jefferson Davis, President of the Confederacy, made a brief stop in Macon on Oct. 30, 1863, en route from Atlanta to Savannah (see Dunbar Rowland, ed., *Jefferson Davis, Constitutionalist: His Letters, Papers and Speeches*, Jackson, Miss., 1923, VI, 72).

[44] Probably the volume of essays on literature, art, and music by Mrs. Anna Brownell (Murphy) Jameson, entitled *Studies, Stories, and Memoirs*.

To Robert S. Lanier [45]

Novr 5th "/63
Petersburg   Va

My Dear Pa:

We arrived here at three O'clock this morning, having been delayed twenty four hours by missing two connections on the route –.

I regret very much that it will be impossible for me to attend to your commission in Richmond –. The train from Petersburg to R. left shortly after we arrived this morning, before daylight: and I was unable to see Milligan and get a pass in time to go over on it –. No other train leaves here for Richmond until to-night; when I, of course, could not effect anything –. Even if I *could,* I should be unable to get back here in time for the Wakefield train in the morning: which, by detaining me here Friday Saturday and Sunday, would prevent my arrival at Camp before next monday night: and so make me too great a trespasser upon Milligan's good-natured kindness –. I am very sorry that it all happens just so right-wrong: but it can't be helped – I hope that you will get the goods released, however, without any trouble –.

Cliff and I will probably remain at Boykin's some months longer –. Emmell and some others are engaged, I understand, in raising a company of Non-conscripts, who are to act as scouts on the Blackwater, and in the vicinity thereof: – their success would obviate the necessity of sending our Field-Squad there –.

We have had a very extensive fit of the blues: but, after much philosophizing, we have arrived at the conclusion that it don't pay, and so we are gradually regaining our wonted equanimity –. Our visit home appears more like a dream than a reality: like a glimpse of a flowery valley seen through a gap in the mountains –.

---

[45] To have arrived in Petersburg by Thursday, Nov. 5, 1863, Sidney and Clifford Lanier must have left Macon by Nov. 3. Lanier's letter to his father was received in Macon on Nov. 10, and forwarded by R. S. Lanier to Mrs. Lanier, in Montgomery, with an appended note concerning the release of some sugar that belonged to R. S. Lanier's brother Sidney. This was the business R. S. Lanier had asked his son Sidney to attend to in Richmond.

I'll write you again in a few days –. Present our kindest regards to all our friends that you meet: send much love, and a thousand kisses to our dear ones in Montgomery: and believe that Sons were never more loving than your

Sid & Cliff –.

To Gertrude Lanier

Boykin's Bluff, Va.
Nov^{br} 16th (63

Well, Darling, we are here again, at our old routine of night-guards, and flag-waving, and gunboat-dodging –. Only now do we begin to realize that there has been a " blue break of beauty in the clouds " of our usual life; and to appreciate the happiness which filled that figurative " Solution of continuity –." Not all the cordiality with which our friends in Surrey received us has been able to dissipate our sadness: Cliff and I, in spite of many resolutions to the contrary, have continued deeply, darkly, beautifully *blue.*

I have been anxious to hear from you, fearing that you might have somewhat misunderstood the advise which I gave you in regard to *our friend* –.[46]

In writing to him, do not wound his feelings by the sudden assumption of a cold tone, which your former letters did not possess –. He is doubtless a man of *sensitive* nature; and would quickly perceive any change in your manner of addressing him –. Deal *perfectly candidly,* with him –. You have told him that you love him; *continue* to tell him so, and to write him lovingly, until you have reason to believe that your feelings have changed –. Meantime, make him appreciate your candor in telling him you are yet too young to have perfect confidence in your knowledge of your own heart – Let him know that, should any change ever occur in your regard for him, (which, of course, you do not now consider probable) you will apprise him of it, in so many words; meantime, you will enjoy the pure happiness of loving and being loved –.

[46] The object of Gertrude Lanier's affections at this time is referred to in her letter of Feb. 26, 1864, to Sidney Lanier, as " Mr. H." Gertrude was possibly still in Montgomery, more probably with her grandparents on Mobile Bay.

Tell him these things, and you will have done *all* that is *necessary* –. Cherie, the worship which a pure man renders to a woman is the sacredest thing, I know of in this world –. *You,* since you return our friend's affection, have now no complications to trouble you but, should a change in your heart ever render it necessary that you should withdraw from your present relations with him, you would then have need of all the reverent delicacy and tenderness of which you are capable –. By writing him as I have told you, above, you would be able, at such a time, to free yourself without doing *violence* either to your own womanly truth or to his respect for you –. If, after a year or two of probation, you and he should still love each other as you now do, so high is my opinion of his moral truth and purity, I would resign you into his keeping without a single apprehension as to your future happiness, at least so far as *he* would affect it –. *Now,* I *could not* do it; nor do I believe that *you,* when the time came, would speak the irrevocable vow without a tremor, caused by the fear that you perhaps did not sufficiently know your own heart –.

I think I have here condensed about all that I would say to you on this subject. I know that you will give weight to my advice: and so I write it with pleasure –. Keep me well advised as to all that occurs between you and your lover; should any difficulties arise, do not act until you consult me –. By the way, would you have any objection to letting me see one of his letters? I am certain I could extend my knowledge of his character very greatly, in that way; and it is an eager desire to *do that,* by no means mere curiosity, which prompts me to make the request –. If you think that neither he nor you would object, send me any one of his letters, in your next –.

The scene, through the window at which I'm writing, is too exquisite for mortal eye –. It is painful to me –. They say, a sight of God would strike a man dead; I believe it, knowing that the pain which I have sometimes suffered, under too much beauty, is only less than death –. The Sun is just setting –. The bay is blue as your eye: and so still is the water, one might imagine it the blue eye of Ancient Maia, in a day-dream of a lover –.[47]

[47] This description suggests the inspiration for Lanier's poem "To —— (The Day was dying; his breath) " (I, 153), which Lanier sent to his father in the letter of Dec. 7, which follows.

Kiss everybody, individually and collectively, for us –, especially dear Grand Ma & Grandpa –. We love you all; and long for you, almost *too* much, I'm afraid –.

Cliff sends kisses – Write me very soon; meantime, rest in the love of yr. Bro.

Sid.

To Virginia Hankins

                    Mantura – – – – –
                       Dec – – –/63

" Now let God be witness betwixt us two "!

Did I not warn you that you would hear strange things about me? Have you forgotten, O Friend, that you promised to despise *all,* until you should receive confirmations or denials from my lips? You thought you " feared nothing " when you wrote –. But did you not, *do* you not, *fear all*?

The humiliating confessions which my letter contained should be *guarantees* to you for the *truth* of it – You *do* believe it! I hardly think you *can dis*believe it! I hardly think you *can* retract your reply to it!

I have asked Mrs Wilson to show you a little poem[48] I scribbled off for her the other day – – Read it & study it until you understand it: and tell me, when I see you again, if you think a *false-heart could possibly* have written it –.

Pardon a very hurried note – – " Patience "! say you; and " patience " also, say I, – – And so we'll wait, friend, till we meet again –.

Truth is a circle and ends where it commenced – – Be this note like it! to which end, I beg again,

              " Let God be witness betwixt us two "!

---

[48] See p. 128 and note 50, below.

EARLY DRAFT OF LANIER'S "TIGER-LILIES," PAGE 39, 1863-1864

Manuscript in the Clifford A. Lanier Collection, Johns Hopkins University

To Robert S. Lanier

Boykin's Bluff, Va.
Dec^br 7th ''/63

My Dear Father:

I have delayed writing you, in the hope that I might be able to send you a copy of the introductory chapter of " my novel ": [49] but I have not had time to write it, and so wait no longer –. After Christmas, I hope to give more attention to the Novel itself.

Our friends in Surrey, extended to us the most cordial welcome imaginable: they have given us several delightful parties: have insisted on frequent visitings: and our relations, up there did not permit us to withdraw our attention, even if we had wished to do so –. All this has occupied much time which I should otherwise have devoted to matters literary –.

In the long night-guards, however, which we have to stand here, my mind has ample scope to expand itself, and it does so, always, with reference to the novel –. I have found it somewhat difficult, amidst the multiplicity of scenes and incidents which would crowd upon me in fascinating succession, to concentrate my attention upon what, I suppose, should be the first aim of the novel writer, viz; the forming of the bare outline of a consistent plot –. I find, however, of late, that the plot, in spite of all this confusion, is taking the matter into its own hands, and is gradually *shaping* itself out into form and comeliness: I think one more guard-night will finish it: and hope to send it to you, together with the introductory chapter, in my next –. Meanwhile I write for you, a little piece which sang itself through me the other day, and which I have given to a female friend in Surrey –. She is a tolerably good judge: and she thinks it very beautiful –. It does not compliment *you,* however, as it

---

[49] By this time, and perhaps largely under the stimulus of literary discussion at Bacon's Castle, Lanier had begun the writing of *Tiger-Lilies*. The difficulty of literary composition in the midst of war, referred to in the third paragraph of this letter, is echoed in a phrase occurring at the end of Bk. I, Chap. III, in the MS. of *Tiger-Lilies* (Clifford A. Lanier Collection, Johns Hopkins University), but omitted in the print version: " and I, here in Virginia scribble, between guard-hours " (see facing illustration and cf. V, 20).

did *her*: and so your judgment will probably be more vigorous –.
There's more in it than you'll see at one reading –.

To ——————

The Day was dying: his breath
Wavered away in a hectic gleam –.
And I said, " since Life's a dream, and Death,
And Love, and all, are dreams – – –, I'll dream "

A Mist came over the Bay,
Like as a Dream would over an eye –.
The Mist was white, and the Dream was grey,
And both contained a human cry –.

The burthen of it was " Love ";–
It filled both Mist and Dream with pain –.
And the hills below and the Skies above
Were touched, and uttered it back again –.

—   —   —   —   —

The Mist broke, down the rift
A kind ray shot from a holy Star –.
Then my Dream did waver, and break, and lift;
Through it, Cherie, your face shone, afar.[50]

Cliff and I are in excellent health and spirits –. We were somewhat disgruntled by the news from Bragg: [51] but not knowing
certainly the position of affairs there, and distrusting the Yankee
reports, we cling to a hope that all is not irretrievably lost in
that direction –.

Tell Mother the socks will be very acceptable: the *knife*
particularly so –. I need one almost every moment –.

Present our loving regards to all our friends: and kiss Mother
for us many times –.

Your affectionate Son,

S. C. L.

---

[50] Texts of Lanier's poems given in his letters are included only when, as here,
detailed comment in the letters themselves makes this necessary. Either Mary
Day (see p. 141, below) or Virginia Hankins was the inspiration of the poem
(I, 153 and note), though Mrs. M. P. Wilson was the " female friend in Surrey "
to whom he gave a copy (see Lanier's letter to Virginia Hankins, Dec. (?),
1863, above).

[51] Gen. Braxton Bragg was defeated by Gen. U. S. Grant at Missionary Ridge
on Nov. 25, 1863, thus losing Chattanooga and Tennessee generally to the
Federal forces.

FROM CLIFFORD A. LANIER TO ROBERT S. LANIER

Genl Barton's Hdqrs
Kinston, N. C.   Dec 30/63

My dear Pa

      You will no doubt be much surprised at this new date – Let me explain – On the day after Christmas, as we rode down to Ft Boykin from the Castle, where we had spent a glorious Christmas day, with feasts & dancing – we received an order from Maj M[illigan] to report at once to Petersburg. With much regret on both sides, we parted from our friends & proceeded to obey. Arrived at Petersburg, an order was handed us from Genl Picket through Maj M directing Bro Sid to Genl Ransom [52] at Weldon, me to Genl Barton here, for the purpose of showing their Asst. Adjt Genls the new system of cypher. At the same time, Maj M gave us most complimentary letters of introduction & told us that, the duty discharged, he would recall us.   I left Bro Sid this morning at Weldon and myself arrived here about dark this evening.   Have met several Officers whom I knew & having reported at Genl B's Hdqrs have been invited to join the mess of his staff. So I am here, in a most comfortably warmed room, trying to realize that I am by myself, out of hearing of Mrs. Wilson's cheery voice & the magic flute, away from the booming of the James River waves, & unable when I please to visit the brunette lady of the Castle.[53]

    Kinston is a pretty little place, full of dashing infantry & cavalry officers.   I have no doubt I will be very pleasantly situated here for two or three weeks. Preparations are being made for a grand tournament & ball by the young men and much to my regret, I will not be as quiet as I wished.

    If you have any money that can be spared, please send us a little.   Love to dear Ma & to yourself & Sister, if she is with

---

[52] In a letter of May 2, 1905, to Edwin Mims, Clifford Lanier stated that both he and his brother were under the command of Gen. Matt Ransom, and added: " I do not think Sidney met him in any individual or social way."

[53] Mrs. Wilson was the mistress of " Harp Hall," Mantura (see note 35, above) ; the booming of the James River waves probably refers to Fort Boykin; " the brunette lady of the Castle " was Virginia Hankins.

you. Loving regards to our friends, the young ladies. I wrote you hurriedly several days ago.

Your Affte Son

C. A. Lanier.

P. S. Ma, I got your bundle of jeans & blankets when we returned after furlough – I am not certain whether I ever informed you. Notify us when you send the next bundle, which direct as usual to Petersburg –   My letters you may send here untill there is a change

C. A. L.

1864

Weldon N. C.
Jany 4th "/63 [1864]

My Dear Pa:

I have just received your critical letter –.
If I could tell you half the pleasure it gave me, I think you
would be more than repaid for the trouble you took in writing
it –. It is, by far, the best thing, I have seen from your pen:–
which certainly possesses the merit of being an *honest* compliment, inasmuch as, considering the severity of the critique,
no such thing as "Mutual-Admiration-motives" could be
attributed to me – !

The little poem [1] was written upon the principle of exciting
the reader's imagination to wander for itself, rather than of
presenting a perfect picture before it –. That the separate
images of which it is composed are *beautiful* I don't think any
man could deny: but I aimed at something higher than that –.
The piece has a double, or rather triple meaning –: which I
shall explain presently – . – –
Aside from the ultimate idea which comes out in the last line,
and which may be considered as at once the germ and the consummated flower of the poem:– the beauty of it, considered as
a whole, as a specimen of imaginative *mechanical* art, consists
in the *pari-passu* progress which the *two symbols,* the Dream
and the Mist, make, towards the culminating conclusion in the
last line –. Like two Will-O-Wisps, they change places: sometimes the mist symbols a dream, sometimes the dream symbols
a mist; *all* the time, *both* symbolize something *else* –.

Which being premised, I proceed to your objections –.
Imagine that I was lying, at Sunset of a Summers-day, on one

---

[1] The first four stanzas of the poem, "To ———," are given on p. 128, above;
the fifth stanza, p. 136, below. R. S. Lanier's letter of criticism, to which this is
an answer, has not survived.

of those high, grassy escarpments of old Ft. Boykin, which you and I admired together –. In sympathy with the dying day; meditating upon the dreamy futility of life, (as youth *will*: which is sufficient for the purpose, and so we won't stop to discuss whether life's a dream!): meditating especially upon the dream of *Love,* which, hitherto had certainly been *unrealized*: under such circumstances,

> " A Mist came over the bay,
> Like as a dream would over an eye –.
> The mist was white and the dream was *grey*" &c. –

You object that I have not, before, substantively referred to the *dream* –.

The omission was intentional –. In composing that verse, it occurred to me, upon reflection that the reader would recognize the omission of such uninteresting *details* as a delicate compliment to his sagacity: and would experience therein a pleasure separate from that conveyed by the beauty of the image, yet heightening this beauty –. You object also that you are color-blind to a *grey dream* –: but you ought *not* to do it, while professing your ability to distinguish blue and grey *Spirits* –. Which, think you, is most *colorless,* a Spirit, or a Dream? Jesting aside, the epithet " grey " was only used as indicating a *sad, ghostly,* hue: and as connecting the dream, by a closer tie, to the Mist –.

You do not like that the " cry " is " *contained* " –. I chose the word after some reflection –. The dreamer cries out in his sleep: so earnestly and so vehemently that the cry absolutely *fills* both the mist and the dream: fills them with *pain* as if it were poured into them, as if they could *barely contain* it –.

The whole piece symbolizes, *Youth* –. Our boyhood sets, rosily, beautifully –. The time of Youth comes on, misty, dreamy, filled with painful uncertainties, with vain anticipations of realizing boyish dreams about life and love &c–. This broods over us silently, like a shadowy, fluctuating darkness: until some woman's face, some *Love,* comes like a Star, and shines through all dreams and mists, and dissipates them, into the clear day of an earnest, loving manhood –.

Of course this ultimate aim of the poem is not to be seen in the four verses that I sent you –. One more verse would bring it out –. When I next feel the Divine Afflatus, I'll write the other verse –. Meantime, I thought the four, I sent you, would do well enough as a complimentary effusion, and would be rather too *didactic,* if the full meaning which I intended were brought out – . – After these explanations, read the piece over and see if you do not like it better –. I have made a rough draft of two chapters of my novel: and have about finished my conception of the plot –. I would send you all these to-day; but am suffering very much with bad cold, and feel too badly to write –

Had a letter from Cliff, yesterday –. He writes that he was splendidly received by Gen. Barton and Staff; was messing with them; and was, on the whole, much pleased –. I wrote you the other day by Jim Hines asking for some money for Cliff and myself –. We will both need it, to pay our mess bills –. Direct to me " care of Gen. [Matt] Ransom, Weldon, N. C."

Kiss Mother for me –. I pictured you, to myself, puzzling over the Poem by the light of her countenance –: and I yearned that I might shadow that same light, for one moment, with a kiss –.

I saw Uncle Melville yesterday –. The battery has just been ordered to Kinston, where Cliff is –. He wishes to know something of his little boy from whom he has not heard in two months –. Write me; and I'll convey any information through Cliff –. Uncle looks very well –. I wanted to write you a long letter: but am feeling very badly –.

Your aff. Son,

Sid.

FROM CLIFFORD A. LANIER TO MARY J. A. LANIER

Kinston, N. C.
Jany 7th 1864

My dear Ma

I wrote to Pa from here, on my arrival, about a week ago. I have heard from you since through Bro. Sid – who received news from Pa – at Weldon. My mission here is ended and I leave tomorrow morning for Weldon, will there await – with Bro. Sid – further orders from Maj Milligan – We confidently expect to be sent back to our *second home* on James River.

I met Uncle Melville this morning. His battery is here, just arrived from Weldon. He is up but by no means well, has a huge sty on his eye and suffers with headache in consequence. I found him squatting around a little fire near the rail-road, & would never have recognised him, had I seen him casually, without knowledge of his proximity — — Tis miserable weather and *his* tents were all hung with icicles — I brought him around to my comfortable room at Hdqrs & talked with him some time — He is now acting as Surgeon to the battery, never did a man have such a number of titles — in the course of half an hour I heard him addressed as Dr, Major, Sgt, Mell — &c. Shall go to see him again this evening — —

There was a grand tournament and coronation ball here day before yesterday. The best part of the performance was the tilt of the "Knight of Dixie" — who with knightly black vizard and pasteboard helmet, mounted on a Rosinante-looking mule made the distance of the run (100 yards) in ten minutes (the required time being 8 seconds) & at a slow walk, gallantly bore off the ring on the little end of a fence-rail.

I am rejoiced that you have better rooms than formerly [2] — Suppose that now you will also have Sister with you — I hope she will frequently seek the society of Mary Day and the girls on the hill. Tell her to give much love for me to them: Love to you all & to HER — Continue to direct your letters to us to Petersburg — — Much love to Uncle Clifford & to Aunt Annie —

Your Affte Son

Cliffd A. Lanier.

To Rebecca Alexander [3]

[Weldon, N. C., Jan., 1864?]

P. S.

Dear, glorious Miss Beck!

What shall I say to *you*, that you won't call impertinent! —

[2] For the past year Lanier's parents had been living at Wesleyan Female College, in Macon.

[3] Previously published in *Ex Libris*, X, No. 2 (Johns Hopkins Univ., Jan.,

Will you believe me if I say that I do not know any dream
of my life which I would rather have realized, than this one
which floated before me when I read Ginna's account of " the
quiet nook where stands the Piano, which the dear, loving
fingers of Beck had wreathed with vines "? I imagined myself
there, looking into two such pairs of eyes as I do not think are
in all the world elsewhere: into yours which are calm and gray
and holy, like a Dawn: into hers, which are mysterious and
dark and full of mystic suggestions, like a Twilight: while I,
like a foolish, glaring Noon-day did nothing but stare for dear
life from the Beginning (the Dawn) to the End (which is,
the Twilight.)!

Well, – it is a poor, *un*selfish dream: and I must content
myself with asking if, sometimes when you two are in our nook,
you will not find time to remember one who has no higher
pride than to call both of you

Friend?

To Robert S. Lanier ⁴

Weldon, N. C.
Jan'y 18th "/64

My Dear Pa:

       Your letter arived about fifteen minutes ago –.
Whether or not it brought a tricksy Sprite of Poesy concealed
in its folds, or whether Phoebus Apollo chose just that particular moment, to infuse the Divine Afflatus into me, or

1941). Rebecca Alexander was a friend of Virginia Hankins, and Lanier had
met her at Bacon's Castle several months before (see p. 116, above). This is
apparently a postscript included in a lost letter to Virginia Hankins, for the
envelope is addressed in her handwriting (to " Miss Rebecca Alexander / Care
of Hon. Mark Alexander / Lombardy Grove / Mecklenburg County / Virginia /
Haste ") and was sent from Bacon's Castle—thus indicating that it was forwarded by her. The post mark has been torn off with the stamp; but the
envelope was dated " Jany 11 " by Miss Hankins. The year must have been
1864, since Lanier did not meet Miss Alexander until the autumn of 1863 (see
his letter of Sept. 15, 1863, above), and since he was a prisoner of war in
Jan., 1865. He had spent Christmas, 1863, at Bacon's Castle (see Clifford
Lanier's letter of Dec. 30, 1863, above); the " nook . . . wreathed with vines,"
mentioned in the present letter, seems to refer to this occasion.
  ⁴ Excerpts previously published by Mims, p. 56.

whether the genial sympathy with my literary efforts, you have
exhibited, worked upon my heart, – I don't know –. What I *do*
know is, that there came across me, somewhat in the manner
of a flash of lightning, the last verse, which, I promised, should
inculcate the idea which underlies the little song –. Listen:

> " So Boyhood sets: comes Youth,
>   A night of painful mists and dreams –.
>   It broods, 'till Love's exquisite Truth,
>   The star of a morn-clear Manhood, beams " !

What do you think of it?

Perhaps I ought to say something in regard to the metre, in
which the song is written –. If you have not forgot your
Prosody, you'll remember that the foot called *Iambus,* consists
of two syllables, a short before a long, the accent falling always
on the *long* syllable. The first line of each of my verses contains
three Iambi: the other three lines of each verse, *four* –. Scan-
ning it so, you'll find it perfect; except that I have occasionally
substituted an Anapaest (*Two* short syllables and a long),
which is not only allowable, in Prosody, but is even considered
judicious, sometimes, as a means of breaking the monotony of
the rythm –. I chose this style of metre, purposely: in order to
try my hand at the *terse* way of writing –. I have frequently
noticed in myself a tendency to the diffuse style –; a disposition
to push my metaphors too far, employing a multitude of words
to heighten the *pat*-ness of the image, and so making of it
rather a *conceit* than a metaphor, a fault copiously illustrated
in the poetry of Cowley, Waller, Donne, and others of that
ilk –. In a short poem, with only three or four feet to a line, it
is impossible to do this: and so I selected the metre, on these
grounds, as well as because it was somewhat unusual, and
might possibly charm by its quaintness –. Here, every word has
to tell: and it is quite a trial, to sacrifice as little as possible of
perspicuity, in order to attain terseness –. I succeeded far better
than I anticipated: it was the first time I ever tried it.

I send you, in a large Official-looking envelope, the two first
chapters of the novel [5] –. They are the first rude draughts, just

---

[5] In the surviving MS of *Tiger-Lilies* (Clifford A. Lanier Collection, Johns
Hopkins University), obviously a first draft, Book I, Chapters II-V, and Book

as I dashed them off, at odd times –. I would copy them, but
have not time to do it: hope you will be able to half-read them,
at least so as to gain some idea of the idea –. I'm afraid you'll
grumble at some of the high talk: but, if you do, just convince
me that it's too high, and I'll lower it –. For, you read me right,
as regards the criticism –. I court it, rather than avoid it –.
No man can expect to write perfectly: least of all, *I*: who have
as yet almost no practice, and who have not been able to find
any one whom I was willing to take as a model –. And so your
criticisms will always please me, other things being equal, in
proportion as they are minute and detailed; not only because
they will be of more benefit to me, so, but also as affording
lively proofs of your regard for the pieces under consideration
and for *me* –. Don't forget, tho', a small modicum of praise
whenever you can conscientiously bring it in: perhaps it is a
shameful confession, but it is *true,* that *this praise,* or rather
the *love* which praise indicates in the praiser, is, or has been,
heretofore, the strongest incentive to exertion I ever knew –.
I'll grow independent of it, however; for gradually I find that
my whole soul is merging itself into this business of writing,
especially of writing poetry –. I'm going to try it: and am going
to test, in the most rigid way I know, the awful question
whether it is my vocation –.

Cliff is with me; and we will probably be stationed here for
a month or so –. He had a very agreeable time at Kinston;
and is looking splendidly –. We are comfortably situated: and
what with our flute and books, manage to get a whiff of the
pure air in the upper art-regions, occasionally, even in this
smoky, money-mad Weldon –. I got your remittance of $50:
and Cliff's will be here tomorrow –. Benson has our bundle in
Petersburg –. I'm very anxious to finish my novel; in the hope
of ekeing out that " Adjutant's pay " – Wonder if it *will* do it?
Kiss them all for us –: I wrote Aunt Jane not long ago –.

Yr. aff. Son,

Sid. L. – [6]

III, Chapters IX-XII, bear evidence of having been torn out of a notebook—
possibly for the purpose here indicated of sending them to his father for
criticism.

   [6] In a letter of Jan. 20, 1864, to Clifford Lanier, R. S. Lanier wrote: " We were
glad to get your letter of the 14th to-day; but you will understand our feelings

From Clifford A. Lanier to Robert S. Lanier

Petersburg Va.   Feby 6th 1864

My dear Pa

Theodore Wells' package with its various contents meets us here tonight, as war-worn and jaded, we arrive from the expedition against Newberne.   It is like a glorious Sun-rise after a very dark night, and with the most eager pleasure we opened and read (and Bro Sid smoked Mamie's cigarettes) the communications.

Well, we marched to Newberne and we marched back again – How representative and frequently repeated is Mother Goose's movement of the " King of France marched up the hill &c c "! Sunday morning [7] Bro Sid & I left Kinston – he, mounted and accompanying Genl Pickett – I – with breeches stuck in boots, pedestrianizing – Halted about ten oclock that night – Blistered feet had hardly stopped throbbing before the march was again begun, soon our advance encountered the enemy's pickets, rushed on them, knocked down one with clubbed muskets and captured the other – their reserve, fifty men, occupied strong works and a block house, these were stoutly defended untill daylight which revealed their intrenchments lining the opposite side of a deep creek spanned by one bridge – Quickly we felled tall pines across the stream below, a party was crossed and then Hoke's brigade charging in front across the Lodi-bridge, the enemy gave way, and rushed pell-mell towards their strong tower of defense – New Berne.   The entire camp of the 132nd N. Y. was captured, new clothing & blankets, horses & wagons & two pieces of artillery, much provision & three thousand barrels of corn – It was a beautiful camp, the Officers quarters built in cottage style and furnished with bureaus, mirrors, curtains and all conveniences – much female clothing was taken – oranges, lemons, nuts &c –   The other two columns advancing by different roads failed to come up in time and the works

when we heard of your bro's being affected with so dangerous a disease as dyptheria. Whilst it is true you both excited & allayed our fears, yet we shall be the happier the sooner we hear from you favorably again." There is no reference to this illness in Sidney Lanier's letters.

   [7] Jan. 31, 1864.

around the city seeming to be impregnable, – having no siege pieces, Genl Picket ordered × × × ×[8] movement and by thinking everything must be safe in Kinston. We will remain here two or three days & then possibly go to our station at Fort Boykin –

Conceive our surprise and pleasure at meeting Sam Knox this morning at Weldon – We journeyed with him from there here – Such relation of different histories for the past three years was never heard. He was going to Richmond. Will return in a day or two & we hope to see him again –

I see that you have not yet received my long letter written from Weldon, containing " GOETHE'S WORDS " – my little poem – I hope that the letter is not lost – Tired and writing in this busy office, I can send you nothing this time worthy to be preserved – Bro Sid has written three more chapters of the " novel " – Much love to dear Ma & Sister – All sorts of happy wishes to the " bride " – [9]

Your Son

Clifford A. Lanier

TO MARY DAY

Petersburg   Va
Feby 28th "/64

Good Friend and Sweet:

Your bird-notes have come, floating down to me, out of my Heaven; – dear bird-notes, faint, far off, beautiful, falling from above; – as if a Star-beam should dissolve into music!

But what a Strange, Protean Bird-of-many-Hues art thou!

You're a Lark; for you sing high up in my sky, and while I hear your song, I cannot see you!

And yet you're a Nightingale; for you sing in (what is to me) the night!

Nevertheless, you're a Mocking-Bird; for you warble the strains of another!

[8] The MS is torn at this point, and one or two words are not decipherable.

[9] The reference is to William Lanier's daughter Sallie, who had recently been married to Capt. Tench Schley.

Moreover you're one of the white Doves of Hilda; for *your* Hilda is *Music,* in whose bosom, while she tends the ever-burning Lamp, you nestle and coo; whereat the Passer-by, far-below, looks up at the Tower, and thinks of Heaven!

And, after all, your wings are like the wings of that Eastern, great Bird, the Roc: for your wings overspread my whole Sky, so that my eager upturned eyes see, in the whole Heaven, nothing but you, O sweet, strange, ever-changing, unchanging Bird! – – – – –

And then came your " Charmers "; which, like the Eastern Fisherman's Genie, have all vanished in a cloud of smoke –. Do you know, I have a passion not only for smoking, but for *smoke* also –. What is Man, but a sort of human Cigarita? Is not our soul enveloped in flimsy flesh, just as the tobacco is enveloped in flimsy paper? Is not Life the Manufacturer who pulverizes the leafy Child-Soul to make it burn easy in manhood? Does not God light this human " charmer " at the fires of Love; – whereat our Soul's-aspirations go floating and curling beau-tifully and gracefully, like Smoke, towards Heaven? And does not our flesh taint the Soul's desires, as the burning paper taints the odor of the tobacco-smoke ! – –

And here are your flowers and your prayers: of which two, " I know not which is sweeter, no, not I ": for the flowers pray, and the prayer is a flower! – In the midst of a troop of beautiful Dream-children born of this exquisite Jessamine-fragrance, I sit regal, like King Oberon, presiding over the Sports of his elfin Subjects –. And my Royal Majesty grows sad enough with thinking there's but one Titania, and you are She, and you are not here!

Friend, Friend, Friend!   How shall I bless you, for all these things which assure me that you do not forget me? Oh, I can-not talk of it –. If one were Shivering in a Winter Storm, and should suddenly look up and see a taper Angel's-hand push through the Cloud, and open a " blue break of beauty," and Toss him a rose with a smile, and direct the Sunbeams on his head – – –, one would hardly bow and then proceed to deliver an oration of thanks! And so, if I'm mute, – – – you know why!*

My life, of late, has been so erratic that I have not been able to write at all: and so you'll pardon this hurried scrawl, and regard it only as one of the thousand ways in which my soul, every day, sighs itself across these hateful thousand miles that lie between you and me –. I heard some sweet things said about you a day or two ago, by Mrs Lamar with whom and her husband and Gen Gordon & wife, I came from Goldsboro, N. C. to this place –.[10] She seems to have fallen in love with you: which fact established one congenial point between us immediately! I enjoyed the trip, with my good Compagions du Voyage amazingly: had not seen John Hill [Lamar] for some years before –.

Good Friend, One-Friend, write to me: having spoilt me *so* much, it would be too cruel not to keep on –. I shall look for your letter eagerly: as the Earth might look for the Spring.

Meantime let me write, on the next page a little poem that sang itself through me, the other day – 'Tis the first I've written in three years: I send it to you rather for your criticism than for your admiration. It is a sort of half allegory –: read it twice –.[11]

* *Note by the Editors*—Aint responsible for 'em; didn't see 'em 'till I turned over the page: can't afford to start over –. They are supposed to be tear-drops: and from their color, were evidently shed during an intense fit of the (light) Blues –. [Lanier's comment on four small blemishes that appear on p. 2 of the MS.—ED.]

To Robert S. Lanier [12]

Burwell's Bay, Va.
March 14th "/64

My Dear Pa:

At last, I have got back to my old Stampingground, and begin to entertain some hope of a little rest from my travels –: and a little time to write and dream in –.

---

[10] The reference to Mrs. Lamar is apparently to the wife of John Hill Lamar, the former Janie Taliaferro, who figures in the letters of 1866 and later as Janie Lamar. Gen. Gordon was John B. Gordon, who had given the commencement address at Oglethorpe when Lanier was graduated in 1860.

[11] Here Lanier wrote out a copy of the poem " To ——," sent to his father in the letters of Dec. 7, 1863, and Jan. 18, 1864. All evidence seems to confirm the statement that it was his first poem in three years (see I, 153; also, p. 128, above).

[12] Excerpt previously published by Mims, pp. 55-56. Burwell's Bay was at

Your letter containing two Fifties, per favor of Cottingham, arrived at the most opportune moment imaginable – I had written to you for a remittance only two or three days before, and was most agreeably surprised at having my necessities met so soon –. Travelling is an expensive business, when meals are Ten Dollars apiece –.

I was bitterly disappointed at missing Aunt Jane and the wedded couple –. I went over to Richmond, on my way back here from N. C., expecting to meet them: but they had left only two days previously –.

I am anxious to hear from you –. Does not the last Military Bill compel you to abandon your present situation, and enter the field? What are you going to do about it?

Cliff. and I are having a good time –. We have a large room to ourselves; and lead the most literary life imaginable –. "Our Bay," in this exquisite opening of the Spring, is rarely beautiful: I shall never sufficiently acknowledge my indebtedness to it, for the beautiful Hosts of Thoughts which arise from it, before my eyes, like exhalations, every day and every night –. I'm a better magician, than Owen Glendower: for I call spirits from the vasty deep, and they don't refuse to "come when I do call" –.[13] Indeed so attached have they become to me, that not even the guttural Ichs and barbarous r-r-r-s of the German, with which I plenteously regale their ears, can drive them away –. If I could only call up a Dutch Spirit, I should be a happy man! For then should I have a teacher, the absence of which, now, grieves me sorely – I am learning to read the language easily; but will hardly be able to speak it fluently, for want of some one to converse with, in the popular idiom –. I have succeeded in obtaining a very good German Dictionary; and have a project on foot for getting some of Schiller's and Uhland's poems –. If you should come across any German works, no matter what they are, seize them for me at any price –. I am particularly anxious to get Uhland, Lessing, Schelling, and Tieck –.

Some very grand projects begin to present themselves to me, in connection with the novel – They are projects too which are

Ft. Boykin, or Boykin's Bluff as Lanier usually called it. The "wedded couple" referred to in the third paragraph was Capt. and Mrs. Tench Schley; Aunt Jane was Mrs. A. P. Watt.

[13] The allusion is to *King Henry IV*, Pt. I.

not only grand, but feasible, and which under favorable circumstances would require no long time to advance to maturity –.
You certainly *could n't* ask me to detail them to you, with this
diabolical pale ink, which scarcely makes a visible mark on the
paper, and has already tried my patience sorely –! – And so, till
I get some blacker ink, Leben Sie Wohl!

Tell Sister I got her letter yesterday – Will answer it in a
day or two: and will show her what a narrow escape she has
had from marrying an Ass –.[14]

Don't publish our poems –. After-a-while, when we have
acquired reputation, in other ways, enough to make people read
our poetry, how do you think a book, entitled for instance.
" Poems, by Two Brothers, of Macon, Ga." would look? –

Hopson is going home, or has gone, on furlough –. If you
should meet him, treat him, for my sake, with as much warmth
and cordiality as possible – Make him eat with you and carry
him round to see our friends –. He is a glorious boy: and has
befriended me on many occasions –. He will appreciate friendship coming from you very highly: I have read him many of
your letters, and he already loves you –.

Kiss Ma for us and write us soon –.

Your Son,

Sid. Lanier

From Mary Day [15]

Macon, April 3rd 1864.

Friend Sidney, *dear* friend, a thousand times have I marvelled
at the careless audacity that sent *such* a letter as mine of last
month, to answer *such* an one as yours of a month earlier.
Nor do I expect to mend the matter in these hasty words – only
I would explain to you how that I was quite sufficiently pene-

[14] The reference is to Gertrude Lanier's letter of Feb. 26, 1864, in which she
stated: " My affair with Mr. H. has been satisfactorily arranged & the matter
closed. . . . My dear brother you were right in saying I was unacquainted with
my heart."

[15] This is the earliest of Mary Day's letters to Sidney Lanier that has been
found. It is printed here for the light that it throws on her and on their early
relationship.

trated by your words to have given you a response as *nearly* worthy as any that *I* could ever offer – and that having seized upon a happy *moment* I wasted it and its fourteen brief companions in preliminaries until the relentless tide of visitors & social calls swept me abruptly from you.   Then – unwilling to delay – I forced myself to finish in a dull distracted interval, and wrote you a few lines of nothings; – clippings from the worn edges of my long restrained heart's message to you. Every remembrance of the failure has annoyed and distressed me, and I've only been trying to discharge all the claims of *duty* which pressed upon me, before composing myself for a long unfettered talk with my " Sir Philip." (Sid, do you know I'm a little *in awe of you?* Intellectually, I mean; 'tis a new mood, " coming over " & " overcoming " me, and 'tis so powerful as to interfere seriously with my ease just at present! *No jest.*)   Friend! your poem has taken possession of me – I've *thought out* some *half*-dozen letters to you on the subject – though I was too weary to pen them. It " sings itself through *me* " all the time – as passages of finest music will haunt me 'till I grow fairly nervous – O, it is exquisite – like German music – we know, at first, 'tis worth a second hearing and a farther study, and it gives present delight, also – but that first delight leaves hardly its *memory* with us; so is it absorbed in the new and ever-growing beauties, which sweet *intimacy* yields. The first two lines are *full,* they mind me of the lifelike, wondrous sketches I've heard that great masters can produce by three or four skilful strokes of the pencil, or sweeps of the brush portraying more, and more vividly than a meaner hand in hours of laborious, minute touches. A most perfect sunset vision – over which I can dream indefinitely!   And the last verse – – I silently bow before it in admiration, but then am compelled to caress it – in love – " Love's exquisite Truth – the Star of a morn-clear manhood." – But I'm on the verge of soliciting *your* appreciation and appealing to *your* taste and admiration, and I must retract – or stop short, lest you forget the poet's name – in one of your wanderings – and bestow such praise on him as might put your modesty to the blush, when you " found yourself." But I must tell you of *one* triumph – over my quiet undemonstrative Papa – (For – I hope you did'nt imagine I could keep yr. sweet song to myself – I'm both *generous* and *grasping*; grasping in seeking due appreciation of you in other minds – and generous, in sharing such sources of delight with *all* the *few* whom I think capable of rendering that appreciation.) I gave your poem for Father's perusal (tho' I thought 'twould be decidedly out of his line, weighed down as he is by business cares and political anxieties) – for I wanted him to know you better you being so dear to me. I silently watched him read and recommence it then left the room; and returning – fully ten minutes later – to my amazement, Father was still intently reading it. Let me add, " to my dismay and discomfiture " – for I concluded that his gentle loving sympathy with all my pleasures was leading him to patiently ponder over something which he found too " misty " to be easily grasped. So I dolefully asked " Reading that still? Can't you see *any-thing* in it? " 'Twixt a laugh and a cry I inquired – when Father looked up with strong but quiet surprise at me – and exclaimed with most unusual warmth and pleasure – " O, no! why it is so beautiful I could not stop reading it! " Or some words to that effect. It took him by storm, at once, and I repaid his good taste by allowing him to read dear Cliff's characteristic and soul-full verses.[16] He was *very* much charmed with them – who could help it? The rhythm is so striking and original – it has a great fascination for me. O, Sid – do you know I've nearly lost my heart (what's left of it) to your friend Mr. Hopson –? He made a first visit to me yesterday morning – and after one hour and a half's *parley* (for I fear the attraction was not sufficiently mutual for me to call it *a siege*, on his part –) I surrendered unconditionally. His presence in church this morning was a sore temptation and distraction to me. Are you amazed – and *shocked?* Moderate your censure! – for I assure you we talked of little else than you and Cliff – and he won my l---1----1--*liking* (that's all I *dare say*.) Just by his warm friendship and unison of feeling with yourselves. Why it was *next* best to meeting you! I've been almost embarrassed since in recalling the surprising freedom with which I talked to him, a stranger, and though he acknowledged it with kindness when we parted – I fear 'twas an impulse of courtesy, and that he

---

[16] The poem " Goethe's Words," mentioned in Clifford's letter to his father on Feb. 6, 1864, above, and probably sent to Mary Day about the same time. The poem was used by Clifford Lanier in his novel, *Thorn-Fruit*, p. 91.

entertains an odd opinion of me. I wish you would write me about him – describe him that I may compare it with my own estimate; for he returns to N. C. this week – and I shall not see him again. Another person you must teach me to know – *tell me more of Ginna H.* Perhaps she might prefer the prefix of " Miss " – from *me* – but I don't *feel* it and *won't* say it – to you. I think of her as often as tho' we were personal friends – and with as earnest an interest. I made Mr. Hopson talk to me of her – a task he willingly undertook. His coloring harmonized beautifully with your own. What, is she thinking of now – and how grows your pleasant friendship? Sid. will you give her my love? I send it in trustfull trust. And now, – to a subject which deeply interests us both. Gussie wrote to you a fortnight since – did she tell you that *Ginnie* is soon to be married?[17] They have never hinted it to me – but I know it quite as certainly – and yesterday I was confidently told that it was to be the 19th of this month which surprised me – for I had placed it somewhat later. I think it is correct – but I've been absent so long[18] that I attribute to that the strict reserve they have maintained towards me on the subject. I've been *fully* assured since Christmas day that the engagement was positive – and she is very happy – no one can mistake it – so I've *tried* to banish all regrets & selfish pain in seeing her lost to us by this fearfully engrossing sentiment. I believe that Capt. Bacon is worthy of her, if spotless character and purity of mind can claim such a prize – for to these, I have heard his gentler friends yield a tribute which they esteem unprecedented. And he loves her fully as she deserves, I might say, *worships* instead of *loves*. He has *never* known a mother or a sister – tho' he is one who would have appreciated them – & his whole life's demand has concentred in this love. He is the soul of honor – and will prove to her the soul of devotion. Thus have my " hasty words " increased and multiplied into a letter – but I believe *you* will not weary of your true friend

Mary.

---

[17] Augusta Lamar's cousin Virginia Lamar was married to Capt. A. O. Bacon. She is hereafter referred to in the Lanier letters as " Ginnie Bacon."

[18] Gertrude Lanier, in her letter of Mar. 18, 1864, to her brother Sidney had written: " Mary Day is expected home next week." Where she had been visiting is not known.

To Robert S. Lanier [19]

Boykin's Bluff, Va.
April 9th "/64

My Dear Pa:

The quick change from the bustling life of Richmond to our quiet, lonely hill here, seems more like the transition of a dream's shifting scenes, than the ordinary contrast of real life –. To *me,* it is like a leaf from the sensuous, to the *super* sensuous, world, – a flight from the land of men to the land of Spirits –. For altho' " our hill here " *is* " quiet and, lonely " to him who sees and hears only with the *physical* eye and ear, yet, to me, who am growing daily more in the habit of looking and hearing with the Senses of the Spirit, there is, here, anything *but* silence and Solitude –. Troops of Spirits, multitudes of Strange, airy Shapes, wheel and hover about my hill, like Sea-gulls about some lone Crag in the Ocean; and these, by long acquaintance, are become familiar Spirits, so that I sit in the midst of them, like Prospero, and am not afraid –. And the winds, here, are never silent: always they are either breathing some low, soft tones, as if Heaven were sending some message by them to her Messenger, the Spring: or they rise into a wild, joyful song, chanting

–. " With an awful, jubilant voice,
As when a mighty people rejoice
With Shawms, and cymbals and Harps of gold,
And the tumult of their acclaim is rolled
Through the open gates of the city afar,
To the Shepherd who watcheth the Evening-Star "; [20]

or they rise, higher, into loud, indignant, scornful complainings: or they Shrill out startling treble notes, like the Shrieks of

---

[19] A telegram from R. S. Lanier to Mrs. R. S. Lanier (Clifford A. Lanier Collection, Johns Hopkins University) sent from Richmond and received in Macon, Mar. (?), 1864, reads " All right boys well." Lanier's letter opens with a reference to a visit in Richmond with his father, who had by this time obtained a military commission. The envelope of this letter is addressed: " R. S. Lanier, care Sgt. Benson, Petersburg, Va. Sgt. B. will please retain this until R. S. L. calls and then hand it to him, obliging S. C. L."

[20] Tennyson, " Dying Swan."

women: or they sink into strange and mournful monologues, as if wailing dirges for the dead that have died in despair, or as if uttering the unimagined agony of those whom Dante places in the lowest pit of Hell, and who, he says, are to be pitied most of all for they have not even " the *hope* of death "–. And then the Wave-noises! – He who has not listened on a Still night, with straining ears, to the Surf beating on a long Shore, – does not know the meaning of the words, – *confusion* of voices –.   The roaring of Lions, the growling of Bears, the snarling of Hyenas, the hissing of Serpents, the war-yells of Indians, the Songs of birds, the cries of men in terror, the Shouts of children at play, the violent Sobs and Shrieks of women, the cackling of geese, the neighing of horses, – all these and a thousand other sounds float to one's ear as if from a distance, strangely commingled and interblended –   It is as if all the men, women, children, beasts, birds, and reptiles of the world had suddenly been proselyted into Howling Dervishes, and had chosen the same moment of time for their infernal devotions –.

Apropos of contrasts: send us the Coffee and Sugar, by Express, to Petersburg –. I have just recently discovered what a " good thing " Coffee is –.

Kiss Mother and Sister for us: and give our love to Hopson, if he is with you –. Write us soon –

Your Son,   Sid. L.

To Mary Day

Ft. Boykin   Va
April 12th "/64

Du Himmel's Liebchen: – will " Himmel " be jealous, think you, if I dare to call you also *Mein* Liebchen?

If she does, I'm a thunderstricken man, beyond hope and doubt! – for I've been calling you that and many another friendly caressing name, the livelong night –. You must know I was on guard, last night: and about Ten O'clock a small faint breeze came out of the South, and passed by me, and moved over the Bay (which has had a sad time of it, poor Thing! for a month or two past, what with the Vernal Equinox and the long Easterly gales that come in its retinue) and whispered something, I know not what, to the tossing waves; whereupon they quickly calmed and fell into a magical quiet: the clouds, meanwhile, moving kindly away so that the Stars might look down and see –. Well; in this unbroken rest under the Stars, my beautiful bay reminded me of *you* –. Its quietude, concealing its depth, – was like *yours*: its pale white hue, with two large Spots that two passing clouds shaded into a deep and tender grey, – made me think of your face and your eyes: it held in its bosom lovingly the Stars of Heaven, as you hold in yours the *Truths* of Heaven, which are the Stars of the Spirit: it sent up graceful wreaths of mist and I thought perhaps *you* were *praying,* then: lastly, it loved me, and so do you!

Voila a perfect picture ! – and I'm tempted to call *you* Miss Bay, and *it,* the Day ! – Didn't you crown my Cap with Bay (leaves) once, on that unforgotten day at " Paradise "? [21] And can't I return the compliment by showering " Bay " upon you?

And don't all the god Story-books pathetically exhort, Children, O, bay your parents? and, O, Ain't I baying my friends, which is next thing to it?

And didn't that dog, that the man " would rather be," " bay the moon," that luminary of night? Ain't I entitled, on the Chacun-a-son-gout principle, to Bay the *Day* itself, if I want to?

Now, maledictions on this " bay "! For my poor head's in as great a maze with the word, as was Capt. Wrogge's wife with the cookery-book! Well, poets have ever been crazed by the Bay: – if I could only be like Aurora Leigh, and " choose *no* bay "!

I seriously fear I shall verify the predictions which my Mother made, when she was teaching me to spell: " Ah me," sighed she. " I'm afraid he will *never* get beyond his b,-a,- ba,s! Thou sad fate! to be drowned in a " b,-a-, ba "!!

Like that " little Lamb " which " Mary (?) had," my only Stock of language consists of that one word " Ba-a- "!

And so not knowing any more puns on " Bay " I'm fairly

[21] The reference is to the October day at Mrs. Freeman's, in 1863.

brought to bay: whither you are doubtless wishing, by this time, that I had never been brought!

Have you read Marius and St. Denis, of Les Miserables? If not, do so: some of my favorite theories are embodied there –. Victor Hugo has dreamed and loved and thought with an earnest Soul: for that reason, if for no other, he is worth reading –. He tells his Story, moreover, with a charming, naive vivacity: frequently rising high above *that* –. I can't find your Charles Auchester, anywhere; to my most bitter disappointment –.[22] I was particularly anxious to read it, inasmuch as I have serious thoughts of writing a book which should have much to say upon the same subject: and I would like, immensely, to know whether any other writer has anticipated my method of treatment –. Wherefore, Mamie, good Mamie, Sweet Mamie, exquisite, unimaginable Mamie, (put your hands on your ears, you know what is coming) won't you just please sit down and write me very soon what Mr Charles Auchester believes about Music " and sich like "? And won't you pardon a letter that's written very hastily, 'midst War's alarms? and tell me the address of our friend Capt. Little?[23] And give my regards to your Father, Bro, Fulton, Ogden and the rest of 'em and kiss Gussie and Sister and true-hearted Mrs Freeman (whose letter I've got) for me? And believe that I am, heart, soul and hand,

Your

Friend?

Cliff Sends a great deal of Love!!!   (see Signboards as

" Sugar
Coffee
Bacon
Nails
&
Groceries ")

[22] Lanier read Elizabeth Sheppard's *Charles Auchester* (London, 1853), and there are numerous references to it in later letters. The character of Seraphael in the novel is supposed to have based on Mendelssohn.

[23] George Little was an army comrade of Mary Day's brother, H. C. Day, and possibly a college friend of Lanier's. He is several times mentioned in later letters, most frequently in letters of Sept. and Oct., 1874.

To Robert S. Lanier [24]

[Ft. Boykin, Va.,] May 7th "/64

My Dear Pa:

I have unexpectedly found an opportunity to get a note through the Yankee lines, by a scout who goes up to Petersburg today –

You need have no anxiety about Cliff and me, if you should receive no letters from us – Our communication with the Railroad has been cut off so far as *regular* mails are concerned: but we will probably have frequent chances of sending letters to you by our scouts, who find no difficulty at all in penetrating the weak line of the enemy –.

Cliff. and I, having received no orders to leave, are going to remain in our present locality, which I do not name for obvious reasons –. Somewhat to our discomfiture, we are probably in the *safest* place in the Southern Confederacy –

The *Spirits,* that filled my last letter to you, fled at the coming of your last to me, like Tom O'Shanter's warlocks at the break of day –. Tell Mother that I shall, at the earliest opportunity, send her a detailed account of the present status of my Wardrobe, of my daily diet, of all and sundry my outgoings and incomings, and of everything else that is noticeable in a " Bushwhacker's " household economy –. Meantime, seriously speaking, I thank you most heartily for your letter, and so does Cliff, for it gave us the prettiest, coziest peep into that dear Home-room, which is now become sacred to us both!

I write hurriedly – Kiss Mother and Sister a hundred times for us: and give our love to Mamie Day and Gussie –. Ask Sister to explain from us to Jennie Lamar,[25] why we have not sent our congratulations to her, " under our own hand," upon the recent happy event, to which we received invitations: let

[24] The address seems to have been deleted from this letter, and the two following, in response to orders from the army censor. But Clifford Lanier's letter of May 14, 1864, to his father bears the address " Still on the Bay." In it he wrote: " Our duty here is to procure information about the enemy & transmit it to Petersburg."

[25] This is Virginia Lamar, whose name is spelled both Ginna and Ginnie in Gertrude Lanier's letter of Mar. 18, 1864, to her brother, in which she refers to Ginnie Lamar's engagement to Capt. Bacon.

Sister Gertrude salute the fair bride sisterly on the cheek for me, as I should have done had I been there — Our love to Mrs Freeman —

Receive all that you could desire from Your Son,

                                        Sid. Lanier

To Robert S. Lanier

                              [Ft. Boykin, Va.,] May 28th "/64

My Dear Pa:

After many long days of suspense and anxiety, we have just got your letter, written twenty days ago, (7th May)—. Having been sent before the commencement of Johnson's retreat,[26] it contained not a word of all that we wanted to hear concerning the state of things, at home, resulting from that singular movement —. What does Gen. J. intend to do? I know nothing of him, except what I could gather from his Peninsula campaign and his short administration in the Vicksburg region:— judging from *these,* it seems to me he is a sort of monomaniac on " abandoning " and " retreating "—.

We hear that the enemy are in a few miles of Atlanta —: and fear you will suffer from raiding-parties —. Meantime, with the utmost anxiety, we await further news from you —.

Am very sorry you didn't receive our letters —. Have written you *four* in the last three weeks —. Doubtless your failure to get them was caused by the recent numerous tappings of the railroads, with which the Yankee Cavalry have been solacing themselves by way of sweet revenge for the shower of defeats which we have poured upon their armies since the opening of the Spring campaign —.

I fear that Major M.'s dispatch, (sent, undoubtedly, with the *best* of motives) overrated the action to which it referred, and magnified your fears as to our future security —.[27] I wrote you

[26] Gen. Joseph E. Johnston began his retreat in north Georgia on May 13, 1864. He was removed from his command on July 18, six weeks before the fall of Atlanta, being replaced by Gen. J. B. Hood.

[27] On Apr. 28, 1864, Major J. F. Milligan had telegraphed R. S. Lanier from Petersburg: " Your sons are a credit to you & a pride to their state. In the action of the 14th inst, their gallantry was particularly conspicuous. Thank God they

an account, somewhat in detail, of the Affair, a month ago: hope you have received it by this time –. I did *not* lose my flute, *nor* the Novel, having taken the precaution to secure them, together with one or two other of my treasured " movables and hereditaments " about my person, in my haversack –. We lost all our clothes, however: apropos of which: – a citizen, who was taken prisoner by the Yanks, on their march down the road, and who accompanied them to our camp, told us, (after he was released) that he heard the scoundrels remarking, as they rummaged our knapsacks &c, " Talk about ragged Rebels! The d – d Rebs have got better clothes than *we* have! " – – The compliment to our wardrobe, however, was but a poor compensation for the loss of it –.

Dear, good Grandpa! As I read his letter, the most passionate yearning arose in me to go to him, and spread before him and about him all that love which these long years of separation have collected silently as a dam collects water, in my heart – How beautiful is his old age! And how I would glory in ministering about it, and in showing him my admiration for those noble qualities which often, in my reveries upon them, have made me stretch out my hand, so to draw them from *his* life into my own –. Old Romans are rare, in these bad days: and that, to me, makes the contemplation of this glorious old man so much the finer sight –. God bless him! And may his happiness be as full as our love for him could ask, or our reverence demand!

I send you a little poem I wrote t'other day –.[28] It is the

---

are well & hearty. Regards to your esteemed family " (Clifford A. Lanier Collection, Johns Hopkins University). The activities of April and May were caused by Gen. Butler's advance on Petersburg, which broke up the Confederate signal line, leaving Lanier's party of scouts cut off. These experiences form the background of the few actual war experiences related in *Tiger-Lilies* (V, 98-136).

[28] The poem Lanier sent his father is obviously the poem " To G. H." The MS copy that he sent to " Ginna " Hankins bears the date May 23, 1864 (Hankins Family Collection, Johns Hopkins University). A quotation from a lost letter by Virginia Hankins appears on p. 6 of Lanier's Ledger (obviously the " note from G. H." to which, as Lanier wrote his father, his poem was " an Impromptu " reply). It reads:

" Do you remember the Brown Bird ' in the Drama of Exile [by Elizabeth Barrett], whose song as he sat on his tree in Paradise, was the last sound heard by Adam as he fled with Eve, ' along the glare '? So, O Friend, do I send my cry for you across these broad stretches of moonlight that lie between us." To

only " Love-song " I ever produced: but the conceit in it brought
me some solace, in these " bitter hours," besides drawing some
very sincere praise from the fair friend who inspired it –. I
send it to you in the hope that you may like it better than my
last, (at least, the *verbal* part and the *prosodial* construction)–.
It was written at a flash, in reply to a note from G. H., and
might be called, strictly, an Impromptu – The " *love* " referred
to in it is merely Friendship, as it were, " called so for short ":
which *she* and I, (perfectly understanding each other, and
growing dearer friends with each moment of our frequent
meetings during the last year) have agreed to do, that so, in
quite an innocent, dove-like, billing-and-cooing way, we might
commit all those delightful little sentimental *extravaganzas,*
which belong to youthful friendship as well as youthful love –.

I have no news –. Our campaign progresses well: but I have
a " heart for any fate "–. Have you ever realized how splendid
is this truth, that, whereas it *is* possible to conquer and enslave
a man's *body*, it is yet quite utterly *im*possible to subjugate his
soul? and that consequently a true man is always, by a divine
right, essentially *free,* since even when bound hand and foot he
may always defy and shame his captors with an unconquerable
heart? It's perfectly glorious! – Deal out a thousand kisses
and loving embraces to our Mother and Sister: and send another
thousand to the dear ones in Alabama –; from your and their

S. C. L.

To Mary Day

There or Thereabouts
[Ft. Boykin, Va.,] July 1st ″/64

On a far, lonely Island, in the vast old Ocean of Silence, with
toil and Slow labor I learn Prospero's art –. . I succeed –.
Already have I subdued my Caliban: – and at this moment I
am uttering the Spell-words which shall bring into my service
bright Ariel, bright, airy Ariel, to whom my only bidding shall

this quotation is added a note in Lanier's hand: " Extract from letter of G. H.
recd at 3. B. Reply on opposite page." And on p. 7 of the Ledger, the opposite
page, is the poem " To G. H.," dated 1864 (see I, 154). The quotation in the
following paragraph of this letter is from Longfellow, " A Psalm of Life."

be, ply thou between me and the dear Home-Shore, my Venice, where once, in being loved, I was a Doge, and where yet, in being loved, I am a Doge, albeit the waves roll many a mile betwixt us –. Ah, thou Home-Shore, that at the same time dost burn in the glow of eternal Sunset and glitter in the dew of immortal dawn, thou Venice whose flowers perfume all my dreams and whose music floats and hovers down all my life as down a Cathedral-aisle, my thought turns to thee and I become a fanatic, I dream of the dear ones who dwell in thee, and who love me, and I become a God!

Friend, my heart uttered this sacred thing; and I could not help transcribing it for you, that you might know how jubilantly, when I dream of home and you, I cry, I am in fellowship with the Gods –.

A kind friend has sent me a Germanbook containing extracts from various German authors, in the original –. It has been the daintiest treat of my life: and constantly in reading it, my thought has been of you –. I cannot resist the temptation of sending you a specimen of its extracts –. The following little song, by Herder,[29] altho' not the most beautiful is the first that occurs to me –. My translation is *perfectly* literal, almost: which, I think far better than the most elaborate *liberal* translation I could make –. It is a

" Spring – Greeting " –

" Softly floats through all my Soul
A lovely, tiny chiming –.
Ring out, thou little Song of Spring.
Ring out upon the distance –.

Chime out, away, to $\begin{cases} \text{the house} \\ \text{my home} \end{cases}$

Where the violets grow: –
And if thou haply see a Rose, –
Give my love to it! "

[29] The " Frühlings Grüss " which Lanier ascribes to Herder is actually *Neue Gedichte*, " Neuer Frühling," VI, by Heine, and is not correctly quoted; but Lanier may have followed an incorrect text, and ascription, in the " Germanbook" given him. The literal translation of the poem sent at this time to Mary Day differs radically from the free translation made at Point Lookout Prison in Dec., 1864, and published by Lanier in 1866, his first poem to be printed. The second translation, from Tanner, has not been previously published. Both are included here because they are inextricably bound up in the context of the letter (see I, 5).

The original is more musical than any piece of German Poetry
I know –. Listen:

> " Frühlings – Grüss " –
> " Leise zieht durch mein Gemüth
>   Liebliches Gelaüte.
> Kling aus, kleines Fruhlings-lied.
>   Kling hinaus in der Weite –.
> Kling hinaus bis an das Haus
>   Wo die Veilchen spriessen:
> Wenn du eine Rose schau'st
>   Sag', ich lass sie grüssen! "

Another, by Tanner:

> " Eine Welle sagt zur andern,
>   ' Ach, wie kurz is dieses wandern '!
> Sagt die zweite zu der dritten,
>   ' Kurz gelebt ist kurz gelitten ' "!

Which I have ventured to versify, somewhat liberally:

> " A wave said to a second, dying,
>   ' Thou too wilt die to-morrow ':
> The second died, to a third one Crying,
>   ' Short life, short sorrow ' "!

Friend, Friend! when we meet, what a delicious time won't
we have revelling in these fairy-lands –

I have received your letters, and, recently, the piece of music
sent by Hopson –. I need not say to you, that all of your words,
breathing so much friendliness, were inexpressibly sweet to me:
nay, too sweet to talk of at all –. They are written in my heart
of hearts: no world-waves of any Sorrow or Joy are strong
enough to wash them out –.

I enclose you a poem which Ginna Hankins handed me some
days ago saying, " send this, with my love, to Mamie Day "–.
You will find it rarely beautiful at the first reading, and more
so, by far, at the tenth: it will repay your deep study –. It's
by an English Anonymous –.

Child, may all friendly Blessings, like the white doves of
Hilda, hover about your dear head: and, in their midst, do not
forget, sometimes to look down out of your tower upon your

                                        Friend –.

My very kindest regards to y͏ʳ Father, & Brother – Where is
Capt. Little? Love to M͏ʳˢ Freeman & Gussie – Cliff sends love
to you – I write very hurriedly –   L.

FROM CLIFFORD A. LANIER TO GERTRUDE LANIER

Dunn's Hill
Petersburg Va.
July 27͏ᵗʰ /64

My darling Sister
            This is a lovely balmy, dreamy, misty morning
and I wish that I could surmount all this intervening distance,
lovingly grasp your hand and talk of all those whom we love.
Having heard nothing from you for nearly two months I was
delighted to get your letter of yesterday, of such late date as the
20͏ᵗʰ I was equally surprised to see it dated from Cokesbury.[30]
How much you have been doing of which we know nothing!.
Let me tell you of our movements. After dodging the Yankees
in Surry so long we were a few days ago ordered up here &
sadly parting with so many good friends, here we are. What
would you give for a new silk dress from Nassau? Or how
would you like to take a sea-voyage? Well I see you are
completely mystified & will explain. The Sec'y of War has
made a requisition on Maj. M[illigan] for Signal men to go on
Blockading ships. The vessels are not yet ready & we, selected
by Maj M to be of the detail, are in the mean time stationed
here at one of the Signal posts around this invested city. We
are at the best post of the line, on Dunn's Hill. Every hour
or two the enemy throw their mortar shells at the devoted city.
Two have just burst below me with a " CHI-BELUNG " and
a hurtling, rushing sound, like that of a startled flock of
partridges.
            Petersburg is one vast encampment, every yard is a bivouac

[30] Gertrude Lanier and her mother were at Cokesbury, S. C., with the family
of Mrs. T. D. (Wilhelmina Lanier) Eason, of Charleston, S. C. On July 26
Gertrude wrote Sidney Lanier from Cokesbury and referred to reports of his
recent illness and thinness.
     In a letter of Aug. 6, 1864, to his sons, R. S. Lanier wrote: " Cokesbury is
about 60 miles beyond Columbia—in the direction of Montvale Springs, & not
more than 100 miles from it as the crow flies."

& every man a soldier. Good news comes in this morning of a
victory by Genl [Jubal A.] Early. God grant we may soon
drive the vandals from Petersburg.   I am glad that you & Ma
are in quiet Cokesbury with good Aunt Mina —   How is Uncle
Tom? We will probably not go blockading for some time.
Write to us very frequently. Forgive this disjointed style of letter
writing for it is hard to compose oneself in this uncertainty.
Love to dear Ma & Aunt Mina, Uncle Tom and the children.
We have seen our friend Hopson & enjoyed a day with him.
God bless you all.

Your Brother

Cliff. A. Lanier

TO VIRGINIA HANKINS

Dunn's Hill, near Petersburg
July 28th "/64

Meine Heiss-geliebte, have you ever dreamed the emotions
of a soul which has just taken its first step into Heaven? Did
not your loving Heart know that when you sealed the thrice-
blessed letter which I have just read, you were closing a fair
Heaven-Gate, which I was to be the first to open?

In this tumult, which is at once wild and familiar, exultant
and humble, sweet and sad and glorious; in this whirlpool of
feeling, which has all the fury of the MahlStrom and all the
grace and glitter of an eddy in a Sun-lit brook; in this strange
enchantment which converts the screaming of Shells into a
music that floats me high up into Heaven,—— I cannot think,
nor write; the morning-wind, which flutters the white page,
(the dear, envied page so lately pressed by *your* hand!) seems
to me " the mighty breath of a coming Genius ": and, like Jean
Paul's Gustav, dazzled, bewildered, breathing such a prayer as
never mortal breast contained before, I throw myself upon the
earth, to dream of my Little *One,* mine own Ginna, in whose
name there comes to me all the freshness of rustling leaves at
Dawn, all the passionate purity of odorous dew on flower-
petals, all the strange music into which Star-beams convert
themselves in a Poet's Soul, all the " Tender grace of a day that

is dead," [31] but that lives again, forever, in my soul, with the most beautiful of resurrections –.

Shall I tell you how, each night, a dainty, white hand, with the sweet blue veins branching over it, presents itself to me in the darkness, and how, when I have seized it, and pressed it to my bosom, and covered it with a thousand kisses, I whisper, " Good Night, Ginna," – and then turn me to my sleep, content, as if I had said a prayer? Shall I speak to you of the thrill that comes to me with my salutation, " Good-Morning, Little One," which I utter when I awake, and which then quivers and glitters like a drop of dew upon the unfolding flower of my life for all that day? Shall I describe to you how all the Stars at night seem to me Love-lights in a myriad brown eyes, that look down on me lovingly and softly, and into which I gaze until my soul fails and grows dim with an infinite, sad yearning to draw near you?

Dearest Brown-Eyes, these things belong to the holy kingdom of the Inarticulate –. In a silence deep as Night, I brood over my dear dream of you; – and I believe that I have a license to die, in having entered into so high a place in such a heart as yours –. And so; – content in a love which has ceased to question itself, and which, self-unconscious as a flower, quietly awaits its own outblushing and unfolding, careless whether it turn out a flower of Love or a flower of Friendship, certain that it will be beautiful and perfect and all-satisfying in *either* event,— — I live, begging that the Unknown One may fold you in his Infinite Arms as lovingly as would I in my finite ones, did not the mysterious Fate-Wall rise so high between you and your most loving and yearning

Colin.

To Virginia Hankins

Petersburg Va
August 1st ″/64

Best Friend, I know that *you* will not grow weary of loving words; and so, altho' I wrote you yesterday by Capt. C[ausey], I cannot resist the temptation of scrawling a short note to you,

[31] Tennyson, " Break, Break, Break." Gustav was a character in Jean Paul Richter's novel, *The Invisible Lodge*.

by Walton, who leaves for the Blessed Land (not of Heaven, but of Surrey) to-night –.

Thou sweetest Little One that ever filled the heart of a man, with what passionate longing do I gaze across this desolated city, across the men and the cannons and the smoke of battle, towards the dear spot which shines upon my soul from afar with a bright, unspeakable holiness, – like the unattainable blessedness of a Star to a lost Spirit – !

Here sit I, and dream of the haunted fields, over which you and I have ridden, in enchanted twilights which, as if by some magic spell-word, compelled our hearts, – as well as the timorous Moon and Stars, to disclose themselves; – and from behind those encircling trees, – arise a thousand exquisite memories, like stars, spangling all the blue of our unbroken friendship and filling my dream with a rare and golden light –. This light is from you; and I, who have been all my life crying, what Goethe only cried at his death, " More light, more light," – bless you for it, with such blessings as I can not utter, with such glowing in my heart as makes me write, for fear of sacrilege –. The sweet words of your letter, hovering, in the light of beautiful and poetic images, were to me the

> " Pleiads rising in a mellow shade
> Like fireflies tangled in a Silver braid " – [32]

I read them right, and believed them all –. It is impossible they should not be true –. And so I do not ask you, continue to love me so, and to write me so –. You *will* do it, you *must*; the dread of that dark hour, in which it should become possible for you to *dis*continue filling my heart with your love and your beautiful words, would forever prevent me from contemplating it – I await, with impatience, the next-comer, who is to bring me another Inspiration, another Rose that perfumes My Soul with all holy and sweet thoughts, from you –. By Petrarch! (and that's a mighty oath, for a lover) do these men, these Waltons and Causeys, know that they carry Star-light in their letter-bags, do they know that their Coat-pockets are full of Heaven, that a whole beautiful and stainless Eden, with all its flowers and fruits and Four Rivers of Delight, lies perdu in the

[32] Tennyson, " Locksley Hall " (misquoted).

enchanted compass of those rough Confederate Envelopes, which they soil with their greasy fingers?

Write me of all that you see or hear or read or think or feel –!

If ever two souls were near together, yours and mine are so –. Out of this soul-proximity arises a sort of right that each should have carte-blanche, as it were, into all the arcana of the other. To share all your thoughts and all your feelings would be at once my most glorious privilege and my most exquisite pleasure.

You know, Little One, that I am *not*

Goethe!

To Robert S. Lanier

Petersburg Va
August 2nd /64

My Dear Pa

I can scarcely express to you the relief which I experienced on receiving your letter yesterday, written July 25th.[33] It had been two month since I heard from you; your letter written on May 24th having reached me just two months after that date –. The papers of day before yesterday announced a Yankee Raiding-party at Clinton, Ga. moving on Macon; and I, not knowing what your capabilities for defence were, supposed that you would have the old tale repeated in which " our forces, consisting principally of Militia, made a gallant resistance, but were over-whelmed by superior numbers, and routed &c &c," and that our beautiful city would fall prey to the barbarians –. But we have, this morning, the cheering news that Genl Iverson has met the enemy near Clinton, defeating him and capturing several hundred of his men –. And so, with our letter from you informing us that you are comfortably situated with our letter from Sister, also recd yesterday, loudly praising the kind hospitalities of Aunt Mina, and with one from Mother full of

---

[33] R. S. Lanier's letter of July 25, 1864, to " My dear Sons " refers to Sidney Lanier's letter of July 1 (lost). With his wife and daughter away from Macon, R. S. Lanier had moved out to Camp Cooper, where he was serving as adjutant to Major Rowland. He reported raids near Covington, Athens, Madison, Eatonton, and Milledgeville. And in his letter of Aug. 6 he gave a detailed account of the repulse of Gen. Stoneman's raid on Macon by militia under Gen. Alfred Iverson and of the victory at Clinton.

all love and holy invocations, we rest content, and for the first time in two long months allow ourselves to think with satisfaction of the dear ones whom we long so much to see –.

Cliff and I have been "rudely torn" from our pleasant abiding-place in Surrey, and will probably remain in Petersburg for some time –. We are here awaiting orders from the War Department to go aboard a Blockading Vessel from Wilmington to Nassau or Bermuda – [34] Meantime we are stationed at a place near Petersburg, immediately in rear of Genl Beauregard's Hd'Qr's, being the terminal Post of a signal line which stretches along nearly the whole front of our army –.

It is not yet absolutely certain that we will be ordered to the blockades: but esteeming it highly probable, we are held in readiness to obey the orders promptly, should they come – It is described to me, by a friend of mine who has been engaged for some time as a signal man in the blockading business, as a most delightful and desirable position, since one is there surrounded by pleasant and agreeable gentlemen, lives well, has plenty of leisure to read, and frequent opportunities to visit friends for a week or two, besides being enabled to make advantageous purchases of useful articles in the cheap markets of Nassau and Bermuda.

Affairs are very quiet here along our lines, tho' it is rumored to-day that Grant is again moving forces to his left, threatening the Petersburg & Weldon R. R. The excitement consequent upon the recent springing of the Yankee mine has subsided; and, beyond a little picket firing and an occasional shell shrieking into the city, an air of Sabbath calm prevails –. I am strong in the hope that the campaign, and, with it, the war, is nearly over –. Grant's repeated failures, and the terrible slaughter of his men (we yesterday shovelled six hundred dead Yankees into their own mine, the grave which they had dug for us!) are already beginning to excite in the mind of our erratic enemy that distrust which has always been the inevitable prelude to a change of Commanders and the abandonment of a campaign –. Several staunch War-papers at the North have recently come out for peace on *any* terms: and I firmly believe that since the

---

[34] The official records of the U. S. War Department show that Lanier was detailed as a Signal Officer on a Blockade Runner, by order dated August 2. 1864.

recent speech of Mr Long at his reception in Ohio, the Peace-party, (and that, too, not the restoration-of-the-union peace party, but the On-any-terms-Peace-party) at the North has ceased to be a phantom, has clothed itself with flesh and blood, has organized into bone and muscle, and has become an earnest and significant reality –.[35]

Yet, I rejoice in the Peace-party, not because of any results which I expect directly from its operations in favor of our independence, but simply because it is an infallible indication of a wide-spreading belief in the ability of the South to *win* its independence *by force of arms* –. The true and effective Peace-party is led, not by Mr Long, but by Gen. Lee. This noble Fugleman, with his ragged constituency, who combine filth with heroism, in such a way as the world has not before seen, who vote by bullet and not by ballot, who thunder from the Earth-works and not from the Hustings; This innovating politician who discards bribery, who spreads not soft-soap, who pulls not the concealed wires, who confers no lucrative positions, who makes no shoddy contracts, who rejects all the old and well-established " mechanical applicances " of Party, that is the man, these are the voters, who are to give us peace and to establish our independence –. Nor have we long to wait, before the end comes –. The North believes that this is the closing struggle; nothing is more curious than to notice how, in all their utter-ances, this idea is unconsciously but plainly presupposed –. The campaign is nearly over; its last battles are to be fought in a few weeks at farthest –. The crisis is come –. The Western Continent is in labor; the awe and agony of child-birth are upon her –. But I believe that by the New Year, /65, the gigantic throes will cease, and it will be announced to the World-Family that another son is born into it –. May all kind Fairies and good Angels preside at the birth of him, and endow him with all manly virtues and graces; so that his career in life may be that of a star in heaven, which

> " Maketh not haste,
> Which taketh not rest,

[35] The peace movement of 1864 gained such momentum that the northern Democrats wrote a " peace-plank " into their platform for the presidential cam-paign, but the re-election of Lincoln ended it. Alexander Long of Ohio was one of the delegates to the Republican National Convention in 1864.

> But ever fulfilleth
> Its God-given hest " ! – –

So! I've written a regular " leader " for the morning-papers –.
I assure you I didn't do it with malice – prepense; more by
token, I don't often bother my head about the chances of
military events –

Gen. Lee held service at his Hd Q'rs. about two hundred
yards from our station, on last Sunday –. Gen. Pendleton
preached; Gen A. P. Hill was present, and some other Officers –.
The table, which held the simple paraphernalia of our worship,
a Bible and a Prayer book, was placed under a noble tree; the
sky was serene: the sunlight was warm and beautiful on the
green grass; a shell shrieked occasionally; a bird flew into the
tree over the Preacher's head and sat and sang; my dog Flag,
trotted composedly around and through the assemblage, rubbing
himself sometimes against Gen. Lee, anon against Gen. Hill –,
and then seating himself in the circle to stare at everybody, this
being the first time that Flag ever attended Divine Service; the
Preacher preached peace on earth and good-will towards men,
dressed in a uniform which was trimmed with blood-red; – all
of which incongruous elements set me into a reverie upon the
illimitable mystery of the World, the end of which has not yet
come – . – Gen. Pendleton is a noble, dignified man of large
stature, and reminds me forcibly of a picture of Oliver Cromwell
which I have seen somewhere – Gen. Lee has the Commander
in every lineament of his face, and motion of his body; his
dignity is graceful and simple, and his firmness which declares
itself at first glance to be impregnable, is relieved by the intelligence and charity which one discovers in his eyes presiding
over it –.[36]

You complain of our having written you nothing of our
situation in Surrey –. This was impossible; since it was of the
greatest importance that our position should be kept secret, as
well as our occupation; and all our letters were sent at imminent
risk of being captured by the Yankees –.

Cliff and I have recovered from our chills and are now in
first-rate health and spirits –. Should we receive the orders

---

[36] See Lanier's account of this service in his memorial address on the death of
Lee in 1870 (V, 274).

which we expect, we have strong hopes of seeing you in a month or so –; but otherwise, we will not apply for furlough until the campaign is over –.

I wrote Mamie Day at the same time I wrote you – Did she get my letter? Ask her to write me –.

I regret more than I can express, the news of John Lamar's death –.[37] Poor Gussie will be inconsolable; she idolized him – If you should find an opportunity to assist them, do so, for my sake –

Regards to any friends who ask after us – Please inquire constantly after Sam Knox who is probably in Gen. Hood's Army –. You could not do too much in the way of befriending him, should he be wounded or otherwise needing assistance – [38]

Write me often –. Our communication will I hope continue uninterruped –.

> With all love,
>> Your son,
>>> Sid. Lanier

To Virginia Hankins [39]

[Petersburg, Va., Aug.? 1864]

We were sent for in order to have us in readiness to go aboard a blockading vessel from Wilmington to Nassau. Meantime Cliff and I are stationed near General Beauregard's headquarters, in little danger except from stray shells. The city lies under us, and the beautiful view we have adds no little to the comfort of our situation. It is just this moment reported that we have to go into the trenches to relieve another party, and so farewell beautiful views and comfortable situations!

[37] In his letter of July 25, 1864, R. S. Lanier had written: "Poor John Hill Lamar was killed recently in Maryland. Willie Le-Conte got home yesterday wounded in the leg at Atlanta on last Saturday."
[38] In his letter of Aug. 6, 1864, R. S. Lanier wrote: "Sam Knox was at Mr. Gresham's—wounded—but has probably gone home."
[39] Previously published in the *Southern Bivouac*, II, 760 (May, 1887), from which it is here reprinted, the MS not being found. The beginning and end of the letter are missing. It is dated from Virginia Hankins's statement that it was Lanier's "first letter after being ordered away," and from its sequence with the preceding and following letters.

H[opson] is encamped about eight miles from the city. Cliff and I rode out to see him the day after we arrived here, and found M. and P. camped next to him. All of us, Cliff, H., M., and I dined with Captain P., and you may well imagine we were a merry party. We confined our talk religiously to a discussion of the dear inmates of —— [Bacon's Castle,] —— from the General, whom we all reverence, to beautiful little Louis, whom we all love. A thousand questions were asked and answered about you all, and we were able to drink a toast to the beloved friends whose affection formed a common tie between us.

To Robert S. Lanier

Smithville, N. C. –
Aug. 11th ″/64

My Dear Pa:

The orders, which I wrote you in my last we were anticipating, came the day after I had sent my letter. We went over to Richmond and reported to Capt. Barker, acting Chief of the Signal Bureau; and after remaining there two days, came down to Wilmington, where Gen. Whiting ordered us to report to Capt. Bain, Signal Officer of the harbor of Wilmington, HeadQ'r's at Smithville, Thirty miles below that place, – on the Cape Fear River –. We arrived here day before yesterday, after a delightful trip down the river, by Steamer; and tomorrow will be put on duty at the Forts commanding the entrances to this harbor, temporarily, until we are assigned to duty on board of blockading vessels –.

With our usual good fortune, we are pleasantly located: and, if we can escape capture by the Yanks, will have a pleasant time – I cannot tell how long we will remain here: but it will, in all probability, be two or three weeks, (possibly months) before we get our vessels – Meantime, endeavor to scrape together some gold and silver, and send it to us, so that we may fit ourselves out, if we should get to Bermuda, with some clothes befitting the civilized life which we are expecting to lead on the blockaders –. Also send me some letters of intro- duction to any leading firms you may know in Wilmington: and get Uncle Sid to do the same –. Should you be coming through

Wilmington at any time, apply at Gen. Whiting's HeadQr's for a passport to Smithville, where you can telegraph us by the Signal line, so that we may come over here, from the forts, and see you –.

We found the Sugar and Coffee in Richmond, and have already enjoyed some of it – [40] Accept many thanks for it: and be a witness to my retraction of all the hard remarks which I made about the supposed embezzlers of the same –.

Write to us, at Smithville, N. C. care of Cap. Bain, Signal Corps. You will pardon a short letter. I am suffering with a severe cold and don't feel like writing. Will give a long communication shortly –.

Our love to all; and a thousand kisses for Mother and Sister, when you see them –

S. C. L–

To Virginia Hankins

At Campbell, August 16th/64

Thou, the pure-white Petal in the centre of a Red Rose which is my heart: – Thou, the soft, cool cloud which a Blessed Wind from Heaven has wafted and left still over my soul as over a lake: – Thou, the immaculate Vestal-flame which needs no attendants, which burns of itself forever, and before which I kneel: – thou, mine own lovely and loving and beloved Little One – – " far-off "!

Thou art *not* far-off: nay, thou art not off at all: for, as I sit here on this Parapet whose base is in the brine, my eye wanders across the old mysterious Ocean, and my thought would follow, did not the dainty white Hand extend itself, to receive with irresistible gentleness draw my soul inland to the Spot where thou art and where I long, Oh God! *so* passionately, to be also –.

Down upon my Reverie there descends a mysterious Sheen from above: – it is your thought come to mine –. And as the moon-beams fall upon the water and blend with it so that we cannot tell whether the moonlight ripples or the water glitters:

[40] In his letter of July 25, 1864, R. S. Lanier had mentioned sending sugar and coffee to his sons.

so I feel your musing blend with mine, into Something which is not you, nor me, nor exactly both of us –. Do you not recognize, *now,* how it is that Robert Browning found that " One *near* to one is too *far* " ? Do not we two, you and I, sometimes become

" One and one with a *Shadowy Third* " ?

– – – – Alas, only sometimes!

My Darling, I look up to you from the low pavement-world, as Kenyon looked up at Hilda in her tower, from the streets of Rome –.[41]

High up there, above all Men and Cities and Forms and Vulgarities and Oppressions, you sit: with your beautiful white thoughts, like white Doves, circling about your head: tending the undying Shrine-Lamp, whose flame is not purer or steadier or warmer than your heart: stretching out your hand for the Morning-Star to salute: – your brow nigh as white as the snowy Forehead of old Soracte across the Campagna yonder, and receiving the early ray of the Rising-Sun nigh as soon as his!

Friend, I am coming up to where you are: only give me yet a year or two to climb in: and then —— and then?

Smithfield, Aug. 24th/64

I have copied this letter out of my heart, where it has lain written to you ever since the date on the other page –. There's a great deal more of it: but I fear you'll complain, like some other friends I have, that I give you no details of any movements but those of my heart –. And so, if I can keep from talking love to you long enough I'll try and

x   x   x   x   x   x   x [42]

vessels were prohibited from discharging their cargoes and confined under a rigorous quarantine of fifteen days, in consequence of alarming report of Yellow Fever at Nassau and Bermuda –. We were temporarily assigned to duty at the Forts that defend this Harbor, and there quietly awaited the develop-

---

[41] The allusion is to Hawthorne's *The Marble Faun.* Lanier had previously used it in a letter to Mary Day, Feb. 28, 1864, above.

[42] A part of this letter (which exists only in a typed copy) is missing at this point.

ments of time –. With which, our prospects seem again to brighten –. Several of the ships, having ridden out their quarantine-term without exhibiting signs of the fever, have been released, and are preparing to leave port – The Lilian ran out last night –: and tomorrow night, two of our party, Nestor Richardson and Lanhorne, go out as passengers on board the Mary Celeste, to bring in new vessels which are now awaiting Signal Officers at Bermuda –. It is understood that a large number of vessels will be ready in a few weeks to commence runnings, and that a large majority, if not all, of our party will be sent out to bring them in –.

Yesterday afternoon I recd y'r letter of the 12th, forwarded to me from Petersburg –. I do not know how to thank you for that, nor how to thank Heaven for *you.* I pronounced the letter which preceded this as the most exquisite I ever received from any woman: but I believe this last is still better. Your words are so inexpressibly sweet that I cannot help begging you to write me more of them and more frequently –.

I have met several old friends, male and female, who are spending the summer here –: and would have a very pleasant time, amidst the kindnesses and attention which they show me, if my heart were not so wholly absorbed otherwhere –. There is no hour in the day in which my thoughts do not turn yearningly to My Little One –: and as I read over and over again the dear words that you send me, I stop to ask myself if it is really I who receive so much love from you, and who am so o'ervaultingly bold as to hope for so much more!

I am anxiously awaiting a letter from the General –. I wrote him, sent him some papers, by Walton: and wrote you a second letter at the same time –. I'm quite certain that the General opened my second letter to you: and I can imagine the stare of surprise when he reads the passionate and loving things with which it was filled –.

Cliff and I had a pleasant time in Richmond. We took the Douglass Sisterhood to hear the music in the Square, and to see the thousands of people assembled there. I, who had Miss Joan, managed to go through the performance with a very distinguished air, in my ragged coat and hideous pants: but Cliff and Cousin Lucy wandered away to the sequestered walks, under the vain delusion that they would be unnoticed, and so, innocent children as they are! – were pronounced an " engaged couple " by everybody in the park –.

Beloved, write me, write me – I wish to bear as many as possible of your sweet words away with me –. Write me: and God keep you for

Your S.

To William A. Hopson [48]

[Smithville, N. C., Aug. 24, 1864]

Ten or twelve Blockade-runners came into Port within a day or two after our arrival here, and were immediately placed in strict quarantine, it being reported that the Yellow Fever was raging in Bermuda, and even that there were cases on board some of the vessels. This proceeding somewhat damped our hopes at first, as we did not like the prospect of being assigned to duty in the Forts protecting this harbor, and awaiting the coming of Frost before we could proceed on our voyages. But, the vessels having developed no serious cause of alarm after riding out a Quarantine-term of fifteen days, are being released and allowed to discharge cargo and re-load. The " Lilian " went out last night; and to-morrow night two of our party, Richardson and Langhorn, go out as passengers on the " Mary Celeste," to bring in two new steamers now ready at Bermuda. It is reported that there are a number of new blockaders in foreign ports awaiting Signal Operators to bring them in; and it is probable that, in the course of two or three weeks, a large majority of our party will sail from the Port for that purpose.

I had a letter from that blessed Brown-eyed child [44] yesterday, which I verily believe to be more beautiful than anything of the sort I ever saw. The letter was forwarded to me by Benson from Petersburg, she supposing me still there. I transcribe a part of it for your edification: " I am glad that *you* see Mr.

---

[48] Previously published by G. H. Clarke, *Independent*, LXI, 1096-1097 (Nov. 8, 1906) ; *Some Reminiscences and Early Letters of Sidney Lanier* (Macon, Ga., 1907), pp. 21-22. It is here reprinted from the latter source (MS not found), which furnishes the bracketed date. Part of the letter is missing—" only two brief paragraphs," according to Clarke.

[44] Virginia Hankins.

Hopson; but I do not forget that the moving of the Signal Corps precludes all hope of *my* soon seeing him again. I do not know how *he* regards it, but it is a very unpleasant fact to me, as you know, Mister Sid. By the way, did you deliver to him the package I sent, together with the *big* bundle of kind messages? etc., etc." Certainly I did; didn't I, Hoppy?

With my usual good fortune, I have met here several of the kind friends that I made two years ago in Wilmington. They are spending the summer here, and have introduced me to all the nice people in this truly pleasant village. Insomuch that every day since I have been here various servants, bearing white-covered dishes of delicacies, or fruit, or books, with notes of compliments from the ladies, " might have been seen " wending their way toward the Signal Quarters where I reside. I'm keeping up the Troubadour wandering about the world with a sword at my side, and a lute (or flute) slung on my back with the ribbon of my ladye-love!

To Robert S. Lanier [45]

Smithville N. C –
Sep 13th ″/64

My Dear Pa:

My little friend, Miss Lizzie Frink, leaves here today for Columbia, where she is going to school: and I seize the opportunity to write a line, to let you know that we are well and that we wish very much to see you here – I wrote you a few days ago, begging you to come here and relieve our ragged necessities: but I fear that you will not get the letter before your furlough expires – Should you be able to come, telegraph us here, when you arrive at Wilmington, and we'll meet you at that place – If you cannot come, do try and send us about a Thousand Dollars wherewith to relieve our naked-ness – When we get to running the Blockade, we shall be able to fix ourselves up in the clothing line together with you and

[45] Clifford Lanier had written to his mother in a letter of Aug. 31, 1864 (from Ft. Fisher): " Awaiting our Steamers, we are doing duty here to acquaint our-selves with the locale of the Harbour and so remain but a week at each Fort and battery."

the rest – I am told that our pay will amount to two Hundred
dollars a trip, in Gold –

The blockading business has been seriously interfered with
by the prevalence of the Yellow Fever at Nassau and Bermuda–:
since the vessels, having to ride out a Quarantine at both places,
can only make about one trip in two months – But it is hoped
that by October, the interruption will cease: it being already
reported that the Fever is raging less violently each day –

Cliff has had a little attack of bilious Fever, but is now well –
Our kind friends here were unremitting in their attentions
during the two or three days that he was in bed, and kept him
supplied with all sorts of nice things; which I, not to be outdone
in generosity, assisted him very materially in devouring –

I have written you two long letters since I heard from you:
one sent to Macon and one to Cokesbury – Hope you have
received them by this time –.

How I should like to drop in among you all at Cokesbury!
The yearning to do so is so intense that I cannot indulge it, for
the pain it produces – We will not be able to get a furlough
until November, at least: but I hope by that time to obtain one
long enough to give us time to visit everybody from Columbia
to Montgomery –.

What will be the future movements of Mother and Sister ? –
Write me very soon and pardon a hasty note from

Your Devoted Son,

S. C. L.

To Virginia Hankins

Smithville, N. C.
Sep. 24th "/64

Little One, Your pure Soul must have swept across a bank
of Love, as Shakespeare's " Sweet South, across a bank of
violets,"[46] or ere it wafted me this dear letter-zephyr of yours,
which comes all perfumed with an exquisite, friendly holiness –
Nay, so entirely are these sweets blended, I cannot know

---

[46] Misquoted from *Twelfth Night.*

whether it is the Holiness that is friendly, or the Friendliness
that is holy; Oh Himmel, I thrill when I think that perhaps both
are true, and that perhaps Friendliness and Holiness mean the
Same thing!

If which be so, some people that I ken owe much holiness to
you –. For here come letters, from two of the Friends that I
love best in this world, full of sweet things for you – . – " But,"
Says Hopson, " to return to pleasant subjects," (he was talking
of the war) –. "You have again heard from Jennie H–. I say
reverently, – God bless her –. My thoughts go out to her from
among these rude scenes more often than she will ever be
aware –. When I think of her I seem to stand in the presence
of a pure white Soul, unspotted from the world, and am
strengthened for my daily conflict with this Soul-crushing life –.
Hers is one of the influences that help me to preserve whatever
is good or noble within me –," &c &c.

And Mamie Day, on this dear fragile paper with the fine
chirography, which is like a love-letter from Oberon to Titania
written upon a Lily-petal with a fairy-pencil, spreads before you
some " cakes and delicacies " fresh from out that most rare
heart of hers –. Her interpretation of the " April Shadows " is
as beautiful as the poem itself –. Is she not good and apt at
drawing " lessons "? She's like a Star which extracts, with a
distant, brilliant beam, perfumes from any flower that blooms
in the night –.

And so, here's a long page and a half which I have yielded
up to convey to you the caresses which *others* are lavishing upon
you; all of which " time and Space " *might* have been employed
in lavishing upon you all those tender things which crowd into
my soul at the call of your name, like Hamadryads and Oreads
crowding from their coverts when Old God Pan Sounded his
reed! Is not this true Greatness of Soul? And does it not make
you feel like sneering at " George Washington refusing a
Second presidential Term," or " Julius Caesar declining the
Roman Crown," or Jean Valjean rescuing Marius from death,
or any other of the commonly-quoted examples of self-sacrifice
and magnanimity?

And, By the Souls of Hero and Leander! – how that tenderness yearns for you on this most beautiful of Autumn-Sundays!
Last night the Equinoctial Storm executed its Grand Finale, in
the most operatic Style, and was hissed off the Stage by the

thousands of waves, who were in a grand turmoil and were apparently very much dissatisfied with the performance –. To-day is as cool and clear and calm and holy as a day in Heaven –. One wish has usurped my whole heart and will not allow me even to dream of aught else: it is the wish that I might spend this long day with *you*, O Thrice-dear Friend, around whom my soul folds itself and remains entranced by the still and un-imaginable delight of *Rest*, like yonder dreaming mists which I see through my window lying upon the far horizon and encompassing the Sea –.

I hope that the Day smiles upon you as upon me –. I hope that all days in the coming years will have for you a special smile which will break through any frown-clouds, be they of the thickest and darkest –. I hope that no night will, for you, ever refuse to exhibit all its Stars, when you call –. I hope that, for you, the Holiness of all Starry Nights and the Brightness of Sunlit days will combine and encircle you in their midst, as in a Sacred Halo, impervious to the Hot Winds and freezing Blasts, which, as passion and indifference, sweep successively through the world –. I hope that your life will be like the lambent light which I have seen on a Sea-wave in a stormy night, serene and clear in the midst of turmoil and darkness, shining more brightly as the wave raged more furiously – –

And I thrill as I speak the words which, when Jean Paul uttered them, must have presupposed *you*: " O never fall, thou Lily of Heaven: and may Four Springs, instead of Four Seasons, open and shut thy flower-bells to the Sun "!

My very kind and warm regards to Miss Beck: and for your-self receive a world-full of such love as you know fills the heart of Your

Friend.

To Mary Day [47]

Wilmington, N. C.   Oct 1st "/64.

Dear Mamie,   The words of your last two letters to Cliff and me were like consecrated Coals from an Altar, warm and holy –.

---

[47] Mary Day had at last made up her mind to marry Major Fred Andrews, and this is Lanier's letter of felicitation to her.

In a letter written from Savannah, Nov. 22, 1864, by Mary Day to Georgia

Well: – the fires on your Altar have been kindled: and Love was the Priest: and *I*, – do not know how to utter to you the sacred congratulations which are in my heart –. I see that there are lingering fears in *your* heart that these congratulations of mine may be somewhat forced, and not so earnest as those of a Friend: and this only adds to the strength of a wish, which already *fills* my heart with yearning, that I might see you once again –. For, were I at your side, I have a word which I could whisper into your ear, and which would immediately and forever set at perfect rest *all* your doubts –. This word seems to me so strangely sacred that I cannot write it: but I know that you will believe me, and that your dear Friendship, confiding in the truth of my words, will cease from its anxieties on my account –.

And so, Child, Darling Friend, to the winds with *this* Grief! Down with the Death's-head that would obtrude its grin at the high, sweet Festival which you are so soon to celebrate!

And now, My Little One, By the Spirits of the Perverse ! – but I envy *both* of you ! – I do not know whether most to congratulate *you* upon winning *him*, or him upon winning *you!* Nor do I know how to escape from this dilemma, unless I regard you twain, in the same light that Heaven does, that is to say, " *as one* " –. Wherefore I address myself to you as " One and one with a Shadowy Third," and, say: O Thou mysterious and beautiful Tertium Quid, that art neither My Friend Mamie nor My Friend A[ndrews], but art yet both of these: Thou exquisite Double-Soul, whom I have never seen, and shall never see, but whom I love with my whole heart: Dear, friendly Wraith, – I am glad that thou art only a Shadow, for so thou wilt inhabit the land where *I* dwell, and I can welcome thee as my own beloved Fellow-Citizen –.

I hope that, for thee, all the eerie denizens of this Land shall have Stars for Hearts and ray out golden happiness upon thee –. I hope that to thee all the Shadows of this Land shall prove to

---

(Shackleford?), she had said: "Would to Heaven that I were like you – and *loved* as you love! I cannot lose myself and my own will in this new affection. I cannot – as yet – return what *I* consider an equivalent (though happily, he is content) and you, who know something of my past, *may* be able to understand how a heart so shocked has failed to recover its natural and healthy action." (From a typed excerpt supplied to the editor by G. H. Clarke from an unnamed source.)

be only " Lustrous Darks " and " Secret Lights " –. I hope that,
for thee, the dim Dawn-light which forever broods over this
Land shall be full of Religion and of Beauty and of Holy
Dew –; and that no Day shall ever arise to chase thee away
with hot excess of Light –. I hope that thy One-life, in which
two lives center, will be as perfect as White Light in which
Three Colors blend: and I hope that thou wilt walk through
Time with so little of its dust upon thee that thou shalt enter
Eternity without even putting off thy mantle –. And I hope
that He whose invocations command the might of the Universe
will be the only One who owns more Love in thy heart than
thy Friend

Sir Philip.

Dear Child I had nearly forgotten that if I do not give you
some " particulars," I shall draw down another torrent of abuse
upon my devoted head –. Tho' verily, my good Mamie, your
abuse was so daintily administered that it e'en sounded to me
sweeter than other people's compliments! So *much* Sugar that
I didn't even taste the Pill!

Know, however, that at the invitation of *Lt. Wilmer*,[48] Chief
of Marine Signals in this District, I have removed from Smithville, where I had been temporarily assigned to duty; to
Wilmington, and am now temporarily in charge of the Marine
Signal Office which has just been established here –, during Lt.
W.'s absence –. Cliff, is with me, and another Friend: we have
little to do, and live a lazy, good-for-nothing sort of life –. We
could have been assigned to blockading-vessels some time ago,
but the prevalence of Yellow Fever at all the Ports to which
our blockaders run determined me to await the coming of Frost
before accepting the position –. The Fever is now said to have
nearly subsided at Nassau: and I shall endeavor to obtain a
Ship running to that Port –. But three or four weeks will
probably elapse yet before we sail –. It is, on the other hand,
quite possible that we will not go at all: inasmuch as there
seems to be indications that the Yanks will attack this place
soon, in which event I presume that the blockading-business

---

[48] In a letter of Oct. 10, 1864, to his mother, Clifford Lanier wrote: " We
occupy a pleasant office here – fronting the water and are much pleased with Lt.
[Skipwith] Wilmer, who is cousin to the Episcopal Bishop of Alabama."

would be nearly or quite closed up –. Should this occur, I have not the remotest idea as to what would be our Movements; but think it probable that Cliff. and I would be ordered back to Petersburg, or perhaps to our old Scouting-ground on the James –. At any rate, you shall be promptly apprised of our changes –.

I have sent your note to Ginna: and I wish I could be near her, to see her mysterious eyes burn as she reads it –. I cannot help expressing to you my earnest admiration of the beautiful thing: it is the best letter I ever saw, either from your pen or any other woman's –. " Love," as I said to you *once before,* " makes poets of us all "!

I have written to Gussie –: but have had no answer – Kiss her for me, and beg her to write to me –. Bear my love and kind regards to all whom you and I love: to *my* Father and *Yours,* to your Brother, to M^r & Mrs Fulton,[49] to Mrs Lamar, and Jennie & Mary Lou. Write me as often as you possibly can – I do not see any people here like you, my Darling Friend: and your letters thrill me with such emotions as few things can awake in me –. I've written a piece that I'm dying to play for you on the flute: Oh Himmel! – *when shall* I?

To Robert S. Lanier

Wilmington, N. C.
Oct. 6th ″/64

My Dear Father:

We received yesterday your letter of Sep. 23rd, from Macon –. I regret that the view which you give both of the *public* and *private* situation is so discouraging: but am very strong in the hope that *both* will wear a decidedly more pleasing aspect in a short time –.

The price for making a suit here is Four hundred and Fifty Dollars: but the tailor " thinks he would get up both suits for Eight hundred "–. Of the amount you sent us, I was so unfortunate as to lose One hundred and Fifty Dollars: and the rest

---

[49] Lanier's friend Harriet Freeman, who had married Thos. W. Fulton on Aug. 16, 1864.

either has been or will be absorbed by our current expenditures for the next month –.

This is certainly not a very cheering Exhibit –. But there is another side of the page, which, it seems to me, will go far towards making a large balance in our favor, if our usual success should attend us –. If I or Cliff were in a condition to cultivate our friends here, it would be the easiest thing in the world for each of us, in a week or two, to get a situation which would pay him from Ten to Twelve Thousand Dollars every month –: the situation, namely, of Purser and Signal Officer on board a blockading-vessel, which commands a salary of Five to Six hundred Dollars in Gold each trip –.

Invitations of all sorts have been extended us here: but we were unable to accept them, for the reason that we had no clothes in which to make a gentlemanly appearance –. Could we have accepted these invitations, and mingled in the Society here, we would have met the controlling-parties of the vessels, and the positions of which I speak would have been offered to us –. As it is, we could not get them, without asking for them, and carrying, in our personal appearance, a strong recommendation to the charity of our benefactors –. This we cannot do: – – and so, as it is not a pleasant thing either to think about or write about, let us whistle the whole matter down the wind –. The Fates, which have certainly been on *our* side for a long time, may favor us again: and should they desert, we will but curse them for fickle Jades, and go to work for ourselves —

The appointment of Beauregard to the command of your department, and the threatening position which our army is reported to have assumed have excited a lively sentiment of pleasure, I think, throughout the whole country –. It was high time that the people were being relieved from the Sinbad's-burden of discouragement which has been hanging about our neck and frustrating all our best endeavors –. You know I never set up for a military prophet; but I think the concentration of all our forces at Marietta, superintended by a little Genius would very soon drive Sherman from our State, if it did not annihilate him before he got out –.[50]

---

[50] In Sept., 1864, Beauregard had been appointed to the administrative command of the Army of the West, but Gen. J. B. Hood remained in active command.

We were glad to hear, a day or two ago, of Mother's improvement in health — I wrote her day before yesterday, advising her against returning to Macon before the close of the Summer Campaign: and, in the hope that she had not left at the appointed time, directed my letter to Cokesbury —.

Our best and warmest Love to her and Sister, with a thousand kisses —. Accept for yourself the earnest affection of

Y^r Son,   S. C. L —

To Robert S. Lanier

Wilmington N. C. Oct 14th /64

My Dear Father:

I had just mailed a letter to you when we received yours bearing date Oct. 3rd —.

It is unnecessary to say that we were no less pained than surprised by the contents of your letter —. I could not dwell on it, for it revives in me recollections which are too terrible to be endured —. I hope I banish them from *your* mind, as I do from mine, when I tell you in so many words, that we are not influenced by dissolute men, that we spend no money for anything, but the barest necessaries of life, that the " great ideas " to which you refer have not deserted us, and that you need have no fears lest we should disgrace the fair name which people have been pleased to give to us —.

The good citizens of Wilmington were thrown into some excitement a day or two ago by a published announcement from one of the physicians in the city, stating that he had just lost two patients with Yellow Fever —. The alarm, however, has almost subsided, in consequence of the continued cool weather, and of the fact that no new cases have been reported in the last two days — We have had two or three Frosts: the weather is still quite cool, and all agree that there is no possible chance of the disease becoming epidemic —. Our office is situated in a cool airy portion of the city, in a few feet of the

---

Hopelessly outnumbered, Hood abandoned the campaign against Sherman and moved into Tennessee on Oct. 16, in a futile effort to cut his lines of communication, and the march to the sea began.

River, and we feel no apprehensions whatever –. Should the disease seem about to spread, we would probably remove our office to Smithville, entirely out of danger – I write thus much to allay any alarm which you might feel, on reading the newspaper accounts –.

Some expectations seem to be entertained by the Commanding Officer at this Post that the enemy will attack us at no distant day –. Of course he has better means of information than I: but I still think that the preparations he is making to repel an attack, are made rather in view of what *may* happen than what seems *likely* to happen –. For I cannot see how the enemy, straining every nerve at Petersburg and Atlanta and St. Louis, can assemble the force sufficient to make any serious attempt upon a well-fortified position like that of Wilmington –. The popular apprehensions of an attack here seem to be based principally upon the fact that Farragut has been ordered to relieve Lee [51] in charge of the blockading-fleet now off this Port: but I do not think that this change contemplates any other purpose than the employment of Farragut's well-known energy, in the work of capturing and destroying the Confederate Blockading-vessels and Privateers which have recently been flocking into our Harbor – At any rate, we will be found, I think, ready, in any emergency: and the enemy will find it a serious undertaking either to stop the Blockaders or to capture Wilmington –.

We have not received any letters from Uncle Sid.[52] though both of us have written him –. Gussie and Mamie owe me letters: and so do Mother & Sister –. Will you be sent to the Field? – Our kind regards to all our friends –. Receive the devotion of Yr Loving Son,

S. C. L.

---

[51] Acting Rear-Admiral Samuel P. Lee, who had been in command of the blockading squadron off the coast of Virginia and North Carolina since Sept., 1862, was replaced in the early fall of 1864 because an attack on Wilmington was contemplated and he was not considered the proper fighting man for the occasion. Farragut himself had to be relieved of the assignment because of ill health.

[52] In expectation of his nephews' imminent departure on a blockade runner, S. C. Lanier (bother of R. S. Lanier) wrote from Montgomery to Clifford Lanier on Sept 28, 1864, and again on Oct. 9, stating that he was willing to turn over to his nephews some bonds to be used for the purchase of goods at Nassau.

To William A. Hopson [53]

[Marine Signal Office, Wilmington, N. C., Oct. 21, 1864]

I wish I knew how to thank you for this good letter that you send me, and which is the best I've ever seen from you. I could not help airing some of its beauties, and so sent copious extracts from it to our friend Ginna Hankins. I've been waiting to hear from her, that I might send you her comments thereon; but the diabolical mails are so slow that I cannot wait any longer, for fear you might think me under the waves.

Cliff sailed last night on the Steam Ship "Talisman" for Nassau. Telegrams from below this morning state that the vessel ran safely through the blockading fleet. She is owned by the "Albion Trading Company," E. Solomon, of New Orleans, partner and resident agent at this place. He was very intimate with our cousin, Major Lanier, of New Orleans, and entrusted to Cliff's care a large amount of bonds, besides giving him letters of introduction sufficient to insure his being well taken care of while at Nassau.

I do not know what time I shall leave here. The imminent prospect of an attack on this place by the Yankees will probably induce the Blockading-firms to keep their vessels in port on the other side of the water, as far as possible. Were it not for this, I should get out very soon, in a week or so; since large numbers of new vessels are waiting at Nassau, Halifax and Bermuda for Pilots and Signal Officers.

Several of our party are now out. Besides Cliff on the "Talisman," Beach went out on the "Hope," Livesay on the "Helen," Culpepper on the "Will o' the Wisp," Barnes on the "Florie," and Langhorne on the "Stormy Petrel" –. Nestor Richardson is at Bermuda recovering from the Yellow Fever –. Eddie Godwin is Signal Off. on the Privateer Chicamauga, now lying at this Port: and Leroy Godwin, his cousin, has just been

---

[53] Previously published by G. H. Clarke, *Independent*, LXI, 1097 (Nov. 8, 1906); *Some Reminiscences and Early Letters of Sidney Lanier* (Macon, Ga., 1907), pp. 22-23 (also, in facsimile, "Stormy Petrel" to the end, p. 24). It is here reprinted from the latter source (MS not found). Clarke states that the letter was given *in toto*; he is also the authority for the bracketed date.

ordered to the Tallahassee –. The latter will go out in a few days –.

Could you, by any possibility, run down here for a day or so? I have something very particular to consult you about –. Oh Himmel! If you knew! – You'd come –. Don't make yourself uneasy trying to guess it you couldn't do it in a million years –

I haven't the remotest idea where you are; and so shall send this to Benson – Write me as soon as you receive it –, addressing " care of Lt. Wilmer, Marine Signal Office, Wilmington, N. C " I am staying in the office, as clerk, with Frank Hyman – being invited to do so by Lt. W. who is a magnificent fellow –

I am Your Own

S C. L.

From Frank M. Hyman to Mary J. A. Lanier

Marine Signal Office
Wilmington Nov. 4 "64.

Dear Madam,

   Your son Sidney C. Lanier, Signal Officer on Str " Lucy " ran safely out on the night of the 1st Inst. He requested that I would advise you when he went out. There is a report today that the " Lucy " has been captured, but it can be traced to no reliable sources. I think it impossible to have read any advices about the " Lucy " so soon after his departure and only mention the report lest, reaching you in any other shape you might give it too much credit. I have written to Mr Lanier at Macon.

Very Respectfully

F. M. Hyman.

Mrs. R. S. Lanier
 Cokesbury S. C.

To Clifford Anderson [54]

Camp Hamilton, near Ft. Monroe, Va.
Novbr. 11th "/64

My dear Uncle:

After remaining for some days on board the Steamer " Santiago " (my captor) I was sent to the Provost Marshall at Norfolk, who assigned me to confinement in the Military Prison at this place. The officers of the Santiago, whom I found full of all gentlemanly courtesy, invited me into their Ward-room, and during my stay with them treated me in all respects with the utmost kindness. I have met acquaintances also here, and am as pleasantly situated as I could expect.

See Judge Ould immediately, and arrange a *special exchange* for me —; [55] also write home and inform Mother how well I have been treated.

You will pardon a very laconic epistle: I'm limited to one page. Send a thousand kisses to Mother and Sister and Father from

Yr. devoted

Sidney C. Lanier [56]

[54] Lanier's uncle, who was at this time a member of the Confederate Congress in Richmond, was the logical member of the family to negotiate for an exchange.

[55] Judge Robert Ould (1820-1881), a Washington, D. C., attorney, who served as Assistant Secretary of War in the Confederacy. In 1862 he was appointed commissioner for the exchange of prisoners.

[56] No letters by Lanier have been found between Nov. 11, 1864, and Mar. 18, 1865. For the known facts concerning his three months' imprisonment at Point Lookout, Md., his release, and his return to Georgia, see Appendix C, vol. X.

1865

To Mary Day [1]

Macon, Ga.
March 18th /65

I'm told you are very ill.

Now, Mamie, those People in Heaven are trying to get you to go back up there!

And I write to beg you, in the most emphatic way *don't you do it!* Write 'em a note of regret, Child: tell 'em you're too unwell to come, tell 'em you have engagem (tisn't *my* fault; how can I write if you seize my hand: and put your fingers over my mouth, in that way?), tell 'em in fine, that *I* have not seen you in, let me see, several Aeons and Cycles of ages at least –: and that's a legitimate excuse for your refusing to do anything in the world, in my (*very*) humble opinion ! – –

So far, when your note, God bless you and it, came –. My Friend, when I look into your pages here, it is as if I looked into the Heavens, at twilight – The words come out, like Stars, one by one, each one tremulous with an intense radiance which connects itself with *me,* – a familiar, *friendly* Lightning –. Mein Himmel ! How these lovely and loving Star-rays do spurn the cold prison-darkness which has been settling round my heart, like a deadly damp Night-fog ! –

[1] Lanier is said to have reached Macon a month after his exchange on Feb. 15, 1865, and immediately on his arrival to have become seriously ill. His letter of Mar. 18, 1865, probably antedates the illness and the delirium of that spring.

Mary Day had been in Augusta, Ga., where she had typhoid fever. On Feb. 15, 1865, Elizabeth Frances Andrews wrote in her diary (*War Time Journal of a Georgia Girl,* New York, 1908, pp. 91-92) that Mary Day was at the plantation home of the Andrews family, in Washington, Ga.: "She is too weak to make the journey from Mayfield to Macon, and all non-combatants have been ordered to leave Augusta, so mother invited her to Haywood." She was there until April 27, when she left "for a short visit to Augusta" (p. 186). She was at this period still engaged to Miss Andrews' brother, Fred.

184

Remember you the Knight in the " Marble Faun," who, when
tired with hunting on hot days, was wont to repair to a Spring
that gushed from a grotto near his castle: and whose lips, when
he bent down to drink, would be kissed by the enamored
Nymph of the Waters? – [2]
Your letter is my Grotto: your words, to me, are cool waters –.
Says the German:

   – – " Life is a Sultry Day –
   The day has made me tired! "

I'm tired, too: of hunting, and of sultriness –. As I bend down
over this letter of yours to drink its waters, your graceful
Friendliness, their presiding Nymph, rises to the surface, and
presents to me her own blessed lips –. Ah, they are moist, and
cool, and fragrant, and enchanting: – and I would I might be
tired every day, if so I might win more of these divine kisses,
which are as soft as flower-breath, which are as sweet, Friend,–
as you —
It may be that my good friend Andrews will purse up his
mouth, and bristle, and look very dignified (which means, being
interpreted, very ugly) when he reaches these words –. If so,
tell him that these remarks are addressed to *your* Friendship,
which is an airy entity, and not to any flesh-and-blood reality
like yourself: tell him I'm in love with the Love that you've
given me, and that I talk lover's talk to *that,* and not to his
betrothed wife –. Tell him, and at this juncture of your
remarks, do me the favor to fillip him on the tip o' the nose,
by way of underscore or emphasis: which I, not being able to
(Sir) Philip him, proceed to write fillip-pics against, – Good
Mamie, I'm a " blind instrument in the hands of a Higher
Power: " I CAN'T help it: it's a punishment: I say tell him
that your Friendship is quite entirely *out* of his department:
Tell him that your Friendship is your Pin-money, which you
are entitled to squander on me or any other trifle to which your
woman's perversity takes a liking; tell him that, if, in the distribution of *you, he* is determined to be Gen. Lee, *I* am equally
determined to be Gen. M –, with a command in the Reserves ! –
Which having told him, – Give my love and warm regards to
him –.

  [2] The allusion is to Hawthorne's novel, *The Marble Faun.*

Mr. & Mrs. Clay are expected here every day: and as they are probably now on the way, I'll send no messages for them –: I'm all afire to see them.

Can you imagine what wayward Fate it was, which led me to go to Augusta, which was *out* of my way, and not to go to Washington,[3] which was directly *in* my way, and which *contained* you –? I did not know you were there – I passed within a few miles of you –. Retributive Heaven! what great and horrible Sin have I committed, that I should be thus dealt with?! I entreat you to believe that I would pursue this apostrophe until I would melt you to tears, – – if I had time –. But I have yet to tell you, that on reaching Richmond I was furloughed *for* Forty Days; (and Forty nights: which awoke in my mind, I know not why, some startling and horrible recollections of the Forty Thieves, and the Forty days duration of the Deluge; upon ground of rigorous principle (for I *never* pun, I do not refer to the

" Forte Dux "

who fortified the unfortunate Fortalice of Troy), "unless sooner exchanged" –. This last clause, which might be called a saving clause, was a destroying clause for me: Mein Himmel, these "clause" is now fastened in my coat-collar, firmly, to drag me back to Richmond: for I see by a telegraphic dispatch in the Papers that I am exchanged, and am daily expecting the orders to arrive for me –.

However, au contraire; I have been very ill ever since I arrived in Macon: and the Surgeons tell me I can get a thirty days extension of my furlough –. Father insists that I shall apply to the Board for this extension, and I have consented; and so it is almost quite certain that I shall be in Macon at least another Month –.[4] Meantime, My Good Friend, your letter is as absolutely devoid of all details about yourself, as those of mine that you scolded so: how are you, how are you going to be during the next month, but, above all, *where?*

---

[3] Washington, Ga., about fifty miles northwest of Augusta.

[4] On Mar. 29, 1865, Lanier's furlough was extended for thirty days more by the Post Examining Board, at Macon, " in consequence of bronchitis, with great disability." The war ended before his extended furlough expired, and he did not return to the army.

Reflect, O sweetest of Preachers, upon thine own doctrines and precepts, and, as the Music-teachers say, Practice, Practice, *Practice!*

Should I not succeed in getting a furlough, I shall make arrangements to call on you, at Washington, on my way back to Virginia: which, in that event, I should resume in a few days –. If I get my furlough, where will I meet you? Are you coming here? if so, when? – if not, why? These questions will furnish you with a sort of nucleus for a blank form, which you will be kind enough to draw up: and then fill out the interrogatories with careful and well-considered replies, duly attested by two competent witnesses (Andrews is *not* a competent witness, being now undoubtedly non comp. Ment.) and a Notary Public –: in the absence of a Notary Public, a long and very loving letter, under your own hand and seal, will be regarded as answering every purpose by the stern eye of the Law, which is *I* –.

" Crazy? " Of course I am –. " Drunk "? Of Course I am –. There are, my dear Friend, certain occasions when a man has an inalienable and indefeasible right to be both drunk and crazy –. With the diplomatic epigrammaticalness of Count Fosco, I proceed to remark, by way of conclusion, that *your letters,* O admirable Woman, make such occasions –.

Accept a Friendship which is as immutable as Love –.

from   Sir Fillip –

To Mary Day [5]

Macon Ga
May 8th /65

My Good Friend:

Until a few moments ago I expected to accompany Harry as far as Madison, and to charge him with a thousand loving messages for you: but have just discovered that I cannot go, and so have only time to scratch off a line or

---

[5] Miss Andrews wrote in her diary (see note 1) on April 19, at Milledgeville: " They began to evacuate [Macon] at dusk yesterday. . . . Sidney Lanier, a friend of Fred's, was there, trying to get aboard one of the outgoing trains. Fred introduced him, but we soon lost each other in the crowd. The poor fellow *is*

two, wherein to tell you that I am at last ascended out of the strange dreams of delirious sickness: that your face and your friendship were present to me, even in my wildest ravings: and that I long for you with such longing as I do not dare to describe —

Come, Child —.

I would come to *you*: but my Mother's perilous condition will not permit me to leave her —.   She scarcely can bear that I should be a moment out of her sight, God bless her ! — and I,

---

Come —. I long for your music, your sweet, dear face, your sympathy, your grey eyes, into which I gaze as one looks into the sky at dawn, — The trees and the flowers here participate in my yearning for you: the leaves do not rustle right, the petals seem to me sad, the great oaks stretch out their arms, as I do mine, and beckon to you, and beg you, come —

For their sake, and for mine, Child, Friend, sweetest Soul that I know, bring all your exquisite thoughts and your tender feelings and mingle them with these other perfumes that at this moment hover about me and remind me of you —.

You will pardon a most hasty note —: and present my regards to the ladies to whom I was introduced but whom I was too ill to *see*, even: and give my love to Maj. Fred: and kiss yourself for me: and

COME!

Sister sends a hundred kisses: and says you may imagine why she has not replied to your dear letters, her whole time being occupied in tending our Mother [6]—. She says, come —

just up from a spell of typhoid fever, and looked as thin and white as a ghost He said Harry Day was left behind sick, in Macon " (*op. cit.*, pp. 157-158).

By May 8, 1865, the Confederacy had fallen, Macon had been occupied by Federal troops; and on that day Lanier applied for and received parole papers from " Head-Quarters, Cavalry Corps, M. D. M.., Macon, Ga." He is described in the document (Clifford A. Lanier Collection, Johns Hopkins University) as 5 ft-10 in. in height, with light hair, gray eyes, and dark complexion.

H. C. Day was returning from Macon to Washington, Ga. Madison is the county seat of Morgan County, Ga., 55 miles east and south of Atlanta. Miss Andrews wrote in her diary on May 10 (p. 237): " Harry Day came over from Macon looking very pale and ill."

[6] Mrs. Lanier's health, bad for some years, had become increasingly worse. She died May 22, 1865, a few days after the return of Clifford Lanier from Bermuda, via Cuba and Texas.

To Mary Day [7]

[Macon, Ga., June, 1865?]

My Dear Mamie:

Sister has gone out to spend the day (at Carrie Weed's) –.[8]

I've been all alone, the whole morning, taking care of the house, and wishing that you'd come down and help me – Why didn't you? –

Will see you this afternoon, I suppose –: and, meantime will send your note to Sissa –

Hurriedly,

Sid.

To Mary Day

[Macon, Ga., July, 1865?] [9]

I should have seen you yesterday, My Dear Child, according to appointment, had I not been engaged –. If I should feel well enough not to bore you will come to-day about half-past two or three –

I thank you very much for your cigarettes – I shall put a loving wish into each smoke-wreath, to float, like a soul in the arms of an Angel, up to heaven –.

---

[7] On May 15, 1865, Mary Day wrote to Lanier from Washington, Ga., that she had not received an answer to a letter sent to him at Milledgeville, three weeks before; and that she was sending by her brother " a little package of cigarettes for your use,"—cigarettes of her own making. Miss Andrews records in her diary (May 13, p. 250) that she and Mary Day had been making cigarettes to sell the Yankees, " but we both gave them all away to the poor Confederates as fast as we could roll them." She also records that Harry Day left Washington on May 20 (p. 264), and that Mary Day left for Macon on June 22, with her brother who had returned for her (p. 305). Lanier's letter is apparently written after her arrival.

[8] Caroline Weed was married, Dec. 2, 1868, to Lanier's friend C. E. Campbell.

[9] The following note was written sometime between Mary Day's return to Macon, on June 23, and Lanier's acceptance of a position as tutor at Mrs. Fulton's, about July 17, 1865.

I would you might have as many blessings as your dear, far-stretching, all-embracing soul ever coveted: – and I send you my

Love.

To Clifford A. Lanier [10]

Scott's Mills
July 24th "/65

My Darling:
I think you'd laugh if you saw me at this moment. In the room at Mrs Fulton's which was formerly a dining room, you would note a remarkable change –: for whereas, in former days Stomachs were stuffed here, – *now,* heads: and, by consequence, the inmates of this room no longer suffer with Stomach-ache, but with head-ache, which is a change for the better, the head being the nobler part –. That is, as a general thing: for, I verily believe, some heads I've seen are nothing but Stomachs in disguise –: indurated Stomachs; ambitious Stomachs; that are looking up in the world: *rebellious* Stomachs, that have successfully risen and overthrown the head: Women's-Right's – Stomachs, that ape their lords and masters –. All of which is said without any reflection being intended upon any of the five heads, which are at this moment taking in provender under my supervision: they being heads in which I discern, I think, a capability of digesting other material besides bread and meat, tho' the said capability has so long been neglected and perverted, that I find considerable difficulty in convincing the owners thereof that they possess it –. However, I do not despair –.
Have only been to town once since I came here, a week ago – Saw Mamie and Gussie and Pa & Sister –. Best of all, received

[10] On July 10, 1865, R. S. Lanier had written to his father Sterling Lanier: " Sidney is to go into the country to our friend's, Mrs. Fulton, some eight miles from Macon – a pleasant place – to teach her five children as private tutor." Mrs. Thos. W. Fulton's plantation, Scott's Mills, was an inheritance from her father William Scott, who had died in 1851. It was located on the Fulton Mill Road at Tobesofkee Creek, about nine miles west of Macon. (It was here that Lanier and Mary Day had visited in October, 1863.)
Clifford Lanier had gone to Montgomery to take a position as clerk at the Exchange Hotel. R. S. Lanier had given up his house to board at the college; and Gertrude Lanier was planning to spend part of the winter in Montgomery, with her grandmother.

your kind and thoughtful present, for which I intend writing you a pretty letter, as soon as I can procure some ink that *ain't* greasy –, like this with which I am now writing, and upon which I utter so many anathemas that the *flow* of my thoughts is utterly *damned* up by the same.

Gussie and Mamie speak of you so lovingly and so much that I if I knew what jealousy was, should certainly indulge in that sentiment a little –. As it is, however, our dear little mutual admiration Society goes on well, and we write our little loving notes, and talk our little love-talk without any disturbance. – Mamie and I spent two mornings with Mrs C. C. Clay: bright, glorious mornings of the old golden sort, filled with music both of tones and souls. Mrs C. sent you " a many messages; she, with Mrs Celeste,[11] are now both in Macon –;

Your cigarettes were delightful, and gave me the more pleasure inasmuch as I have become unable to smoke a pipe in consequence of my illness, and so am confined to these, cigars being out of the question –.

They have prohibited me from studying, on account of my health, which is seriously impaired – I think that Consumption has laid its bony finger upon my life: but am not yet certain –.[12]

Kiss 'em all twice 'round for me: and give Aunt Janie Three, 'cause she's de biggest!

S.

To Mary Day [13]

[Scott's Mills, Summer, 1865]

My Child, If there is any moment in which you seem nearer to me than another, it is when I have drawn my desk to me, at night, to write – The sweetest and most effective inspiration

[11] Mrs. Hugh Lawson Clay.

[12] In a letter not completely dated, but which apparently belongs to this period, Gertrude Lanier wrote to Sidney: " God save you from consumption! " Mrs. Fulton had reported that he was improving, but Gertrude urged him to take exercise, and his medicine, and as much whiskey as he pleased. When what whiskey he had was gone, she promised him more – some bourbon that was a present from Mary Day.

[13] Letters and notes (most of them undated) that were exchanged by Mary Day and Sidney Lanier during the summer of 1865 are written in language that

I ever knew has been your ready sympathy with all my written thoughts, a sympathy which never yet failed me, and upon which I always rely with absolute confidence – At *this* moment, so near do you seem to me, that I half scorn the idea of writing to you – Do you not know my thought? Is not every chamber of my soul open to you, (except the dark Blue-Beard room, which contains my sins, and which I do not let you enter because I fear it would make you abandon the whole mansion, in affright?)

O Child, O Child, you fill my heart as full of sweet strange soft light, as the world is now, of moon-light – All feelings, all thoughts, stand in long, holy trances, like the trees out yonder, shivering sometimes with a sacred half delicious, half-painful tremor – In this Heavenly stillness, the Earth dreams, and does not speak: but from the water yonder rises, as from an altar, many a silent Wreath of Mist, floating up to the moon –

So, O sweet Giver of my Light, rise up prayers and blessings and caresses from my heart to thee –. Hear the prayers! Receive the blessing! Answer the car——S.

To Mary Day

Macon, Ga.
September 1st ″/65.

My Dear Mamie:
I came in last night, on a short holiday, and your good letter fell on me suddenly, like a flower, from a tree, upon a lake –. Like such a flower, it shall meet its shadow! For it was tender and kind: and mine shall be so –.

is affectionate, and that suggests intimacy and understanding; but they are hardly the love letters of an engaged couple (the one here printed is representative). And yet there must have been some local gossip to the effect that they were engaged, because on Aug. 14, 1865, Virginia Hankins wrote to Clifford Lanier: " Mr. Price is staying at Mantura, but he could tell me but little about you; through him I learned of Mr. Hopson's expected marriage & of ' Brother Sid's ' – How strange it all seems to me – " (At some time during the summer of 1865 the Day family went to Wesleyan College to live. Mary Day's letter of Aug. 7 is dated " The College.")

I'm glad you like " the Tournament "–.[14] Your idea of a picture for each verse is a good one and takes me – Imagine it, in a dainty blue and gold edition, of Derby and Jackson, on fine thick paper, with a fair steel engraving for each verse! O fair Vision, and oh most visionary Vision!

Yet, the cacoethes scribendi which has long possessed me is now beginning to superinduce the Cacoethes publicandi–. I am working hard on ye novel, and hope to bring it out before three months roll round. –

If you have a chance to make a conquest of any Newspaper editors, or Magazine proprietors, or any of Mr Harper's Brothers, do captivate them, for my sake: [15] and when you have brought them to that (awful!) stage of infatuation in which your word is law to them, then tell them that I'm a perfect Stunner, in the way of genius: impress them with the idea that money is to be made out of me, (a Golden Calf am I!): tell them that when my book is published, every book puff they give it shall (like the old traditional " rule ") work both ways, urging forward my book, and propelling their prosperous sails (Sales!) into the haven (which is also the Heaven) of your favor –. Such puffs should be called " Trade-winds," eh?

I have a long letter from Ginna –. The poetry in it thrills me as no other poetry ever did – She has lost her mother: like me, she " feels a Mother-want about the world "–. She mourns divinely –: if An Angel should die, its Angel-Friend surviving would wail just so – Her sighs go through my heart like the West-wind through a tree: they make a music, so, in my soul, which is, I think, heard in heaven – I wish very much you would write her – She says in her last line, " I am what I was in the time that is gone ": which surely is token that she is your friend – Take her in your heart and wear her there, like a bud in a vase: God bless her, (and you) when she blooms she'll fill your vase and all the rest of Heaven with perfume, which is the Otto (not of roses but) of a Holy Soul –

[14] The composition of this poem, " The Tournament: Joust First," and several others written at Scott's Mills that summer marks the first renewal of Lanier's literary activity since the close of the war (I, 6).

[15] Mary Day was in New York, visiting her cousin A. Foster Higgins. She had left Macon on Aug. 19. In spite of his jesting, Lanier was apparently hoping to finish *Tiger-Lilies* in time for fall publication.

If I had known that my little song would convey any reproach to you, I would not have given it to you – It was not so meant: it should not do so – Poor Heart would not rest quietly in his grave, if he knew that his dying words were ought but sweet message to his ladye-love – God send, his Ghost may not take to walking, and haunt you! [16]

I have taken a little holiday today, to be with my dear ones – Hopson is spending the day with me: he leaves to-night for New York, and will call on you there –. Do treat him kindly, and show him some attentions –. It is a deep heart he has, and a loving: and you are in it — You may kiss him, for me –

Receive, Good Friends, all sweet messages – Let them float to you, like Summer-clouds, which however white and soft they seem, still are filled with lightning – this love-lightning of my words is not dreadful, but will be your servant, like Ariel; whom I send you, with fair greetings from his conqueror and master, The rightful Duke of Milan (you're Milan), Andrews is the Usurper, (Hang him) and I am

Prospero.[17]

To Clifford A. Lanier

Macon, Ga.
Sep 1st 1865.

My Darling Cliff;

Your letter and the box of cigarettes came a few days ago –. I thank you for both of them –: the letter more than the *latter* –.

I am working hard at Yᵉ Novel: I have three chapters more finished, and a whole host of others in my head – I've also been wooing the music, and send you one piece which is highly regarded in our little circle. I have written the words and music

---

[16] Mary Day seems to have accepted " The Tournament: Joust First " as a song addressed to her, but that Lanier also intended it to be an allegory of the late war is confirmed by his use of it in " The Psalm of the West," in 1876.

[17] It seems evident from the conclusion of this letter that Mary Day still considered herself engaged to Fred Andrews.

to a grand Wedding-Hymn [18] for Gussie; she says it is equal to Mendellsohn –. I think she is a – story-teller, but you'll like it –.

Are you coming over? Do, O Sweetheart-Brother; I never know how I love you, until you are away: I yearn for you – Come, if you can –. Father and Sister join me in entreaties: perhaps they might go back with you –.

Meantime, I am selected as the only Bridegroom's-man, to stand up with our dear couple –. This greatness thrust upon me brings like other high conditions, a train of expenses –. I cannot appear on that occasion in aught less than black broad-cloth and a white vest; for the matter must be down in black and white – These blacks and whites have however given me the *blues*: for I have not the golden wand wherewithal to exorcise such

> " black spirits and white
> Blue spirits and grey "! [19]

I do not like to ask Mrs Fulton or Father for they are both hard up for money –. Can you lend me Fifty Dollars for a month? If it will inconvenience you, don't hesitate to say so –

I send you Ginna's letter – There's enough poetry in it to fill a book – She says she has written you; have you rec^d?

I have two letters from Frank Hyman –, addressed to the firm of S. C. & C. A. L –. Your trunk is at Frank's, Warrenton [N. C.] – He is to be married: will send for trunk as soon as possible –.[20] Dora Brown, from whom I have three long letters, is sojourning at Boston: she has your box –, and sends you a great deal of love –.

---

[18] The words, but not the music, have survived (I, 155); the draft in Lanier's Ledger is dated " Scott's Mills, July 1865," but the final draft was apparently not completed until shortly before the wedding of Augusta Lamar to James Monroe Ogden, which took place on Sept. 19, 1865.

[19] A traditional song, appearing in Thos. Middleton's *The Witch* and in *Macbeth*.

[20] One of these letters, dated Aug. 14, 1865, has survived. Clifford Lanier had left his trunk with Hyman (a fellow member of the Signal Corps at Wilmington) when he made his last trip on a blockade runner in Dec., 1864. Dora Brown, referred to in the following sentence, was apparently a Wilmington friend of the Laniers. She is also mentioned in Sidney Lanier's letter to Clifford of Sept. 30, 1865.

Kiss 'em all for me: I long to do it for myself — Receive all fair-breathed blessings from the soul of Your

S. C. L.[21]

If you can spare the money, send by express immediately — The wedding takes place in two weeks: and I have to wait before I can give my measure to the tailor —. Gussie has written you to come — It is to be a small, very private, and very recherché affair.

To CLIFFORD A. LANIER

Macon, Ga.
Sep 16th "/65

My Darling:

Your kind letter enclosing [fifty dollars arrived] [22] last week; and I should have replied sooner, but being in the country, had no opportunity to send letter — I came in yesterday with Harry Day who has been spending a day or two with me; and will remain until Gussie is married, which eventful ceremony comes off at 3 oclock of Tuesday afternoon, next —. The happy pair will proceed to Augusta on a short bridal trip, and will return in a week or so, to go to housekeeping —.

Gussie had set her heart on your coming, and almost wept when I showed her your letter announcing the impossibility of that event —. I too had hoped to see you: and was bitterly disappointed that you couldn't come —

I hope sincerely that you will keep up your studies —. I see that Gen. Lee has accepted the Presidency of Washington College, at Lexington, Va. —: the military school, you remember, in which Stonewall Jackson was a professor, and to which our young friend Mark Hankins [23] had gone when we were at Bacon's Castle —. How would you like to go there, & devote your attention to the Mathematics, and become a Civil Engineer? Or have you any taste that way? — Or what was the m[er]cantile life to which [you referred in] one of your letters, not long

---

[21] With this letter Lanier sent his brother a copy of "The Tournament" to which he gave the title "Love and Duty," here omitted.

[22] This letter seems to have been mutilated deliberately, perhaps primarily to destroy reference to money for Lanier's dress clothes. The restorations, in brackets, are conjectural.

[23] One of Virginia Hankins' brothers.

since? Write [me in] full about these things –. I am very busy writing poetry, Music, and ye Novel: and hope to publish before many months –. Should I succeed I might be able to furnish you money to go there –.

We are all grieved at Aunt Lucy's loss, and Sally's illness; [24] and hope the latter will be much better when this reaches you –

I had a letter from Mamie day before yesterday: 'twas short, but enclosed a sheet of poetry from Adelaide Proctor, and a beautiful photograph of the Mater Dolorosa –

Your last two letters were fine; and I think you will make a splendid writer, if you practice –. Keep a small blank-book in your pocket and note on it every idea, whether fantastical, comic, or poetical, that occurs to you – You will find them all come to use; it is to me an indispensable thing, and has been the practice of all authors – . – –. Kiss 'em all for me with a thousand blessings on every one of the dear heads,

from Your Bro

Sid. –   Turn over

I append my two last poems; I have set them both to Music, and have written them down: they are now in Gussie's hands – The Wedding-Hymn is a duett, with Contralto Solo –. The Morning-Talk is sung, the first verse by Contralto voice, the second by Soprano voice, (both with flute obligato), and the last verse a trio chorus – two voices and flute –. I have also put on [paper several other] flute-p[iec]es: beside digging at [the novel, so] you see I'm not idle, what with [scho]ol teaching and all –.[25]

To Mary Day

Macon, Georgia –
Sept. 16th "/65

My Dear Mamie:
          I've just received your letter enclosing the poems of Adelaide Proctor's, and the Mater Dolorosa –.

[24] Mrs. William Lanier had lost an infant son; Sally (Mrs. Tench Schley) was her daughter.

[25] The texts of the " Wedding-Hymn " and " A Morning-Talk " have been here omitted (see I, 155, 156).

If all sorrow were as beautiful as this most exquisite embodi-
ment of Sorrow, I should surely prize it, and clasp it to me,
with as much fervor as Miss Proctor did *her* sorrow, which had
a grace unknown to any gem or flower –. But alas! – Do you
know that this word *sorrow* is used to denote two things which
are as different from each other as " Star-fire from Street-mud " ?
There is a grief, a wounding from the Surgeon-hand of God,
which we can accept and cherish, as a treasure – The loss of
a dear friend by death, being beyond our control, is a grief
which we may keep in our heart to bind us always to death and
heaven –: and so of a painful sacrifice – which we may make
for one we love –. But the case is very different if our sorrow
proceed from our own sin –. The sorrow that comes from a
sacrifice or a friend's death is *not* a sorrow – It hath in it,
(to me) a not unpleasant sadness; in which good hopes lie
concealed – Aye, Mamie, rich, brave, sweet hopes float out from
this sadness, like perfumes from a sad colored flower –.

But the Sorrow which comes from a sin that we despise when
we have committed it, burns, stings, is bitter, maddens –.
Black cannot mean also white: the word sorrow cannot mean
both these things that I've spoken of –. And so this picture,
which is called the Mater Dolorosa, never did *mean* the Mater
Dolorosa to me, but I always interpreted it very differently –.
The Sorrowful Mother would be following, with her eyes, the
rising Stars of hope and love –, whatever agony expressed itself
in her mouth, and in the melancholy hood and drapery – The
picture is too exquisite to praise: but it's wrongly named –.

I wrote you by Hopson and hope you've seen him ere this –.

Miss Bowen is come: and Miss Chappell – Gussie is like
a bird out of the cage –. The ceremony comes off at 3 O'clock
of next Tuesday Afternoon, after which the doves fly away to
Augusta –

My " Wedding-Hymn " is written, Music and all: and Gussie
says it will immortalize me –. I have also written another
piece, – consisting of a Contralto solo and Soprano solo (with
flute obligato), and a *chorus* (?) or two voices and flute –: and
have sent the Music to Ginnie – Bacon, (to whom it is dedicated) – to learn –. I append the words: 'tis called

A Morning-Talk,
Overheard and transcribed by an eavesdropper,
One S. C. L. – –

.   .   .   .   .   .   [26]

I've also written the Music to Tennyson's " Song of Elaine," in Idylls of the King – [27]

And so you see what a flood your inconsiderate opening of the flood-gates is like to pour upon the world! Child, thou didst not know what thou wast doing, when thou saids't to me " write! "

You'll be sorry to hear that the Wood-larks have stopped singing – I think it must have been somehow bruited abroad amongst the wood-lark community that a Chiel was among 'em takin' (*their*) notes, and they were afraid he'd prent 'em – Fortunately, they stopped too late: for I had already written down something like their warbling, in good legible black and white –.[28]

I like Adelaide Proctor –. She's deep and tender and true-womanly – It's perfect woman-poetry that she writes: delicate, dainty, sweet, tremulous with sweetness, like the air over a rose –. Commend me to her –: I thank you for the poems very much –

Well –: give me your blessing and let me go – I have much to do this morning – I am to appear, as Ogden's Bottle-holder, in good clothes; and they are dressing me up so fine. I have serious ideas of urging Mary Lou [Lamar] to embrace this, probably the only occasion in my life when I'll be dressed well, and double the number of doves –.

Bye-Bye: I kiss your hand –.   Write me –

Sid.

---

[26] The text of Lanier's poem is here omitted (I, 156). The music has not survived. The dedicatee was Virginia Lamar, Mrs. A. O. Bacon.

[27] This musical composition (first conceived over three years before—see p. 51, above) has survived (photo, Henry W. Lanier Collection, Johns Hopkins University).

[28] In the letter to his brother Clifford on Sept. 30, which follows, Lanier announces the completion of a flute solo called " The Woodlarks." No copy of this musical composition has yet been found.

Harry spent the day with me yesterday –: he is looking better, and the change improved him still more – we 'are much together –

To Clifford A. Lanier [29]

Macon Ga.
Sep 30th "/65

My Dear Cliff:

I got your letter a few days ago, and embrace the first opportunity of replying to it; being in town to-day, spending my little holiday with Gussie, who with her liege lord is snugly esconced in Mrs Ralston's (formerly Dr Franklin's) fine house – Mrs R. is gone away to remain some time, and Gussie takes her house in the meantime – The house is elegantly furnished, and they are as happy as any two turtle-doves of your acquaintance –.

I have been busy with my brains since I wrote you –. Have a new song out for Soprano voice, Music by me, and words by Tennyson, the "Sweet is true love, tho' given in vain, in vain," [30] &c – I have also a new poem upon "the dying words of Jackson"; – [31] a letter from a rural darkey to the white man what prints de papah; [32] and another chapter to the novel –. I have little leisure; not a spare moment in the day-time, having to hear some Thirty classes every day – [33] Consequently I have to do all my writing at night, and my failing health prevents me from sitting up late – It almost maddens me to be confined to the horrible monotony of Tare and Tret (it ought to be called Swear and Fret!), and B-a-k-e-r, Baker, when my brain is fairly teeming with beautiful things, at least, things that seem beautiful to me –.

[29] Excerpt previously published, *Chautauquan*, XXI, 408 (July, 1895).
[30] A photostat of this original musical composition, entitled "Song of Elaine,' is preserved in the Lanier Room, Johns Hopkins University.
[31] "The Dying Words of Jackson" (I, 156).
[32] "*Timeo Danaos* (White Man What Prints de Papah)" (V, 200).
[33] Lanier's school, which originally consisted of Mrs. Fulton's five children (Charles H., Ellenora J., James S., Rebecca, and Roberta—all by her first husband, Robt. Freeman), had apparently been increased by the enrollment of children from neighboring plantations.

I'm also out with a new flute Solo, called The Wood-lark, and think of writing a series of Vogel-lieder (Bird-songs) for the flute –, with piano accompaniment –.

And so, enough about me –.

I thing you mistake our ideas here, in reference to your future avocation –. Father and I have had several talks about it –; and I think we both agree that the best life for you is the mercantile –. I wrote you the letter in reference to the Civil Engineering, under the supposition that you disliked mercantile affairs, and would prefer a professional life –. If you keep at your literary tastes, (as you will certainly do, for your nature demands and *will* have some better eating than corn-bread); ten years from now, (by which time you will, if at all successful in business, have acquired something to go on in life) will give you that practical experience which will enable you to give a solid gold setting to the gem-fancies which now flow so easily and beautifully from your pen –. Of course, if you get so good a salary as that you now have, you ought to remain in the Hotel next year –: I only wish I were doing as well.

I have a letter from Dora [Brown], since I wrote you; she sends you a great deal of love –. Thinks of going to Virginia to live, but doesn't say what part of it –.

Gussie got your letter and said fine things of it – She is just come from Augusta, and will reply soon –. We had a Musicale at her house last night, and some company –. I walked home with little Mary Lou, who is as sweet and piquante as – as – as (Mein Himmel! as what!) as a Star-beam, slightly tight –!!!!!! The moon-light and stars and things went near to make me fall at her feet –.

Kiss dear Aunt Janie for me, a hundred times – I long to see if she's got too big for me to fling my arms round her –. I suppose all the rest will be gone to the bay ere this reaches you – Love to Uncle Abe and Bulger.[34]

Write me fully about all you think and do –; and believe that I am

Your

S.

[34] Abram P. Watt, husband of Aunt Jane Lanier, was one of the managers of The Exchange Hotel, Montgomery; Bulger was probably his son.

TO MARY DAY

Macon, Ga
Oct. 15. "/65.

My Dear Mamie:

Your letter arrived too late for me to take any " action in the premises "– Child, you're an Artful Dodger: you're a Humbug: you're a delicious Delusion, such a delusion as one likes to hug to one's breast, tho' ! –

I scarcely know what to say about the poems – Of course, if you succeed in getting them published (which I doubt), I shall be pleased –. I would have taken some steps towards publication myself: but was waiting until I could get written enough pieces to authorize a beginning: believing, with Mendellsohn, that no Author, with pieces of this sort, could produce any strong impression on the public mind, except by submitting a continuous series of them: calling attention to them, so, by mere qua*n*tity, and leaving their quality to be then fairly criticized and definitely settled –. With this view I have continued writing " little pieces," and have two or three more, since I wrote you last –.

I am obliged to your " Soul " for his favorable view of the little poems –: and more so to you for writing " so touchingly " about me – Child, what did you tell him? You must not talk *too* touchingly about me, tho': for then the people will get sorry for me –. Dear, don't let the people get sorry for me –.

Your Father, as I understand, expressed his trunk from Washington, and it is not yet arrived – So I have not yet rec'd your kind presents –.[35] You have long ago exhausted my soul of thanks, and so I won't thank you for them: but if I were a flower I know which way the grateful odors would float!

I've spent some pleasant times with Gussie and Ogden in their nice home –: that being my H'd Q'rs nowadays, when I come to town –. Gus. Bacon has been quite ill for a month past; and has just left, with Ginnie and the baby, for Mitchell County, where they will spend some weeks –

[35] Mary Day had sent Lanier " a package of music," and also " a box for Gertrude," as R. S. Lanier wrote to Clifford Nov. 2, 1865.

I've visited your friend Mary Plant several times since you left; we get on well together, – considering that she is a black-eyed woman, and I never get at my ease with *them* –! But I like her, and wish she were a little more earthy, so that the black eyes wouldn't pretend, all the time, as if they were looking past me, a mere man, into Heaven – It will come, tho', when she falls in love: an event which I most devoutly wish to see – [36]

Of course you're having a time which can only be characterized by the word Bully – Don't I wish " I were with thee," there? – Tho' *that* would create a bully time for me, anywhere –

I should have sent you a letter by Harry; but he left quite " unbeknownst " to me –

I shall be curious to hear if you get the pieces published: and shall expect to hear from you soon –

Do write, Child, a great long letter to your

Friend.

To Mary Day

Macon, Ga
Oct. 25th "/65

My Dear Mamie:

I am about to leave the city for Mobile Bay, whither it is thought advisable for me to go, in order to recruit my failing health – My Grandfather & family are spending the winter there: and he writes us such glowing accounts of his situation and such urgent invitations to come that, " by and with the advice and consent of the physicians &c," we have concluded to go, Sister and I –.[37] I shall probably be gone about one month, and then return and go to work –.

---

[36] Mary Plant was married to Marshall de Graffenried on Oct. 6, 1875.

[37] On Oct. 15 Gertrude Lanier wrote to Clifford that her brother had decided to give up his school, because of his health, and would join his grandparents, and his uncle William's family, at Point Clear, Ala., on Mobile Bay. Apparently he gave up his position as tutor at Mrs. Fulton's plantation at some time between Oct. 15 and 25. Thos. W. Fulton, acting as guardian for his step-children, in account with the estate of Robert Freeman, deceased, made the following entry for Oct. 25, 1865: " Mr. Lanier for tuition of children 3 months . . . . . . $90.00."

The object of all which unusual details is simply this: — I'm told that your " lovyer so bold " was in town a few days ago and threw out some dark hints about a speedy marriage — Unfortunately I didn't see him, and so I'm going upon mere hearsay: *but* —, of course I want to wait on you, upon that occasion: and so I must beg you to write me immediately the when and the where (*not* the where*fore*!) and the how and all about it, so that I may shape my somewhat-erratic movements accordingly —. Now don't fail me, Cherie: address me here, whence, Father will forward my letters: don't remember exactly what my address will be —

Gussie has been quite ill for several days, but is up to-day, much better — Cousin 'Liza has also been in bed for a week, with fever: but is said to be recovering —. She has been at Ogden's house, all the time —

I have not yet had the pleasure of seeing any of your kind presents — Mr Day has not said anything about them: and so I conclude the trunk containing them has not yet arrived —

I have your letter containing the sweet, tranquil hymns, and your sweeter little sermon — Child, I do not know why I say it, but there rises to my mind only this: who shall read a human heart? Who can read his own heart? God help all Struggling Souls and Sorrowful hearts!

I'm very glad that you enjoy my letters, and that they touch people's hearts —. I wish, when I am writing my book, that I could, in my mind's eye, transform the world into *you,* and write *to it* under that impression —. I never write well, unless I have at my heart the consciousness of someone's perfect sympathy —

You will pardon a short letter to-day — I have much to do — Miss Mary Plant is inveighing heavily against you, for writing me *twice* to her *none* —

Bless me, love me, write me — — —

(MS in Bibb County Court House, Ga., Office of Ordinary). Lanier's tenure thus ran from about the middle of July to the middle of October, room and board included. In her letter to Clifford, Gertrude sent him a copy of her brother's poem " To J. L." (Janie Lamar), apparently inspired by Mrs. Lamar's impending departure for Virginia. It was the last poem written at Scott's Mills (I, 8).

From Mary Day

New York. Nov. 1st 1865.

Dear Friend –

I acknowledge two kind letters from you – The last one demands an immediate answer, and I grieve that it must be a brief one. You are not so well! you know what I feel when you suffer. "*People* are not sorry for *you,* dear –" and I did not even know that I had written touchingly to my friend – save in speaking of your delicate health – You were right to speak so gentle a warning – I respect it – & have done so – if I know aright. I shall not be married *before* Jan. 15th. I wish I could write to you to-day, but my thoughts are, and have been, perfectly formless and incoherent – I think between Jan. 15th & Feb. 1st – in Macon – I know no more at present. I bless you for all your goodness – and am your loving and humble friend,

Mamie.

Kisses to dear Gertrude and Cliff.

To Virginia Hankins

Mobile, Ala –
Novb 15 "/65

I wish with my whole soul that the Post Office Department had but one neck, and that I could have the pleasure of wringing it; – how I should gloat to see the miserable fat carcass covered with battening vultures!

I got your first letter, written in reply to my note by McClellan – Since then I have written you two letters, each one with my Soul in it – Last night I recd a letter from you, bearing date *inside* " Bac. Castle, *September* 12th "; and postmarked outside, " Richmond, *Oct. 28th* ": in which you announce that you have not heard from us, and do not know whether yr first letter ever reached us! [38]

---

[38] Apparently Sidney Lanier and Virginia Hankins made efforts to get in touch with each other immediately after his return to Macon. But this is the earliest

This is almost too much –. If I were a woman I should cry:
if I were a profane man I should surely *give* utterance to some
" *Cuss-word* ": being neither, I only grieve, Sweet, rare, noble
Ginna, – with such regret as laughs bitterly at all attempt to
express it, – that you have not, ere this, read the tender, loving
words which both our hearts poured out to you as soon as you
could be reached –

Friend of my inner Soul, My own exquisite Brown Bird, how
sad is this song that you send me! – Great God, it settles over
my heart, like a rain over the ocean, and blots out all sights and
sounds there, except the sight of grief and the sound of
weeping – My blessed Bird, they haven't sent *you* out of
Eden, too?

Does the " Mother-want about the world" cloud my sweet
One's wonderful eyes, so that she cannot see that she still
dwells in the Heaven that pure hearts make for themselves?
Ah, Little One; I shudder when I obtrude *myself* in this connection: and yet I cannot help, for my life, again flinging, as I
have so many times before, at your feet, an infinite tenderness
(*infinite* is the word), a loyalty that never has failed in word
or deed or thought for one moment, a respect that is as deep
and wide and full as the Sea, a wild and fierce and thrilling
kind of Friend's-love which I never felt before, which I never
wish to feel again, so completely, so sweetly, do you fill all the
requisites that my soul asks – Let the world die and go away,
let Time exhale into the blue of Eternity, let Doom-trumpets
blow and wail, let me be on earth or in hell or in heaven: – still
shall my heart be full of this love, still shall I yearn to be near
you –, still shall this glorious feeling triumph over eternal fires,
or mingle, not over powered, with the eternal sweetness of
Heaven – My heart fails, my words fail, let silence come: – but
believe me, and love me, Ginna –.

⸺ ⸺ ⸺ ⸺

You will be surprised to see my date from " Mobile " –

My sister and I came out here, about two weeks ago to spend
the winter: my health having been seriously impaired by expo-

---

of his post-war letters to her that has survived; and none of her letters to him
either during the war or shortly after have been found—the earliest preserved
being that of Oct. 24, 1867. All of the letters mentioned in this paragraph
were either lost in the mails or have disappeared since.

sure on my way home from Pt. Lookout – It was thought that the Gulf Coast might avert the Consumption which threatens me, and so Sissa and I have come here; where we are most delightfully situated, being about Twenty miles from Mobile, (just across the Bay,) in full view of the great ocean, surrounded by loving friends, (Grandfather and Grandmother are living here), and feasting upon the most delicious fish and oysters – Cliff is still in Montgomery, doing well –: and will pay us a visit here in a few days when we are to have a grand family reunion –. C. has written you several times, also to the Douglasses: to whom, a letter-full of love and kisses from both of us –.

I saw Miss Dolly Chappell several times, a week or two ago: she was staying with my Friend Mary Lou Lamar, in Macon, and asked after you, *so* sweetly; and a long talk we had about you completely won my heart – I have also heard fine things of you from Maj. Hudson, of Gen. Elzey's Staff –. God bless you, Little One!

Mary Day, now in New York, writes me that she would write *you,* if she knew your address; which I send her – By the way, how did you get that strange idea of my marriage to Mary Day? – [39] She *is* to be married shortly, but *not to me*; She has been for a long time engaged to Maj. Andrews, (She had told me of it before I left you) and will marry him shortly. – Hopson will probably commit matrimony before a great while – No such luck for *me!* My sister bids me send a good, long, loving kiss from her – How I wish you could see her as she sits by me! Her eyes are larger even than yours, and as blue as Heaven – Love her – – –

To Clifford A. Lanier

Point Clear, Ala
Nov 25th "/65

My Darling:

Surely no one in the whole world wishes for you at this moment half so eagerly as I – All of my best thoughts and feelings bring you to my mind: – and who could help feeling

[39] Intimated in a letter from Virginia Hankins to Clifford Lanier, Aug. 14, 1865 (see note 13, above).

purely and thinking good thoughts in this exquisite place, under these matchless skies which have scarcely been marred by a cloud since I came here, by these fair waters which seem to have little to do except to reflect the sun and the stars, that is, to be beautiful!

The Yacht is just come from New York, and I have already become a good sailor – Of all sports, sailing is, to me, by far the most enchanting, and I enter into it with my whole soul – The Yacht performs finely; and, so far, has beaten any boat here – Uncle Will [40] and I have been out several times, on long excursions down the bay; and yesterday we returned from our first trip in the Yacht to Mobile –

Uncle Sid is improving slowly, tho' quite feeble yet – He seems to be much delighted with this place, and I think will get well here if anywhere –

I have a couple of letters from Pa, and one from Ginna Hankins, which last I enclose –. She seems not to have rec^d our letters to her yet: which almost makes me want to say a cuss-word against the infernal P. O. Department –. Have also letters from McNeill, Harry Day & Mamie, and a wee bit note from little Mary Lou (whom the Angels guard), which sends a special love-message to you –

Grand Mother says Uncle Sid's *carpet*[-bag] did not arrive with the other things – It is in Watt's Store – She wishes you to fix it up and send it by Father, who expects to be on sometime between now and Christmas.

Who else will be employed by Uncle Abe in the Office, besides yourself? If he has engaged no one, couldn't I get it? Write me what you know about it –

My destitute condition is the Death's Head at all my feasts – It drives me hard, day and night, towards the grave – Two months more, like the two months gone, will put me yonder beside Mother –. To which, personally, I don't know that I would have much objection: being deeply convinced that nothing could exceed the unceasing sufferings that I endure all the time in secret –

You'll pardon all this, Cliff; and I won't write so any more,

---

[40] William Lanier was co-manager (with A. P. Watt) of The Exchange Hotel in Montgomery.

nor would have done so now, had it not been to you, My One
Beloved, that my heart leaped up to show itself – Mayhap the
Times will brighten; if so good; meantime, I have one consola-
tion, that, dark or bright, I am unfailingly

Your Faithful

      Sid [41]

[41] Clifford Lanier replied, Dec. 3, 1865: " I did not dream that there were
such bitter drops in that fountain, whose flow is usually so beautiful. Courage,
My Boy. We can quickly sweeten them." He then presented a choice of positions for the coming year. First, a clerkship in the Exchange Hotel, " with
such a salary . . . as would enable you to support most comfortably yourself and
another." Second, a position as book keeper and cashier in a business house in
New York, recently offered to Clifford Lanier by a friend: " He talks eloquently
of my advantages of study, & of association with literary men, access to books,
&c . Would you like this, if I should ask him to transfer his offer to you? . . .
Your best hope, Sir, is in your pen. Then the best thing is to go to New
York."
  But R. S. Lanier, in a letter to his son Clifford, Dec. 5, 1865, discouraged
acceptance of the New York job, which was promised for only one year: " You
might then be tempted to try the untried *sea of letters* in which so many poor
Bohemians have drowned themselves. Better tempt the Muses by gas-light
wooing, with your breeches pocket lined with Greenbacks." (See also note 1,
1866.)

1866[1]

To Virginia Hankins

Exchange Hotel, Montgomery Ala
Jany 14th 1866

Sweet, high-Souled, pure-Souled, Sad-Souled Ginna. My Little One, My Sacro-Sanct Woman. My Blessing out of Heaven!

O Flower, I do not see how They had the heart to crush thee, even for the sake of the perfume that exhales from *thine* oppressed heart:—and I strive and Struggle to get to thee, and I swear that God is the only One that could ever have kept me from thee so long—: and if I think of it one moment longer my heart will break and my soul will be dark as the ————

———— Time after time have I written you – I have recd three letters from you, each of which announced that you had not heard from me – Despairing of reaching you I was about to postpone any attempt to talk to you until I could do so in person, when a lucky accident presented me this opportunity of sending a letter to you –

A gentleman presented me his card yesterday, inscribed " Mr Tinsley, of the Spotswood Hotel," and of course, when we fell a-talking my first question of him was, did he know General

---

[1] No letters by Sidney Lanier written between Nov. 25, 1865, and Jan. 14, 1866, have been found. On Dec. 17, 1865, R. S. Lanier had left Macon to join his children for Christmas in Montgomery or at Point Clear. On Jan. 10, 1866, having returned to Macon, he wrote Sidney that the money he expected to find on his return had not arrived, and that he was therefore, to date, unable to send the money his son wanted—apparently to start a store of some sort in Montgomery with his brother Clifford. On Jan. 16 he added: " Having received your brother's telegram—not to send the money you wrote for I did not write you further on the subject. But I hope you were not disappointed in going on with the business you thought would pay so well." But Lanier had apparently by this time joined his brother Clifford as a clerk at the Exchange Hotel, although he seems from the first to have regarded the position as a temporary one.

Hankins of Surrey? At mention of the name, another gentleman standing by, (it was in the Hotel Office) turned quickly round and said, " He is my cousin!") We shook hands, Mr *Graves,* Mr Tinsley and I, and had a pleasant talk: and the upshot is, that Mr Tinsley pledges himself to get this letter to you if possible – He returns to Richmond in the morning, and so I'm scratching of this hurriedly to-night – May all the Gods assist him to bear to you this message of unfailing and unforgetting and ever-deepening love from your faithful and half-worshipping Friends

Sid & Cliff,

Who expect you to write them here, as soon as possible –

To Harriet (Freeman) Fulton

Exchange Hotel, Montgomery, Ala.

Jan'y.   22nd, 1866.

My dear Friend:

I should have written you long ago:—but I have somehow felt the greatest reluctance to saying anything upon the subject which I knew I should have to speak of in my letter to you.

The truth is, Necessity has driven a wedge into my life, and split it in two. Whereas I *used* to live wholly to make beautiful things, I *now* live *half-ly* to make *money*: and I hate all half-way things, and so I don't like to talk about it. – Don't let's talk about it – Requiescat! Schweigen! it is finished! –

I scarcely know how to thank you for your offer,[2] which was so much more liberal than I could have expected, or deserved. – *That,* however, pleased me all the more: for I attributed the liberal proposition rather to your love for me, than your estimate of my real services: and I had rather be loved than *prized.*

---

[2] To induce Lanier to return to his position as tutor at Scott's Mills, R. S. Lanier rad reported in his letter of Nov. 29, 1865, that Mr. and Mrs. Fulton had offered him a salary of $1000, besides board, and " a *good* horse . . . & feed for him." In his letter of Jan. 10, 1866, he had added: " Had a long talk with Mrs. Fulton the other day. She laments your decision—but thinks you did right. Said she would have offered better terms to have secured you—had bought a good piano in expectation of you."

Indeed I thank you very much for all your kindnesses to me: I find it hard to say no to you.

Father writes me that the mill is like to prosper, and is about to produce a favorable *turn* in your fortunes. — Bully, say I! — and one good *turn* deserves another. You're in better luck than any that visited the wildest dreams of Micawber: for he only wanted something to turn *up*: while *yours* turns all round. The *Millenium* is come, to you: you'll be a Millionaire. As a Mill-owner, *old saws* will perhaps be profitable to you: and so I send you some, to wit: —

Do not grind the poor: but grain.

Produce, as far as you can, the (A1) *flower* of our Southern chivalry.

Never get mealy-mouthed.

Issue cereals like (the) Dickens! (*vide. "All the Year Round"*)

" Toll slowly "!

Your damn is your oath: but, if your dam break, not on that account is your oath broken.

Let your mill-wheel be a common weal!

If your *flour* rise well, then will it be a-rose!

A circular " saw ":

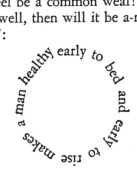

An upright " saw ":   Honesty
is
the
best
policy.

I'm afraid you wish devoutly that you could *run* all these saws. —

-- All in the dark, I feel a dim presentiment of strange things happening -- What?

My love to your Goodman and all that remember

Sid. Lanier.

To ——————————? [3]

[Montgomery, Ala., February, 1866?]

My Dear Sir:

I think there is surely no greater stumbling-block in the way of free and earnest utterance than that euphemistic *superlative-ism* of our day which, having exhausted all the strong expressions of our language upon trivial occasions, has left none but weak words wherewith to express strong emotions –

To the man who saves my life I cannot say, " Sir, a thousand thanks," because I should say as much if he only handed me my hat: nor could I say " Sir my heart will swell with eternal gratitude &c," – because (reverencing time-honored customs!) I should say *that* if he but toasted me at dinner: so that, under the circumstances, one prefers to abandon speech, which the World's bad men have reverted into " a method of concealing thought," to grasp his preserver's hand, and to say – nothing.

The hope of doing this, – of taking your hand, and looking into your eye, in person, – has for twelve months prevented me from writing you: but, it has now withdrawn itself to an indefinite distance, and I fear to be longer silent, lest you will think me totally insensible to all your kindness.

And yet, it is only to interpret this silence by rendering its reason, and not to say ought, that I write – No true emotion is voluble: of all emotions Gratitude does most halt and

---

[3] This is a draft of a letter (dated from internal evidence) no other copy of which has been found. It was probably addressed to Judge Russell, whose daughter Mary had married Lanier's uncle, Sidney C. Lanier, referred to in this letter. (Clifford Lanier in letters to his father on Dec. 1 and Dec. 10, 1864, had suggested Judge Russell as a likely intermediary in securing his brother's release.) Another bare possibility is that it was addressed to a distant cousin, J. F. D. Lanier of New York, who, according to family tradition, assisted in securing Lanier's release from prison. A third possibility is Judge Robert Ould (see note 55, 1864).

stammer when called on to utter itself forth –. In how poor a case am I, my dear Sir, who, wishing to say all things to you, am driven after much awkward prefacing and generalizing, only to render pitiful excuses for saying nothing!

You, if you have ever had a benefactor whom you reverenced so highly that you were *content* to be under obligations to him, will pardon me if I say no more, and understand me if I beg that I may write you and hear from you, sometimes –

Uncle Sid tells me that you understood the necessity which compelled me to address you, in my prison-letters with so much more familiarity than my acquantance with you justified: a great relief to me, since I expended considerable ingenuity in endeavoring to hint to *you*, and *not* to the letter-inspectors, the true state of affairs –. The mode of my release, with which I hope some time to amuse you prevented me from announcing it to you by letter: – which I was the more anxious to do since I suspected, from your last letter, that you were probably on your way to Point Lookout at the time of my departure –.[4]

What will the Radicals do with us? It is fortunate that most of us here are so entirely occupied with earning our daily bread that we have little time either for regretting or foreboding evils – The luxury of grief is beyond our means: and provisions are too scarce in our citadel to support any Cassandra or other Evil-prophet – Is it not well?

To Robert S. Lanier

Exchange Hotel
Montgomery Ala
March 21/66

My Dear Pa:

Your good letter in reply to the Photographs [5] was duly rec^d and read to an admiring and enthusiastic audience. I'm glad you liked the pictures: tho' they don't do the girls justice at all.

---

[4] Traditions concerning Lanier's release from prison are obscure and contradictory, and the " mode of my release " is explained only in the brief statement in Lanier's letter of June 11, 1866, to M. H. Northrup: " Some gold, which a friend of mine had smuggled into the prison in his mouth, obtained the release of both of us." (See also Appendix C, vol. X.)

[5] One of the photographs referred to is apparently the group picture taken on

As far as the criticism is concerned – if I had known that it was to be submitted to a solemn conclave of the musical Cognoscenti I should have been decidedly more elaborate in the preparation of it: tho' the factitious glamor of triumph thrown upon it by the magnificent discomfiture of my fair opponent will, I hope, conceal its real meagreness.[6]

I've just returned from a flying visit to New Orleans where I've been playing the carpet Knight to Aunt Jane and Carrie Ligon.[7]

We had a good time: saw many pretty things and heard some fine music – I especially enjoyed a visit to the Vesper Service at the Catholic Cathedral.

My health is better since I returned, and I hope that the warm weather will relieve me of the cold from which I've been suffering so long.

On our way back we paid a visit to the point (Clear) and took Uncle Will by storm. Had a glorious haul with the seine and caught a barrel-full of sheep-head, trout, spots &c.

Gen. Smedes, of St. James Hotel, New Orleans, has bought Pt. Clear Hotel, and Uncle Will is to run it this season. It is to be thoroughly refitted and refurnished, and they expect to make the investment clear, this season. The Hotels in New Orleans are doing the most smashing business: and I would I could run one of 'em for just one year.

I'm sorry to hear that y'r business has declined but I believe it is the case universally and so don't complain. *We* are quite dull.

Cliff and I have been wooing the muses, being incited thereto

Lookout Mountain in 1866 of Sidney and Clifford Lanier, Carrie Ligon (later Mrs. Edward Varner), and her cousin Wilhelmina Clopton (later Mrs. Clifford Lanier), first reproduced by Alfred Allen in *Mid-Continent*, VI, 83 (May, 1895). Other possible photographs may have been the one of Lanier in Confederate uniform, first reproduced by M. H. Northrup in *Lippincott's*, LXXV, 302 (Mar., 1905), or the picture of him used for the engraving on the title-page of *Little Ella*, sheet music published in Montgomery in 1868. (The last two are reproduced in the present volume, pp. 228 and 379.)

[6] The "criticism" was probably of a performance of *Traviata* or *Martha*, in Montgomery, by a company that played later in Macon (see R. S. Lanier's letter of Feb. 23, 1866, to Clifford Lanier). It was possibly published in a Montgomery newspaper, but has not been located.

[7] Carrie Ligon of Tuskegee, Ala., was a distant cousin of the Laniers and a first cousin of Wilhelmina Clopton.

by the manifold lovely charms and graces of our pretty cousins of Tuskegee. Cliff went over with Carrie and spent a couple of days, returning last night, after a most uproarious good time. Says the Tuskegeans fêted him to death. Cousin Dave Clopton has formed a copartnership with Judge Stone and will settle here, bringing his family over in the fall. I should not be surprised if Bob Ligon follows suit.

Am sorry to hear of our Darling's illness, and hope she has quite recovered by this time. Give her a thousand kisses for us: and ask her for me, please to write me something of my Sweetheart.[8] I've not a word from her in a long time: has she forgotten me?

I enclose ye little Poems.[9]

Write me often. Love to Uncle C & family, and all friends from

Sid. L.

To Robert S. Lanier

Exchange Hotel
Montgomery Ala.
March 24/66

My Dear Pa:

        With no news to tell, I scratch a hasty note, to inclose a little poem,[10] which is by neither Cliff nor me, but —

---

[8] " Our Darling " was Gertrude Lanier. " My Sweetheart " seems to have been Mary Lou Lamar, a younger sister of Lanier's friend Augusta Lamar Ogden, for Gertrude Lanier's letters of this period to both her brothers indicate that Sidney was supposedly in love with her. On the other hand, the reference may have been to Mary Day, who had broken her engagement to Fred Andrews; but although she wrote to his brother Clifford twice in April, she apparently did not resume correspondence with Lanier before Aug., 1866.

R. S. Lanier kept his son informed about his friends. On Jan. 10, he had written: " Have seen Mary Lou several times—she looks well. Mamy Day comes to table occasionally: but there is something preying on her mind, I think, something more than physical ailment—it seems to me." And on Mar. 10 he wrote to Clifford: " Mamie is spending a few days at Mrs. Fulton's—She has improved of late. Seems more cheerful."

[9] The poems sent with this letter have not been identified. It is possible that they are the poems included in Lanier's letters of Mar. 24 and 26 (see notes 10, 12, and 13, below), omitted by mistake from this letter.

[10] " To ——— ('Twas winter when I met you first)," by Sidney and Clifford

by both of us. I like it better than anything we have yet done, singly. It is more simple, less involute, more passionate, more full of broader meanings.

Hope Sister is well – Don't hear from my Sweetheart – Has she cast me off?

All well here – Business duller than I ever knew it. Merchants, Lawyers, farmers, Hotel, – all sick.

Love to everybody.

Sid. L.

Poem on other side. Show it to Judge Nisbet,[11] but don't publish it: Cliff & I are getting up a volume.

To Robert S. Lanier

Exchange Hotel
Montgomery Ala.
March 26/66.

Dear Pa:

Here's our best: on the other side.[12]

The partnership works well. Write us what you think of the poems.

All well: Wrote you yesterday, enclosing poems.[13]

How's Sister. Our love to her and all.

Hastily,

S. C. L.

You must read it three times, and then get Uncle C to read it to you, aloud.

Lanier, a copy of which in the autograph of Clifford Lanier was sent to Virginia Hankins (see I, 213).

[11] Judge Eugenius A. Nisbet of Macon, in whose memory Lanier delivered an address in 1871 (V, 277).

[12] "A Song (Day is a silver veil)," by Sidney and Clifford Lanier (I, 213).

[13] Two poems by Sidney Lanier alone: "To Willie Clopton" (I, 158), and "To Carrie Ligon" (I, 159).

To Robert S. Lanier

Montgomery   Ala
March 30th/66

My Dear Pa:

Here's another one,[14] by me *individually.*

Write me what you think of it.

We're all well. Cliff and McDaniel [15] have gone out hunting to-day; and are having a good time with the snipe.

Business dull as dull can be, in every department of trade.

I believe this is my Fourth to you since I heard from you. Write me.

Sid. L.

From Robert S. Lanier

Macon Ga.   April 11, 1866.

My dear son:

Yours of 8th inst. came to-day. I will reply to it at once as you hold me in your debt.

What I stated in my last letter in regard to a want of competency to determine correctly the merits of the pieces submitted to me is no doubt true, for I have been too-long diverted from the line of thought & reading which would best qualify me for such office. I *ought* to distrust at least some of the views offered, though, on the other hand, the danger was that I should lean to favorable views. What I had to say was more the result of taste than an application of the rules of the art of poetry. Discussions on the former would perhaps take a wide range & not reach very definite conclusions. The general impression my letter was calculated to make is, I think, not far from what it ought to be: but the truth is there were so many things to be said that were not said for want of time & space that this impression was hardly as clear & vivid as it might have been. Shall I concentrate all my powers on the " Sea Shore

---

[14] " *Will* ' all be right in a hundred years? ' " (I, 159).
[15] Another clerk at the Exchange Hotel.

Grave"?[16] Perhaps I had best do so, & will send you the result in a few days. I have got a sabbath school speech to write for the young representative of the Methodist church for 1st May & that will take up two or three of the ensuing nights.[17]

In the poem last referred to I notice perhaps a verbal error in the first verse, 2 line ends—" shore "—4 line ends " me." Was that intended? I suppose not—as elsewhere the alternate lines rhyme. Let me know.

Gertrude & I are very well & so is Lamar-tini,[18] who I see once to thrice or oftener every week. Gertrude sees her oftenerer, & as the latter has intimated to me none of those capriccios you refer to I do not think they exist. Indeed I have noticed nothing but what tended to show that former impressions were in active force. Gertrude has a pleasant time with her friends, & is very lively, & sweet. She would pet her old father – if he would permit it. She is now more to him than mere daughter. She is his affectionate friend & companion.

My business has been very fair since the month commenced. But after May court the summer will be very dull. I read with regret the accounts you continue to give of business in Montgomery. Wont somebody tell us something about Grandpa & Ma – where they are & what doing, & of William & Lucy?

Hurriedly your father
R S Lanier.

Love to brother C. & all the family.

To GERTRUDE LANIER

Montgomery Ala
May 4th /66

My Darling Sissa:

We got your beautiful letter, and read it with more pleasure than I could well describe to you. Your flower-

---

[16] " A Sea-Shore Grave " was written by Sidney and Clifford Lanier in memory of their mother (I, 214).

[17] In Apr., 1854, Sidney Lanier himself, aged 12, had been the Presbyterian Sunday School orator at the annual celebration of the Macon Church schools. On a similar occasion in the late 1860's, he also wrote an address for one Master McKay entitled " What I Know About Flowers " (see Preface, vol. I).

[18] The reference is to Mary Lou Lamar.

symbols were fine and very appropriate to the fair souls they represented.

I have been in quite a whirl of excitement since I wrote you last. You must know that, some weeks ago, the ladies of Montgomery formed an association for the purpose of giving a set of Tableaux and Concert, the proceeds of which were to be devoted to the purchase of a plot of ground where might be interred the remains of Alabama soldiers buried in Tennessee during the war. A supper, of all sorts of good things was to follow each performance. – Well: time rolled on, and the tableaux were given and, the first night after, came the Concert in which Cliff and I played a duett, and I a solo. We were both inspired by the most brilliant audience I ever beheld, and played well –. The duett was encored enthusiastically; and so was the solo. Besides these were some choruses, and vocal duetts and trios, by other ladies and gentlemen of the city, which went off splendidly, and the concert closed with a grand Supper at which everybody in town was present, including us. Compliments and congratulations poured in on Cliff and me from every quarter; and we extended our acquaintance indefinitely.[19]

I hope that Father is better than when you wrote. Are *you* as fat as when you left Pt. Clear?

Tell Pa I am looking for his criticism of the last poems I sent him.

I suppose you enjoyed yourself hugely, in the beautiful expanding of the Spring, at Mrs. Fulton's. I should like to have been there to wander through those magnificent woods with you. When you see Mrs F. do remind her that she owes me a reply to my last letter to her.

---

[19] There were apparently other concerts that month. A letter to Lanier from Vittaria Bailini, Columbus, Ga., May 16, 1866, indicates plans for a second concert on May 29, featuring Mme. Bailini, and refers to letters from Mrs. Montgomery and Mrs. Ludecus. The former was Mrs. Mattie Montgomery, the friend who had found Lanier on the flag-of-truce steamer bearing soldiers for exchange to City Point, Va., in Feb., 1865 (Starke, pp. 68-69). Lanier's song, *Little Ella*, not published until March, 1868, but "Dedicated to Ella S. Montgomery . . . May 10, 1866," was addressed to her daughter and may have been performed publicly about the date of composition. A note from Mrs. Montgomery dated May 14, 1866, reads: "Messrs. Lanier will please accept the accompanying Bouquets,—from their friends & admirers, Little Mother & Ella."

Am glad to hear of Father's continuance of good business –
Ours has plucked up a little in the last week: but only temporarily, I suppose.

Love to all friends that inquire for me

from   Your Most loving

Sid.

To Milton H. Northrup [20]

Exchange Hotel
Montgomery, Alabama
May 12th "66
address so.

My Dear Northrop:

So wild and high are the big war-waves
dashing between '61 and '66, as between two Shores, – that,
looking across their "rude imperious surge," I can scarcely
discern any sight or sound of those old peaceful days that you
and I passed on the 'Sacred soil' of M[idway] – The sweet,
half-pastoral tones that *should* come from out that golden time,
float to me mixed with battle-cries and groans – It was our
glorious Spring: but, My God! the flowers of it send up sul-
phurous odors, and their petals are dabbled with blood.

These things being so, I thank you, more than I can well
express, for your kind letter. It comes to me, like a welcome
sail, from that Old World to this New one, through the war-
Storm. It takes away the sulphur and the blood-flecks, and
drowns out the harsh noises of battle. The two margins of the
great gulf which has divided you from me seem approaching
each other: I stretch out my hand across the narrowing fissure,
to grasp yours on the other side.

[20] Previously published, with omissions, in *Lippincott's*, LXXV, 305-306
Mar., 1905), by M. H. Northrup, whose introductory note stated: "On the
return of peace and the reëstablishment of postal relations throughout the South,
while still ignorant of [Lanier's] fate, I ventured a letter to my friend of antebellum days. A prompt response followed, inaugurating a correspondence that
continued at irregular intervals for years." Northrup had been a friend of Lanier's
at Milledgeville, 1860-1861 (see note 9, 1860). (For excerpts, more correctly
printed, see Mims, pp. 64-65.)

And I wish, with all my heart, that you and I could spend this ineffable May Afternoon under that old oak at Whittaker's and " talk it all over "!

I am glad that you continue to be of the gay troubadour-craft of letters: and especially congratulate you upon occupying so complimentary a position in our guild, as that of Correspondent to the World, which, by the way, is the only N. Y. paper that I take.

You must know that Clifford and I lost all we had, and have been compelled to go to hard work for our living. We have, however, through kind friends, obtained positions with good salaries, so that we are free, at least, from the pressure of immediate want. In the moments that we can spare from business we continue our studies, with even more ardor than while we had plenty of time to devote to them.

Cliff has finished a novel,[21] written entirely during intervals snatched from business: and I am working upon one which I hope to finish ere long. We also hope to get out a volume of poems in the fall, written by *both* of us, conjointly.

You will laugh at these ambitious schemes, when I tell you that we have not yet offered for print a single thing! But, we have no newspapers here with circulation enough to excite our ambition: and of course the Northern papers are beyond our reach. Our literary life, too, is a lonely and somewhat cheerless one; for beyond our father, a man of considerable literary acquirements and exquisite taste, we have not been able to find a single individual who sympathized in such pursuits enough to warrant showing him our little productions. So scarce is " general cultivation " here! But we work on, and hope to become, at least, recognized as good orderly citizens in the fair realm of letters, yet.

There's so much to tell you, and so much to hear from you! Our adventures (I say our, for Cliff and I were by each other during all the war) would fill, and possibly *will* fill, a volume: and I do not doubt that yours will prove equally varied.

Let me have them; and if you will keep me posted as to your whereabouts, I'll keep up a talk with you.

I'm thirsty to know what is going on in the great Art-world

---

[21] *Thorn-Fruit,* published by Blelock & Co., New York, 1867. Sidney Lanier did not finish his novel, *Tiger-Lilies,* until the spring of 1867.

up there: you have no idea how benighted we all are – I've only recently begun to get into the doings of literary men, through the Round Table,[22] which I've just commenced taking.

Write me soon: and believe that I am always

Yr Friend

Sidney Lanier

Clifford sends kind regards. Many of y'r old friends at the college were killed in battle. Will particularize some other time.

TO VIRGINIA HANKINS

Exchange Hotel
Montgomery Ala
May 13th "/66

Dear, Most-sweet, Ginna, I wish, often, with more earnestness than you can well imagine, "that I had a commodity of good names" to call you by; – sweet names, that would be each a love's-declaration in itself; – names as passionate as Rose-odors and as tender as Heaven; names full of my soul, which I could send to you like ships full of freight. They would be so much better than these poor words, which, as I write them, seem to me to fall on the paper like so many rain-drop-blots, weak, vapid, and tasteless. But I can't pronounce any such names: – except on my flute, and you're too far, alas, for that: and so, Child, content yourself with vapidities.

How do I yearn to spend one of these long ineffable May mornings with you, in a ride through those green alleys in the blessed woods that surround you! And if I might but sit on the shore there with you, as we sat, that sunset, and send my soul on a voyage down your unfathomable eyes to look for the mystery of the Beautiful and the Sorrowful!—

What is this talk of Marriage-bells? – *Your* Marriage-bells? – *Yours*, Ginna?

---

[22] *The Round Table: A Saturday Review of Politics, Finance, Literature, Society, and Art* was published in New York from Dec. 19, 1863, until July 30, 1864; and from Sept. 2, 1865, until July 3, 1869. The editors, during the period in which Lanier not only subscribed but contributed to the *Round Table,* were Dorsey Gardner and Henry Sedley.

I do not grasp this idea, at all – My mind is not large enough to concieve of your – Marriage. It is something which has not occurred to me: the possibility of it seemed about as remote as that of a silver Star fluttering down to yoke itself with a stone, or some other earth.– But then – you were joking and I'm a fool————

I often think my heart will break if I do not see you soon. You're the only one, of all the friends I ever had, (and they've been many) with whom I connect nothing earthy, in whom I see no fault. I address prayers to you as to a pure-white Soul that has chosen, I know not why, to unveil Itself before me. My Soul stands forever uncovered, with bent head, before you, reverencing, worshipping, as much as you will receive. O One-friend, my soul is a sea, to which you are the flowery shore –: my thoughts come running shorewards, wave after wave, and climb as high as they can towards you, and bow, and then sparkle away in a death-ecstasy, as if, having reverenced *you,* their life-end was fulfilled, and nothing left them but to die.

I bless you: and pray for some words from you – You do not talk to me as you used– You are not afraid? – *I* am not, of you–. I would trust you with my salvation– If Heaven were mine, I had as lief you administered it as I. Whatever I am or have been to others, – to you I am always your wholly-loving, reverencing, longing

L.

The package and y'r letter are received – We thank you very much – Cliff will write shortly – Our love and regards to all with you. Hop is not to be married soon, I believe –

S.

To Virginia Hankins

Exchange Hotel
Montgomery, Ala.
June 9th /66

Ginna, did you see the stars yesterday, just after Sunset, how they all flocked out of the East, streaming Westward, until they drowned themselves in the late-remaining glow of the Sun?

So, O my Little One, do my thoughts throng to you, over yonder, and lose themselves in a rosy sweetness when they reach you – If only I, – I mean the flesh-and-bone *I*, – could go, too, and reach you! Himmel, Himmel, why has God tied all this matter, clog-work, to our Souls? –

I *want* you, *so* much! I've not seen anybody like you, before nor since I met you. I know some that love Beauty as *much,* but none that love Her so *well,* as you. I know some with souls as airy and as fleet of wing: – but none so strong to upbear heavy weights, nor so pure to breathe the fine upper air where we love to dwell.

Child, you're better than a Star, for your rays, being bright and pure, are also warm and passionate.

You're better than a flower, for the adverse Seasons, instead of killing you, only make you sweeter and stronger.

You're better than a bird, for I understand your Songs.

You are too fine for this world: but I'm glad, glad, that you are not too high to see and answer your

Yearning and Loving

S.

To Milton H. Northrup [23]

Exchange Hotel,
Montgomery Alabama
June 11th "66

My Dear Northrop:

I have to thank you for your promptness in replying to my letter, as well as for your kind expressions in regard to its contents. Since I like *friendship* better than all things else in the world, I'm well content to believe that y'r complimentary terms originated in *that,* rather than in any merit of what was written.

---

[23] Previously published in *Lippincott's* LXXV, 307-309 (Mar., 1905), and excerpt in Mims, pp. 54-55. The outline of Lanier's military career, as given in this letter, is not correct in detail, and his estimates of time are usually wrong. These inaccuracies are corrected by letters written during the actual experiences of the war (see note 13, 1862, above).

I proceed to give you a very condensed " syllabus " of my war-experiences. In June, of '61, 1 enlisted as private in the 2nd Georgia Battalion of Infantry, then stationed amongst the marshes of Sewall's Point, Va, immediately opposite Ft. Monroe. Here we played " Marsh-Divers " and " Meadow-Crakes " for Six months, our principal duties being to picket the beach: and our pleasures and sweet rewards-of-toil consisting in Agues that played dice with our bones, and blue-mass pills that played the deuce with our livers. Unless you 've had a real James River chill and fever, you'll utterly fail to appreciate the beauties of the Situation.

We were next ordered to Wilmington N. C., where we experienced a pleasant change in the Style of fever; indulging, for two or three months, in what are called the " dry shakes of the sand-hills," a sort of brilliant tremolo movement brilliantly executed, upon " that pan-pipe, man," by an invisible but very powerful performer.

We were then sent to Drury's Bluff: and, from there to the Chickahominy, participating in the famous Seven days battles around Richmond — Shortly afterward, my regiment went upon a special expedition down the South bank of the James, and, after a little gunboat-fight or two, was sent to Petersburg, to rest. While in Camp there, I, with Cliff and two friends, obtained a transfer to Maj. Milligan's Signal Corps; and becoming soon proficient in the System, attracted the attention of the Com'd'g Off. who formed us into a mounted Field Squad and attached us to the Staff of Maj. Gen. French.

After various and sundry adventures, in that capacity, we were ordered to proceed to " The Rocks," a point on the James near its mouth, opposite Newport's News, where we remained about a year and a half, acting as scouts, and transmitting our information across a Signal line which extended up the river to Petersburg. Our life, during this period was as full of romance as heart could desire. We had a flute and a guitar, good horses, a beautiful country, splendid residences inhabited by friends who loved us, and plenty of hair-breadth 'scapes from the roving bands of Federals who were continually visiting that Debateable Land. I look back on that as the most delicious period of my life, in many respects: Cliff and I never cease to talk of the beautiful women, the serenades, the moon-light dashes on the beach of fair Burwell's Bay (just above Hampton Roads), and the spirited brushes of our little force with the enemy.

The advance of Gen. Butler upon Petersburg broke up the Signal line, but our party was ordered to remain, acting as scouts in the rear of Gen. B.'s army. By dint of much hiding in woods, and much hard running from lair to lair, we managed to hold our position and rendered some service, with information of the enemy's movement.

From here, My Bro. and I were called by an order from our Sec'y of War, instructing us to report for duty to Maj.-Gen. Whiting, at Wilmington. Arrived there, we were assigned to duty on Blockading Steamers, as Signal Officers; Clifford on the " Talisman," I on the " Lucy." Cliff made three delightful and adventurous trips: from Nassau to Wilmington: was wrecked, on the last voyage, and just saved his life, getting on a federal Schooner just in time to see his Steamer go down. He went then to Bermuda, and was on the point of sailing for Wilmington as Sig. Off. of the St'r Maude Campbell, when, hearing of the capture of Wil[ming]ton, he went to Havana, thence, after a pleasant time of a month with friends in Cuba, to Galveston Texas, whence he *walked* to *Macon, Ga*: arriving just in time to see our Mother die. I, meanwhile, ran the blockade of Wilmington, successfully, but was captured, in the gulf-stream, by the Federal cruiser Santiago de Cuba, carried to Norfolk, thence to Fortress Monroe, and Camp Hamilton, and at last to Point Lookout, where I spent four months in prison. Some gold, which a friend of mine had smuggled into the prison in his mouth, obtained the release of both of us. I made my way home, by a long and painful journey, and, immediately upon my arrival, losing the stimulus which had kept me going so long, fell dangerously ill and remained so for three months, – delirious part of the time. I had but begun to recover, when Gen. Wilson entered and occupied the city (Macon, Ga.). Then Cliff came; then we buried our Mother; – who had been keeping herself alive for months by the strong conviction, which she expressed again and again, that God would bring both her boys to her, before she died.

Then peace came, and we looked about, over the blankest world you can imagine, for some employment – My Brother first came here, as book-keeper, of this hotel: I meanwhile spending the winter at Point Clear on Mobile Bay. In January last, I came here –.

And so, you have a very outlinish outline of my history.

Your letters do me more good than you imagine – Himmel! My dear Boy, you are all *so* alive, up there, and *we* are all *so* dead, down here! I begin to have serious thought of emigrating to y'r country, so that I may live, a little. There's not enough attrition of mind on mind, here, to bring out any sparks from a man.

I offer you my sincere congratulations upon the flattering proposition made to you by y'r friends in Syracuse –.[24] From what I know of you, I should think that the life of a journalist would suit your temperament and talents exactly. Success to you, Monsieur le Feuilletoniste! And may the Devils be kind to you.

I won't weary you. Write me: and accept the constant regard of Y'r friend

                    Sidney Lanier

Cliff. sends kind regards.

To Milton H. Northrup [25]

                    Exchange Hotel,
                        Montgomery, Alabama
                        June 29, '66.

My dear Northrop —

            The cadaverous enclosed is supposed to represent the face of yr friend, together with a small portion of the Confederate-graycoat, in which enwrapped he did breast the big wars.

I have one favor to entreat; and that is, that you will hold in consideration the very primitive state of the photographic

---

[24] Apparently Northrup had been offered the editorial position with the Syracuse *Courier* which he accepted several years later.

[25] Previously published, *Lippincott's*, LXXV, 309 (Mar., 1905); Mims, pp. 65-66. With this letter Lanier sent a copy of the familiar *carte de visite* photograph of himself in Confederate uniform (see facing illustration).

LANIER IN CONFEDERATE UNIFORM, 1866

Courtesy of Miss Alice Northrup, Syracuse, New York

art in this section, & believe that my mouth is *not* so large, by some inches, as this villanous artist portrays it.

I despair of giving you any idea of the mortal stagnation which paralyzes all business here.   On our streets, Monday is very like Sunday: they show no life, save late in the afternoon when the girls come out, one by one, and shine & move, just as the stars do, an hour later.   I dont think there's a man in town who could be induced to go into his neighbor's store and ask how's trade: for he would have to atone for such an insult with his life.   Everything is dreamy, and drowsy, and drone-y — The trees stand like statues: and even when a breeze comes, the leaves flutter and dangle idly about, as if with a languid protest against all disturbance of their perfect rest.   The mocking-birds absolutely refuse to sing before twelve o'clock at night, when the air is somewhat cooled: and the fire-flies flicker more slowly than I ever saw them, before.   Our whole world, here, yawns, in a vast and sultry spell of laziness.   An " exposition of sleep " is come over us, as over Sweet Bully Bottom; and we wont wake till Winter.[26]

Give me some idea of the internal " modus agendi " of a paper like the " World."   As day-editor, for instance, what would you have to do?

It is possible that Cliff or I may go North in the fall, with bloody literary designs on some hapless publisher.

I anticipate much pleasure in meeting you if it should be *my* lot to go.   Meantime, do you know Judge Russell?   If not, and you should need him, call and tell him you're my friend. He's a friend, and distant connection: My Uncle married his daughter.[27]

Cliff sends love.   Write me often.   Y'r letters always wake me up from that sleep which I share with my torpid fellow-citizens here.

Y'r Friend

Sid. Lanier.

[26] The allusion is to *A Midsummer-Night's Dream*.   The depressing conditions in the South after the war are reflected in a number of Lanier's writings, notably in the fragmentary novel " John Lockwood's Mill " (V, 231).

[27] In a letter of May 27, 1866, to his sister Gertrude, Clifford Lanier referred to the death of his Uncle Sidney, in New York, " about the 15th April "; his wife, Judge Russell's daughter, Sidney Lanier saw several times in New York in later years.

To Robert S. Lanier

Montgomery, Ala
July 1st/66

My Dear Father:

We recd your and Sister's letters yesterday, for which we had been looking a long time. Mr Watt, however, had heard, at the Chalybeate, Ga, that you were at the Indian Springs! [28] and we attributed your long silence to the heavy demands made upon your time by the gayeties of the Watering-place.

I had written you, in reply to your strictures on the War-chapters: [29] but suppose you had not received my letter as you make no mention of it.

Things go on quietly enough, here: the regular monotony of our life being a little changed, since yesterday, by the arrival of Uncle William, Grand Pa & Grand Ma. The grandparents are in the very highest condition of health: I should put Grand-ma down at about 350, Nett. While this amount of flesh is somewhat uncomfortable, during these Tartarean days, yet the discomfort may be compensated by the reflection, – that she'll save firewood in the winter. Uncle Will, tho' hardly so fat as when we left him in the winter, is still in good case, and armed with full many a quip and jest which he lets off, after the manner of the Fire-by-file. He reports considerable increase in the Company at Pt. Clear.

How is your business, now?

Cliff and I write our little effusions, and have settled into

---

[28] A resort about 35 miles northwest of Macon.

[29] The reference is probably to a long letter from R. S. Lanier to Clifford Lanier, June 22, 1866. In addition to the criticism of *Tiger-Lilies* here alluded to (see V, xxxv), he had urged his sons not to devote themselves exclusively to poetry and romance, but to turn their attention to the more practical branches of literature, " political essays, social questions, criticism, history &c." And he proposed as an immediate subject of study: " *North American Civilization as illustrated by the War*. . . . (Its illustrative conduct towards Mr. Davis being the central idea all through.)" He concluded: " Or if you insist on poetical composition – then I pray you read Spencer's Fairy Queen & . . . let its splendid allegories suggest a new mode of attacking the *demonalogy*—if I may so call it—of the Purito – Blue-nose – oh! – Radico-Abolitionism of North America. . . . Oh! what a chance here for immortality! "

quite sober and staid citizens. Cliff has finished his novel, and
has already begun a new one, on what, he says, are scientific
principles. I have evolved some ten Chapters, since those I sent
you: and lack about ten more to finish.[30]

We have here a Literary Society, which is just beginning to
flourish finely. Upon the invitation of some of the members,
Cliff and I have joined it,[31] and have already taken some stand.
I made a speech last night, which has brought out several
congratulations.

I wish sincerely we could be with you, but the state of our
finances will scarcely admit such an expenditure as would be
necessary. And so we wait and hope.

I should have been very glad if Sister had gone with the
party she mentioned to Lookout Mountain. Some travel would
help her immensely, in giving new subjects of thought.

No news. All send love and wishes that you could be here.

Sid. L.

To Robert S. Lanier [32]

Exchange Hotel
Montgomery Ala
July 13th "/66

My Dear Father:

The notes from you & Uncle Clifford are rec[d]
and " digested."

As far as regards your (and his) suggestion in regard to *the*

[30] In his letter of May 27, 1866, to Gertrude Lanier, Clifford Lanier had
written: " Bro Sid and I are working, I only in revising—He is writing nearly
a chapter every day: and never have I read anything that surpasses his writing in
beauty and purity. You cannot imagine anything more delightful than our
reunions at night, when we show each other all the beautiful thoughts we have
conceived during the day. Yet we are not secluded, two or three of every seven
evenings are spent in making music for, and knowing, the good people here.
I have changed somewhat my reclusive habits and, without dissipating, am striving to be sociable. Our only disadvantage is the absence from you and our
beloved Father."

[31] See the note from Daniel Fraser to Sidney Lanier, Montgomery, July 11,
1866, informing him of his election to the Montgomery Literary Society.

[32] Excerpt previously published, Mims, pp. 81-82. R. S. Lanier's letter to
Sidney Lanier, July 4, 1866, is in criticism of Book II, Chapters I and II, of
Tiger-Lilies, and refers to a similar letter written by Lanier's uncle, Clifford
Anderson (which has not survived). Their criticisms, which Lanier apparently
had requested, are sufficiently implied in his comments on their letters.

propriety of expressing individual opinions of the Author in other ways besides the utterances of the characters in the book, – I think perhaps you have failed to appreciate the distinctive feature of the *Novel,* as contrasted with the *Drama.* The difference between these two great methods of delineating events is, simply and only, that the Novel permits its Author to explain, by his *own mouth*, the " situation ": whereas, in the Drama, this must be done by the characters. But even a written Drama *tends* towards the Novel: for it has *stage-directions*: and a Novel is nothing more than a *Drama with the stage-directions indefinitely amplified and extended.* And if the Author of such a Drama choose to insert, in his stage-directions, his individual opinions as to the best positions &c upon the Stage (which, in the Novel, is the World, & men & women the players), these opinions are regarded as the advice of one who, writing for the stage, may be rightly supposed to know more of it than common readers and common players. And this natural view of the question is enforced by Authorities and precedents without number. The epigrammatic apophthegms of Victor Hugo; the polished man-of-the-world's advice of Bulwer; the erratic " Extra-leaves " of Jean Paul: the shallow but good-natured moralizings of G. P. R. James: the shrewd old-man's talks of Thackeray: the vigorous sermonizings of M[rs] Browning, – all these attest the legality of the expression, by the Novel-writer, of his own opinions in terms as such, outside of that indirect utterance of them which appears in the " poetical justice " of the Denouements.

The " error in fact " to which Uncle C. alludes can surely be nothing more than some obscurity in my assignment of the *time when* the war-feeling overspread the country. It is stated that " in the early Spring of 1861," – this war-wind began to blow &c: will not this do very well, as pointing to the 12th of April, of that year, when the Sumpter gun was fired, which set the whole country in a blaze?

I believe I must agree with you both, as to the propriety of mentioning living persons by name – I was dubious about the good taste of it, at first: but the temptation was strong to hit 'em a lick as I passed by.[33]

---

[33] The surviving MS of *Tiger-Lilies* mentions several living persons by name, omitted in the print. For an account of this and a history of the composition of

I begin to see the end of the novel. The story assumes a far soberer tone, as it progresses: and I have, in the last part, adopted almost exclusively the *dramatic,* rather than the descriptive, style, which reigns in the earlier portions, interspersed with much *high talk.* Inded, the book, which I commenced to write in 1863 and have touched at intervals until now, represents in its change of style almost precisely the change of tone which has gradually been taking place in *me,* all the time. So much so that it has become highly interesting to *me*: I seem to see portions of my old self, otherwise forgotten, here preserved. If the book should possess no other merit, it will perhaps be valuable, to others even, on this very account: being the genuine and almost spontaneous utterance of a developing mind, which, says Carlyle, would be interesting even if the mind were that of a hod-carrier!

Cliff has only a few pages to write, to complete the revised copy of his book. We think, now, that we will publish in the same volume under one title.

We get on quietly – Aunt Jane has just returned from the Point. Grand Pa & Ma are spending a day or two with us.

We echo your wish that we could be together this summer but I don't see the chance for it, unless *you can come* here. Can't you?

Our love and kisses to Sister. How I long to fold her up, once!

The family unites in love to you all. Our congratulations to Uncle C. on the accession to the future army of the country.[34]

Sid.

To Milton H. Northrup [35]

Exchange Hotel
Montgomery. July 28th ''/66

Mah Deeah Bawah!

I should have written you earlier; but I've been seriously ill ever since I received y'r last; – too ill to think, much less to write.

the novel—mentioned in the following paragraph—see the introduction to *Tiger-Lilies* (V, vii-viii, xxxv-xxxvi).
[34] A son had been born to the Clifford Andersons on July 4.
[35] Previously published, *Lippincott's,* LXXV, 310 (Mar., 1905).

I thank you, very sincerely, for your card of invitation and for your " Phot." I do not know anything I wish more earnestly than that I could have attended the one, and saved you the necessity of sending the other. But: Hope is the Anchor of the Soul, – and I'm an Anchor-ite! – For all I have, i' the world of my seclusion, is, some score or two of big and little hopes, many of which, I doubt not, will be but poor dependencies and drag i' the sand, when foul weather comes.

However, as yet, they lie rusting in the mud of my cave: and my anchorite's-prayer is, morn and night, that the Fates may soon blow fair, so that I may at least *weigh* my anchors.

Sick men, you know, are always selfish! I *started* to talk about *you,* not myself.

This is a good head, you send me, and covered with ringlets fair to see. *Long* may they *wave!* – – A wish, appropriate enough for what will, I hope, be always locks, streaming free, like a battle-flag, in the front of that long line of us who fight for truth and our Ladye – love, whose name is also Fame. –

I'm glad you found the letter of enough interest to make it worth publishing:[36] if all publishers saw with your partial eyes, – I'd be an author. By the way, do you know the editor of the Round Table? I'd like to send him a poem or two, occasionally: or an essay; – but I dread " rejection " like a mad lover! I had seen the article you allude to, ("Duties of Peace ") before I rec^d y'r letter. I thought it by far the most sensible view of the situation that I had yet seen.[37]

You'll pardon a poor letter: no bone in me but aches, no nerve but tingles, when I cough, shaken by that old Bronchitis I caught in your inhospitable Point Lookout Prison, there.

Write me soon. Cliff sends love. We're getting up a Literary Club here.

I'm y'r Friend

Sid: Lanier.

[36] Apparently Northrup was at this time correspondent of the New York *World* (or *Express?*), but a search of the files for the summer of 1866 failed to reveal any contribution by Lanier. (Courtesy of Mr. H. S. Parsons, Library of Congress; Mrs. F. T. Goldstein, New York State Library, Albany; Mr. J. E. Downes, New Jersey State Library, Trenton. The files of the Syracuse *Courier and Union* were also searched, courtesy of Mrs. Grace B. Lodder, Syracuse Public Library.)

[37] The editorial, " The Duties of Peace," in the *Round Table* for July 7, 1866,

MARY DAY IN 1866

Charles D. Lanier Collection, Johns Hopkins University

From Mary Day [88]

Lookout Mt. Aug. 5th
1866.

I offer you, Sidney, what I refused to you three years ago. The *desire* that you should care for it may make me fear lest you should not — and yet, the friendship of your response to my message forbids to pride the privilege of doubting your welcome for this poor representative of poor me. If you will permit it, it seems right to incur the pain of mentioning one

is quoted in part by Mims, pp. 76-77. Strangely enough, Lanier makes no mention of his own poems published in the *Round Table* of July 14, 1866—" Spring Greeting " and " To J. L." [Janie Lamar] (I, 5, 8).

[88] This letter, the first from Mary Day in nearly a year, requires some elucidation. When they had first met in the spring of 1863 (" three years ago "), she had felt obliged to refuse his suit and apparently his request for her photograph because of her engagement to Major Fred Andrews. But friendship was granted, and for the next two and a half years a considerable correspondence ensued (more than a score of Lanier's surviving letters to her during this period are included in the present volume). Their last meeting had been in Aug., 1865, at Scott's Mills, Mrs. Fulton's plantation (see note on " The Tournament: Joust First," I, 6) ; Lanier's last letter to her was on Oct. 25, 1865, and Mary Day's last to him was on Nov. 1, 1865. In this she had announced that her marriage to Major Andrews would probably take place the latter part of Jan., 1866. But the date was postponed, and late in April she had broken her engagement; the " time of mental darkness and spiritual torture " here referred to was the four months of her indecision during the winter of 1865-1866, when, at her father's instance, she suspended correspondence with Lanier (" an intercourse which he supposed might supply another element of strife to my disordered nature "). By the summer of 1866 she had partly regained her composure, and overtures were made for a renewal of their correspondence (" my message and your reply " seem to refer to such overtures made through the medium of a friend, probably Clifford Lanier, with whom she had renewed correspondence as early as Apr. 21, 1866, rather than to actual letters now lost). Finally, on Aug. 5, 1866, she wrote to him, offering as a symbol of her altered status " what I refused to you three years ago . . . this poor representative of poor me " (see photograph, opposite, by the Eagle Gallery, Lookout Mt., Tenn.—also Clifford Lanier's letter to Mary Day, Sept. 10, 1866: " Sid has the [picture] you sent ") ; but her indecision was still such that she did not mail the letter for more than a week after it was written (the envelope is postmarked " Aug. 14 "). Because of the vagueness of her communication and because of what Lanier had suffered from the indeterminateness of their relationship from the beginning (it was not until her letter of Oct. 11, 1866, that she gave him anything like a clear account of her broken engagement and her true feelings for him), it was more than six weeks before he could bring himself to a direct answer to her letter on Oct. 6, 1866, and nearly a year after that before their reconciliation was complete.

thing which may make your acceptance of it more pleasant. There was a time of mental darkness and spiritual *torture* which left me utterly apathetic towards all things human. At that time my dear and loving Father judged it safest for my restoration to thought and feeling that I should be cut off from an intercourse which he supposed might supply another element of strife to my disordered nature. My apparent indifference and hardness — (in silence) confirmed him in this opinion, when he spoke to me of it, so gently. In truth, I did *not* care. I never wished to see you and would even have avoided you, had I been consoled by the remnant of so much courage as to resist *any* portion of the destructive fate which I beheld hourly advancing to crush me. For tho' everything was pain – the *most* exquisite pain came from meeting the *nearest* and *dearest* – The presence of strangers I could endure with comparative composure. What followed is known to both — the estrangement, the silence, which has, later, seemed like that " silence of life, more pathetic than death's." — God's light has shone in upon my darkness – His mercy has banished my despair — His counsel has been granted to my prayer — and pointing to a new and difficult path, – He has led me into it, saying " this is the way " — and while I walk therein with frequent pain of self-upbraiding and regret – I yet walk undoubting, grateful to reach the true way, altho' so late, and joying in its million wayside flowers, its pure — free — air. When I could, rightly, I spoke to you — and rather an evasion I felt it. So much so, that for both his sake and yours I was, last month, fain to quiet my conscience by writing to Father the exact words of my message and of your reply – hoping that it would not meet his disapprobation – and expressing (somewhat too wilfully, I fear) a firm conviction of my *right* to do what I had done – He replied with great kindness that " he had no wish to express any displeasure on account of it —" but had determined to acquiesce in whâtever might be my wishes in regard to my two friends of whom he wrote. He *therefore* approves this little gift with which I wish to present you, if you have not ceased to value it. I do often idly dream of meeting you, but my prevailing impression is that I shall never see you again — although that seems most improbable, should we both live. Nor do I think that you desire it — Could I but be assured of this — it should be so — for, believe

me, whatever may be your wishes, THEY ARE MINE — Meanwhile — separation shall not chill my firm regard, – nor,
through its length alone, reconcile me to itself.   Whatever
hopes or happiness the present bestows, or the future holds for
my friend – he will find them shared by a heart which — however unworthy – does sincerely desire his happiness and good
above all things in this world.   For once, Sidney, in a selfish
life, I have learned to prefer and rejoice in the welfare of
another being – above my own gratification and happiness.
Whatever be your joy, I will thank God for it — e'en though
weak lips falter — and I *will* be blessed in knowing you
happy — God ruling in my heart.   I will watch you, Sidney,
with prayer and aspiration; in your world-life, in your poet-
sphere, in your home affections and surroundings————
I *linger* so; yet – 'tis my pen, and my woman's way –   You'll
understand them. It is always hard to say to some, (be the
blessing for weeks or for years) — "Good Bye."

To Robert S. Lanier

                              Exchange Hotel
                              Montgomery Ala
                              Aug. 10th "/66

My Dear Father:
                    At the last meeting of our Literary Society I
was chosen one of the public Disputants, in a debate to come
off two weeks from Tuesday next. The question is, "Was
Louis Napoleon justifiable in establishing the monarchy in
Mexico." [39] I'm on the negative side of it: & scratch off this
hurried note to ask that you will collect and forward to me by
Express, as soon as possible, anything you may have seen,
regarding the history of the Maximilian affair – I know almost
nothing of it and shall debate principally the moral phase of
the question. Yet, the other side will be certain to go into the
facts of the case, and I wish to be prepared to meet them.
Wrote to Sister yesterday by Mr Salisbury.
Aunt Jane goes to Point Clear to spend a month, to night.

[39] A speech of 25 pages on this subject survives in MS (Clifford A. Lanier
Collection, Johns Hopkins University).

We'll be lonely enough when she goes: but what with business and books, we haven't much time to think about the good dinners and suppers she gives us in the back-parlor.

Y'r good letter came yesterday and we thank you very much for it – I could almost believe our separation a good thing, since it brings to me such sweet expressions of love and encouragement. I should, however, insist upon your coming here, this summer: but the place is so terribly unhealthy, and that, too, with your peculiar bilious forms of disease, that I should really fear to see you come here – Cliff. and I have so far escaped: but it has been by exercising the utmost prudence – We never go into the Sun, and are very strict in diet. I should go up to Tallassee [40] and spend a month there, but it would cost me 25 Dollars, besides the loss of a month's wages: and I can't afford it – I gained a pound or so, in my five-days frolic up there! The air is pure and mountain-like, and braced me up splendidly –

All well –   Hastily,   Sid. L.

To Virginia Hankins

Exchange Hotel
Montgomery Ala
Sep. 25th '/66

O Ginna, Ginna, Why?

Here I've written letter after letter [41] to you, each of which, I hoped, might fall upon you like a raindrop, coming, (not, indeed, from Heaven, but) from my Heart that was full as any cloud could be: Ah, I hoped that each drop was trickling down, to serve for the drinking of many a Rose-root lying perdu there in your Soul; every one fell surcharged

---

[40] A town of 1,500 feet altitude on the Tallapoosa River, about 25 miles northeast of Montgomery.

[41] Besides the present one, at least six of Lanier's post-war letters had reached her—two notes (dated Apr. 4 and June? 1866) in addition to the four letters already printed in this volume. But the earliest letter from Virginia Hankins to Lanier that has survived is dated Oct. 24, 1867; whatever others she sent were lost in the mails or have disappeared subsequently. The photographs mentioned in the following paragraph had been sent to her by Clifford Lanier in his letter of July 3, 1866.

with my love, and you know how Love is a genuine " Bloom-evoking" Agent: (all of which disjointed talk you are humbly requested to disentangle; and then to read further that) in spite of all these love-showers which I have rained upon you, I have not received any such response as gardens give to clouds: if flowers have bloomed, no crimson and no rose-perfume has come to eye or nose of mine:—in short, we have had no word from you in,—in—in—well, in several cycles and aeons of centuries, certainly, measuring by Heart-throbs –

We sent you some pictures: one of Mamie Day, and one of you; – I should regret *so* much if they are lost! – For we only lent them to you, and were going to frame them daintily for our future dream-inspirations, if the Fates should continue to separate us.

Which may all Benevolent-Hearted Powers forbid! No day passes in which I do not yearn for you: nothing beautiful, nothing noble, nothing high—presents itself to my soul, without bringing you, nay, everything fine comes preceded and authorized by a sanction which *you* have unconsciously given.

Aye, more than that. I never endure a trial without remembering that *you* would smile approval if you knew it: and I never fall *beneath* a temptation without begging pardon of you: as I do, now, humbly on my knees, O Sweetest, O Purest, O Strongest, for all I ever did that was unworthy of you or of your passionate-loving, true-hearted

S.——————— [42]

To Gertrude Lanier [43]

Montgomery, Ala.
Sep. 26th /66

My Darling Sissa: How I wish that I could travel with this letter and get a kiss from those sweetest sisterly lips that were ever red!   Indeed it seems as if a cycle of ages had passed since

---

[42] On the reverse side of this letter Virginia Hankins wrote down from memory seven lines of Tennyson's " Break, Break, Break," ending:

" But the tender grace of a day that is dead
Will never come back to me."

[43] Excerpt previously published, Mims, pp. 73-74.

I had a caress from you: and mein Himmel! – if times don't get better another cycle will roll round before I get any more.

Well: – we take refuge from the menacing " No! " of nature, in dreams where nothing is impossible: and so, if I cannot clasp my own well-beloved real flesh-and-blood Gertrude, can at least call up from that vasty deep that men name " The Past," the blue eyes, and the milk-and-rose cheeks and the most fair forehead that you bear so well and maidenly. Waver these never so indistinctly before my dreaming eyes, they yet sanctify me and bless me and inspire me.

O, Blue eyes, and rose-cheeks and white forehead, forever glimmer before me, through the Smoke of Life! – Followed man ever so sweet or so high a banner as this Red White & Blue?

He that conquered not, so fair a flag as this leading him, surely should have somewhat that was dastardly in his soul!

I've just returned from Tuskegee, where I spent a pleasant week, part of the time with Bob Ligon and part with Dave Clopton. They petted me to death, nearly: but I endured it with Christian resignation!

Indeed they were all so good and so kind to me, and the fair cousins were so beautiful that I came back feeling as if I had been in a week's dream of Fairyland. Willie & Carrie spoke of you often and lamented that you could not come, – I however, was glad, on *some* accounts, that you did not: which I may tell you some other time.

The hotel at Point Clear is closed for the season, and Uncle Will comes up here probably to-morrow. Aunt Lucy has already left the point, and, after spending a day or two here has gone over to Robinson's Springs,[44] where Sallie Schley has been spending the Summer. Grandfather has bought a house at the Springs, (Robinson's) and he and Uncle Will, with their families, will winter there. 'Tis expected that the " North & South Ala R. R." will run near the house, in which event it will be somewhat valuable, and a very pleasant summer residence in future.

All here have been ailing a little with bilious attacks – except *me!* Who am usually regarded as the most delicate of 'em all.

---

[44] A resort in Elmore County, Ala., about 12 miles from Montgomery.

Letters from Charleston give doleful accounts of the broken bone fever: all Aunt Mina's household down with it, but getting better.

Bus. dull. Rec^d Pa's short letter. All send love: and I send

My Heart.

To Robert S. Lanier

[Montgomery, Ala., Oct. 6, 1866?]

My Dear Pa:

I send you a poem [45] I wrote a day or two ago, at the request of a young lady friend, on her birthday. Cliff declares it equal to Tennyson, and I am pleased with it. Write me y'r opinion – Wrote you a day or two ago: and Sister.

"Biz." improving a little, but very slim still. All well. No news.

Hastily,   Sid.   (over)

Sent a letter of introduction to you, presenting Maj. Edmondson.[46] He is a Charlestonian and is a great friend of Uncle Tom's: [47] is now representing Richardson & Co, of New York, Publishers of several Southern books – I had some pleasant talks with him, and found him possessed of considerable cultivation, and a fine store of travelling experiences.

I send a little poem of Cliff's, written on the fly-leaf of a copy of Tennyson which he presented to his sweetheart on her birthday, – the same to whom my poem is written – I think it very fine.

Love to everybody,

Sid.[48]

[45] "A Birthday Song. To S. G." (I, 9). The dedicatee was Sallie Given, whose father was the lessee of the Exchange Hotel in Montgomery. The copy of the poem in Lanier's Ledger (Henry W. Lanier Collection, Johns Hopkins University) is dated Oct. 4, 1866; hence the conjectural date of this letter.

[46] Lanier's letter to his father on Oct. 1, 1866, is a brief note introducing: "Maj. Jas. N. Edmondson, formerly of the Confederate Army, and now engaged in the interests of the 'Southern University Series,' of Text-books, which are being published by the Professors of the University of Va."

[47] Thomas D. Eason of Charleston, husband of R. S. Lanier's sister Wilhelmina.

[48] Clifford Lanier's poem "To S. E. G. with a copy of Tennyson" was also

To Mary Day [49]

Exchange Hotel
Montgomery Ala
Oct. 6/66

My Dear Child, Be many sad hours, be infinite weaknesses and self-upbraidings and unsolaced regrets, be a thousand unmanlinesses and turns of Resolution, be a continuous stream of tenderness and of doubt as to my right to be tender, – be all these the witnesses of the earnestness of my soul, be they the apologists for the trembling of my hand, – as I reply to these the first words from you to me in so long and so sorrowful a time.

But the words come slowly to me. Y'r letter awoke many memories which slept. As if out of graves; pale in their cerements, wondering at the alien day, they came to me. Dear Mamie, I knew not what to say to *them*: I know not what to say to you!

I know, well enough, what to *feel* — to you.
But a Feeling, which is infinite, and therefore in its nature inexpressible: – and an Idea, which is *definite,* that is to say bounded and circumscribed and easily embodied in words: – these are *so* different!

And I have so few ideas, and so many feelings, about you! It seems to me as if I knew you as well as I know anything: and knew you so by a blind intuition, totally independent of any reasoning process.
Well ——————————————.

inclosed. In a letter of Oct. 9, 1866, commenting on the two birthday poems by his sons, R. S. Lanier wrote to Clifford:

" You could hardly tell me anything better than that Sid's only ' doctor ' is doctor Resolve-to-finish-his-book. . . . I trust the latter will be tickling his palate when I come to see him Christmas—as I hope to do. I wish then to see you both, to talk over business prospects, &c, to get some more charming readings, to hear the flutes & guitar—to drink in those delightful strains of the organ I can now almost hear. – By the way, does Sid. play the organ regularly or only as the spirit moves? It is as natural for him to land in an organ-loft as it is for a bird to hop into a tree. If he has time to practice I have no doubt he plays well."

[49] This is clearly Lanier's first letter in reply to Mary Day's letter written on Aug. 5, 1866 (but not mailed until Aug. 14); for she later chided him for waiting " six weeks " to answer (see Mary Day to Sidney Lanier, Oct. 16, 1866).

Let me say that I *do* desire to meet you, again. At such a time, perhaps a momentary flash of Heaven-light out of those old brilliant *first*-days might dazzle my eyes which have been all unused to such light, since then: but I should recover, and the succeeding Earth-light, displaying you as my faithful friend and me as yours, would still be delightful and not too strong for me.

You know Mrs Browning says it is only true love which dares to chide a child. Perhaps it may be proof of my friendship if I dare to chide *you,* a little.

You analyse yourself too much, Little Mamie! The struggle to understand one's self is good: but it may be pushed too far, and then it is terrible. Why?

Well, it is because one is one's self to-day, and is *not* one's self tomorrow. It is because the only consistent quality in man is his inconsistency. The Sun shines every day with white light, but men are prisms, of varying structure, and one day we show red, another blue, and another yellow. When we have by analysis found out a thing about ourselves; – expecting to find it again tomorrow, we fail, and are amazed. Imagine this perplexity occurring not day by day but minute by minute, and you may see how inextricable is the labyrinth in which we involve ourselves by over-nicety and over-frequency of analysis. Should you think, *now,* that this is humbug; – I will but ask you to remember it – One day you will find it true.

The remedy?

Feel more, and think less! yield yourself up to the blind and vague delight of your music and your pictures: or to the blind high sorrow of them, if they bring *that* to you as they often do to me.

Question not so minutely the Infinity, which is *therefore* the *Vagueness,* of the Soul and its passions and thoughts. If Apollo fly down and enchant you with his Lyre: if an Angel take your hand and lift you up to where the air is fine but so pure that it is painful for grosser breathing: – will you catechize the Divine Player, and examine the mechanical construction of his instrument and make him explain it to you? Or will you feel the Angel-wing betwixt finger and thumb, to see whether it be of veritable Feathers-of-Heaven, or only a wooden flying-machine?

Let us, who surely have seen and known some genuine Beauty and genuine Sorrow, – let us trust these more, let us go blind-fold where they lead, sometimes, and not tear away the sacred bandages in order that we may speculate, geologically and topo-graphically, upon the Land to which, and the route by which they conduct us. – – – –

We have made a thousand friends here and all people are kind to us. But we do not see any like *you.*

And I well know that *you* see none more faithful than

Y'r Friend

Sidney Lanier

FROM MARY DAY [50]

Marietta. Oct. 11th 1866.

I think, to-night I have some beauty — I am not vain, nor think it *mine,* no, no! I've heard so often that happiness makes women beautiful, and I looked, to see, and it was true. For to-day, I received *your* letter, Sidney —

Forgive me – I had grown so proud through silent waiting that I could send you no message when last I wrote to dear, dear Cliff: and still, I did you justice – I approved all you did – or left undone – your life-words, and your silence, equally. To-night, I am too solemnly glad for sleep – I would rather lie still, still – in sight of watchful stars and holy heaven, holding my treasure of thought – of feeling. I cannot lose it in uncon-sciousness – Our Father in Heaven cannot wish *that*; – ah, there have been so many nights for sleep, oblivion — so few for happiness, these fourteen months! [51] My weary heart, stopped in its latest struggle, drops down to rest like tired child, upon this letter's heart. It would have failed me long before, Sir Philip, but it took for sword and staff the bygone letters, the dearest things left to me on earth. Yet, O gentle Teacher, I

[50] This letter is included because it gives the clearest available picture of their relations during the past twelve months and because it seems indispensable to a full understanding of Mary Day's character and personality, which was so closely bound up with the rest of Lanier's life.

[51] That is, since their last meeting, in Aug., 1865, at Mrs. Fulton's plantation.

have learned some truths — (*burnt in*, as by fire) you wot not of – and this, – you've set the seal on it, – is one –: " the only consistent quality in man is his inconsistency."   Therefore, my staff would sometimes bend beneath me, and the sword fall, like false steel, from powerless hand – and then the hands – forsaken – could only clasp and reach for *God,* saying – " Thy Will, not mine – I beseech Thee!   I know Thou lovest me more than all – stay my soul on Thee! "   Oh, His Love, His Infinite Love! can I ever distrust it more? —

You tell *me* — " Feel more, think less? "   And *I* upbraid myself for never having a thought, for living wholly a life of feeling. This is very strange.   You're right – I'd surely want to satisfy myself about the Angel's wing – It has been already a great puzzle to me – *what* they're made of!   Only once or twice however.   Indeed, Sidney, your're talking to the woman of eighteen and twenty-one, you once knew,[52] and not knowing me now, since " all His floods have gone over me," you take me for the same exactly, whereas it is so different a person that my *sister*-friend, dear Lilla,[53] took it for a stranger when she came to me last May, and had to study each inward feature, once so familiar to her loving eye.   You, too, are changed – more tempered and patient, stronger, and more concentred, a man's true growth, a *true* man's growth, I thank *Him* for that, too.   There has been such a blank sometimes when I wished to think of you – such ignorance of your life and progress – its force, its scope, its direction – – 'twas very painful.   And you, I infer, have felt some of this also, about — — your child.

O Sidney, it has been the deepest, fiercest year a human life could hold, without destruction – No *words* could ever tell it – much less – the pen.   Nay, I'd never *have* you know it, lest in very *pity – compassion*, it should darken *your* heart, as it often does my life.   To live in visible, conscious *Eternity,* shut out from God, for four long months – is awful, I have found, to a soul in the flsh – The unseen World—and, oh, terrible sight! my own unveiled heart – as *in God's pure sight* — all, laid out forever beneath my maddening gaze –

" *Hopeless* grief is *passionless –* "

[52] That is, in the spring of 1863 and the summer of 1865 (Mary Day was born on June 10, 1844).
[53] Probably Lilla Hazelhurst.

I attained even to *that* depth. What awful fascination draws me on to look into its blackness and form it into speech? Lets leave it – my dearer Heart – God's light gives life – Christ is not only the Truth, the Way, the Light; He is *the Life* – away from Him we *die,* as branch cut off from Vine: some, inch by inch, and some, like me, beneath hotter suns – in quick – scorching ruin – Ruin of *mind,* of *affections* – the heart one blank – incapable of comprehending Love – of seeing Beauty, its collateral.

> Flee we, dear one, to *our Life,* our Redeemer!
> " He will forsake thee, oh, never –
> Sheltered so tenderly, *there.*"

——— There are things so hard to speak – Sir Philip, I want to be *true-womanly — towards* you, and *before* you, while I live. When I fail in that, in *your* eyes, I pray God to let me die. I thought last year that the failure *had* fallen upon me, and perhaps, tho' I knew it not, at first – it was that which was ruin to me. So – now – I strive to tell you some truth, of which few words ever pass my lips, and I plead with you to look upon the revelation with knightly honor and reverence, and shelter me in your heart from any slighting thought, however I may merit such –

I cannot find a phrase to displace the one which rushes from my heart — " I am free." When a woman says *that*, she has never been bound, save in honor – And yet *that* is wrong, for it is in *dis*honor, oh, most sad and low dishonor, when love is withheld and hand and troth are given. I have no one to blame save myself, and mistaken influence around me which meant to work for my happiness. He [54] is true, unselfish, manly; there has never been the hour when my simple request would not have released me, with but one question from him – " Do you not love me? " *Equal* love, he did not demand – his own was so great, it sufficed him — (& then – he never knew me, at all) but – the best I *had,* to give. I honestly thought I gave him the best left to me – which was *friendship* and *reason's* approval – until God taught me better. And I – *I shame to speak it –* I thought it dishonor – *impossible,* to break my pledge; and yet could think to marry one whom I counted

[54] Fred Andrews, her former fiancé.

on "*learning* to love " –   O, I bow my face, and cover it, at
such a thought!   My ignorance was surpassed only by God's
wisdom; my weakness by His Power; – my recklessness, by his
Love.   It seemed – later – when I became *aware* I *could not,*
even, be what I had promised — it seemed so awful to wreck
a true, full-freighted heart, that *it* helped to craze me too, and
I dwelt in that silence, frozen into absolute silence, while he
waited, pityingly, forgivingly – suffering, on my restoration to
health and reason.   Life returned, and with it – responsibility –
near on to April –   The Spring saw my resurrection – every bud,
like to my spirit – bursting with its fullness of riches, its beautiful, new, undeveloped life – The glory of that Spring, surely can
never return to me –   *The Father's* smile upon me – pardoned,
received, crowned with blessings of the Saviour's sacrifice!   My
precious Father's and Brother's tender, patient waiting re-
warded, *everything* a joy, because upon it was written – " Unto
the Lord – " —   Late in April – I believe – The only remaining
weight was lifted by my beloved pastor's counsel and aid,
following my full confidence.   (I had been so long blind, I
dared not see a new path, all for myself.)   I wrote to that dear
and honored friend, with pain intolerable and condemning,
and prayed absolution from my pledge.   It was granted far
more promptly than it was asked –   There could be no veritable
doubt to me, concerning his reply.   — I cannot yet forgive myself the injury I have done his life – if I dwelt upon it, no sun
could shine to me; and still, I humbly thank the guiding Hand
which prevented a *greater* wrong, the greatest of all wrongs,
and one irreparable.

So much tender love has been shown me; so much generous
friendship — even from his cousin, whom you know – *especially*
from her — upholding and comforting me in what I have so
often uncharitably condemned in others, – trusting me, through
all adverse appearances, even my own self-abhorrence, setting
me forward on my new path, with such gentle hands – ! ought
I not to be very humble !
You, alas, know partly, how unworthy of it I am –   Even so –
turn not from me – Sidney – Sidney!
My story is done — we are at this present – Of intervening life,
I trust me not to speak – to you.   Yet have I written it to you,
more than once; – letters I have *willed* to you when I shall rest

in the last sleep; the outflowings of hours when I could bear Silence no longer.[55]

I seek a blessing for you, ere we part – but, alas — is any mine to give you – ———

The *Valediction* rises to me, with its great heart and full impotence – and *that* I cannot bear – I must *do* for you — or, at least try – and fail –

Yet, the strength of the weakest hand may sometimes rescue, and its little wealth *may* meet some life-hour of need. For such hour, dear, I wait – When it comes, call

Your Child [56]

[55] Two other letters from Mary Day to Lanier survive, dated Sept. 8-10, and Oct. 8-12, 1866; but it seems reasonably clear that they were " diary " letters, not written to be mailed, and not actually sent until later, for the following reasons: (1) In subject matter and tone they are much more forthright and passionate confessions of love than her sense of modesty permitted in her other letters. (2) In the present letter she refers to " letters I have *willed* to you when I shall rest in the last sleep," and in her letter of Oct. 29, she says she is sending him the record of her heart—" The letters I told you were to be sent to you when I was dead." (3) Both of these " diary " letters are without envelopes and are so folded that they fit with the letter and envelope of Oct. 29 and with none other written during this period. (4) None of Lanier's letters seem to be in answer to them until his letter of Oct. 31, which answers them specifically, with phrases quoted *verbatim* and with the significant statement: " I think I know, *now,* that you loved me." (In her " diary " letter of Sept. 8-10 she had unequivocally confided that she had been sure of her love for him " since the very hour when I closed my letter [end of Apr., 1866], which asked for release from my former pledge "; and in that of Oct. 8-12, she said: " I do love you so passionately, my love burns up the words and leaves me speechless. . . . Tell me that your heart *is* mine, that you are *not ' my friend.' "*)

[56] The renewal of correspondence between Lanier and Mary Day is somewhat complicated by the existence of six further letters from him written during this autumn, which were set aside in later life (1915) by his widow and clearly marked as not for publication. The Lanier family have generously made these letters available for the Centennial Edition, so that the record may be as complete as possible; but the requirements of scholarship accord with their preference that they should remain in manuscript. They have almost no factual content (the few facts that they do contain are utilized in the notes), and they throw no new light on the inner or outer narrative of Lanier's life. The painful misunderstandings of two whose love had been thwarted from the beginning by circumstances, the tortured soul-searchings for guilt that did not exist, the self-accusations and unintentional woundings—these are matters of interest solely to the recipients of the letters. The only points that need to be recorded, perhaps, are that the dozen surviving letters from Mary Day during this period (Oct.-Dec., 1866) show her with candor and without reserve declaring a love that she fears is hopeless because it is so belatedly confessed, and that the half-dozen letters which Lanier wrote in reply show him slow to believe in and return a love denied him previously.

To Virginia Hankins

Montgomery Ala
Oct. 14th "/66

Good Ginna, You must know I'm the Organist of the Presbyterian Church, and today's Sunday, and I've been playing. Now if you had sat by me this morning, you would have recognized in my Voluntary, my answer to your letter; indeed, the Organ is the only thing I *could* answer it upon; – not, oh not, upon this paper! Spirit that I love, Oh Saintly Soul to whom I dare speak my soul, why were you not there?

These brutish miles of hard earth that stretch between me and you, – what have they to do with you and me?

Tyrannous miles: a bas les Tyrans!

Today I would see your face and eyes and hands. It is the very passion of hunger that comes over me, – of hunger for you in the sweet body. Today I am not content to know, as I *do* know, that your Spirit is here: but I yearn ceaselessly with heart-swelling and sighing that I might walk the fair solemn fall-fields with you, as we walked them once. If all the true-blessed-ness of the world were before me for choice, I'd take – – – that I might ride with you to that sand-point where we saw the sun go down into the water, one day. The tiny foot-tracks you made there in the sand, remain impressed on my heart; the multitudinous seas that dash upon me from the main of the world do not efface them.[57]

Would it not be strange and too sweet, to go over that moment again? Then (I *now* know) we were no more than boy and girl; – *since,* – Royal Sorrow has struck his kingly *Accolade* upon us, and knighted us, in the grand and most high

(These omitted letters, with conjectural datings supplied from internal evidence and by reference to the entire sequence, are as follows: from Lanier—Oct. 27(?), Oct. 31, Nov. 1, Nov. 13, Nov. 16(?), Dec. 25-31(?); from Mary Day—Oct. 16, Oct. 29, Nov. 2-4, Nov. 13, Nov. 16, Nov. 20, Nov. 28-Dec. 1, Dec. 8, Dec. 9, Dec. 15, Dec. 17-21, Dec. 25.)

[57] In the autumn of 1863 Lanier was stationed at Boykin's Bluff, Va., only a few miles from Virginia Hankins's home at Bacon's Castle. The occasion here referred to may have been the one commemorated in the poem he addressed to her at that time: " To ——(The day was dying, his breath)", the text of which is given on p. 128, above.

Order, Man and Woman. I would *so* like to see the Woman –
Ginna. I who so deeply reverence the girl – Ginna whose face
flushed in the rose-glow that came down from the Sun and up
from the red water, that day! If God grant me live to see such
another, I envy not man nor Angel.

Of course your Brother's policy was the only right one –. His
challenge being refused, he is right before the world: any
honorable man would call his enemies by no better name than
contemptible cowards: and their plea that he was no gentleman
is but a flimsy fortification which may indeed shelter them from
his bullet, but can*not* shelter them from dishonor and the contempt of brave men.[58]

My regards to all that remember me. What wedding is it you
speak of? How fare the married couple of Mantura?[59] Write
me a gossipy letter about the folks there: *but put as much love
in it as you can,* Dear!

Don't hurry about the pictures; we only wanted to know they
were safe. Keep 'em as long as you please. Cliff sends his
heart and I send

Thine alias Mine.

To Robert S. Lanier [60]

Montgomery   Ala
Oct. 14th ″/66

My Dear Pa:

Your letter has been received and, on the principle
that all's well that *ends* well, has afforded me much pleasure –
in the complimentary terms with which it concludes.

---

[58] Apparently a reference to the political dispute in which Virginia Hankins's
brother, J. D. Hankins, was involved, and which led to his death a short time
after the date of this letter. (See, below, Lanier's letters of Nov. 5, 1866, to
Virginia Hankins and to his father.)

[59] Lanier's Macon friend and army comrade, Jim Price, had married the widow
Wilson of "Mantura," Surry Co., Va., earlier in the autumn (see R. S. Lanier
to Clifford Lanier, Oct. 6, 1866).

[60] Apparently an answer to a letter from R. S. Lanier to Sidney, early in Oct.,
1866, now lost. But it also serves in part as an answer to R. S. Lanier's letter to
Clifford, Oct. 9, criticizing the two poems written by his sons addressed to
"S. E. G." (see note 45, above). The correct title of the Swinburne poem here
quoted was "Rondel" (*Poems and Ballads,* 1866).

As to y'r preface, I won't have a word of it. Although it may sound, in view of your complimentary expressions, like a reciprocity treaty for *me* to say so:– yet, I'm quite certain that you not only have *not* lost your critical taste, with increasing years, but that you are, among all the men I know, the only judge to whom I dare submit any such poem as the one I sent you. Indeed, if you were totally devoid of taste, and my poem did not produce in you some feeling of the Mystery of Beautiful Things that surrounds us daily and nightly, – why, I'd quit writing, forever.

That the poem was somewhat obscure is quite probable; – especially to you, who read Addison. But to me, who read Swinburne, – how different!

Mr Swinburne has suddenly shot up into the foremost place among modern poets: I transcribe one of his poems, that you may see how it looks, in *writing,* instead of *print*: and compare it with mine, as regards obscurity of the two.

A Lyric –   *By Chas. Swinburne.*

These many years since we began to be,
What have the Gods done with us? what with me
What with my love? They have shown me fates and fears,
Harsh Springs, and fountains bitterer than the sea,
Grief a fixed star, and joy a vane that veers,
        These many years.

With her, my love, with her have they done well?
But who shall answer for her? Who shall tell
Sweet things or sad, such things as no man hears?
May no tears fall, if no tears ever fell
From eyes more dear to me than starriest spheres
        These many years.

But if tears ever touched, for any grief,
Those eyelids folded like a white rose-leaf,
Deep double-shells where through the eye-flower peers,
Let them weep once more only, sweet and brief,
Brief tears and bright for one who gave her tears
        These many years.

What think you of that?

We are all well. I get on slowly with the book: but, I believe, surely – I'm certain it is much improved, since you saw it: it is as if the first part were written by a boy and the last part by a man: and I think I'll let it stay so, if only as a true and faithful representation of growth. As such, if it possessed no other value, it would be a curiosity of literature.[61]

Cliff gets on well. It is a pretty poem he sent you: sweet and rich and dainty. With some practice so as to acquire dexterity in forming his dainties into unities, in crystallizing his chaotic richnesses, – he would be a good poet.

We await your arrival with great impatience. Ask Sissa to write me another gossipy letter – I wrote her a lover's yepistle not long since –.

Our love to all who remember us.

                                        Sid.

To ROBERT S. LANIER

                                Montgomery Ala
                                Nov. 3d/66

My Dear Father:

            Sister's letter was received a day or two ago, and read with great pleasure. We are glad that she heard the Opera and enjoyed it. Cliff and I were there, in full force: and had a good time tho' we found much that was in our opinion reprehensible and false in the presentation of the music. If I ever get any influence in the world I'm going to commence and keep up an earnest crusade against the Italian opera, as at present existing.

We have all suffered more or less with the inevitable breakbone fever. Sallie is just recovering from quite a severe attack of it. Rest of us now well. Grandpa was over to dine with us today, meeting Uncle Will and Aunt Lucy who returned from a trip to Tuskegee last night.

I've been playing the organ at the Presbyterian Church for

---

[61] For this discrepancy in style between the first and last part of *Tiger-Lilies*, and a history of its composition, see V, vii-viii, xxxiii-xxxiv.

several weeks –. Yesterday Dr Petrie came down and offered
me the situation of permanent organist there: which I accepted –
Don't know what the compensation is, but suppose it'll get me
a suit of clothes –

Could Cliff and I borrow any money from you next January?
We are very desirous of endeavoring to get into the Hotel on
our own hook, next year: but fear that it will take more capital
than we can borrow.

How will you come out on the year's business? Let me know
your financial condition,

No news here. Business dull, and cotton flat.

Who is in Macon, that could deliver a fine lecture before our
Literary Society? Somebody with reputation enough to draw a
paying crowd, for instance.

Love to everybody, and a thousand kisses for Sister

                    from

                        Sid. L.

          To Robert S. Lanier

                              Montgomery, Ala.
                              Nov. 5th "/66
My Dear Pa:

            I have been requested by Ginna Hankins to write
a little In Memoriam, to her brother recently killed in an unfortunate " Affair " at Surrey Court House.

I send the enclosed for your opinion.[62] It's the best thing
I've written: approaching more nearly my ideal of simplicity.

Wrote you yesterday. All well, but Sallie, slowly improving.

          Hastily

                    Sid.

[62] " To Captain James De Witt Hankins " (I, 10).

To Virginia Hankins [63]

Montgomery Ala
Nov. 5th 1866

Dear Little One, I send you a little piece I've written, and
beg that you will publish it, if you like, in the Petersburg and
Richmond papers. I think it the best thing I have ever written:
and *you* will, when you are as old as I am. I like such an " In
Memoriam " better than an obituary such as is usually inserted
in the papers: for the reason that no one reads obituaries and
that everyone expects what they contain. This tribute of our
friendship to your brother will at least bear witness how we
lament him and how we love you.

Indeed, we love you so that our eyes and our hearts grow too
full to speak to you.

Sweet, it utterly breaks my heart that I cannot fold You up,
now, from all this grief, from all this dead drudgery which
fits you no more than a body fits a soul.

Aye, it breaks my heart — It breaks my heart, Ginna – I cannot speak, nor write, now.

Receive thou the sad yearning Soul of

Thy

Friend -

To Mary Day [64]

[Montgomery, Ala., Dec. 9-15?, 1866]

My Darling Mamie, Imagine an Avalanche descending Blanc
by wild Tiger-leaps, spreading its terrible tiger-claws to seize
the world with, and glittering deadly along with the cold
ferocity of utter desperation ——— ——

[63] An undated note to Virginia Hankins, probably preceding this by several
days, also survives. In it Lanier says: " The favor you ask shall be done: it will
come better after a few days are past."

[64] Excerpts previously published incorrectly (misdated October, 1866), *Scribner's*, XXV, 622 (May, 1899); reprinted in *Letters* (New York, 1899), pp.
65-67. This letter is here included since it does not belong to the series set
aside as not for publication (see note 56, above), and since its factual content
forms a necessary part of the record of Lanier's life at this time.

And then imagine that the terrified Villagers below, as they knelt and gazed upward in a last prayer, should suddenly see this avalanche dissolve, midway of its last leap, into sweet rain and mist, hovering downward full slowly and gently, – administering drink to the violets instead of death to the Villagers, falling from the Clouds as Despair and quickly mounting to the clouds as Thanksgiving!

So – your last letter follows your first four.[65]   It is beyond me to bless you for it: but the Unknown will do that.

I was replying to your letters when your last came. See what I wrote! I, too, was crazy: – but, Child, your words were too much: some of them were even *cold,* to *me!*

Well – Away with all that – it is Night-talk, it is dank and terrible: – here is the Morning, let us talk in the light: here are flowers about us, with dew and odors, let us enjoy them; we are tired wandering in the Dark, here is Nature, a rock covered with moss. Sit with me and rest: our ears are full of Night-sounds, let us send in Music like Michael to chase these Devils out of our Heaven: –

Old Night that tormented'st us,
Adios, and God give thee better favor ! ————————

Why, how you write, these days ! Your dainty letters breathe and stagger with beautiful things like a Spring with more flowers in her lap than her jaunty apron would hold! [66]

[65] Apparently the reference is to Mary Day's letters of Nov. 13, Nov. 16-20, Nov. 28-Dec. 1, Dec. 8, Dec. 9. (The conjectural dating of Lanier's letter is arrived at from the fact that it seems to be an answer to these five letters—see notes 67-69, below—whereas it, in turn, is clearly answered in her letter of Dec. 17, detail for detail.)

These letters show that Mary Day was gradually achieving some peace of mind. As early as Nov. 13 she had written: " I will try to be to you what you wish— what is pleasant to you—what you are to me;—only, it takes time to learn, and you who know how can teach me. I do not say I can—I do not know how much I can do—but you may judge that *something* is already gained—

" After the first blow, my heart was incredulous—and then rebellious, but the bewilderment of those days is passing from me." (The reference is to Lanier's letter of Oct. 27?, which she called her " death-letter," since he had said: " Thinkest thou this is Love, that visits thee so late? . . . It is but Tenderness.")

On Nov. 28 she had added: " I . . . write this note in order to bring you healing for any wound that I may selfishly have inflicted in these last letters. . . . Since then—*all the time*—I have found great peace."

[66] This was apparently prompted by a reminiscence in Mary Day's letter of Nov. 13, written from Scott's Mills, " where we have spent many golden hours."

Ten years ago ('gad, Mamie, how glibly I say that! "*Ten years ago*," quotha! — 10 + 15 = 25 !!!) — Ten years ago I said one day that whereas Memnon's statue sang when the light struck it, therefore Memnon's Statue was but a statue and not a man, for men sing and become poets when *the Darkness* strikes Them. Is it not so? *You* never in your life wrote half such a poem as in this next-to-your-last letter ! — [67]

Where am I ever to start, to answer these thousand things that I want to talk to you about! I turn from one to t'other helpless –. Dost thou remember the fate of honest Tim O'Donahue, who dhramed that he wint to Hell and the Divil (rest his sowl) offered him hot whiskey punch and cold whiskey punch and he tuk so long to tell which he'd take that he *woke* and got nayther of 'em ?

Mindful of this terrible catastrophe, I plunge, – and beg to know how heard you of George Petrie, my old friend and class-mate, and the brother of our Dr Petrie, of Montgomery, Pastor of the Church here –? Was it through George Little,[68] and where *is* George Little, and is he still Professor at Oakland or, as I hear, State Geologist of Mississippi, and if so what is his

---

She was spending some days at Mrs. Fulton's plantation, trying to comfort her in the recent death of her husband (see Gertrude Lanier's letter to Sidney, Aug. 14, 1866), and reading *In Memoriam* with her: " I carry it . . . the precious volume of Tennyson . . . , daily, into the woods with me—or by the old bridge, of many memories. Yesterday I could brook nothing in it save ' St. Agnes Eve ' and ' Break, break, break, on thy cold stones, oh Sea! ' I have treasured that same sweet volume near four years, and often wished I could ask her to exchange that copy with me:—but now, it is endeared to her—and it can pass, like the rest. I doubt if—when I am an old woman, (assuming I shall endure long years)—I shall ever be able to look at the last pages of the ' Princess ' without returning, as in trance, to the wooded banks of this loved place and resting, in fancy, once more amid the fresh beauty of Springtime, as on the Sunday afternoon [in 1863?] when your fingers and voice committed the words to faithful Memory:
" ' But the tender grace of a day that is dead—' "

[67] Though several of Mary Day's letters of this period are written, at least in part, in verse, her letter of Dec. 8, seems to be the one here referred to.

[68] George Little, with whom Mary Day's brother Harry had served in the army, was teaching at Oakland College, near Port Gibson, Miss. Later (1874) he became State Geologist of Georgia.

This paragraph was in answer to a query in Mary Day's letter of Nov. 13 (and was in turn replied to in her letter of Dec. 17). The following paragraphs, on music and organ-playing, echo the same letter.

address and would he give a copper to hear from me and who's
his sweetheart *now?*

You are right to cultivate Music – Cling to it, it is the only
thing, the only *reality,* left in the world for you and me and
many another like us – It will revolutionize the world, and
that not long hence. Study it intensely, give yourself to it, *you*
can enter the very innermost temple and Sanctuary of it, *you*
will always be a Priestess there. The Altar Steps are wide
enough for all the world, and Music inquires not if the Worshipper be Vestal or Stained, nor looks to see what dust of
other Shrines is upon the knees that bend before her. She is
utterly unconscious of aught but Love which pardons all things
and forgives all things and receives all natures into the Warmth
of Its Bosom. I look to hear you play divinely when I shall
see you again.

As for *my Organ*-playing, you would be wofully disappointed
to hear me – It is all so new, the fingering and pedal-playing,
and base-notes and stops &c &c, and I have so little time to
practice , – that I have as yet not acquired anything like such
mastery over it as would enable me to render Music in fit style
for *you* to hear. I know however that you would like some of
the little melodies which I improvise sometimes before service,
because you would *understand,* and recognize the hand which
was *so* proud, the first time It knew that It could delight you
with its work.

Dear Child, the poem you sent me is nothing less than
delicious. Whenever I read it, all sorts of delicate adjective-
combinations float into my mind –. I call it, dainty – crystalline –
A mellow radiance plays and wavers through it, like the red
spot in an opal – The man who wrote that poem, (a friend says
it was James Russell Lowell; but *I* could have sworn some
woman wrote it !) was, of the enviable sort who *enjoy* music –

You and *I* – – would not " enjoy " such an Organ piece as is
there described – Our souls would be like sails at sea: and the
irresistible storm of Music would *shred* them as a wind shreds
canvass, whereof the fragments writhe and lash about in the
blast which furiously sports with their agony –

Therefore I, except in some supremely-happy moment, could
never write a piece like this, wherein one finds nothing of that

sorrow-tone which forever winds like a black thread through the glittering brocade of Music – — –   In the copy you send me, the *third line from the last* runs; –

   " To the delighted Soul, which abyssed " – &c.[69]

This is defective in Metre: – have you not left out a word? And what is it? – I so wish I could tell you what rare pleasure the piece gives me! I kiss the hand which sent it – 'Tis a dear hand, and feeds my soul daintily through the bars of life: –   Fair Fingers, that hold sugar between the wires of my cage, – I'm but a Raven, yet I love sugar, *so hold,* and I croak to ye, more, more, more ! –

   You ask of my hopes and prospects – Both are dim, but brighter than they were – You will be glad to know that, so far as the material comforts go, I live quite luxuriously, and in the way of quarters, feed, and " good harness," – I may be said to be well stabled and groomed: – a simile which reminds me that I wish for you every afternoon, when Cliff and I mount our two fine horses and gallop over some beautiful English downs that surround this place – — My Hope is, to work hard next year in my present business and go to Oxford, England, early in "/68, with Cliff, to study two years in my profession.[70] *Now,* I study little – I have much sitting-up at night, and if I even sit down to write a letter, I go to *sleep,* – –. as you observe!

   This is why I do not write you oftener; but in the summer I shall have plenty of leisure –

[69] James Russell Lowell, " A Legend of Brittany." A transcript of part of this poem had been sent to Lanier in Mary Day's letter of Nov. 28-Dec. 1 (probably Part Second, stanzas XXIX-XXXII, which treat of organ music) ; the line here quoted should read: " To the delighted soul, which sank abyssed." Her reply to his comments is contained in her letter of Dec. 17.

[70] This dream—probably to study either literature or law—was as futile as had been the one at Oglethorpe in 1861 of going to Heidelberg to become a professor. In her reply of Dec. 17 Mary Day asked: " Sidney, *what* is ' your profession '—? Please tell me, for indeed I do not know. And *what* is your book? Are you unwilling to trust me with one word concerning it? If only I had it to read!" (She had apparently heard of *Tigers-Lilies* only indirectly through Macon friends or family.)

See, Friend! while my soul dreams of you, my eyes go to sleep!
There is, in this, nothing for you to

Forgive – !

Thought I'd send you my wild letter, but 'tis not worth it –.
Love to everybody.[71]

[71] The year ended with another disappointment for Mary Day. In her letter
of Nov. 28-Dec. 1 she had asked for " the inestimable boon of a Christmas visit
from ' Sid and Cliff.' " In her letter of Dec. 17 she renewed her appeal, saying
that his family and friends were suspending their own plans until they knew
whether he was coming. But in a postscript, dated Dec. 21, she added: " I
know, now, that you are not coming. . . . May Christmas be bright and glad to
you."

Lanier did not go to Macon for Christmas. Instead, his father went to
Montgomery (see Gertrude Lanier's letter to Sidney, Dec. 25, 1866), and was
probably the bearer of Mary Day's Christmas note and gift—" a portion of
myself "—to Sidney; he was certainly the bearer of Sidney's answer (the envelope
is subscribed " Kindness RSL "), which indicates that the gift was a lock of her
hair. (Lanier's answer is numbered " 1 " in the series set aside by Mary Day
Lanier in 1915, which would place it in the early autumn. But in its warmth
of tone it fits more accurately as No. 6 of this series; and its specific reference
to her Christmas gift places it after Dec. 25.) Mary Day's letter of Jan. 2-3,
1867, acknowledges receipt of Lanier's answer. R. S. Lanier had probably
returned to Macon about Jan. 1; his letter to Clifford on Jan. 12 states that he
had been too busy to write since his return, concluding: " Will only add: I came
home prouder than ever of my dear sons & with more confidence than ever in
their success. Sid's improving health also makes me happy." He and his daughter
had moved back to their old rooms at Wesleyan College (see Gertrude Lanier to
Sidney, Jan. 12, 1867), where Mary Day was also boarding.

1867

FROM SALEM DUTCHER [1]

Augusta, Ga., 5th Jany, 1867.

Sidney Lanier Esqr.
   Montgomery, Ala.

My Dear Lanier: –

   Prior to leaving Milledgeville for this festive burgh I wrote you, but, as no reply has yet been deigned, presume the length and dulness of my epistle cast you into a syncope. This is, therefore, to arouse you from so criminal a lethargy and inform you with what regret I should renounce the acquaintance of a man after my own heart, fond of even the abstrusest studies and yet not utterly disdaining the small creature comforts of a hot punch, late supper, and segar. By the same mail which takes you this I forward copies of three papers containing those Essays on Truth whereof I once told you. Nos 1 and 2 are freely at your disposal but I must beg

---

[1] At some time toward the end of 1866 Lanier had met Salem Dutcher, five years his senior, who, during the next few years seems to have been recognized as Lanier's best friend. Not much is known of Dutcher. He was possibly a native of New York State who had lived in the South. (In a letter to Lanier, Jan. 5, 1868, he refers to "Tennessee—home of ye hours of my youth.") He may, even at the time Lanier met him, have been a correspondent for the New York *World*, for which he seems later to have worked as editorial writer.

At the time of their first meeting, Dutcher was probably in Montgomery, the capital of Alabama, to report on the session of the state legislature for his New York paper. From Montgomery he went to Milledgeville, the capital of Georgia; and from there he returned to Augusta, which he called home, though his mother and sisters lived in New York. The letter here printed is Dutcher's second letter to Lanier. The first (referred to as having been written from Milledgeville) has not survived and was probably never delivered.

Only one of Lanier's letters to Dutcher has been found (Oct. 26, 1867). At the time when the family were collecting letters for the Scribner volume in 1899, Clifford Lanier reported: "Dutcher has not preserved any" (see his letter to Mary Day Lanier, Feb. 23, 1899).

some care to be taken of No. 3, that being the only copy I have to complete my series. Read them at some time when, mentally speaking, you feel, after the fashion of an ostrich, able to digest ten=penny nails, and should I chance to meet you again we will enter upon their merits through the Menstruum of a smoking toddy. Since I wrote you, have been hideously cast about on the sea of life – *this* simile you, of course, never heard before – and am only just now considering myself home again with my books, my papers, and my pipe. In a few days, however, must tempt this self-same sea again, having received divers invitations to deliver a certain lecture of mine in some of the principal places in my State. But what saith the Poet

"———— nunc vino pellite curas:
Cras ingens iterabimus æquor." [2]

In the course of these projected peregrinations it is not impossible I may come so near the Alabama line as to be tempted into a descent upon you. Montgomery has divers attractions for me, not the least among them being the fair ones who honour the earth by there taking up their abiding place. G – d d – n ’em is my constant bi=fold prayer. I'm forever
Heaven bless
getting into hot water about some petticoat with a little lump of perfection inside it and yet despite at least nine thousand separate and distinct formal resolves to eschew ’em, my motto still is

" Dulce ridentem Lalagen *amabo,*
Dulce loquentem " [3]

Can't help it I give you my word, Lanier. Toward men am generally ice and have the reputation among that spotless race of being proud, stuck-up etc, but to a woman melt in a moment. For some months I kept a petticoat in my room once – brought there, however, by another fellow, a most debauched and insidious person – and for the whole time that relic remained was known as the most amiable of created beings. But, if you will, write to me – my address is here, glass box No. 116 – and if you positively won't, at least hold me in kindly remembrance. I left a copy of Gª Laws for 65-66 at your house – in the office – as also two copies of the Ordinances of the Alabama Conven-

[2] Horace, *Odes,* I, vii.   [3] *Ibid.,* I, xxii.

tion of 1865. Please preserve them for me (they are of value)
till I come or write. It has struck me that, perhaps, your pride,
for you are Spanish that way, as also in your cast of face, took
fire at what you might have deemed too irreverent allusions to
a certain fair one you wot of.[4] If so, acquit me of anything
more criminal than an occasional recklessness – reaching no
nearer the heart than the tip of my pen – that is wont to carry
me unto terrific heights. Commend me very kindly to the
demoiselle in question, as also my regards to Mrs Watt and
the masculine element of your family.

Herewith accept my fervent supplications you may see the
error of your ways – a thing I will not say, as said a divine once,
I doubt most d — n'bly.

Yours

Salem Dutcher –

To John B. Tabb [5]

Exchange Hotel
Montgomery Ala
Jany 20th/67

My Dear John Tabb:

After various fruitless inquiries, I have
tonight, by accident, met Mr Selden, of Virginia, who knows
and kindly agrees to ford this letter to y'r address.

I'm just *infinitely* glad you're studying Music, (as Mr S. tells
me) and hope yet to hear you play. Study *Chopin* as soon as

[4] Dutcher's allusion may have been to Mary Day; but was more likely to one
of Lanier's friends in Montgomery, possibly Anna Howard (see notes 13 and
36, below).

[5] After the close of the war, John Banister Tabb, whom Lanier had known
as a fellow prisoner at Point Lookout, Md., from Nov., 1864, until their
release, in Feb., 1865, went to Baltimore to study piano. At the time of this
letter, however, he was visiting an aunt in New Orleans. Lanier was apparently
under the impression that Tabb was in or near Richmond, Va., as the reference
to the "Medical College" seems to be to the well known "Medical College of
Virginia." This letter, it seems clear, was never delivered; and Lanier and Tabb
did not meet or correspond after their release from prison until ten years later,
in 1877, when their friendship was resumed. After this, it lasted unbroken until
Lanier's death.

The Mr. Selden mentioned as the bearer of the present letter was probably a
guest at the Exchange Hotel.

you become able to play his music: and get his " life," by *Liszt*
(the Composer) – 'Tis the most enjoyable book *you* could read.
I scratch this off very hastily. Write me immediately, giving
y'r address – Send y'r letter, Ut Supra.

I'm always Y'r Faithful

Sidney Lanier

Go to the " Medical College " and inquire for Henry Howard,
of Ala – telling him you know me – you'll find him a pleasant
friend – Have you forgotten old Pt. Lookout? I wait for letter –

S. C. L.

To Gertrude Lanier

Montgomery   Ala
Jany 30th/67

My Darling,   How rapidly the time glides away when one is
busy! Here it is two or three days since I got your sweet little
rose-petal of a letter that was so fragrant with Love, and I am
just answering it, tho' I had made most solemn resolutions to
reply by return of mail.

I am working hard on the novel and hope to finish it in a
Couple of weeks. The copying and recasting will then take me
a month. And so I hope, like the poor old Wintry Earth, to
blossom forth this Spring!

I am infinitely pleased that you are acquainting yourself with
the thoughts of great men. You, My Dear Child, have the most
immense advantage over any one I know in this respect, and
you should improve it. I mean: — most people, arriving at
your age, find themselves under the necessity of educating, or
rather of *re*-educating, their *hearts,* and not their *intellects.*
Youth, – Mein Himmel, what a terrible thing that time of Life
is! It is like a wild Wind-gust rushing down and blowing one
off the land: and one revels in the intoxicating velocity of one's
motion and the delicious delirious up-and-down of the Sea's
surge, – until, when far out at Sea, beyond Sight of Landmarks
or Lighthouses, it suddenly occurs to him that he is going
Somewhere, and questions rise thick upon him like the dead
sailors that thronged about the Ancient Mariner in the lonely

Sea. These questions are:— where is one going, and where's the Compass, and how is one to use it![6]

That is to say, what does one *love*, (for one goes where he loves, and it is always true that Home (be it Heaven or Hell) is where the *heart* is) and how shall one attain to the Beloved, and further how shall one employ the means given one for such attainment?

Well:— *you,* Bless you My Sissa! — you have somehow kept in sight of your Land (which is Heaven) all the time, and have kept your Heart steadfast and true, and you do not *now* need to find out what is worth loving and to educate your heart to love it.

For all of which, Let the Heavens be festooned with rainbows!

I am sorry enough that we couldn't be at the Concert. I believe we are to have one here, in a short time: at which I am expected to perform.

Aunt Jane rec y'r letter — She's looking well, and having a good time with the Legislators. Sallie [Schley] is also improving and is really beautiful. Uncle Will still digging gold.[7] Grand Pa heartier than he has been in a year or two.

All send love to you and Father. I write to Mamie by today's mail. How is she? — If she should be very ill, telegraph *me immediately.* Her last letter made me anxious.[8]

God keep you.

Bro. Sid.

[6] This metaphor seems to be the germ of an early undated draft of Lanier's poem " The Ship of Earth," first entitled " Fear at Morning " (I, 15). The charting of his own career was still somewhat uncertain at this time. In addition to the abortive plan of going to Oxford to study, he may have given some consideration to the tentative offer by Mr. Gresham and Judge Nisbet, of Macon, to become a professor at Oglethorpe University, which they were hoping to revive. (See R. S. Lanier's letter to Sidney, Jan. 29, 1867: " I told them that I was under the impression you had other aims & that in the present condition of the College, no salary they could feel able to offer you would be likely to induce you to alter them; but that I would make known their wishes & you could write me on the subject.") But no letter by Lanier mentions this scheme for the resurrection of Oglethorpe, which, indeed, came to naught. Instead, Lanier's aspirations were turning seriously to the profession of authorship, as revealed in the following letter.

[7] William Lanier seems to have gone to California, and to have been literally digging for gold.

[8] Three letters from Mary Day during this month survive: Jan. 2-3, Jan. 16-18,

Tell Father Cliff. and I want the *Horace,* and the 2 Vols. Lempiere, Class-Dic. Please send them by Express, if no other way.

TO MARY DAY [9]

[Montgomery, Ala., *c.* Feb. 15, 1867]

An I were to be hung for the doubt, Good Mamie, I could not tell which was the Sweeter flower, your letter or the violets in it!

These both breathe a sacred fragrance about my soul: they make me as a star up to which floats incense from some wondering world – full of worshippers down below.

I am glad that you cling to those " first – days." There are not many moments when I dare to think about them. Nothing like them will ever come in my life again.

and Jan. 20, 1867. In the second of these she said that she had been suffering from chills and fever; in the third she announced: " I have been much worse . . . It is not simple chill & fever but also a remittent fever." This would account for Lanier's anxiety.

Lanier's letter to Mary Day here referred to ("I write to Mamie by today's mail ") and acknowledged in hers of Feb. 2 has not been found, nor an earlier letter acknowledged in hers of Jan. 20. But her letter of Feb. 2—which revels in memories of their first meeting in the spring of 1863, and which echoes warm phrases from his lost letter of Jan. 30—seems to indicate a nearer approach to reconciliation than had been achieved previously.

[9] This is Lanier's first letter to Mary Day in 1867 that has survived (see note 8, above). It is undated, and the envelope bears no postmark. At the top of the MS and on the envelope is written in Mary Day Lanier's later handwriting: " Robinson Springs, April 1867 "; but the date is unquestionably wrong, and the place is probably wrong also.

The conjectural dating is arrived at from the following evidence: (1) the first three paragraphs are clearly in answer to her letter of Feb. 2, (2) this letter in turn is answered specifically in her letter of Feb. 21, (3) and he refers to her here as " Eve," as he does also in a Valentine poem entitled " To MD " (I, 164), which bears the date Feb. 14, 1867. (Strangely enough, no reference is made to this poem in any of Mary Day's letters of this period, though the attached envelope indicates that it was sent; it is hard to explain how she passed by in silence his avowal that she was:

> " The real woman, whose first touch
>   Aroused to highest life
> My real manhood. Crown it then,
>   Good angel, friend, love, wife! . . .
> We two together shall bind up
>   Our past's bright broken dream."

The present letter was not so hopeful.)

Is not each man a devil, and has not each some Heaven from which he has fallen?

Those First-days are the Paradise from which thou, Sweet Eve, O Sweet Eve, – and I, – have been expelled.

Perhaps our Friend Christ, when he unlocks the other graves, will also reopen for us this ineffable Eden whereof our memories now dream and dream. Ah God, Ah God, clarify my Soul and clarify my Heart till they be crystalline pure, – so that I may reenter the old Heaven, when Thy time comes!

Pray for this, Eve.

I have to tell you what I hope you will keep a most profound and inviolable secret for a week or two: not even disclosing the same to Sister or Father: – and for my life I can not tell why I should wish so whimsical a thing, either! – Yet, keep it. Know that I have finished my book: and that a perverse Fate, in all probability planning my destruction, impels me to seek a publisher. I have lain by, long enough: the humor is upon me to go into the great world, as into a gypsey's hut, and try my fortune. In two weeks, at longest, I shall have copied and arranged my Mss. I shall then pass through Macon on my way to New York, and submit my book to you and divers others, for criticism: to *you,* first.

And now; finger on lip, Child! and God guard thee with His Sanctity.

Sidney.

To Mary Day [10]

[Montgomery, Ala., Feb. 23? 1867]

My Dear Mamie:

Your telegram was received this morning, and I hasten to write you, tho' with faint hope that my letter will reach you before you leave Macon.

[10] Lanier's letter is undated, but the envelope is postmarked Feb. 23 (Saturday). Moreover, Mary Day's letter of Feb. 24-26 (begun on Sunday before she left Macon and continued on Tuesday aboard a boat from Savannah to Brunswick, Ga.) acknowledges receipt of his letter and informs him that she is en route to visit her friend Lilla Hazelhurst at Waynesville, Wayne Co., Ga. In a previous

In the next two weeks, I hope to be in Macon, where I shall spend a day or two: on my way to New York. I hope to find a publisher for my book, in the big city: in which fortunate event I shall quickly return and spend some time in Macon. Failing, — God knows what I *shall* do.

I cannot speak of my disappointment at not meeting you. It is hard.

But you have not even told me where you were going. Write me soon as you receive this.

I hope to get some testimonials which will ensure me a *hearing,* at least, in New York. If you have any friends connected with the publishing houses there, leave letters of introduction for me. Where is Mrs Clem. Clay staying? She was in New York a short time ago. You will pardon this illegible scrawl: but I have written in a great hurry.

Thou knowest that I am always

Sid Lanier

To Robert S. Lanier

Montgomery Ala
March 3rd /67

My Dear Father:

Hoping every day to arrive at some definite conclusion which I might announce to you in regard to my movements, I have delayed writing to you until this time; when I have the pleasure of telling you that towards the last of next week, or the first of week after, I shall pass in upon you, at Macon.

I had hoped to surprise you: but I see that Mr Vedder has let out my secret.[11]

letter dated " Thursday Night " (Feb. 21) she had told him of the same plans; but the accompanying envelope is postmarked Feb. 23 (Saturday), indicating that her letter probably did not reach him until Feb. 25 (Monday).

Both of her letters are filled with regrets over circumstances which made it impossible for her to remain in Macon and with plans to come back in time to meet him on his return from New York.

[11] Lanier had not informed his father of his projected trip to New York, but a Mr. Vedder, of Macon, who had been in Montgomery on business, had brought the news to him (see R. S. Lanier's letter to Sidney, Feb. 17, 1867).

My indetermination until now has been in consequence of the unavoidably erratic movements of a friend of mine who wished to go to New York with me, and who will assist me very materially in my mission there. This friend, (Salem Dutcher, of Augusta, Ga) has just been appointed a sort of Minister Plenipotentiary of the publishing-house of Richardson & Co, New York, and is now travelling in their interest. – But I'll give you particulars when I see you.

The humor is upon me to go and try my fortune in the big world. I cannot but indulge it.

Grandfather passed through a day or two ago, on his way to Pensacola, where he must needs go and spy out the land, to see whether it would pay to go down and occupy there.

He suffers a little from the gout occasionally, but is otherwise quite well.

Uncle Will still plodding in the mud after gold.

Aunt Jane in New Orleans, where she has been sojourning for a couple of weeks on a pleasure trip.

I shall bring the novel, which is now finished and within a day's work of being ready for the press: and shall submit the same to you and Uncle Clifford and the Judge,[12] for criticism. If you have tears to shed &c.

Hastily,

Sid.

FROM SALEM DUTCHER [13]

Montgomery, Ala., 13th March, 1867

Dear Siddy –

After you left I took to my bed and there remained all day, Alfred bringing me my meals, whereof I could eat nothing, and dosing me with congress water and citrate of

[12] Judge Eugenius A. Nisbet.

[13] Interesting sidelights on Lanier's life in Montgomery at this period occur in the surviving letters of Salem Dutcher. For instance, in his letter of Mar. 20, 1867, Dutcher wrote (from New Orleans): "Immediately on arriving Sunday morning last I went to a Catholic Church and as I saw the poor devils of Creole men and women crowding round the altar or pattering their prayers in the rocky aisles I could not but think of that parlous oration of yours delivered one night in thy sanctum upon the great benefit poor, pale, washed out women seemed to

magnesia. Toward night I rallied and Cliffy and self walked out, stopping for a moment *en route* at Anna's. She, poor child, was as pale as a ghost and presented generally a most dilapidated appearance. Last night after supper the hotel became unbearable. Cliff was busy – my stomach was too weak for either cigar or julep and, to escape madness, I went to see Anna and talk of you. Being most entirely and inexcusably in the wrong myself, I of course forgave her freely for iniquities she never dreamed of and we chatted till half past ten.

To=night I leave, though not yet determined whether to go to Jackson or New=Orleans – but withersoever it may be will write you speedily. The Low=Browed I have not seen nor is it likely I will, only having remained over in order to wind up some business I could not attend to yesterday. Since you left it has seemed to me that every body has been pointing the finger of curiosity at a grown man almost in despair at a temporary separation from his friend and brother — also a man and a soldier. But my dear boy thou – for let me adopt that endearing old style — thou hast been unto me my Jonathan my Benjamin, my preserver. He is like sweet, generous wine, I said to A. and we laughed as I told her the tighter you got, the purer and more loving your talk became. Thanks to him who giveth us the victory not a drop of liquor has this day passed my lips going in or an oath or a *fly blow* coming out. Cliff says little but goeth about his business in his usual quiet, grave sedateness, and yet

derive from being in a Church—why or wherefore they could not, for their souls, relate." Again, on June 5, 1867, Dutcher wrote (from Augusta): " Since last night came to this place where I abide some serenaders who, in discoursing sweet music to a damsel overhead, did bring to mind, as I lay in my basement room, divers recollections of that time wherein I went with thee the rounds of Montgomery. Here as there, the violin and guitar and clarion (or clarionette) and banjo softly linked their several tones, but nowhere in the medley did I hear the voice of the flute—and, in thinking of the absence thereof, thou camest into mind straight way."

From the evidence of the present letter (Mar. 13), Lanier probably left Montgomery for Macon on Monday, Mar. 11. Dutcher's letter suggests that a farewell party for Lanier had been given in his room at the Exchange Hotel on Sunday night. Anna Howard, mentioned in this letter, was apparently a guest at the party, but she had probably left after Lanier's uncle, Abram Watt, the proprietor of the Exchange, objected to the noise. She was a Montgomery girl who was a friend of Lanier's at this time, and probably sister to the Henry Howard mentioned in Lanier's letter of Jan. 20 to Tabb. (See also note 36, below.)

I do fancy he would last night have wept had the balance not been preserved by a most huge bouquet of sweet flowers from his beloved. Mr. Watt said to me – in half apologizing for coming to your room which the hideous din there made entirely justified him – that you did not think he liked you as well as he did Cliff and in the office he did not – you were not fit for it you should be a lawyer, that you had ability and nerve – saying this latter after yᵉ manner of yᵉ aged some three or four times over and had the stuff of a man in you only needing a rough bout with the world to bring it out. Dear Sid – I think him right in one thing – *Be A Lawyer.* The field is glorious and I know, for all the overplus of imagination you have, logical power and mental systematism are large within you. Let litera-ture be the rose that adorns the statue but let the statue be of marble and of steel. Life is not all flowers. Take Law as the backbone of your future and let letters be " the limbs and out-ward flourishes " — Anna says I must put her in this letter and send her to you – so accept a pure little child. And herewith, my brother Sid, farewell. May God keep thee from fly blow and all evil things – turn your brain to the Law and keep some warm corner of your brave heart for

Salem.

Write me to New Orleans
　　Care Sᵗ Charles.

To JANE L. WATT

Macon Ga
March 14th /67

My Darling Auntie:

　　　　　　　After a thousand trials and tribulations incident to the change in the schedule, I am at length here, safely esconced in No 30 of the Lanier House, with a delightful view out of my one window comprehending a vast range of back-alley, bricks, dirt, a livery-stable, and one tree and a half in the distance.

　　And Mein Himmel! The infinite loneliness and desolation weighs upon me as Mount Etna weighed upon poor Enceladus. Every man, (I've been here fifteen hours and haven't seen as many people!) has a long, long face, the corners of the mouth thereof being in a state of indefinite downward extension, and the eyes showing uncertainly through a round million of crow's-feet. Each store has a single clerk in it, who stands peering through the glass-door like a cannon through the embrasure of a casemate. The bar-keepers, — I entreat you to believe that my knowledge of these individuals is derived entirely from distant inspection — sleep in sweet and undisturbed security upon their counters, and the rum-suckers upon tick have not the daring to wake them. The cars come into the depot on tiptoe, as it were; and the engineer blows his whistle with a tremulous hand, weakly, full feebly, not to disturb the sabbatic quiet which reigns over the poor city. There is no chaffering nor bargaining even among the Jew-stores! and Jewry may say here, what it could never say except from necessity, " I never 'aggles! "

Do you ask what it means?

It means the Sherman Bill.[14] ——— ————

I found Sister and Father well, and expecting me anxiously. Sister returns you many thanks for your nice present, and will write you.

I've been asleep ever since I arrived and have seen few friends yet. Shall sally forth to meet them, when I have paid my little tribute to the dear ones with you, there. My God, Child, how I miss you all!

————

Tell Cliff. to send by Express (Billy Mitchell will fix it) the blank book I left on the table in 61.[15] Under the circumstances,

———

[14] Lanier's article on this topic, echoing the above paragraph in detail, was submitted to the Syracuse, New York, *Courier and Union* (see his letter to Northrup, Mar. 15, 1867, following), where it was published on Apr. 8 (see V, 209). In a letter of Mar. 7, R. S. Lanier had written to Clifford of this bill: " The faces of men & their affairs look gloomy since the final passage of the ' Military Bill.' It is difficult to say what course we should take. Perhaps it is best to leave the matter to Providence & to the calm counsels of the Governors of the states—who are most likely to suggest the safest measures. Meantime we may accept with quiet dignity what we cannot prevent. The best manhood is seen in adversity. Since there is nothing we can do that will not be construed to our disadvantage we ought to be careful to preserve what is about all that is left to us—our self-respect."

[15] The reference is to Lanier's room at the Exchange Hotel. (See Salem Dutcher to Lanier, Mar. 10, 1868: " Ah! let me not think of 61 or 60 was it,

it is wonderful that I came off at all, – eh? Cliff will tell you how unexpected, and at the same time, how gratifying was our parting frolic. Do apologize to Uncle Abram for the noise, it being our first offence.

Write me. Kiss everybody, and believe that I'm always

Yr Loving

Sid

To Milton H. Northrup [16]

Macon, Georgia, March 15, '67.

My dear Northrop: Would a little series of letters like this, in which, as they go on, I would like to enter the pathetic to some degree, be of any value to you? Being temporarily out of employment, I am moving about Alabama and Georgia visiting some friends, and could write you from different places. If you accept, send me a copy, and make any suggestions, for the business is new to me.

Write, and know that I am always

Y'r friend,

Sidney Lanier.

To Mary Day

Macon Ga
March 16th /67

My Dear Mamie:

It is a desolate place: you are not here: I will not speak of it.

My movements are as yet undecided, and so I cannot appoint

where with the small aid of books and music all about we sat in easy chair and had talk.")

The " blank book " requested may have been the literary " Ledger " which still survives (Henry W. Lanier Collection, Johns Hopkins University), containing many of Lanier's early compositions.

[16] Previously published, *Lippincott's*, LXXV, 310 (Mar., 1905). For the newspaper letter, here referred to, see note 14, above. A search of the files of the Syracuse *Courier and Union* reveals no further letters in this series.

a time for you to return. A friend of mine, who will assist me very materially in my projects, is to go to New York with me. He is now travelling in the West and may not be here for some weeks.[17] I await him here: the probabilities being that we shall leave Macon in three weeks from this time.

And so, spend your visit pleasantly, Little Mamie: we will meet, somewhere, this summer. *I* promise it.

I took tea with Gussie last night, and we had some music. Her voice is a little improved, I think, since I last heard it. I played for her: and she gratified me with her old groans and sighs wherewith she was wont, in times gone, to testify the agony of her delight. Bless her! She was very sweet, and kissed me warmly, and didn't talk more baby-talk to little John Hill [18] than my strong constitution could bear.

I'm told Janie Angel [19] is with you. Kiss her for me, and say the sweet things I would say if I were there. How would I love to wander in the Spring-woods with you and her! It would be too sweet.

I have not yet called on your friend Mr Reese,[20] but will do so when the weather has moderated and I am thawed a little. It is now too cold and wet to think.

Child, Child, when great desolation is upon me, my heart turns towards you. I would I were near you today, that I might rest a little.

God, God

L

[17] The reference is to Salem Dutcher, who wrote to Lanier from Mobile on Mar. 15-16, and left by boat for New Orleans on Mar. 16.

[18] Augusta Lamar Ogden's son, John Hill Ogden, named for her brother and Lanier's friend John Hill Lamar, who had been killed in the war (see note 37, 1864).

[19] Janie Taliaferro, the widow of John Hill Lamar, had accompanied Mary Day on her visit to Waynesville.

[20] The Rev. E. F. Rees, rector of Christ Church, Macon, throughout Lanier's life. In answer to Lanier's request for letters of introduction to New York publishers (see his letter of Feb. 23, above), Mary Day had written on Feb. 24-26: " Grant me, in my bitter disappointment, the *hope* of being indirectly instrumental in your success. Please, the *first* day you spend in Macon, call on my dear friend Mr Rees, who promises *most* gladly to give you a full letter to an Editor-friend, John Henry Hopkins—He says Mr. Hopkins' word will carry great weight in your favor—that he is a man who is deeply interested in everything treating of *Music,* especially, and art in general; and that *he* can command *Mr. H.'s* attention for you."

To Clifford A. Lanier

Macon Ga
March 19th /67

My Darling Cliff:

I'm struggling hard against the blue sentimentals and so I'm not going to tell you how infinitely lonely I have been since I left you.

The weather has been so bad since I came that, up to Sunday last, I have seen very few of the Macon people. Since then, however, a sunshiny day or two has brought them out, and I have been in a perpetual handshake. Every one inquires after you warmly: and I have fallen into a most parlous formula of reply to these interr[o]gatories. For instance, I meet Smith.

" How are you, Sid! Glad to see you."

" How are you, Smith."

" You look fatter than I ever saw you. How's Cliff?"

" O, Cliff's hearty; not so fat as usual, tho. Cliff and I are like Jack Spratt and his wife, one of whom could eat no fat, the other no lean.– Cliff fattens in the summer, and I in the winter!!!!"

I hope you see the beauty and point of this simile. I have made it do duty on at least a hundred occasions. You would be astonished to see how gracefully it covers a " See you again," and the retreat thereafter.

I've spent one evening with Gussie, and had some glorious music. We all (Father, Sister and I) take tea with Gus. Bacon tonight and with Ogden tomorrow night.

I played the organ at our church last Sunday at the night-service. Of course, everybody looked up as soon as I commenced the voluntary, and enquired who is it. After service, while I was playing the march, a crowd gathered round me in the Organ-loft, to whom I played for an hour: Gussie sang some pieces to my accompaniment, and we had a good old-fashioned time of it.

I have been busily writing ever since I came here, and besides a huge letter to Northrop's paper,[21] will get off, today, a batch to some other papers.

[21] See note 14, above. No similar letters to other newspapers have been found.

Do go and see Mary Wyman [22] and tell her that I remembered
her in my letter to you: and endeavor to cultivate her as much
as possible. She likes you above everybody, there, and will be
delighted to see you. She doesn't talk much, but you can converse on anything and see that she is listening and appreciating
all you say.

I've written Anna Howard.

Mamie Day is not here, and will not be for some weeks: is
spending the spring at Waynesville. Harry [Day] is here, and
called on me in a very cordial manner.

And that's all about *me*. Write me quickly. My One-
Beloved; Ah, how I yearn for you!

My love to all.

Sid.

To Clifford A. Lanier

Macon Ga
March 21st 1867

My Darling:

        I enclose you the prize-advertisement of the Mobile
" Times," which I have just recd in a long letter from Salem, at
Mobile. He has seen Major [Henry] St. Paul, the editor of the
" Times," and spoke to him of me, without knowing that *you*
had any serious designs against ye *same*.[23] You will observe that
the Mss. is to be sent in by April 1st, which is now close at hand:
Will you be ready? Write me.

---

[22] Mary Wyman, of Montgomery, was a friend of Lanier's, referred to in a
letter of May 4, 1867, from Salem Dutcher, who saw her in New Orleans. A
carte de visite photograph of her—with an inscription by Lanier dated Aug. 15,
1866—survives in Lanier's pocket book (Charles D. Lanier Collection, Johns
Hopkins University).

[23] Lanier's story, " The Three Waterfalls " (V, 213), may have been written
at this time and submitted in the Mobile *Times* prize contest. (Dutcher had
suggested in his letter of Mar. 15 that Lanier submit a short piece of " six to ten
pages of thy letter size ' handwrite,' unless it should occur to promulge upon a
novelette of some three to four times that length." And Clifford Lanier's reference in his letter of Mar. 22 to his brother's *feuilleton* suggests the same possibility. But a search of the files of the Mobile *Times* for this period—through
the courtesy of R. J. Usher, Howard-Tilton Memorial Library, New Orleans—
reveals no contributions that could be ascribed to Lanier.)

It is my wish that we should do something *together*. Send me all the little poems that you think or write, and I will put enough labor upon them to give me a sort of proprietory interest in them; then, signed with our two somewhat romantic *cognomina* they will go before the public charming as to their ends, like a little dog with blue ribbon tied round his tail. I'm in earnest, tho'.   Work on.

Wrote you a day or two ago. How is Anna? Go to see her, when you have time. I have written her.

Letter from Aunt Jane yesterday.

Love to all.

Hastily

Your

Sid.[24]

To Clifford A. Lanier

Macon Ga

March 22nd /67

My Darling Cliff:

Do you remember the long essay I read before the Literary Society, on " The New Time? " [25] I think 'tis in the lowest drawer of the bureau. If you can find it, please send it immediately *by Express.*

Wrote you yesterday. All well.

Hastily

Sid.

[24] On Mar. 22, 1867, Clifford Lanier wrote his brother, forwarding a letter of Feb. 2 from " our erratic Keeble " (probably Charles Taliaferro, brother of Janie Lamar) offering Lanier a position teaching music to " fifteen Virginia misses " at Leesburg, Va. Clifford suggested that, since this was on the way to New York, " It – the whole scheme – might fill up till July, when the proceeds thereof might waft you, through all sorts of summer recreations with Ginna [Hankins], to Gotham in September." But the plan did not materialize.

[25] Published as " Retrospects and Prospects " in the *Southern Magazine,* in Mar. and Apr., 1871 (V, 280).

To Clifford A. Lanier

Macon Ga
March 30th/67

My Darling:

Y'r letter came this morning. I'm very glad you're getting enthused again about the novel.

A note from Salem received this morning announces that he expects to be here about the middle of next week. I wish to meet him in Montgomery: as I have yet to collect the note on Uncle Sampson.[26] I hope, also, that Aunt Mollie[27] will be able to go on to New York with us. Salem will probably pass through Montgomery on Monday or Tuesday. Please exert yourself to meet him on the train and *stop him there.* I shall leave here for Montgomery on Monday morning (this being Saturday), and hope to meet you at the dêpot sometime Monday night. Don't know what time the train arrives. Be at the dêpot anyhow, so as to stop Salem in case I should not arrive.

The gossip about Anna saddens me.[28]

Bye-Bye. I hope to kiss you shortly.

Hastily

Sid.

To Milton H. Northrup[29]

New York
April 11th/67.

My Dear Northrop:

Is there any likelihood of your visiting New York shortly? I shall remain here at least two weeks longer; and would be most happy to see you.

[26] A brother of Sterling Lanier, hence Lanier's great uncle.

[27] The widow of Lanier's uncle Sidney C. Lanier.

[28] In his letter of Mar. 24, to which this letter is the answer, Clifford Lanier made allusion to the farewell party for his brother in Montgomery, referring to the " corner room . . . which still echoes Dutcher's shouts! ". Of Anna Howard he wrote:

" Anna, saith Gossip, has been sent in the Country for being too *fast*. Having rode Ham Metcalf out one evening and walked Mrs. Lewis out the next, she is put up for a mark and said archer, Gossip, draws his myriad bows."

[29] Previously published, *Lippincott's*, LXXV, 310-311 (Mar., 1905). There is no evidence that Lanier and Northrup met on this trip.

Sent you a little light communication from Macon, Georgia, two weeks ago. Intended to write a series of them which should grow more sober as it progressed and gradually lead into a heavy discussion of the situation. Left Macon too early to receive any answer from you.

I have serious designs against the publishers here: but, as yet, have only skirmished afar off, without making any direct attack. Do you know any of them personally?

Do come, if you can, and let us have a " parlous " old walk and talk through these streets whose busy life is a thing that fills me full of dreams every day.

I have a pleasant room at No 7, Great Jones St, a few feet from Broadway. Brother Clifford sent regards by me.

Your Friend

Sidney Lanier

TO ROBERT S. LANIER [30]

New York

April 16th/ 67.

My Dear Father:

Pending the arrival of my friend Salem Dutcher I've been endeavoring to domesticate myself in this big city. Yesterday I climbed to the top of Trinity Church

Lanier returned to Montgomery on Monday, Apr. 1, and had a brief talk with Dutcher, who was passing through on his way from New Orleans to Macon. Dutcher wrote him that night to confirm plans for meeting in Montgomery " by either Thursday or Friday next " (i. e., Apr. 4 or 5). But when Dutcher arrived on Friday morning, Apr. 5, he found a letter from Lanier stating that he had gone on to New York. On Apr. 9 Dutcher wrote from Jackson, Miss.: " You say you will await me in New York and defer active operations till I come. When that will be, my dear boy, I do not know."

[30] Excerpt previously published, Mims, pp. 79-80. A letter of the same date to Mary Day is here omitted since it consists largely of a similar account of Lanier's impression of New York, from Trinity Church steeple. But it also contains a reference to Emerson's forthcoming volume, *May Day and Other Poems*, and a passage which implies that Lanier had been hearing some music in New York: " By the way, send me a letter to your old teacher Mr. [Charles] Haase. I wish to hear him play. I can beat, all easily, any flutists I've heard yet."

A somewhat earlier letter to Gertrude Lanier reflects the same attitude—what R. S. Lanier referred to as his son's " bewilderment " (see his letter to Sidney Lanier, Apr. 17); but it exists only in three fragments too brief to justify publication.

A letter from Clifford to Sidney Lanier, Apr. 16, refers to a letter (not found) in which Sidney had given an account of a " divine bath of Music."

steeple: and mein Himmel! What a view! – Yet, the grand
array of houses and ships and rivers and distant hills did not
arrest my soul as did the long line of men and women which,
at that height, seemed to writhe and contort itself in its narrow
bed of Broadway, as in a premature grave. Like a long serpent,
humanity here twisted itself and turned itself about and crawled
up and down, as if Nature, like a mischievous boy, had thrown
it upon the hot coals of desire and disappointment to laugh
at its ludicrous pain. From a thousand steam-jets, this serpent's-
agony of life hissed an impotent protest.

Is it possible to believe that this Broadway serpent, in the midst
of his torture, forgot not to display and flaunt his scales, which
were mostly of brilliant hue? Red, blue, gold – or what seemed
gold –, the colors shone and mingled: and this for his own eyes
to admire, since Broadway swears there is no other world but
Broadway –

—— All of which is gloomy enough, – and for that reason I'm
sorry that it is true. I have not seen here a single eye that knew
itself to be in front of a heart:– but one, and that was a blue
one, and a child owned it. 'Twas the very double of Sissa's eye,
and so I had no sooner seen it than I made love to it: with what
success you will hear. On Saturday I dined with J. F. D. Lanier,
(of Winslow & Lanier, Bankers).[31] We had only a family
party: being Mr Lanier, Wife, Sister, Miss Anthony (don't
know her connection with him), Captain Dunn (Mr L.'s grand-
son, and *aide de camp* to General Grant through the war) and,
last and best, little Kate Lanier, eight years old, pearly-cheeked,
blue-eyed, broad of forehead, cherried i' the lip, only child of
Mr L. and present wife.

About the time that the Champagne came on, I happened to
mention that I had been in prison during the war.

[31] James Franklin Doughty Lanier (1800-1881), a distant cousin of Sidney
Lanier, had removed from Madison, Ind. (where his home is maintained as a
state monument) to New York in 1848, where he became senior partner in the
banking firm of Winslow & Lanier. That he had to be identified to R. S. Lanier
suggests that the latter had not at this time established the connections he later
maintained with the firm. Sidney Lanier may have called on his New York cousin
without any letters of introduction, though his grandfather Sterling Lanier, being
a first cousin of J. F. D. Lanier's father (Alexander Chalmers Lanier), was probably acquainted with this northern branch of the family.

" Poor fellow! " says little Katy, – " and how did the rebels treat you? "

" Rebels? " said I, " I'm a rebel, myself, Kate! "

" What! " she exclaimed, and lifted up her little lilies (when I say lilies I mean hands) and peered at me curiously with all her blue eyes a-stare: " A *'live* Reb! "

This phrase, in Katy's nursery, had taken the time-honored place of bugaboos and hobgoblins and men-under-the-bed. She could not realize that I, – a smooth-faced, slender ordinary mortal, in all respects like a common man – should be a 'live reb. She was inclined to hate me, as in duty bound.

—— I will not describe the manner of the siege I laid to her: suffice it that when I rose to take leave, Katy stood up before, and half blushed and paused a minute – With a coquetry I never saw executed more prettily, " I know " said she, " that you are dying for a kiss, and you're ashamed to ask for it. – You may take one! " The ripe little lips were held up, and I pressed a long one on them, dreaming of Sissa. As I rose, – for I had to kneel to reach her, – " your moustache " whispered she " is *so* much softer than those bristles of Papa's! "

And so, in triumph, and singing poems to all blue eyes, I said good-night amidst the most cordial invitations to make myself at home in the house.

On Sunday I dined at Judge Russells.[32] But I must reserve it for another letter: until I have, as the Codifiers says, digested it!

I have made no literary attempt yet. Carleton is not here, but is now on his way, from Cuba, via New Orleans and Montgomery. I have seen Vedder, who promises me an introduction to Carleton. Barney Smyth took me through the Stock " Long Room " 'tother day. It was rich. Will tell you about it some other time.

Address me at No 7, Great Jones St, N. Y. I board here with some friends. Love to all.

Sid.

---

[32] Judge Russell was the father of Lanier's Aunt Mollie (Mrs. Sidney C. Lanier), who had returned to New York to live after the death of her husband. The " Carleton " mentioned in the next paragraph was probably a member of the publishing house of George W. Carleton & Co., New York.

To Clifford A. Lanier [33]

[New York, Apr., 1867?]

My address (No 7, Great Jones St. N. Y.) so that he may communicate with me as soon as he arrives here. Have you sent the book by Express addressed as above? I've made no effort with the novel yet, but am quietly posting myself about the doings and localities of this great city. So far, I can beat all to pieces any flutist I've heard. I'm skirmishing with the Literary Bureau about a place. Have serious ideas to deliver a lecture for the Southern Relief: and of delivering another (for my own relief) before Northrop Society in Syracuse. Also think of getting together a " flute orchestra " and airing the same in Steinway Hall: it would pay. So, you observe, my head is full of projects: but I await the issue of the novel business.

Do you know whether the " Times " of Mobile published the little pieces [34] I sent 'em? Write me. They were for the Sunday Times, the literary vehicle of the daily.

Aunt Mollie is well, and little Russell better.[35] Mrs *Sibley* has just arrived; Gen. Sibley boards at the same house with me: but I rarely see him. John Stokes is here, running with Bill Knox. Burt Caffey also illustrates his native state.

Kiss 'em all for me.

Sid.[36]

---

[33] The first part of this letter has not been found. That it was addressed to Clifford Lanier seems indicated from the reference to sending a " book by Express " (see Clifford to Sidney Lanier, Apr. 16, 1867). The fragment opens with a request to give his address to some one whom he expects to come to New York—apparently Salem Dutcher. Conjectural dating from the fact that this address was changed to Lafayette Place before May 1 (see Dutcher to Lanier, May 4, 1867), and from internal evidence which seems to place it about the middle of April.

[34] See note 23, above.

[35] In a fragmentary letter to Gertrude Lanier, written *ante* Apr. 17, Lanier had said: " I called to see Aunt Mollie yesterday, and found little Russell quite ill with something like Pneumonia."

[36] During this period Lanier was depressed by an anxiety which is not revealed in the letters to his family, but which is reflected in a letter of May 4, 1867, from Salem Dutcher, who wrote in part (answering a lost letter from Lanier): " Your letter of the 1st has just reached me and I see plainly that you are ill at ease. I wish that I could help you, but in the strife wherein you are engaged it is plainly a duel with sorrow, where all that a man can do for his friend is to

To Robert S. Lanier

New York
May 7th 1867

My Dear Father:

Hoping day after day to get some definite news in regard to my project, I have delayed writing in order to communicate it. But I am firm in my conviction that it would be infinitely less troublesome to negotiate a colossal foreign loan than to-procure the publication of one modest little novel: and I do not now expect to know certainly the result of my efforts before the first of next week.

I have just returned from a trip to Annondale, a village on the Hudson about a hundred miles above N. Y., where Hoppy [37] took me to spend Saturday and Sunday with his brother, Professor Hopson of St. Stephens College. These two days were so filled and crowded with beautiful sights and sounds that I count them two of the very happiest of my life. It is an enchanted land, up there: and the Caatskills are the good Fairies and the river plays Rip Van Winkle in a spell and the old mansions and exquisite grounds of the Aspinwalls, the Living-

---

put him on the ground, strengthen his purpose by kind words, cheer and enhearten him. . . . The nature of some of your griefs I can in part conjecture. You are troubled about your book. . . . Another source of disquietude I can also dimly see peeping out in your fervent and most ethical disquisitions upon Duty. He, my Siddy, who speaks largely upon that theme is infallibly thereunto moved — if such be not his *work* as preacher or moralist — by the pinchings of passion, which would draw him from what he deems right, but most nauseous, to what he deems wrong but is sensible in the very roots of his hair is a joy ineffable. As I cannot help you, save feebly, in your other trouble neither can I, with the best will possible, do much for you here. But this at least I *can* do — to warn you to look closely at this self same Duty and learn how much there is of God and how much of man. Sacrifice not yourself to the Right, ere you know and feel and are in your heart and brain and soul and without peradventure or misgiving satisfied that it *is* the Right."

Further reference to "that feminine entanglement" occurs in Dutcher's letter of May 17, written in answer to a letter from Lanier of May 8 (now lost). Lanier's "disquietude" was largely a result of his sense of obligation to Anna Howard, to whom he seems to have made a proposal of marriage by which he felt bound. (See his letter of June 15, 1867, to Virginia Hankins, below.) Veiled references to this unhappiness, and to Anna Howard, occur in several of his letters to his brother Clifford.

[37] Lanier's Macon friend and comrade during the war, W. A. Hopson.

stones, the Montgomerys, the Bartons &c., all stand and stretch away in a dream. I wished for you and Sissa & Cliff a thousand times.

Your letter accompanying paper with my little squib was received: [38] also yours containing copy of card, which shall be attended to.

I am rejoiced to know of your improvement in health and sincerely hope it will be permanent. I am very well: and frequently do my six or eight miles a day on foot: which, on these hard unelastic stone pavments is equal to treble that number on common ground.

I've been patronizing the Astor Library here, and have found it a mine of delight.

Tell Sissa I read what she wrote anent the blue-eyed Katy – to the same and family, whereat they were much delighted and expressed great desire to know the sisterly writer. I shall write the darling shortly: and will here only express my unfeigned pleasure and gratification that she has found a worthy man [39] to join heart and hand with.

Shall be busy running about today.

Love to all:
from
Sid.

Tell Mamie her letters have rayed in upon me: and I will try and send some answering beams shortly.

S.

My address is changed to " No. 7. *Lafayette Place.*"

[38] On Apr. 27, R. S. Lanier had forwarded to his son a copy of the Syracuse *Courier and Union* containing his article on the Sherman Bill (see note 14, above). He had also shown it to the editor of the Macon *Daily Telegraph*, who reprinted it, with editorial comment. (No file of the latter paper for the period in question has been located.)

[39] Gertrude Lanier had apparently sent Sidney the same news that she had sent Clifford in her letter of Apr. 24,—that Mr. Edward B. Shannon of New Orleans was coming for an answer, and that she was going to say yes. He was ten or twelve years older than she. It is not certain where she had met him, for Clifford seems not to have known him and—as Gertrude wrote Clifford— " Papa does not know him. Brother Sid thinks he has seen him once."

To Mary Day

New York
May 8th 1867

Sweet " Twin-Heart,"   Dear Twin-Heart, what is there in my soul that is fair enough to be spoken to thee?

And again what is there in my soul that is *un*fair enough to be spoken to thee?   For the sweet things that store themselves up there continually for thee are *too* sweet and *too* large to speak, and only if they were *less* so were it possible to say them.

And yet my soul is a-wild to talk to thee.

Let me tell thee that thou camest to me, t'other day, in a most rare sweet fashion.   Good Mamie I saw thee rise up in a mist-wreath out of one of the Catskill mountains, and float over the gleaming Hudson and alight on the swell of sward where I lay quivering and shivering with the beauty there; O Little Mamie, I tingled with the beauty; like a bell on a sea-buoy, the waves of beauty shook me to and fro and dashed me up and down till every nerve rang again. –   And so, as I said, thou didst float over to me and stayed with me: and thou and I had *such* a ramble, through the enchanted grounds of old Aspinwall and the other princely neighbors of his, there.

Like as not, thou wilt not remember being there with me: so perverse is woman! But it was on last Saturday, Child: and Sunday, too: twice, didst thou exhale like an odor from these vast mountain-flowers and waver over the water to me, and ramble and gaze and sigh and thrill with me at all the beautiful things of that Fairy-land.

And it was very good of thee to come to me at such a time, for of all the people in the world I had rather thou hadst been with me then than any other.

Stay with me, stay with me, Other-Soul: my four walls into which I am again cast, like a prison, by that tyrant Life, – are full desolate, they oppress me with the lonely gloom of a grave, and chains seem to extend themselves and wind their heavy links about me. O Thou who hast been to me at once Good Fairy, good Child, good Beloved, and good Friend, – strike off these cold manacles which freeze and bruise my soul.

Turn, O ye gray Eyes that bring the light after you like the gray Dawn, turn and look upon him who kneels all bound and sorrowful in the dark! Thou seest, Friend, my heart is like a mountain which, however sun-lit its top may be, hath yet full many a ravine that is dark and rocky and gelid and filled with serpents.

Know that *thou* seest this: *and thou only.*

My book is not yet determined upon.

I know not when I shall see thee.

God saith to me nothing so plainly as that He will keep thee and guard thee until thou and I have met again.

Bless thee, bless thee, Little Child.

Lanier.

Address:

" No 7.
    Lafayette Place."

To Gertrude Lanier [40]

La Fayette Place
New York
May 17th 1867

My Darling, Darling Sissa:

Father's first dispatch never reached New York, for some reason: and so, until yesterday, when I received his second one, I knew nothing of your marriage.[41] Immediately upon hearing of it, I repaired to the telegraph offices and searched them through, but was assured that the Telegram of the 11th had not reached New York, and so I was compelled to wait until I could have it repeated. Meantime I made superhuman exertions to so arrange my affairs as to get off to-night. You must know that the best firm of Publishers

[40] Excerpt previously published, Mims, p. 18.

[41] R. S. Lanier had written to Clifford on May 9: " For reasons connected with his business Mr. S[hannon] desires the affair to be brought to an early conclusion & I suppose the time will be about the 1st June – possibly earlier." Later the date was set for May 21, and Lanier was urged to come home for the wedding. His telegram, referred to in the next paragraph of this letter, is quoted in his father's letter of the same date to Clifford: " Impossible to come. Too sorry. Will write to-day."

in New York has made me propositions in regard to the book I brought, which, I am assured, are very favorable: but my acceptance of them depends on my seeing Mr J. F. D. Lanier, who is now in Washington and will not return for some days.[42] I found that I could not possibly go there and return to New York in time to get off to-night. I spent last night in an agony of doubts, of conflicting propositions and plans, determining one moment to give up my whole scheme, asking myself the next moment if this would be right when I am progressing so favorably: My heart drew me to you, and yet argued on 'tother side as well, for, God knows, I work, in this matter more for you and the rest of my best-beloved ones there, than for myself. Wearied out with a conflict in which my whole soul drove me first this way and then that, I resolutely expelled my heart from the conference and allowed my judgment to decide the matter. The decision, after a calm consideration of the advantages (to *you, child, not* to myself) of going and of remaining, was clearly in favor of the latter course. I therefore telegraphed Father this morning that I could not arrive in time, and with the saddest heart I ever had, and with the most bitter murmurings of a man against the cruel necessity which compels me to be the only saddening and saddened one on an occasion when I would have your joy as free of defect as Heaven itself, – I sink back to my work and, as one should say grace before a battle, write *you*: You, O my Vestal-Sister, who have, more perfectly than all the men or women of the earth; nay more perfectly than any star or any dream, represented to me the simple majesty and the serene purity of the Winged Folk up Yonder. These Folk only come down in Visions: therefore I know that my life *is* a Vision because *you* are in it.

And imagine with what indestructible loyalty I shall clasp the left hand of him in whose right hand you have laid yours! Since I knew that he loved you I have been bound to him by that tie which unites those who kneel about a common altar.

As the Romans presented the freedom of the city to a conqueror: and as this husband of thine has conquered a whole earth since thou art at once warm-souled as the passionate tropics and serene-tempered like the middle climates and pure

---

[42] The publication of *Tiger-Lilies* was paid for by Lanier with money borrowed from J. F. D. Lanier (see note 48, below).

like the icy zones: so present I to him the freedom of my heart, a gift which combines all civic, military and religious honors.

Believe therefore, Sister Mine, that on that night when thou standest by this man for marriage, thy brother, at once full of sadness and of delight, will be also at once kneeling afar off here, and standing close beside thee there. Nay, since Heaven is but one, and since, in the body, thou wilt stand and I will kneel before Heaven that night, it will but be as if we were on opposite sides of the same Altar.

And over this Altar, in the midst of my invocations, I whisper to thee and to him who weds thee that I am, to both, always

Faithful

Brother Sid.

TO ROBERT S. LANIER [43]

Norfolk, Va.
June 9th 1867.

My Dear Father:

Being a day ahead of time, I could not resist the temptation to run up to Bacon's Castle, where I might minister a little comfort to the deep affliction of my beloved friend, Ginna H. To my great disappointment, I find I cannot by any means get up the river until tomorrow, and so I am a prisoner here in dreary, wet, dismal, burnt-up Norfolk for the day. It is, furthermore, possible I may be delayed in returning, (I hear the boat-connections are not sure): therefore do not feel any anxiety if I should not arrive before Tuesday or Wednesday night.

But Mein Himmel! How do I grudge each moment that I spend away from you! This two-month's bout I've had is like

---

[43] On June 3 R. S. Lanier had written to Clifford: "Had a telegram from Sid this evening stating he had succeeded (in having his book published) and would be in Macon next Monday. Do not know whether he has formed plans for the future or not. Suppose not." Instead of arriving in Macon on June 10, however, Lanier stopped off en route and paid a brief visit to Virginia Hankins, whom he had not seen since the autumn of 1864, and to whom he apparently had not written since Nov. 5, 1866.

the recent fight in California,[44] where one round lasted thirty-eight minutes: it is certainly the largest and hardest round in *my* record as a pug. in the big Ring.

I'm terribly tired:

" Der Tag hat mich müde gemacht "!

Which any German who has dealt out Lager on Sundays will feelingly translate for you.

Got Mamie's " question," and will answer the same in person.

Faithfully   Your   Sid.

To Virginia Hankins

Macon Ga
June 15th "/67

In the still temple of your grief [45] I fear me that my rough man's-tread rang full harshly: – and yet, – O Vestal whose name even when I write it calls all my blood rushing into my heart – and yet, I was but trying to steal silently in, and kneel at your side, and pray with you while you prayed, and offer you my knightly service and knightly love, for life and death, when you had come out of the temple.

Listen. Long ago, in the heat of a dreadful passion, I spoke some words to one who has held me honor-bound by them – since.[46] These words chain my honor, as yet, from marrying another: but *not* from loving another, Thank God who is very good!

Prospects arise that I may be released entirely before long.

And, fired by so sweet a hope, my heart leapt up when I saw you, and must needs whisper love to you in dark sentences, half-fearfully, half-mournfully, but wholly in earnest.

[44] Probably one of the prize-fights of John C. Heenan, to whom Lanier referred in *Tiger-Lilies* and in " The Three Waterfalls " (V, 22, 218) and in " Peace " (VI, 251). Lanier was fond of prize-fights and frequently used metaphors drawn from them, though it is doubtful if he ever saw a major contest.

[45] The reference is to the death of Virginia Hankins's brother (see note 47, below).

[46] Though the evidence is not conclusive, the reference seems to be to Anna Howard (see note 36, above).

Somehow, since we parted, this half-fear and mourfulness are gone. Did you notice, child, that the Sun came out that day and glorified all the by-past rains?

And so, full boldly, full unreservedly, I proclaim now in your ear that I love you faithfully and loyally, that you are my One-Dream of Roses, and my One-Rose of Dreams; and that on the day, (now very near I hope,) when I am free man, I shall beg you, in such loverlike and manly way as my love shall show to me, to dispose my life and my heart as seems good to you.

O my great love, my great love; an you will have it or not, my heart is lighter since I have uttered it, and, if *your* heart be any lighter also, then am I a man consecrated forever, by having lifted one little mote away that kept the sun from you.

Surely, it would be too exquisite, if, having loved you so long without one word of hope from your lips, I should now hear one such word. Yet, I will not ask it, nor blame you a jot for withholding it; nor, – if your heart refuses, being ice to me, to give back the image of my love which shines yearning into so sweet a lake, – can I love you any less for that.

I desire but one thing: it is to win you to my Wife.

I know but one thing: it is that I love you.

I fear but one thing: it is that you should not love

Me!

To John Hankins [47]

Macon Georgia
June 15th ″/67

My Kind, Honored Friend:

It has been a misfortune that I have many times had occasion to deplore very deeply, – that on those very occasions when I most earnestly wished to express the emotions which filled me, my tongue should obstinately seal itself up, and my silence should seem to color the suspicion of my indifference.

I can scarcely recall any moments when this default of speech

---

[47] General Hankins was the father of Virginia and J. D. Hankins—the death of the latter being the occasion of this letter of condolence (see notes 58 and 62, 1866).

has occasioned me more regret, than during those which I recently spent at your house. Indeed this regret is rendered even more poignant by the fact that I had purposely postponed, until I might see you, the utterance of that broad sympathy, that high esteem, that deep gratitude, which have been among the liveliest sentiments of my nature, since I knew you.

In such a conjuncture, you may imagine how deep is my dissatisfaction that I must content myself with the poor solace – of writing to you that I could *not* write any thing to you!

For how can I make you know the stir which was in my heart, when I became aware of your long and weary misfortunes and your terrible afflictions? Or how show you the veneration with which I regarded your manly fortitude in the endurance of so great sorrows?

Or how reveal to you the gratitude which grows upon me with the growing memory of your kindnesses, – which I cannot number?

Take therefore, My Dear General, the inability to express these things as an evidence of their greatness: nothing more, nor less. Believe that few things would render me more happy than the privilege of showing, by some *actions,* how much I am bound to you. Believe that if there be any possible service I could render you, I am at your command, and will respond instantly and cheerfully to your call.

And know that through all changes of country, of fortune, of death, or of time, I am

Your Friend

Sidney Lanier.

To CLIFFORD A. LANIER

Macon Geo.

June 15th "/67

My Darling Cliff:

Having placed the publication of my book upon a secure footing, I did not wait to arrange the details, but left the Mss. in the hands of an agent in N. Y. who will take care of my interests. By the unanimous advice of all those whom I consulted, the publication is delayed until the First or Middle of September next, that being the opportune time for the fall trade.[48]

How do I wish that I might sit with you this long Summer day, and discourse to you of all the marvels I have seen!

Best would I like to make you the sharer in all the experience which I have gained anent our darling scheme of authorship. This you shall have in detail when we meet: meantime, be it sufficient for me to assure you that, after many rebuffs, after much weariness and waiting, after long conferences, after many shrewd peeps into the mysteries of that complex thing called publishing, after great deliberate reflection upon all I have seen and learned, —I have come to the conclusion that we may, both of us, with safety indulge the anticipation of some honor and some profit from our efforts already made and to be in future made, in the book business. I am calmly yet perfectly confident that it is in our power to attain at least a rank as high as any hitherto attained by American authors: all of which I say, not from any flippant motive, but from the consciousness that in order to fulfill our duty, it is necessary, 1st we should propose to ourselves a definite object, 2nd we should thoroughly examine and comprehend the resources available to us, and 3rd we should work, *together,* and very *earnestly,* for the most effective disposition of these resources.

There is so much to be said, in the details of these general propositions that I will not pretend to speak of them further in a letter. But there was one feature in the remarks made upon my book (and *my* book is so much *yours,* and my *thought* so much like yours, that I consider what is said of one as equally said of the other) which stood out prominently, and I may briefly mention it. That was: *great capacity, needing very severe training.* I feel that this view of our efforts already made is a true one, and while the " training," hitherto, has seemed impossible, yet I hope that it gradually will come more within our reach. At any rate, to know that *this* is our main want, and not any *radical* deficiency of power, – is something gained and may

[48] The " secure footing " for the publication of *Tiger-Lilies* may have been a tentative agreement, concluded the following month (see note 62, below), with Hurd & Houghton, Publishers, of New York, to publish, advertise, and distribute 900 copies, for the manufacture of which Lanier would have to pay $800.00. This sum he borrowed on a note from J. F. D. Lanier (see J. F. D. Lanier's letter of Oct. 14, 1868).

make us strive more continuously to remedy a defect so (*comparatively*) unimportant.

If I succeed in some little projects I shall run over to see you, but will for the present remain here. Am staying at Uncle Clifford's. I play some solos at a concert here on Tuesday night next: Gussie's.[49]

My " Tournament " appears in the Round Table for June 8th. I send him, to-day, " Joust II." [50]

I stopped in Virginia, on my return, and ran up to see little Ginna. The spectacle of her quiet devotion and her self-sacrifice, and the unutterable things in her wonderful eyes, was almost too much for me. In the two days I spent with her, I thought my heart would break with a new yearning tenderness which seized upon me and possessed me like an Afflatus from Heaven. In the event of certain occurrences, My Dear Cliff, – certain occurrences will occur!!!!!

And this expression, – which conclusively reveals my fitness for the Chair now occupied by that diplomatist, Mr Seward – [51]

[49] This was undoubtedly the fulfillment of plans that had been announced in Mary Day's letter of Mar. 1, 1867: " Gussie [Lamar Ogden] wants you in April for a concert . . . for a fund to raise a monument to her brother's memory " (see note 37, 1864).

The concert was not actually given until one night later. A program survives: " Ralston Hall. / Grand Concert! / Vocal and Instrumental. / Wednesday, June 19, 1867." Lanier is listed for two flute solos: " La Favorite de Vienne," by Terschak, and " Le Ruisseau," which is ascribed to Lanier himself as composer. No copy of this original musical composition is known to exist, and no reference to it occurs in Lanier's letters or elsewhere. Other performers were " Mrs. Ogden " (Augusta Lamar) and " Mrs. Bacon " (her cousin Virginia Lamar). A notice in the Macon *Daily Telegraph* on the morning of the concert, June 19, said: " We wish we had space to speak of Mr. Lanier's wonderful musical talent. He is an author and a poet; but not alone with his pen does he unburden his soul. The poetical utterances of his flute address themselves to every sentimental nature, and thrill with exquisite pleasure. . . . He will perform a concerted piece with one of the Professors, but we trust he will not withhold one of his own weird improvisations." A second concert by the same local performers was given at Ralston Hall, June 28, 1867. A surviving program lists Lanier for two flute solos: *Fife and Drum* (anon.) and *Swamp Robin*—the latter an original composition by Lanier which has not survived, 'hough it is mentioned in later letters. (Both programs and the newspaper clipping are in the Charles D. Lanier Collection, Johns Hopkins University.)

[50] " The Tournament: Joust First," now first printed, had been composed two years before, in Aug., 1865 (I, 6, and note) ; " Joust Second," just written, appeared in the *Round Table* on July 6, 1867 (see Lanier's letter to his brother Clifford, July 12, 1867, below).

[51] William Henry Seward, Secretary of State, 1861-1869, and one of the chief supporters of President Johnson's reconstruction policy.

reminds me that whispers come of some marriage-intentions on your part. My Beloved, I am *so* earnest, when I beg that you will *not* think of marrying for a year yet. Will you? Write me: for I have many things to say to you in such a connection.

General Hankins, Ginna, Lt. Woodley and Joe Norsworthy, spoke of you constantly with the utmost kindness, and sent many loving messages. I saw many other friends, about whom – when we meet.

Aunt Janie's letter came to me, just as I started. Kiss her and God-bless-her for me, and say, I'll answer soon.

I send an embrace for all the dear ones.

Sissa's felicity gushes and runs over in a letter to me this morning.

I'm very busy. Write me.

Your   Sid.

Woodley sends you his Photograph: and I, " Joust Second " of the " Tournament," – in my next.

FROM MARY DAY [52]

[Macon, Ga., June 16, 1867]

A thought of this Sabbath afternoon which, (first one of my life) has " sung itself " in broken strains through me. 'Tis *from* thee – *for* thee, *to* thee – for it is

Thy Child's.

June 16th.

The Bequest

The love that did inform all life
For me again has heavenward soared!
Was there such need with thee, dear Lord,
Of this pure love, as in my strife?

[52] This note from Mary Day, inclosing a poem of her own composition, seems partly in answer to his poem " The Tournament: Joust First." For it is subscribed: " To ' The Tournament.' Part I."; it quotes a line from that poem (" My love to my Belovéd! "); and the MS copy in the Charles D. Lanier Collection (Johns Hopkins University) has a notation in Mary Day Lanier's later handwriting: " My first & last poem. While the first enchanted love seemed dead:—' strangled at my bidding.' M. D. L." (For a discussion of the auto-

Do angel souls more radiant shine
Since this rare glory, banished hence,
Redeemèd from the bond of sense,
Once more, in heaven, invites with thine?

O Father, hast Thou left thy child
Of hope bereft, all joy fled — ? —
Be still, O Soul, in this thy dread,
And wrong not Heaven by sorrow wild.

Heart left thee not so poor – his best
Was willed to thee as it behooved;
He sighed – " *My Love* to my Belovèd! "
Thou wast beloved: 'tis thine – be blest!

To Gertrude Lanier Shannon

Macon, Ga
June 16th /67

My Darling Sissa:

The spectacle of your happiness, which your good letter so plainly reveals, is to me the sweetest sight of all sights in earth or Heaven and I dwell upon it with a rare pleasure such as comes to a man few times i' this life.   To you and to me this spring has brought a new flower which is as strange as it is beautiful: – for it blushes like a Rose, and yet it is pure as a white Lily, and it is modest as a Violet and yet ambitious as any Sun-flower !

My book is to make *congé* before yᵉ startled public about the middle of September next, in time for the fall trade. I have been seriously debating whether Christian duty does not require me to warn the railroad-people of the immense requirements for freight-transportation likely to ensue upon the clamorous demand for " Tiger-Lilies " which will soon come up from all parts of the land.   But selfishness intervenes: – and if the railroad-facilities should fail under the exigencies of the occasion, – the blood of the stock-holders be upon their own heads !

biographical significance of " The Tournament: Joust First " see the note in vol. I. Mary Day apparently fancied that this poem, written at the time of their parting in Aug., 1865, still symbolized Lanier's regard for her.)

My hands are full of work for the summer, and I shall not be able to recreate during the hot term. I know not yet whether I shall remain to cheer the loneliness of Father, or go to Montgomery to assume my parental guardianship over Cliff, who, poor boy, needs some care more than ever, if, as rumor says, he is over head and ears in love.

If New Orleans, in June, is like New Orleans in March (when I was last there) you will, by a little ingenuity, be able to make yourself perfectly independent of steamboats and cars. Tame two of those colossal Musquitoes ! – You can then harness 'em to some chariot, and go flying through Heaven like the old Goddess drawn by doves: or you might even recline between the wings of one of 'em and sail about like the Arabian sitting on the great bird Roc !

These moonlit nights would be fine for such travel: and I entertain great hopes of seeing you descend majestically on our hill, soon, and alight in the midst of us.   For Heaven's sake, be certain to *tame* the beasts thoroughly, before you bring them here. Himmel ! Imagine them breaking loose and preying upon our weak citizens ! The loss of blood would leave blacks as pale as whites, – and society would be disorganised, for the Radicals couldn't tell their own !

—   I send you a thousand kisses: Two of which you may distribute among your husband and your kind friends.

Sid.

To Mary Day [53]

[Macon, Ga., June 19?, 1867]

Dear Mamie:

Please send the " Favorite de Vienne," – which I am to practice at the hall this morning –

Have you read the Telegraph this morning? – Sympathizing

[53] One of several undated notes written to Mary Day in the summer of 1867, this seems clearly the first; conjectural dating from the request here made to borrow " La Favorite de Vienne " to practice for the concert (on June 19) and the reference to Lanier in " the Telegraph this morning " (see note 49, above).

Mary Day, having returned from her prolonged visit to Waynesville, was boarding at Wesleyan College. R. S. Lanier still lived there, and though Sidney

with young Jacky Horner, whose adroit use of his thumb has brought his name down the ages, I cry out

" O, What a brave boy am I ! "

Bye Bye, – Twin.

See you tonight.

Sidney Lanier

To Clifford A. Lanier [54]

Macon Ga
July 1st "/67

Dear Clifford,   Thou knowest how Grief is wont to make a parlous choking i' the throat, – and I am only got rid of it this morning, so that I can talk to thee.

I see, then, plainly enough, that thy decision is irrevocable, and so, weary at the very first step, I start my poor little race alone, alone and heavy-laden with burdens thou wot'st not of.

That thou art about to bring another flower into my garden, – does not make me sad, and I only told thee to wait because I knew the soil for her, and remembered it must be a rare dainty loam of love and luxury for her to thrive therein, and feared thou might'st be unable in so short a time to procure the latter of these two materials, which has to be brought from a far countrie, namely, from the Future. But thou knowest best as to *that* matter, and so, as thou wilt bring her so soon, I must needs parade all the flowers in my heart at the gate thereof and lead the welcome-chorus of this sweet company wherewith they greet her who is to be a right Princess among 'em since she comes holding *thy* hand.

---

was staying for the present with his uncle Clifford Anderson (only three blocks away), he undoubtedly called on her shortly after his return. A surviving piece of sheet music ("Nocturne pour Flute ou Violon et Pianoforte par A. B. Fürstenau," Charles D. Lanier Collection, Johns Hopkins University) seems to belong to this occasion, for it is annotated in Mary Day Lanier's later handwriting: " The first flute and piano music I played with Sidney Lanier when I was Mary Day, in June 1867, in the College parlor, in Macon."

[54] Excerpt previously published, *Chautauquan*, XXI, 409 (July, 1895). The occasion for this letter was the announcement of Clifford Lanier's engagement to Wilhelmina Clopton, daughter of Judge David Clopton of Alabama, who was a distant relative of the Laniers.

O my Tube-Rose and my Red Rose; My King and Queen of all flowers, grow, grow i' the Southwinds only, and under the temperate Suns and the tender rains: The Heavens, which are full faithful to beauty, distill a special and most exquisite dew for you, which shall not fail you at mornings nor evenings nor in the hot middle of your day.

My Campanulae, my Bell-Flowers, whose silent chimes ring me upward, – grow 'till your top-bells get in among the stars and live on the fire of 'em for dew.

My Climbing-Roses; Love is a lattice, from here to Heaven; grow over it and shade the Cottage of our Life, climb it till your sprays lean over by the Great white Throne and burst into blossoms there as white as Heaven. So, when lying upon the earth-grass, and feeding, – as I must forever, – upon its un-nourishing and most bitter roots, I may sometime look up: and mayhap, at this same moment, the passing wind of an old love may shake some leaf or petal of yours, and drop a drop of cool Dew of the Upper Land upon my hot mouth, – which, howbeit with parched and leathery tongue, yet mutters always Blessings, God's-Blessings, Dew-Blessings, Sun-Blessings, Rain Blessings and Southwind-Blessings upon you who have always been all these blessings to

Your

Sid.

To Clifford A. Lanier

Macon, Georgia
July 2nd "/67

My Dear Cliff:

It is right you should know something of the enclosed affair. I beg you therefore read the within letter to A. H.[55] and then transmit, by your own or some safe hand, to her *immediately.*

---

[55] Undoubtedly " A. H." refers to Anna Howard. Clifford, of course, had known something of this affair from the beginning (see note 28, above). He was also the first to report that it was reaching a satisfactory solution, as he had written to Salem Dutcher some two weeks previously:

" —— is in a condition indescribable, wishes she were dead, vows vengeance on Sid, statelily calls him Mr. Lanier– when she does not speak of him as her ruin– and– and, and is preparing to wed a Mr. Metcalf." (Quoted in Salem Dutcher's letter to Sidney Lanier, June 17, 1867.)

I am quietly working over here. Father busy at Court. We look for Sister on Friday [56] next.

Wrote you yesterday.

God bless you.

Hastily,

Sid.

To Mary Day [57]

[Macon, Ga., July 5 ?, 1867]

Niñita, Niñita !

That is all I dare.

─────────

If Sister does not come, I shall wander up to Hilda's Tower about half-past Six. At half-past five, I go to the Dêpot to receive the expected Shannon & Lady.

─────────── which Jim is in a hurry, wherefore

I am

& C.

To Mary Day

[Macon, Ga., July 6 ?, 1867]

O Niñita, O Niñita !

This is become my Form of Morning-Prayer: and when I wish to make it a Morning-Thanksgiving also I say

O *Mia* Niñita:

[56] Mr. and Mrs. Shannon were on their way to Saratoga, New York.

[57] This note and the next two are dated by reference to the arrival of Lanier's sister, Mrs. Shannon, which in his letter to Clifford of July 2, 1867, he had said would be on " Friday next "—*i. e.,* July 5.

" Hilda's Tower " is apparently an allusion to Hawthorne's *Marble Faun,* to which Lanier refers elsewhere in his letters. " Jim " was probably Jim Holt, a negro who worked for Mr. Charles Day, the bearer of this and other messages sent by Lanier to Mary Day at Wesleyan College. (Five other notes from Lanier to Mary Day survive which undoubtedly belong to the summer of 1867 and probably to this same month, July. But since they cannot be dated with exactness, and since they are trivial in content—chiefly references to meetings—they are here omitted.)

Water those flower-smiles
and keep them dainty for me; – for Little Sissa is come and I
must go sing for *her* this morning, and may not see thee till
afternoon: but I have a project to bring us all together at
Gussie's tonight; – thee, too –

——————— And Oh, Niñita, The morning shall some day
fall like a dew-drop and glitter i' the flower-bell of thy soul: –
and I am

Thy   Friend.

To Mary Day

[Macon, Ga., July 7?, 1867]

How shall a man divide himself?

I have an engagement at Mrs Lamar's at Ten to play a long-
contested game of chess to its conclusion – ! ! ! —; in other
words, ! ? ; : . ! – (Vide Champollion, & cf. Poe on Cryptology [58]) –. After solemn meditation, I do not see exactly how
I can do anything but take my position, at some point exactly
in the middle between Mrs L's & Mrs W[hittle?]'s: and therefrom commence, (like the ball at the centre of the Earth, in
Comstock's Philosophy) to oscillate between the two extremes
of my world, in never-ending motion –
Sissa sends you a kiss –
God bless you, Child! – .

To Clifford A. Lanier

Macon Ga
July 12th "/67

My Dear Cliff:

I enclose a letter which you may read, and forward
immediately to Col. Stansill, whose address I do not know and
am not able to procure. You can learn it probably from Gov.
Patton, or at any rate, from Clanton, Clerk of the House.

[58] Jean François Champollion (1790-1832) was the founder of Egyptology and
the first to decipher the Egyptian hieroglyphics. Poe's well-known interest in
cryptology, which began with a series of articles in *Graham's Magazine*, 1841,

Anna has written me a very noble letter, and I judge, from some expressions in it, that I am indebted to *you* for what, amidst all your life-long goodness to me, is perhaps the best thing you have ever done for me.

For which, and for my great love I bear you, – how do I chafe to embrace you! Yet that must be a week or two distant.

The conclusion of " the Tournament " appears in the Round Table for July 6th. You'll like it, as I do, better than anything I have yet done. I am

x   x   x   x   x   x   x 59

directness of construction at which I aimed, the poem is successful. There is not an involute sentence, nor an indirect phrase in it. If you can send it out to Grandpa I would be gratified, thinking it might please him.

How is ye Tube-Rose maiden? I send her a thousand kisses, and it shall go hard but I will personally caress her dainty petal-cheeks ere long.

If your arms be long enough, I would be glad if you would put them around ye waist (Waste!?) of Aunt Janie for me, and suggest in ye ear of ye same how she is, upon ye book of historical record, in my debt for a yepistle I sent her no long time since.

Whereupon, if she be up to her epoch, she will gently whisper in return, that I, Sidney, have written thee, Clifford, *three* times since thy pen scratched paper for me: and so, since thou art in conviction of being a lazy lout, I will end, by way of sympathy to thee from

Thy Brother –

is fully treated in W. F. Friedman's " Edgar Allan Poe, Cryptographer," *American Literature,* VIII, 266-280 (Jan., 1937). The reference in the following sentence is to John Lee Comstock's textbook, *A System of Natural Philosophy,* which Lanier had studied at Oglethorpe.

59 The MS has been torn at the top of page 2. Apparently only one line is missing.

To Virginia Hankins

Macon, Georgia
July 16th 1867

In this moment, when I have just read your magnificent words, that unfathomable ocean which you saw, with its waves full of stars, comes surging over me and in the ecstasy of so billowy a ride over life I do not judge nor think nor *know* but one thing: that is, that I do love you entirely.

———— And now that I have read your letter over and over again, I still know not what to say to you, except that I do love you entirely.

Listen. The freedom which I expected to come, has arrived. I am untrammeled. I have been so, two or three days.[60] The idea of throwing myself utterly at your feet was so exquisite, that, like a butterfly with but one flower, I have hovered about this one rose, and made myself wantonly drunk on its sweetness. Just as I was about to yield my flower and consecrate it by giving it to you,—comes your letter.

What shall I say? Here am I, arrayed on one side, against those that are Father, Brothers, and sister, to *you*, on the other!

I am not now calm enough to remember whether it was in this connection that Christ declared, the woman must leave all these and cleave to the husband.

Nay, I am arrayed against what is dearer to me than even these kindred of yours that need you: namely, against yourself. For you have here said to me "– if I allowed my heart to take its own course, devotion would be dimmed by the bitterness of regret." Upon this one line in your letter I have built the hope that you might love me, or at least that you *wished* to love me, for that, tho' you probably were unconscious of it, is the only interpretation possible of "*its own course*" that you will not "*allow* your heart" to take:—and yet this line strikes me down more cruelly than all the rest, for it suggests to me that even if I pursued you and compelled you to love me (as my great love persuades me, with the egotism of all love, *might*

<hr>

[60] Lanier's letter to Clifford, July 12, 1867, clearly indicates that Anna Howard had released him from his promise (see also note 55, above).

be done), even *then,* a wild doubt might invade the sweetness of your wifehood, and poison it by suggesting that you ought, perhaps, to have continued the sacrifice of yourself upon the family altar. See, in what a dilemma of terror this places me! If I cease to beg you, I must give you up: if I continue, and win you, I *may* cloud the glory of your martyrdom, and sometime you might turn from poor me, aye, even from my yearning arms, and cast a longing gaze towards the burning star of Sacrifice which I had plucked from your forehead but which still shone in the sky of your memory!

O My God, My God, what a place is this into which Thou hast led me! My love must fight my love: if I love on, I may lose my Love,—if I lose my Love, I *must* love on!

O my Sweet,—it is a time when out of the Deep of Bitterness the man calls to the woman to come and help him. Help me, Thou Little Ginna whom I purely love!

———— Thou knowest what sort of glamor-scales be upon Love's eyes: or rather,—that Love weareth *mirrors* for spectacles, whereby, thinking he seeth the world, it is only his own eidolon and shadow: and so, it may be that I have seen more than thou intendedst in thy letter, and that thou wert only kindly rejecting and tenderly putting aside One whose great love weighed upon thee and made thy trembling heart speak sweetly, where it *would* have spoken decisively. If this be so, I thank thee very much, My Rose-Woman:—and I love thee all the same, and, *sans* wifehood, *sans* thy love, *sans* everything that love demands, I will continue to love thee, because thou hast the greatest Soul, and the whitest heart, and the deepest eye, and the fairest cheek, of all women.

Continuing so and knowing that I will erelong get more words from thee, I am

Thine.[61]

[61] This letter and that of June 15 seem to constitute a proposal of marriage by Lanier to Virginia Hankins. Her letter to which this is a reply has not survived; but it seems clear from the echoes in Lanier's letter that she had refused his offer solely because of the obligation she felt towards her brothers and sisters, who had been motherless since the summer of 1865.

Two poems written at this period (but not mentioned in any of Lanier's letters) may have some bearing on Lanier's love for Virginia Hankins: " Eternity in Time " (I, 12) and "Strange Jokes " (I, 167), composed on July 20 and **21, 1867.**

To Hurd & Houghton [62]

Macon, Georgia
July 22nd 1867

Messrs Hurd & Houghton,
Publishers etc:
   Gentlemen:
           Two weeks since, I wrote your Mr.
Albert Houghton, enclosing an " Agreement " intended to con-
sumate an arrangement for the publication of my " Tiger
Lilies."
   Having received no reply, I fear that my letter did not reach
you: and, – as the time draws near when I should send you the
MS., in order to publish, as was intended, by September, – I
write to request that you will inform me whether my letter was
read, and what is the latest moment at which I may send you
the MS. in order to secure its issue at the time mentioned.
   Begging your early attention, I am

                  Very Respectfully, etc.,

                  Sidney Lanier

To Virginia Clay [63]

Macon, Georgia
August 6th 1867.

My Good Friend: The Opticians say: – when one looks
steadily at the sun a minute, the image is so strongly impressed
upon the retina that one will still see the sun, and nothing *but*

[62] Before leaving New York, Lanier had apparently come to terms with Hurd
and Houghton for the publication of *Tiger-Lilies,* but had not signed a contract.
On June 20, E. G. Parker, Superintendent of the American Bureau for Literary
Reference, wrote to say that Blelock & Co. (the publishers of Clifford Lanier's
Thorn-Fruit) wanted to publish *Tiger-Lilies,* and gave their terms. Lanier
answered this letter on June 24 (letter not found), and Parker wrote again on
July 1 presenting Blelock's terms in greater detail, with favorable comment. On
July 12 Parker wrote that he was sorry that Lanier had not found these terms
satisfactory. Then on July 20 Hurd and Houghton wrote, apparently in answer
to Lanier's letter of early July (not found, but referred to in the present letter),
that they would want the MS of *Tiger-Lilies* as soon as possible, by Aug. 15
at the latest. Finally, on July 25 Parker returned the MS to Lanier, who
forwarded it to Hurd and Houghton for printing. (For a history of the
publication of *Tiger-Lilies,* see V, viii-ix.)
[63] The wife of Senator C. C. Clay of Alabama, and a friend since 1863.

the sun, even when one has turned away one's eye from the glittering heaven to the most dull and muddy earth.

Now, you're to show this letter to Mr. Clem. Clay: and *that* command will exclude from your mind any rising suspicion that I am but in the mad lunacy of lying love, – when I tell you that I, who saw your face first shining in that fair hope-heaven which the early years of our war unrolled over my head, seem still to see it, framed not By Heaven! as of yore with the glory of battles and the halo of high dreams, – but yet glowing in a sky which Misfortune has besmirched and mottled with all manner of muddy streaks and spots.

Himmel! Does the horrible bubble of the big war-waves still roar in *your* ears, as in mine? Does that tremendous sibilation of the wave-froth, which used to transform each surge into the likeness of a Serpent whose hissing tongue was immeasurable and whose malignity was unfathomable, still curdle *your* blood, as it does mine? Are your flowers all flecked with blood which that sea of it dashed upon them? And when this resurrected Tempest of the old war assails you anew, is it your habit, (as mine) to stand on the shore and uplift your hands over the bloody waters, and cry across them to some friend that has power to speak the storm back into stillness?

——Yet, I pray you believe that I did not wish to raise this storm-ghost when I commenced this letter to you: indeed I started with far more peaceful intent.

You must know that for two years past I've been working hard at my old favorite Metaphysics: and that I begin to desire some opportunity to discover how the system, which I have dug up toilsomely in my cave, will suit the needs of practical men for work. Simultaneously with the birth of this desire, I hear that the Chair of Metaphysics, in the University of Alabama at Tuscaloosa, is vacant: – and I'm going to run for it. I have to beg therefore that, through Mr. Clay, you will find out precisely when the election of Professors is to come off, and advise me.

Of course, I'm not going to ask either of you to recommend me to the place, until I've given you some testimonial of qualifications for it. With this view, instead of the ordinary letters from friends used upon such occasions, I have preferred to adopt a more satisfactory method, and have written a meta-physical essay, which I shall shortly cause to be published in pamphlet form and sent to those whose assistance I desire.[64] This will at once enable you to judge for yourself of my fitness for the place, and will free you from any sense of restriction, by previous pledge to me, if other and fitter candidates should offer. For I am quite sure that I love my profession with so sincere a passion that I will most cheerfully see you aiding any other who could discharge the duties of it better than I.[65]

Allow me to beg, therefore, that you will not consider this letter as imposing upon you any obligation of old friendship: but that you will read my Essay when it arrives, and, if you like it, make what recommendations you please to the trustees who have the appointment in hand: writing me, meanwhile, to say when the meeting of the Board occurs, and where.

I had great hope that my book, which is now in the press of Messrs Hurd & Houghton of New York, would be issued before this election. A letter from the publishers announces that they will issue about the middle of next month: – will that be in time? The book, (by name " Tiger-Lilies,") altho' a novel, contains some popularized metaphysical discussions which might assist towards an estimate of my fitness for the Chair of Philosophy.

—Here, then, are six pages about me! – But *I* would be glad enough to have six about *you*: – won't you give them to me?

Miss Mamie Day, who sits by me as I write, sends you her heart: but I – – – cannot consent and so I absorb this sweet ray, as a leaf absorbs light passing through, and will only transmit to you some green jealous ray of love.[66]

[64] This essay may have been "Retrospects and Prospects" (V, 280), for which the American Bureau for Literary Reference had sought a publisher in vain in mid-July; the MS was returned to Lanier at his request on July 30 (see E. G. Parker to Lanier, June 24, July 12, 23, and 30, 1867). Or it may have been one of the metaphysical essays drafted in Lanier's Ledger (V, xlix, note 95).

[65] Lanier seems to have made plans also to apply for a professorship at Oakland College in Mississippi as well as at the University of Alabama. To this end he secured from his uncle Clifford Anderson a letter of introduction (dated Aug. 9, 1867) to L. Q. C. Lamar, a native of Georgia but a resident of Oxford, Miss., and U. S. Senator from his adopted state. The letter, which still survives, was apparently never presented.

[66] Lanier was apparently by this time engaged to Mary Day. In her reply to Lanier's letter, Mrs. Clay wrote (Aug. 21, 1867):

" And so you write love-letters to me with sweet Maime by yr. side, who sends

— And if this letter has bored you *too* much: – why, count it one of the many afflictions of the war, which threw you and me together: and, as you burn it, for a pest, watch the smoke that arises from the burning: for that, – that smoke – is

like
> Your Friend   Sidney Lanier.

To Mary Day [67]

> Exchange,
> Montgomery   Ala
> Aug 10th 67.

Thou, My Heart-of-a-Rose, what may I say to thee that will make thee know how utterly I dwell among stars, thinking I shall wear thee on my breast so soon?
Of thee, Father and I talked and talked as we rode. I would thou hadst heard him! He loves thee nigh as much as I do! And pronounced *thee* the rarest of the World's women, and *me* the happiest of the world's men.
And, last night, I lay with my One-brother at bosom clasping hands, and showering rain-drops of diamond dreams upon thee and Willie until ye both glittered through our talk and shone as if some Frost of Heaven, Crystalline pure, were sparkling about ye.
We did not sleep till near sunrise: and before we slept, we arranged fully our programme. –At the same moment, thou and I, and Cliff and *his* Tube-Rose, are to be married and pronounced one: aye, all four of us, but one. We then meet at Atlanta, and go to Lookout immediately, and to such other

---

her love, & you won't let it come! To *me* Sir, more than any other mayhap, shd. *your* thanks & love forever flow, that she is not this hour Mrs. Fred. A. away down in Mississip. where never more cd. the witching tones of even your divine flute reach her!

" I wd. *never* make a match, 'tis too hazardous. But I wd. *conscientiously* try to break one. ——

" Are you in love with her, ' or any other woman'! Do tell me – I love her dearly – & if you only had a Prof.'s chair, & a piano, & health; I think you two wd. be most harmoniously one! "

[67] This is apparently Lanier's first letter to Mary Day after their engagement. He had left Macon for Montgomery a day or two before.

places as our well-beloved brides and Queens may elect. The particular month and day, the same well-beloved Queens are to select, as is their high prerogative: but we're both to do some powerful pleading for a very early moment.

My Darling, Thou and I, and Cliff and Willie, in the mountains together, for some weeks, married !!

— This is worth living a lifetime for. The Hope of it irradiates my life: the certainty of it (and God will not have the heart to break this Dream: I would thou knewest my utter Faith which does not admit a human probability in the matter) sanctifies my Soul.

O Christ, Christ. I cry continually in my soul,—draw my Beloved into thy Bosom where is Love for all, until thou shalt yield her to mine where thou hast given her Queenhood and utter Royalty !

— And so thou must know I am already famous *here*, in Montgomery, and the shower of kind words, of congratulations, of compliments to my little poems (all of which have been republished here,) is become even painful. My arrival is noticed in this Morning's papers ! Whereat Father protests that there is Humbug rampant in the family, and I rebut– that he is but angry because they didn't mention *him* too!

And if, thou couldst but see our Family, here!

They had expected us: and had all come in from the country to welcome us. I would I might picture to thee the tall stately women, the sweet wifely faces, the chubby children, the hubbub of Cousins, Uncles, Brothers, Aunts, the congratulations to *me*, the proud relation, amidst beaming eyes, of what fine things each had heard said about me, the re-embracings and fortieth-time kissings, the gradual subsidence into little groups, and sweet home-talk of all the haps of the years since we last met. Through it all I was half-wild with the yearning to sit there amongst them and hold my arm about *thee*, Wife, and see them pet thee and love thee.

My heart is all back there with thee, and I cannot send it: but I will wave some breath of the incense of the glory and the calm that envelope my soul, to thee.

I am Utterly

Thine Own.

Thou mayst write me here, Exchange Hotel. Cliff wrote thee yesterday, before we came:

Thou!   Mine! [68]

To Mary Day [69]

Robinson's Springs,
Near Montgomery, Ala. August 15th 1867

My Darling:

      Y'r telegram has just reached me, under cover from Cliff, in Montgomery.

No letter from you:– and I've written three!

I imagine all terrible things: and work on, with a vacant calm in my heart which will kill me, I think unless some kind word from you shall sound through it, shortly.

———— " Personal Information Gained."

Upon holding a conversation with Dr Petrie whose son is now a Prof. at Oakland, I learned that the college was in the most rickety financial condition, and that Prof. Petrie altho' he had already served a year, had not yet been able to obtain all his salary, insomuch that without outside resources he could not have maintained himself & wife. This would not do for me: I immediately determined to revoke the acceptance which I had conveyed to Little by telegraph: but on account of my visit here, have delayed to do so.

Meantime, a principal is wanted for the Academy of Prattville, a fine manufacturing village 15 miles from Montgomery.[70]

---

[68] In her answer to this letter Mary Day wrote (Aug. 12): "Wilt be so outrageously practical as to enlighten me a little? Is Oakland all abandoned? Or do Oakland professors travel about for weeks whenever the fancy moves them? Is *Lookout* a warm resort for the winter months, and (the hotel being closed before Nov.) dost thou propose to 'build thy nest' in a veritable tree – icicle-hung? Or dost intend to be patient until Spring? I wait, most impatiently, all these answers."

[69] Lanier's letters to Mary Day of Aug. 12 and 14 are here omitted, being brief love-messages. In the latter he announced: "Tonight I go into the country a-visiting my aged ancestors." (Lanier's grandfather, Sterling Lanier, had bought a country place at Robinson's Springs, 25 miles from Montgomery)

[70] Prattville had been established as a manufacturing village in 1838, and it remained the industrial center of the state for many years—in fact, until the Birmingham boom of the 1870s. The founder, Daniel Pratt (1799-1873), was a

I went there yesterday. The academy is new, is fitted up with improved furniture brought from N. Y. cost $12000, and is the best I have ever seen. The Prest of the B'd of Trustees told me I might confidently expect 150 scholars at an average tuition of 50 Dollars a year: three assistants being usually employed. I liked the place, and go over tomorrow, (Prattville being 7 miles from here) armed with letters from Governor Patton and other prominent men, to announce my name as candidate, at the election which comes off Aug. 28th. This leaves me free to work, and accept offers, meanwhile.

What is McClellan [71] doing, in Macon?

Y'r telegram reads: "Ask Brother to write immediately all personal information gained." The insertion of a semicolon would change the whole meaning. I know not if I have misconstrued, with my usual "wooden"-ness. Do, when you get this, telegraph me at "Exchange Hotel, Montgomery," and say merely, (if you are well) "all right," over any name. Father and I will return on Tuesday next: and I shall expect to see you that night.

Cliff and I are anxious that our weddings should come off by middle of September next. Will it be possible?

I write in the greatest haste, to catch the mail.

My Darling, My Darling, My Rose, My Queen, My Beloved, I long unutterably for thee and I am

Wholly

Thine.

colorful figure. A New Hampshire carpenter, he migrated South as a young man, set up as master builder, and during the 1820s designed and constructed some of the finest houses in central Georgia. In 1833 he moved to Alabama, where he soon turned his attention to manufacturing. In his model village, whose plants were the pride of the state, he had a grist mill, lumber and shingle mill, cotton-gin, cotton mill, foundry, carriage factory, tinshop, woolen mill, and mercantile establishment—capitalized in 1858 at over half a million dollars. Thus at the outbreak of the war, in 1861, he was the first great manufacturer of Alabama and one of its wealthiest citizens. Though opposed to secession, he threw in his lot with his adopted state, served in its legislature, and organized and equipped the Prattville Dragoons. At the end of his life, during Lanier's residence in Prattville, he had turned his energies to Birmingham. (See S. F. H. Tarrant, *Hon. Daniel Pratt: A Biography*, Richmond, Va., 1904.)

[71] Apparently Jas. B. MacLellan, a friend of Lanier and the Days, who was now teaching school in Macon (see note 104, below).

To Mary Day

Exchange Hotel
Montgomery Ala
August 17th /1867.

The slow mails at length have brought me thy breath-of-a-Tube-Rose, O My Queen: here am I kneeling, and adoring thee, for this queenly grace.

Now may all the silver-clouds of morning melt themselves into a throne for thee: and I would the Morning-star might be hand-maiden to thee, and 'tire thee for him who shortly comes to lay down his life and body at thy feet: at thy feet, where his heart has been lying this long, long time,—this weary wild time that has crept in between thee and me.

—— I wrote thee yesterday, and I fear me that my yearning told itself in over-sad terms: –but thou wilt pardon my *Love,* for it was my Love that spoke.

And thou wilt only say to thyself,— Ah, how utterly mine is this Heart, this deep Heart, which, having no other merit nor grace, is yet always *deep,* and hath all its depth filled and lit by me!

And thou must know that, in the worldly way, my prospects are flourishing, albeit yet inchoate: and that it *is* possible our Heaven-day, which is my Wedding-day, may postpone itself till Spring, tho' God forefend! —and I'll work harder than mortals use to bring it on before that time:— and thou shalt be informed in ample time to array thee suitably, and shalt have at least a month beforehand, whenever it may be, all the time exercising thy queenly prerogative of choosing and determining according to thine own high pleasure: and the next two weeks will determine my work for the coming year: and when I wrote thee of Lookout, we expected to take thee and t'other Queen there before the 1st October: and, howbeit some difficulties thou wottest not of have presented themselves, we are not yet by any means hopeless: and Willie is very sweet but clamors outrageously " Time, Time," like a Second in a Prize-fight: and I shall see thee on next Tuesday night: [72] and

---

[72] Lanier left Montgomery for Macon on Aug. 20. This paragraph is in answer

thou art, of all sweet things, the sweetest, and of all rare things, the rarest, and of all good things, the goodest: and I send my love to him that hath the honor, not to say the brass, to call himself thy brother: – as also to him whom thou,– as I hope also I, one day– callest Father: and I am socially, individually, collectively, politically, financially, absolutely, totally and immediately thy

Longing and Loving

S.

TO HURD & HOUGHTON [73]

Macon Ga

August 21st 1867

Messrs. Hurd & Houghton
    Pub & C.
       D'r Sirs:

           Your favors, containing receipt for my draft, and announcing arrival of my MS. came promptly.

I am also in receipt of y'r Mr. A. G. H[oughton]'s letter advising against appointment of Agents: which advice I of course will regard as conclusive.

Circumstances render it necessary for me to change one or two sentences in the " Dedication " of my book: [74] and I trust this is the only alteration I shall have to make. Please forward proofs to me at this place.

If I had y'r Announcement, I could have it extensively noticed by Editors South.

What will be the trade-price of " Tiger-Lilies "?

Very truly &c.

Sidney Lanier.

to Mary Day's letter of Aug. 12 (see note 68, above). Two brief love-notes, written on Aug. 18 and 19 are here omitted.

[73] Previously published, Starke, p. 85. Aug. 7 Lanier had written asking Mr. Houghton's advice concerning an application of Havens & Brown of Macon to be agents for the sale of his book in the South.

[74] *Tiger-Lilies* was published without dedication. It is possible that Lanier had originally dedicated it to Virginia Hankins, who was intimately connected with its inception.

To Virginia Hankins

Macon, Ga. Aug. 23rd 1867.

Now by all the love you have ever borne for me or any one, —
by all the brave sweet things wherewith you have filled your life
as it were a vase full of flowers, — by all the high endeavors
that you prayed for in my life, — by that meeting I long for, —
by whatever of holy memory or of yearning anticipation lives
in the past or in the future, — I charge you send me straightway
this sad-faced picture you " had painted on porcelain " for me.
Let it be sad as a grave, — is it not framed with Heaven? Let
it be white as a tube-rose, — is it not pure as Love? Let it be
serious as life, — is it not sweet as death?

White-faced, white-handed, white-souled One, send me the
porcelain picture, to keep me always at prayers, to murmur its
mute eloquent Amen to my humble life-endeavor, to shed the
grace of a lily over my rude weeds, to go with me, as the Poet
went with Dante through Hell, through Purgatory, and
through Heaven.

— I have shown the picture of you and little Mary [75] to
several friends. I would you had heard them cry out at the
sweet face, the dainty hands, the rare waist, the exquisite *pôse,*
the far-off gazing eyes, the Evangeline's hair, the unutterable
calm, — of *you!* Tomorrow I go to Montgomery, Ala: and will
show Cliff. how beautiful Sorrow has made you. O how beautiful, how beautiful, Thou Saint this side of Heaven, Thou
Purified before death, Thou Sweet special beloved of Christ!

And so, if my heart have any more rein now, it will cast
away the poor cold ink and put its blood, which is warm, on
this page.

Your friends'-letters *will* " impart restfulness " to me. Send
them often, Ginna: send them very often.

I know not now when I shall see you. It will *not* be in the
fall, tho'.

I am he, O Ginna, who

Waits.

---

[75] Virginia Hankins's younger sister. The picture " painted on porcelain " was
apparently never sent (see Lanier's letter to Virginia Hankins, Nov. 23, 1867,

To Robert S. Lanier [76]

Exchange Hotel
Montgomery Ala
August 25th/67

My Dear Father:

I'm here, after a pleasant trip. Found all the Aunties & Sallie Schley in, on the wood-wagon and on a frolic. They have gone back to Robinson this morning: wagon was full, and so I go on horseback this afternoon.

—Should any letters come, do forward them *here*.

—Weather very cool, and threatening rain.

No news.   Cliff well & sends love.

Hastily
Sidney –

Aunt Mina says please look at enclosed picture and send it back to her – Says, – isnt it pretty?

To Clifford A. Lanier [77]

Macon, Ga
Sep. 5th 1867.

My Darling:

I'm here; and have corrected 75 pages of proof-sheets: and that's all the news.

Father has suggested the idea to me that you would perhaps

below). Two pictures of Virginia Hankins survive in the Charles D. Lanier Collection, Johns Hopkins University, but neither of them fits the description here given. A third, owned by the Hankins family, is reproduced in the present vol., facing p. 106.

[76] Lanier had returned to Montgomery for the election of the principal of the Prattville Academy. A brief letter to Mary Day of the same date (here omitted) begins: " Sunday Morn. Just after the organ. I go this afternoon to the country."

[77] Lanier had gone back to Macon, after his election as principal of the Prattville Academy on Aug. 28. Mary Day, in her letter of Sept. 12, quotes a letter from her father to her: " His election unanimously when he had a number of competitors was really a triumph." Lanier's first duty in connection with his new position was to find an assistant; he tried to secure first Janie Lamar's brother, Charles Taliaferro, then Ned Peck, a Montgomery friend who had removed to Bridgeport, Conn., sometime before Mar. 29, 1867 (see Peck's letter of that date to Lanier).

like to go into the school at Prattville as my assistant. It occurred to me that you were certainly doing much better, pecuniarily, where you are, in consideration of the *board* which will probably be offered to yourself & wife: and I do not know that we can afford to buy the happiness of living and working together at so high a price. It would be *too* splendid: and we might write a parlous book, together: but it would be a bold venture right into the heart of the storms. Write y'r views. Nothing is yet heard from Janie's brother. Get Ned Peck's address, & send it to me: I must fall back on him, in the last resort. He would make a fine assistant, and I doubt not, would come.

Mamie left, this morning, for Mʳ Munroe's summer-residence, near Griffin, where she will remain for a month probably.[78] I hope to get through with the proof-sheets by the 15ᵗʰ of this month, and will start immediately for Montgomery.

What news from " Thorn-Fruit "?

Scott has sent me word that he is publishing my little *jeu d'esprit*, " The Three Waterfalls " in the August number of his Mag. which is not yet out.[79]

Love to everybody. Don't forget to send me Ned Peck's address, *immediately*. I want to write him, conditionally.

Kiss Willie for me. Pa sends love.

Sid.

To Mary Day [80]

[Macon, Ga., Sept. 6? 1867]
Friday

Dear Ninita, Sweet Rose of my life, since thou hast left me, I am utterly without any flowers, and the days which have been ranging themselves around me like dainty vases full of *thee* are

[78] Mary Day's friend Bannie Kell, daughter of Capt. John Kell, who had been with Semmes on the *Alabama*, had married J. N. Munroe, of Griffin, Ga. Their summer home, near Griffin, was called " Sunnyside."

[79] The Rev. W. J. Scott, Editor of *Scott's Monthy Magazine*, of Atlanta, in the Aug. and Sept. issues of which appeared Lanier's " Three Waterfalls " (V, 213).

[80] The three pages of this letter were decorated with whimsical pen-drawings, here omitted since they are of no apparent significance and since they would be difficult to reproduce.

This is one of fifteen surviving letters from Lanier to Mary Day (addressed

now become mere empty cups that I would rather break than keep if I did not know that one will presently come and bring thee again within its sanctified rim. Let that day come quickly, O Sweet Heaven, and may the sky, that morn, spread its blue mantle for the Sun, as Raleigh spread his cloak for the Queen, so that the royal feet of the Sun of that day shall take no harm from the rains of earth beneath!

This morning the floods descended insomuch that thy Hal,[81] (whom I am now courting in default of thee,) and I did fill us a foaming jug of Ale and conveyed the same into our parlor, into thy parlor and mine, where we three, – The jug and Hal and I – held conclave from breakfast till dinner. Even in midst of chess, which I played better than usually, Thy sweet eyes shone before my eyes, and thy wonderful soul was there at its windows, and mine sang serenades to thine above. Thou art very good, Child, to stay with me so, and I will turn the poem of my life into a Petrarch's-song to thee. This song shall be glad as a bird's, for thou lovest thy Petrarch, – dost not?

Here comes today a letter from Hurd & Houghton with the cheerful news that a book – a wee, wretched, misborn and thief-named book, a Sunday-School book, mark you ! – is just out, named " Tiger – Lilies " ! [82] – and the said H & H. suggest that I change the name of my book, for that the present author is ahead of me and by the rules of trade has right to his title and might trouble us if mine be sent forth as was intended ! And

to " Sunnyside ") which seem to belong to Sept., 1867, though they have no dates except the days of the week. Conjectural datings have been arrived at by internal evidence and by reference to four surviving letters from Mary Day dated: Sept. 12, 16, 23, and 25, 1867. Two of Lanier's letters which contribute nothing to the narrative of his life have been omitted.

[81] Mary Day's brother, Henry Coit Day.

[82] The letter from Hurd and Houghton here referred to was written on Sept. 2 (hence the conjectural dating of this letter, since Sept. 6 was the first " Friday " thereafter).

No such book as is here described has been found, nor does the Copyright Office have a record of one. (Courtesy of F. R. Goff, Rare Book Collection, Library of Congress.) In this connection should be cited a letter to Lanier on Oct. 26, 1868, from a stranger, Caroline Parker, stating that an acquaintance of hers by the name of Helen A. Miller, of Cannonsville, N. Y., declares that she is the author of *Tiger-Lilies,* first published in Macon, Ga., and subsequently sold to Hurd & Houghton. But Mrs. Parker confesses that she thinks Miss Miller's story is " the fabrication of an overactive brain."

so, I fear me, my Tiger-Lilies fade, and I must get some other flowers to lay on my book's bosom. Tell me the name of some mountain-sister of thine, My Flower! – that I may consecrate my book with it.

————

Also comes a letter from Prattville announcing that M^rs [A. D.] Morgan will take charge of our Primary Dep.'t, in consideration of a salary of eight hundred dollars a year, and expressing the hope of the same that our intercourse will be pleasant.

————

And nothing is come yet from Janie's brother.

And so thou knowest all I have done and thought since thou hast left me in the dark – .   O my passionately-beloved Wife-to-be, O my One, my One, my heart is full of

Thy Heart.

Hal was sick yesterday. Well to-day.

I played with the Musical Club last night. Mrs Smith[83] is working herself to death on S————S !

And thou art my One-Beloved.

To Mary Day

[Macon, Ga., Sept. 10? 1867]
Tuesday

My Darling, My Darling, there is in thy letter a Tube-Rose Sweetness which hangs and sways over my soul as if a mist, saturated wtih perfume, lay over a valley.

    There is not in my frame a nerve but thrills at this moment with an intense fire, and my love glows in my soul like the red spot in thine Opal. My Sweet, My Sweet, O my Very Sweet, imagine that the infinite blue sky should distill itself into one perfect dew-drop! – So has my life distilled itself into one love.

————

[83] Mrs. Cosby Smith was the wife of one of the professors at Wesleyan and the confidante of Mary Day. In Lanier's letter of Sept. 8(?), 1867 (here omitted), he added: " Mrs. Smith plyeth ye sewing machine with vigor and creepeth in to breakfast loomingly, as if she were a mile long and I do not like the slippuz which she weareth 'em without heels whereby they flip-flop."

And oh, but this dewdrop of mine is itself a world, and hath its lightnings upon its outer rim, and at this moment these lightnings flash and flash, and dazzle me with a light which is like the intoxicating ray of thine eyes, and deafen me with a dainty thunder which is nought besides the sound of thy name.

Sweet Vine, how hast thou crept and grown upon me, and wound me round about with blessings of wonderful leaves, and buds, and wreathing tendrils, and faint Solemn perfumes, and sacred wavering shadows, and fleckings of holy lights – between-leaves, and the tender glory of the woods-loneliness in which thou, being one with me, bringest me at once the joy of company and the exaltation of Solitude.

O Thou Christ that hast trained this vine upon my lonely Soul in the desert. Keep the leaves green with the tears thou hast shed in gardens, and shine with smiles like the Sun to ripen the purple fruit of my Vine, the passionate-purple spheréd Fruit, which is Love!

This is the prayer that I pray for my darling Wife-to-be, and there is no Soul but Christ's that knows the great yearning of my uplifted arms to fold themselves about the only Waist in all the world might fill and rest and satisfy them.

Today, the more I talk to thee, the more is my heart full. My Soul is all tense with longing, – too tense for the arrowy words, like a bow bent too tight for shooting. Is it possible I shall not see my Darling for this long time, this age of three months? [84] Not look into my Saxon-eyed sea-deep Soul? Not feel the lithe twining of my long, music-filled, electric fingers? Not draw backward the great black gloriole of scented hair from thy sweet brows, to make more room for kisses? Not sit calméd in the awful Silence when my love comes rushing in a cloud and lays hand upon thy head and mine and upturns his grand face to the stars and so creates of thee and me and himself, a marble group that is yet steadily aflame with such serene fires as light the silver stars? Comes no ray from thee, O My Silver-Star, through these three thick cloud-months?

[84] That is, until their wedding day, which had already been set for Dec. 18 or 19 (see Mary Day to Lanier, Sept. 12, 1867). Mary Day, who suffered periodically from malarial chills, was spending a month in the country to regain her health and did not plan to return to Macon before Lanier's departure for Alabama to assume his duties as principal of the Prattville Academy at the end of September.

And now, at another word like this, my heart, which is weak with much longing and tender with an infinite tenderness for my sick Beloved, will utterly break. Since thou art gone, I am not strong. Thou art my Strength. Thou art also my Beauty. If I say beautiful things ever, it is because I am an Organ, and thou hast played upon me. I strenuously desire to live, so that I may give tone to thy soul. Make music upon me and wake the world and serenade the Father above. O thou deep and loving Soul!

If thou hadst been mine when "Tiger-Lilies" was started, what a book should have been there![85] The world will not forget the next book I write. I will put *thee* upon paper and have thee daintily bound. Thou shalt light more faces than thou shalt ever see, and thou shalt startle more souls than thou canst ever count, and thou shalt stand upon the top of this century, as upon a pillar, pointing to Heaven with the hand that wears my wedding-ring. – I prophesy, thou seest!

Comes a letter which I enclose, knowing it will please thy loving heart to see how my little efforts win way gradually. I do not at all know the writer: have never heard of him before.[86] I have seen thy friend Mrs Wallen[87] twice since thou left'st me in the dark. Last night I played the twilight through for her: and am to take tea with her on Friday. She talked of thee: and told me of such sweet words that thy Mr Reese spoke of thee to her yesterday, that I shall go and talk some

[85] A passage in Lanier's letter of Sept. 8(?), 1867 (here omitted) suggests that Mary Day, as the original of "Felix Sterling" in *Tiger-Lilies*, was at least partially inspirational of his first book: "And here are some proof-sheets of the Masque-ball Chapter which please me, because they talk of thy gray eyes, thy ' Saxon Eyes, like two unsounded oval seas with silver mists upon them and sylvan mysteries within them!' and Father protests 'tis the best chapter in the book, and I do not say him nay."

[86] This letter from an unknown person, which has not been found, was referred to by Mary Day in her letter of Sept. 12 as "thy Baltimore favor." This and other evidence leads to the conjecture that it was an invitation to write for a new magazine just established in Baltimore, *Southern Society* (see Lanier's letters to Mary Day, Sept. 16(?) and 22(?), 1867, and to R. S. Lanier, Sept. 29 and Oct. 10, 1867, below).

[87] Mary R. Wallen, a resident of Macon and an invalid much loved by both Sidney Lanier and Mary Day. She is referred to in Lanier's Johns Hopkins lectures on the English novel (IV, 48-49) as "The White Flower," and is sometimes referred to by the same phrase in his letters. (See also I, 204, note.)

love to him shortly.   I take tea with Gussie tonight. Tomorrow,
to Mʳˢ Ligon's: night after, to the Musical Club: Saturday to
Clare's,[88] and Aunt Fannie's. Thou seest, *J'ai ma vie arrangée*!

I have been, all day yesterday, poking about amongst old
books and old music, preparing for my campaign in October,
and have arranged the schedule for the whole course of my
three School-departments. Have also examined and selected
the text-books for the entire school: a job of jobs! Have written
to the Publishers to make more exact inquiries about the second
Tiger-Lilies, and see if I cannot retain my title without piracy,
in consideration that *my* book bears imprint " Tiger-Lilies; *A
Novel*," which *could* not be the case in a sunday-school book.

Thou wilt discover that I have not been idle, and that I can
drudge, even in the dark.

I cannot call myself by any name further from thee

Than   Mamie!

To Mary Day

[Macon, Ga., Sept. 12? 1867]
Thursday

My Darling Half-My-Heart,   If our Whole Heart, – I &
Thou – were but there in the woods! Thou must give my very
deep love to the trees and ask them if they are not sorry, too,
that this half is not there to make love to them. To sit under a
tree with thee! – *That* makes me a poet.

— And, as I was saying, Miss Carroll [89] is a woman and
dreams " garlands and ribbons." For, while the charge of
redundancy is always quite tenable as against my *prose*, it is
not at all so, against my poetry. I think Miss C. must surely
have seen some of my letters, and gotten her idea of them
mixed with that of my poems. There is no single poem of

---

[88] Clare de Graffenried, throughout life a friend of Lanier, and an intimate
during his Baltimore residence.

[89] Mary Carroll, apparently a Griffin friend of Mary Day, whose poem and
whose criticism of Lanier's poetry—here referred to—had been forwarded to
Lanier by Mary Day in a letter now lost (see Lanier's letters of Sept. 11(?)—
here omitted—and Sept. 15(?), below).

mine which is not as simple in diction, in word-arrangement, and in thought, as any ballad of Burns'.

But *every* letter of mine is " redundant ": and that, in a *letter,* is not a fault. And all my prose is redundant: I have grown so much in the last six months that I would write quite differently in another book: tho' my tendency to a profusion of metaphors is deep-rooted, and I shall have much trouble in the matter of sarcasms launched against me. But Miss C. has not seen any of my prose, except perhaps some letters. Mein Himmel, in a love-letter, in the very Tropics of Passion, would she cut down the wonderful boscage, and deaden the vivid green of the bird-feathers and turn the red roses into gray ones?

Her poem to thee is very good and I would like to know her and to play for her. She writes like a sweet woman, whose life had not been very full of anything, neither full of what she craved nor of what she hated. I can well imagine how, when *thou* art with her, she would stand like a thirsty flower-cup drinking rain, – for she has a deep and needy heart, apparently. — I have found " Thy Sweetheart " and told him thou hadst sent a kiss to him, – but *I* could not give it to him! Ah, how he raved at me, and swore " twas the hardest fate a mortal ever bore, that he should be, as it were, upon the very marge and threshold of thy kiss and yet not have power to take it! A blind man in heaven! – And yet I had rather be *only near* THY kiss than possess and riot in any other's. Thou sweet Wife-in-the-sweet-Future! Thou Star, afar off in the dark, rising over the high white rocks that crown the mountain of my life's endeavor! Thou wilt rise and stand still over me, and shine on me forever, – wilt not?

I started, for fear thou wouldst tire of too much love-talk, to write thee a calm letter; but thou seest how my Love *will* seize the bit in his teeth and run off with me. I tell thee, May, the young worship of my boy's-heart is come to scatter dew on the full Rose of my man's love. It is too sweet – I love thee utterly: and I find no pleasure save in telling thee so, over and over.

And now thou must look on t'other page: I don't like to write criss-cross!

I send thee a note from Janie. No news of her brother. Sissa expects to leave New Orleans immediately, in a letter

received this morning. I get applications for the place of
Assistant. A friend has brought me a copy of the Tournament
which he cut from a stray copy of the *Iowa* " Pioneer "! [90] Thou
seest how my little waifs go travelling: it is pleasant. Hal and
I play chess *ad nauseam*: even game betwixt us. 'Oggy and I
drank Claret, and eat sardines and anchovy sauce: he's a fat,
greasy-chopped rascal: tried to sell me a new household
Lamp: [91] Mr Sam Coleman's baby, over the way, was just dead
and we dared not play: Gussie was very sweet: I was very
stupid: Mary Lou pretty, hypercritical, and sleepy: Janie on the
Angel rôle: Buddy loud: Dinah dark: smoked four cigarettes:
left at ten: fell a prey to musquitoes, and fell asleep at three
A. M.

The White Flower [92] shall see us one-flesh if it be possible.
Janie spent day and dined with Mrs Cosby Smith. Had long
talk with Mr Bonnell: [93] good man: cultivated: no Methodist,
by a jug-full: deep in Thorough-Bass: suggested some valuable
ideas to

Thy   Lover.

To Mary Day

[Macon, Ga., Sept. 13 ? 1867]
Friday.

My Darling Niñita, 'Twas McClellan said *J'ai ma vie arrangée*
and I am glad thou compassionatedst the Sayer, for there is
surely to me no more mournful phrase a man could speak than
this same. To have arranged one's life is to have forfeited the
aid of the Fairy Future, is to abandon the glorious hope which
cheered and sustained the oft-dejected Soul of Micawber, is to

---

[90] In his letter of Sept. 11(?) 1867 (here omitted), Lanier had written:
" My Tournament has found its way out to the ' La Crosse Democrat,' Brick
Pomeroy's paper! What a journey . . . for my poor little poem! "

[91] In Mary Day's letter of Sept. 12, 1867, which crossed in the mails with this
one, she had expressed a desire for a lamp like the one " Mr. Ogden brought
home the other day." Thus " Oggy " was undoubtedly J. M. Ogden, husband of
Augusta Lamar. In this paragraph Lanier is obviously describing the " tea with
Gussie tonight" mentioned in his letter of Sept. 10(?), above; the others
referred to as being present were all members of the Lamar family.

[92] See note 87, above.

[93] The President of Wesleyan Female College, Macon.

make friends with that poor tame-souled Spinster named
Content, is to be, as it were, a vegetable with digestive appa-
ratus. McClellan got the phrase *not* from the " French Country
House " but from *Balzac.*[94]

I *will* go to the Cottage, which I *have* neglected since June; [95]
and Jinnie *is* sweet and true; and so art Thou!   There!

I have already begun some conditional negotiations with a
friend of mine, to secure him in case Taliaferro should fail.
He is Mr Edward Peck, now resident in Hartford, Conn.   A
fine fellow is he, and a man of much culture and more industry.
As for Miss Lundie, [96] there is no place to put her in unless
the present Chief of the Primary Dep't should need another
assistant: for which place I already have applications, one of
which comes from no less a personage than Carrie Ligon of
Tuskegee.   Little Carrie hath conceived a high resolve: albeit
her Father is wealthy and is now in quite comfortable condition,
she would grapple (quotha) with some of the stern realities,
and is wild to play a part in the drama of life.   As if, By the
Rood! – she were not already playing a part, and as if every
emotion that swells her little idle heart were not a sterner reality
than all the hard knocks in the world, and as if the brutal
necessities of life would not hammer away to blunt her sensi-
bilities soon enough, without her interference! – Still, if the
place should be vacant, in default of Janie, I'll employ Carrie:
she's thoroughly educated, and has never left off studying:
and is altogether of a self-reliant resolute turn that would bring
success to her as a teacher.

And so, as I was saying, Thou art to be my wife on the 19th
of next December.   O Thou who art to be my Wife! – About
this phrase my whole life flowers, as the corolla spreads petals
around its pistil.   O May, like all Mays, thou bringest June to
me, June, full

[94] This paragraph is in answer to Mary Day's letter of Sept. 12, 1867. The
phrase attributed to Balzac has not been located. *A Week in a French Country
House* (London, 1867) was written by Adelaide (Kemble) Sartoris.   The " oft
dejected Soul of Micawber " is an allusion to Dickens, *David Copperfield.*   For
the identity of McClellan see note 71, above.

[95] In her letter of Sept. 12 Mary Day had urged Lanier to call on Capt.
Augustus Bacon and his wife, the former Virginia (or Jinnie) Lamar.

[96] Miss Julia Lundie, sister of Mrs. Cosby Smith, recommended by Mary Day
in her letter of Sept. 12. For the identity of Edward Peck see note 77, above.

" Of nightingales all singing in the dark,
    And rosebuds, reddening where the calyx split."

Sweet nightingales that will never be dumb in the dark! Rare
rosebuds that will forever be buds and never shed a petal! –
God is very good. Let us praise Him with love and works.
Let us convert our grave – Thou and I will have but one – into
altars, upon which we shall lay a perfect life of endeavors like
a round garland of flowers. Then will death be like that short
Northern Twilight which separates two long days. — Tonight
the earth hath wheeled of a sudden into some broad ray that
shoots out from Heaven. The beauty of it is to me, without
thee, intolerable. Such sweetness is too much for one heart:
it demands all the depth and all the resources of two-in-one.
Nothing very beautiful is endurable to me unless thou art with
me. Thou art my Height and my Depth and my Breadth: I am
narrow and shallow as a grave, wanting thee.

Thou wilt see in the Round Table Hal sent thee, a review
and an advertisement of GUYOT'S GEOGRAPHIES, just issued.
I intended, but forgot, to take the *names* of the *books,* and the
address of the publishers. Do thou look carefully, and send
me the title, exactly, of each one, – there are three, I think –
and the name and number of the publishers, in thy next, on
Monday. It is probable I will leave for Prattville on Tuesday
morning.

Thy views are precisely mine on the marriage-day question.[97]
As matters now stand, in the way of schedules, we *could* reach
New Orleans by Sunday morn. — No proof sheets – Thou wilt
see " Tiger-Lilies " announced in Messrs Hurd & Houghton's
list in thy Round Table. – Thou shalt have privacy in The
Home – .[98] Niñita, Niñita! How I long for thee! Dost long
for

Me?

[97] In her letter of Sept. 12, Mary Day had suggested changing the wedding
date from Dec. 18 to Dec. 19, if this would allow them to reach New Orleans
by Sunday morning.
[98] Mary Day had written on Sept. 12: " I would be *willing* – – to share our
home with Lilla [Hazlehurst], Clare [de Graffenried], or Janie [Taliaferro
Lamar] – if it were best so to do; I can think of no others."

To Mary Day

[Macon, Ga., Sept. 15? 1867]
Sunday.

Sweetheart, I pray thee take all the beauty thou hast ever *seen* in thy life, and all the beauty thou hast ever *dreamed* in thy life, and all the beauty thou ever *hopest* to see or dream, and fling these into some warm-passionate moment of thy soul as thou wouldst fling three roses into a crucible, and distill from them some unutterable Rose-Attar of Beauty, – and thou wilt have somewhat like the divine Yearning in which my Soul is steeped, today.

Thou and I have sat together at night when the starlight and the darkness and the silence were like three sisters singing to us. Dost not remember how we have sometimes seen a star plunge into a cloud, and lie still in that sweet bath, daintily breathless with the plunge, glowing faintly, the silver fires half-quenched? So has my Soul gone into my Longing: and that " I " which hath just dressed Father for the Church and which now sits here gazing through our gap to the distant tree-ocean on our hills over yonder, – can scarcely see the " Me " which is thine, and which is now half-obscured, dwelling in a great dun cloud of the Want-of-*thee*.

O Soul of My Soul; – If I might but lie all this September day at thy feet, and watch the thoughts ascend and glow and fix themselves in thine eyes, as the stars rise and stand still and shine in the twilight. – Sweet Twilight-Gray of thine Eyes! This is my Knight's-color; and my soul shall wear it in this Tournament of Life. Who is so brave that he will win from me the scarf which is the color of thine eyes, O Thou Ladye – with the loyal Worshipper? The time will come when I will flaunt this scarf in the sunlight of other lands, and wave it over the bowing heads of peoples that love it; and I will proclaim it the color of the eyes of my Love. Sweet, thine eyes shall look serenely down an age and the after-world shall turn to gaze into them, as into a gray and most dewy Dawn. Be it my one aim of life to paint thee vividly, Thou Dawn that none shall see as I do: Kind Heaven, Sweet Heaven, give me poet's-power to limn my Love faithfully for the world to see!

— Last night, near Midnight, I sat in that poet's-glen around which we have set our dead, as it were Violets set round about a Lily. Dear, the leaves were still as my heart, – but not as empty, alas, as my arms: for every tree-top held his thousand green hollows full of moonlight, and the silvery torrent over-flowed, and dripped and trickled through the vine-leaves, and streamed between the parted boughs, and lay in liquid flecks and silver pools on the jet earth beneath, serenely sparkling in an utter calm of content. Here sat I and wondered why thou *wouldst* not come down out of the gleaming tree-top where I saw thee sitting just above me. If thou wouldst but have leaned and placed thy sacred hand upon my head, Sweet! – I think it was very wrong in thee, that thou wouldst not come to me and consecrate the needy, needy arms which I upstretched to thee! — This from

Thy Worshipper.

—— I think to leave here on Tuesday, possibly Wednesday. I had spoken to Hal about the propriety of my visiting thee, when thy sweet invitation came like an echo to my words. But this echo broke my heart; for I fear it is impossible; and yet, and yet, I will try as I never try for anything else, to bring it to bloom: *not* the echo, but this bud of a visit. I have much work, tho', it is *work for thee*, My Beloved, My Beloved: and I must not leave it, even for my yearning.

I hope to so arrange matters as that I may teach a music-class of 15 or 20 scholars myself, in intervals of school. This will at once increase receipts and diminish expenses. Janie has a letter from Taliaferro, written before he had received her letter containing my proposition & sent more than a week ago. He begs her to get him a situation; she sends me word that I may consider it settled he *will accept,* and is willing to accept for him in advance. Janie is sick at Mrs Fulton's: I go out to see her this afternoon. Thou shalt know the result of our con-ference. – Clare was out: will go again tomorrow: ditto, ditto, Nisbets. Mrs Smith is as long and as good –, Bro. B[onnell] as greasy –, the corn-dragon as ferocious and as affectionoate –, and the bread as heavy—as ever. The only changed thing since thou hast gone is the ale-cask which is far lighter of heart, – and so are *not* Hal & I. While I write Mr Sneed is up from

church and says he heard Mr Munroe [99] tell Hal thou wert in
fine health, and wert to have a side-saddle. O, God Bless Thee,
Wife-of-my-hopes!

This, from

Thy Sidney.

My poor Salem sends me a short note full of grief.[100] He
arrived too late. " The only being " says he " whom I have
unreservedly loved all my life: my one hope, my ambition, —
is just consigned by my hands to the ground." I have written
him.

I send thee Mary Carroll's letter and poem: [101] also one from
Sissa.

Janie was gone to Mrs Fulton's when thy note came, and I am
to carry it out this afternoon.

— I know not if thou wilt ever read anything in this scrawl:
but thou wilt see love in it. Thine electric touch on my heart
makes my hand quiver so when I write to thee! It is done as
in a dream. Ah, how I want my wife, my little Rose-of-wives.
My Niñita — Wife, my Darling!

I will try to send thee a letter for Lilla [Hazlehurst] soon.
I love her nigh as much as

Thou.

To Mary Day

[Macon, Ga., Sept. 16? 1867]
Monday.

My Darling Darling Niñita I am so concerned about these
terrible chills that I can think of nought else. They make me
wild to have you wholly mine so that I may scare them away
with the thunders of my supreme love. I know thou art very
sick because when thou *hast* been so, thou wert cruel to me.

[99] Mr. Sneed was one of the editors of the Macon *Telegraph*; Mr. Munroe,
the husband of the friend whom Mary Day was visiting in Griffin.

[100] Salem Dutcher had been called to New York on Aug. 28 by the sudden
illness of his mother, who died before his arrival (see his letter of that date to
Lanier).

[101] See note 89, above.

" Happy will it be " say'st thou " if I remember to miss thee, so pale and useless a flower! " – Surely, surely, thou art very sick. " I will change the scenes," say'st thou " and write my beautiful things and be loved "—! – Poor, poor Niñita, how very sick thou art, that thou canst write me so!

— Of course I will write for the Baltimore man,[102] tho' I have not yet fully determined what I will send him. Perhaps the essay " Prospect & Retrospect," retouched a little, would suit him.

Probably a month will yet elapse before he will want anything. In today's Round Table's " Literariana " is a line concerning thee and me. He speaks of Messrs H & H's Fall List of publications: " . . . . . and Tiger-Lilies, a novel, by Prof Sidney Lanier, not unknown as a poet by the readers of the Round Table." [103]

— My " Three Waterfalls " appears this morning, in a first instalment comprising about half of it, in Scott's Monthly. The abominable fellow has muddled it terribly, by changing my spelling, my punctuation, my paragraphing, my dashing &c &c. Thou wilt receive it.

The name of Tiger-Lilies is *not* to be changed: a letter to-day advising me against it, and suggesting, in case of difficulty, the feasibility for changing for the 2nd Edition. I am preparing a series of advertisements for various newspapers. 21 pages of proof – sheets today, which I will submit to Mr Sneed, as basis of a puff.

McClellan wishes to send a copy of the critique on Tiger-Lilies to Miss Brewster, Author of " St. Martin's Summer," which book is classed with mine and " Charles Auchester " in the critique. She's friend to McClellan.[104]

---

[102] See note 86, above. " Retrospects and Prospects " was not published until 1871, in the *Southern Magazine* (V, 280).

[103] This notice appeared in the Sept. 14, 1867, issue of the *Round Table*. " The Three Waterfalls," mentioned in the next paragraph, appeared in two installments in *Scott's Monthly Magazine* for Aug. and Sept., 1867.

[104] A two-page MS critique of *Tiger-Lilies* survives (Charles D. Lanier Collection, Johns Hopkins University) signed " I. [J.?] K. M." Because of a statement contained in it (" the musical descriptions are of that kind to make the book exceedingly popular among the lovers of ' Counterparts,' ' Charles Auchester,' ' St. Martins Summer' etc."), this seems to be the critique here referred to. A contemporary copy by Mary Day says that it was a report written

Last night I walked out to Mrs Fulton's and spent the night with her & Janie. Janie was better, and Mrs F. was more like her old self than I've seen her in a long time. I squalled and bawled and sung and cut capers on the floor and made Janie rub my head. Mrs F. wishes Norah [105] to be my Assistant Music-teacher: – I am yours Truly!

As for Miss Weber [106]: – I'll begin the music-class myself, and whenever it becomes a definitely paying thing will be able to make secure propositions to some good teacher.

—   I have to pack my books. Terrible job. Will not leave till Wednesday, hoping to get definite news from Taliaferro. In event of his accepting, he and and Janie are to telegraph me immediately, and are to arrive by Thursday preceding Oct. 1st at Exchange Hotel in Montgomery.

And so, here's a muddle of a letter for thee! Thou seest, when I work for my Niñita, I am not idle!

———————————

Sweet, O my Too-Sweet, my heart tingles to feel thine throbbing. Ah, My God, My God, bring me soon to my Be-loved! I have no thought, no heart-throb, no eye-glance, no movement of hand arm or brain which is not thine and works under the love of thee as under a sky. O my Mamie, My Mamie, my heart is too lonesome: I shiver to think of the three lonely months: I bless Lilla who comes to thee, and I would I had some Lilla to soften the rude solitude in which I must work. But my love, my great love, my passionate, rosy, mysterious, heavenly love, brings no suffering which is not a wild joy to me, thinking that it is for my fine Miranda, my wonderful Mary, my Diamond-Flower.

earlier in the year by the reader for the American Bureau for Literary Reference (V, xi-xii). The author of the first two books was Elizabeth Sheppard, and of the last Anna Maria Hampton Brewster—all dealing largely with music. (For the identity of Jas. B. MacLellan, see note 71, above.)

[105] Mrs. Fulton's daughter, Norah Freeman, who had been Lanier's music pupil at Scott's Mills in 1865, and who lived with the Laniers in Baltimore several years later.

[106] Miss Weber was a native of Tennessee who had taught piano in Macon.

To Mary Day

[Macon, Ga., Sept. 17? 1867]
Tuesday.

My Darling, I have been steadily at work since breakfast this morning on proof-sheets which have come crowding upon me. I have not yet finished, but snatch a moment in which to sing to thee that I love thee whole-heartedly, and that I am joyful to work for thee so hard, and that I am sorrowful to think of thy chills, and that Hal has sent thy note to Dr. Hall and transmitted thee, I believe, some medicine this morning which he rose at six to run to the drug-store for, and that I love thee, and that I am better pleased with the later chapters of my book than with any others and that I love thee and that I cannot possibly come to thee alas, alas, since today is the 17th and I know not if I can even get off tomorrow for Montgomery, so that I will probably be delayed until the 20th before I am at Prattville, being obliged to spend at least one day in Montgomery to rent pianos, to buy – thou knowest what! and to sell consignments of Tiger-Lilies, and I have not yet had any school circulars struck off having delayed in order to have the assistants' names to publish and this last delay renders it absolutely necessary I should be at Prattville for the purpose of making timely arrangements for pupils wishing to board in the village, and many other purposes, and that I love thee, Child, Ninita, and I go to get a sweet place ready for thy dainty occupying, and that there will be no moment of time in which I will not be dreaming of thee while laboring for thee, and that thou hast forgotten to give me the address of the Publishers of Guyot's Geographies, and that thou has also naughtily forgotten to tell me about the chills in thy letter of today, and that I have now to go out and dun Rev. W. J. Scott for the money that should rightfully compensate my labors upon ye parlous " Three Waterfalls," and that thou art right about little Sissa [107] and

---

[107] On Sept. 9, 1867, Gertrude Lanier (Shannon) had written to her brother Sidney: " I am just a little bit jealous– . . . because I found out that Mamie-dear, had been monopolizing you, so entirely that even ' little Sissa ' was most forgotten– . . . but if she'll write me a sweet long letter– immediately– I'll be real good– and will tell her how much I love her in my next letter to her." Lanier

shalt wait until she writes to thee tho' I think thou hast misconstrued a little her form of expression which is a habitual
one with her and that thou art not too proud but thou must
cease for my sake to think about the matter at all because I love
thee, Little Wife, and I care not if the rest of the world go
hang so thou remainest to be my wife and lovest me utterly
and, so caring, think little of aught else whether praiseworthy
or blameworthy of friendship, and that I have the sweetest
plans to learn French from thee by a new system, and have
found some books on Calisthenics to send for, and have written
this note at 400 miles an hour, but not too rapidly to bless every
word thine eye shall rest on and envy every spot thy lithe fingers
shall touch and breathe a prayer through every line that will
rise and caress thy forehead when thou readest these pages of
thy passionate – longing

Lover.

To Mary Day

[Macon, Ga., Sept. 18? 1867]
Wednesday.

My Darling Veiled-One, whom the Present presents to me as
my Ninita and the Future hides from me as my Wife, *I* would
thou wert now my very own, for I am forespent with toil and I
am faint with yearning, and wert thou lying in my arms—which
thou dost consecrate since thou callest them " dear " arms,—
meseems I would be at rest and the morrow would find me
fresh and world-loving and happy and strong. I am not so
selfish that I may rejoice in what thou callest " the pain of
missing me," nor am I so unselfish that I may say I would not
have it so. Thou wouldst be the first and last thought of *my*
waking and sleeping life, also, if there were any first and last
to that which doth not end nor begin with any day or night,
but stretcheth continually through my time. I think thou
need'st not fear that I will love any one much for the mere

had inclosed this in his letter of Sept. 15(?) to Mary Day, who replied on
Sept. 16: " My own Darling– I will not pain you– will I?– by feeling that little
Gertrude ought to write *to me*– first– on the subject of our tenderer relationship.
. . . tell her, ' that indeed she must not visit upon *me* your delinquincies in
correspondence– for it is an old familiar sin of yours . . .' "

"comfort" I may receive from her household ministrations, since thou knowest that to me comfort is only the machine which lifts me above the distractions of *dis*comfort and leaves me so able to think and grow in manliness and strong love: and I swear to thee that my life has little greater sorrow than comes to me when I think that poverty will compel me to accept *thy* work in the household matters and will prevent me from placing thee on that high throne where I would have thee to be utter Queen, where thy dainty fingers should have no heavier duty than to make the Chopin-music which thou and I love, nor thy mind other care than to revel with mine in that beautiful Soul's-Paradise whose gate now stands closed, nor opens, save for money.[108]

———————   ———————

I have so much to do this afternoon that I must not talk much love to thee.

Called on Mr Reese this morning and had a pleasant chat. Found Miss Clare and Miss Roberts there. Paid a pleasant visit to Mrs Ligon's last night.

I leave in the morning for Montgomery.

I am glad thou wilt wait for the likeness, and thou shalt have it as thou wishest. In the flush of our wedding-days,— there is the time for me to look well! It shall be done then.

Bye-bye, and bye-bye, a thousand times: dream thou the thousand kisses I would shower upon thee, rest thou on my love, be not jealous of any in my outer heart when thou hast *all* the inner heart of my

Heart.

To Mary Day

Montgomery
[Sept. 20? 1867]
Friday.

Thou Dear One,   Today is the first, since a long time, that I have been dumb to thee. O the miles, the grim stolid miles, the hateful, unmoved, unloving miles,—why stand they betwixt me and Thee? I know not, I know not: — God is great.

[108] On Sept. 12 Mary Day had written to Lanier: "You would be touched to

I came here last night from Macon, and leave this afternoon
for Prattville. I wait anxiously to hear from Janie. The
Chicago Papers copied the Tournament. Cliff's Thorn-Fruit
will be ripe in a week or so. Aunt Janie (Mrs Watt) has had
a chill or two – A Gentleman over from Prattville today gives
encouraging prospect of the school. There is not a subscriber
to Scott's Magazine in Montgomery. Have just been visited by
a gentleman wishing me to go on a speechifying campaign in
favor of the Conservative Party. Declined, with violent and
paroxysmal thanks. Letters from Anna Howard & Ginna
Hankins. Have seen Mary Wyman. Am negotiating for a
piano. Have gotten up a parlous " Circular " which is now in
press. School Calendar for years '67 & '68: bothered me terribly
to get it up: why don't they have 13 months in a year, at once?
12 of 'em only occupy 48 weeks; and 4 weeks to spare is
inconvenient.

——   This muddle very accurately represents to thee the Olla
Podrida which has filled the five business hours since I got here.
To write thee, in the midst of it, – is like finding an oyster in a
Hotel-stew: a thing at once impossible, ridiculous and unprofit-
able. And yet, O my Darling, My work plays about fantas-
tically in front of the love of thee which is the background
where stands the prime mover of all the puppets and the
fantoccini: aye, the prime-mover, *Thou*. My Attar-of-Life. For
what saith M. de Lamartine? – " –Everywhere it is from the
fireside or boudoir of a lettered, political, or enthusiastic
woman, that an age is lighted or an eloquence bursts forth.
Always a woman as the nurse of genius, at the cradle of literature. When the *salons* are closed, I dread civil Storms or
literary decline." [109] Sweet, Sweet! my *Salon,* my heart, is
empty, thou art not there to entertain the sweet visitors that
come out, of the the royal woods and down from the pure aris-
tocratic skies. And yet, from *thy* " fireside," I think " an age
will be lighted." O God, kindle the fires quickly on *our* hearth:
I am a'cold!

mark the development of my ' housekeepers-spirit,' – my examinations of cooking-
stoves, pantries, store-rooms, &c,– and my pathetic inquiries as to ' light-bread '–
' tea-cakes '– ' tomato soup ' and ' baked apples '– would stir your sympathies.
Ah! how many a solitary cry I see, in vision, awaiting me! Sidney! I feel *borne
down by the weight of cans already!* I'm not laughing– indeed."
[109] The quotation from Lamartine is typical but has not been specifically located.

An now little Wife, God keep thee in his love, as it were
in the core of a rose, petal-folded, incense-calmed, peaceful-
hearted, wifely-souled, dawn-eyed, beautiful: until I come and
nestle there with thee in the very heart of the Rose of the Love
of God, a joyful, proud, uplifted

King of Thee and Slave of Thee.

To Mary Day

[Montgomery, Ala., Sept. 22? 1867]
Sunday.

Where's the bosom of my wife, – that I might rest my head
and rest my heart, weary with anxiety and grief? Thou
knowest, Darling, I am in the midst of affliction. My poor
violet-eyes, my beloved Sissa, has lost her husband, and is now
ill with yellow-fever.[110] A telegram today announces that she
is pronounced out of danger: but I cannot see anything save
her bleeding heart. Her lonely cries ring in my ears. God
must needs have an infinite heart, if He can stand by quietly
and see and listen to these things. I have not an infinite heart.
My heart is sick. My heart is tired. O, Other-Heart, Other-
Heart, mayhap two of us might endure it. Where art thou?
In this moment I cry to thee and it seems that all my soul is
gone out into the dark world to find thee.

So soon as our Sissa is well enough to travel we will bring
her to us. A thousand cares of business oppress me. Alas, alas,
an 'twere not that *thou* livest and art to be my wife, I fear me
that these cares would go uncared for.

We are to have daily telegrams from Sissa, advising us of
her progress. Thou shalt know.

I return to Prattville in the morning – Have been there and
found out what was needed in the house that seems to me holy
as a temple since it is to be *thy* home and mine. Have ridden
nearly forty miles horseback since yesterday morning. I enclose
thee "Prospectus" of "Southern Society."[111] As for the Guyot's

[110] Mr. Shannon's sudden death from yellow fever occurred on Sept. 21. Mrs.
Shannon recovered.

[111] See note 86, above, and note 113, below.

Geographies: – Hal's note just rec^d says thou hast sent the slip. Thou are very careful and good, Darling Niñita: And I, – I am sad, and I long for thee unutterably, and I kneel and worship thee, and I would thy hand were now upon my head. Send quickly a little love to

Thy Lover.

To Mary Day

[Montgomery, Ala., Sept. 24? 1867]
Tuesday Night.

My Darling Heart. I have ridden another forty mile o' horse-back since I wrote thee night before last, and I'm so utterly fagged and so ineffably sleepy that I can scarcely hold pen or see line. But I scrawl to thee that I love thee infinitely, and that I have a man-servant and a woman-servant hewing and scrubbing and sweeping and dusting the little temple in Pratt-ville which is to hold thee. I have done a thousand things yesterday and today. Have distributed circulars, have " seen " parents, have called on my Assistant Mrs Morgan, have found her a fine woman and a tall, and have discovered that I'll like her extremely, have hired a cook, have negotiated for a dining-room servant, (a man) have bought crockery and b – d-ch — rs, have drawn up and signed rent-notes, have played on a most wretched and altogether horrible flute to the accompaniment of an altogether horrible and most wretched piano, have dis-coursed a red-haired and smirky country-girl upon " various topics of interest," have met an old college-mate with a patch on his eye whilk was in battaille extinguished, have sent a telegram to New York to inquire if my Grandfather can lease the Southern Hotel which is now " for rent " and about which thou art to keep thy finger on thy dainty lip if my envy of the aforesaid happy finger will let it stay in so sweet a place, have dreamed of thee along forty miles of the loneliest road in christendom, have determined to have our washing done *out* to avoid the traditional horrors of a " wash-place " on the lot, have refused mildly but firmly to employ a nurse whose father (colored) met me on the street and begged me to hire her and

then begged my pardon when I informed him of the heinous
nature of his request, have also "jewed" down the price of
cleaning out the grass in our flower-garden from five dollars to
two and a half, have looked for a letter from thee which has
probably missed me and gone to Prattville, have come back to
Montg'y to get a whole infinitude of things & to hear from
Sissa, have blessed thee and worshipped thee and yearned for
thee all the days long, and have only space left (not to speak
of eyesight) to send thee mine entire

Heart.

To Mary Day

Montgomery.
[Sept. 25? 1867]
Wednesday.

My Darling Niñita your note is just come. I have been detained
here by the necessity of hearing some=thing from Janie. I
waited till this afternoon, and, despairing of getting any news,
telegraphed her that I could not arrange matters at all if I
delayed longer to employ my assistant. She replied promptly
by telegraph that nothing had been heard from her brother
and that I must not wait. I *coudn't* wait, – my presence being
indispensable in Prattville, and so have employed Mr [Nick]
Williams, a teacher of some years experience tho' now only 21
years of age. He is a fine modest young fellow, knows French,
Italian & Spanish, has good address, was a popular teacher, is
a man of progressive ideas, good-looking, highly companion-
able, and ready for work. I am much pleased with him, and I
hope great things from our companionship. He will be a great
addition to our stock of language.

I did not notice anything at all unusual in Janie's reception
of y'r letter, and I can't imagine what could possibly wound
her from *you,* hope you are mistaken.

I return to Prattville in the morning early and will write you
from our home as soon as possible. I've hired a *man*-servant
who is accomplished as a dining-room waiter and as a cook:
and have secured an old family-servant as cook who, I doubt

not, will prove a treasure to us, and will keep her dep't in cleanly style.[112]

Darling, Darling, how I long for thee! I have been *so* tired today, physically and morally. Men are such horrid things! – which remark might have been uttered by any school-girl. Ah, if I might rest my heart upon the heart of my wife!

A telegram tonight advises us of Sissa's continued improvement and of a letter which when received will post us fully. My poor soft-souled faithful-hearted Sissa! I say to myself, O My God! – and then I do not dare think about it – further.

Thy " languor " and " feebleness " distress me and disquiet me beyond measure. I would I might bear thee up, Sweet Weak One, whom my soul would envelope as the skies envelope the world. Write to

Thy   Lover.

Write me at " Prattville, Ala."

To Clifford A. Lanier

Prattville Ala
Sept 26th 1867.

My Dear Cliff:

      I've at length rented a team, after infinite trouble. Put Robert Hill aboard, then ask Bob Watt to fill the order I left with him and put the provisions in the wagon, sending word meanwhile to Miranda to get herself & Jim ready. Please see the whole establishment on; & don't forget a bundle in Aunt Jane's room, with which warn them to be careful, as it contains glass. Send also the guitar, (the one Willie has) & case. Also the violin; also the text-books of all sorts that I saw in y'r room, if you can spare them.

This, I think, will finish all the trouble I have to give you, for a while at least. Send any letters or packages by Miranda.

Hastily

Sid. L.

---

[112] Referred to in later letters as Miranda. (See also Mary Day Lanier's letter to Fred Alvin King, Autumn, 1891, Appendix B, vol. X.)

To Mary Day

Home.
[Prattville, Ala., Sept. 29, 1867]
Sunday.

There is here a little river which does the mill-work. At twilight, last night, when this stream had done its day's toil, I saw a long white mist steal over the hills and creep close down and lay its cheek lovingly upon the cheek of the water. The white mist is the water's Niñita.

Du Himmel! *I* have worked harder all this week than the stream has. Today, when my twilight-of-the-week is come, my Sunday, why comes not my White Mist to nestle near me, to thrill me with soft cheek against rough cheek? I would some happy wind might float thee here, My Niñita, so that thou might'st enter into thy home and fill it entirely with thy presence: it needs thee: *I* need thee. Ah, My God, how I need thee! Thou woudst fear to imagine, if thou *couldst* do it, how lonesome I am. My heart is tired with incessantly peopling its solitudes: I cannot dream ought but loneliness, my Soul creates nothing but sad, single-ghosts, the hills seem divorced from the sky and the trees from the hills. I fancy the stars at immeasurable distances from each other. Nature is still God's garment but God is not now wearing it, there is a certain truculency and fierceness in the grind of bough on bough and the patter of leaf against leaf in the capricious fall-winds, my roses that peer in my window are half-wrinkled and show like the painted faces of aged spinsters – The want of thee distorts my soul. Mine eyes are fixed on thee, and see all else awry.

I am here, thou seest, at home: but everything is yet to do to make it like veritable home. I find here a charming old-fashioned Secretary, upon which I am writing: while a hundred books look at me from its upper compartment. I try to draw a rough ground-plan.

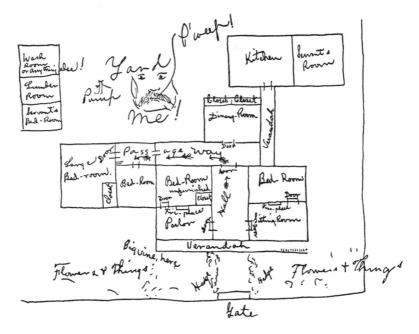

The rooms are small, but conveniently enough arranged. Dining-room quite small, but only needing a curtain or two and carpet to make it quite cosy. I have drawn the "Hall" too wide. 'Tis all done hastily. The plan, I fear, gives *too large* an idea of the house: 'tis a small house. The parlor, sitting-room and "large bed-room" are very nicely furnished: & two other bed-rooms tolerably. Plastering badly cracked in places: I hope to paper it before a great while. Two or three very beautiful Chromo-Lithographs adorn the Parlor & sitting-room walls.

I commence school on Tuesday next, tho' the repairs upon the large School-room are not yet finished — Prospects good; but the terrible decline in the price of cotton and the consequent "blues" of the planters will probably keep many away.

I long very much for some sweet words from thee. Our mail here is tri-weekly. I will surely get something tomorrow! I find no soul to whom I can talk our talk. I suspect that, besides Mr Hazens (Presbyterian Minister, now gone North for his family who have been spending Summer there: to return middle of next week), thou and I will be alone. I care not at all for this; so *thou* are with me.

I pray to hear that thou art getting strong and well. I must work so much away from thee in the days to come! I cannot bear thou shouldst be sick then.

God keep thee, My Beloved, for

Thy   Lover.

To Robert S. Lanier

Prattville Ala
Sunday [Sept.] 29th 1867

My Dear Father:

After a week of incessant work, during which I've ridden nearly a hundred miles on horseback, I am at length established in my new home, and, I doubt not when the newness is worn off, will be comfortable enough. I have just drawn off and sent Mamie a ground-plan of our house, which will probably interest you if you'll make her show it you.

I wrote you from Montgomery three days ago. Have heard no word from Sister since then. Our tri-weekly mail comes in tomorrow and I hope to have my anxiety relieved then.

My School-prospect is good. I fear however that the recent decline in cotton, which has spread the blues over all the farmers here, will cause many to keep their children at home.

I have been fortunate enough to get Miranda for my cook. She is so careful, so thoroughly faithful and honest, and so economical, that I am congratulated by all upon having secured such a treasure. I have a man, also, who will take care of the dining-room and the house-work, besides attending to the Academy-building. Miranda brings Jim with her, who is quite a tall fellow, and makes himself very useful.

I found that I could not possibly afford to wait longer upon Janie's brother, and so telegraphed her some days ago. She replied that nothing had been heard from Taliaferro and I immediately secured a young man from Georgia, Mr Williams (of Merriwether County) who was first-honor man at Erskine College S. C., and has been teaching some years, tho' now only twenty-one years of age. He teaches French, Italian & Spanish; and, after a long talk with him, I find myself much pleased. I have advertised to teach a Music-class between School-hours, and will probably increase revenue somewhat in that way.

I inclose Prospectus of "Southern Society." My name appears in tolerably good company.[113] Have you seen anything of Scott? The amount will be about 33 Dollars for the whole piece.[114] This would be a great help to me just now. Do stir him up, as soon as you get time.

Present my regards to Uncle Clifford & Family, & all inquiring friends. Send me the Telegraph occasionally, I'm terribly lonesome. Clarkie [115] comes over on Monday, to board with me.

Your Loving

Sid.

TO ROBERT S. LANIER

Prattville Ala.
Oct. 10th 1867.

My Dear Father:

I've been so busy, day and night, with organizing and assimilating the heterogeneous elements that compose my school, that I haven't had time to eat or sleep as much as I would have liked.

I have 61 scholars, and it is probable that the first *frost* will increase this number by 25, since, in consequence of the prevalence of summer chills in the village, the country people have refrained from sending their children until healthier weather. I have succeeded beyond my expectation in systematizing the school, and feel confident that in a few weeks I shall make a model institution of it.

I live very plainly and frugally, tho' comfortably enough. Work seems to agree with me: and, in the matter of health, I have nothing to complain of.

Do stir up the Rev. Scott, and stir him up mightily, even unto the payment of the Thirty-three dollars which he ought me and which would be pleasant to receive.

---

[113] Others announced as contributors were: Paul H. Hayne, Henry Timrod, John Esten Cooke, Father Ryan, John R. Thompson, and Mrs. Margaret J. Preston. (See Lanier's comments in the following letter and in his letter to Northrup, Dec. 16, 1867, below.)

[114] The price promised for Lanier's "The Three Waterfalls" by W. J. Scott, editor of *Scott's Monthly Magazine*.

[115] Lanier's cousin Clark, son of William Brinton Lanier of Robinson's Springs.

I have nothing from Sister. Love to all. Rec^d y'r " Southern Society." Poor thing, isn't it? Write to y'r Loving

Sid.

To Mary Day [116]

Prattville
Friday [Oct.] 18/67

My Darling Niñita, That hadst not heart to call thy self Niñita, I fall on my knees before thee and cry to thee humbly that my work for thee hath left me *no time at all,* no *single minute,* Niñita, in which I might worship thee in other ways.

Darling, there is nothing sweet for me now save to write thee: all things else are bitter; think how bitter have been *my* eleven days in which I have not spoken to thee! Even on Saturday and Sunday, what with choirs and churches and visitors, and collecting, I had no moment. From 8 A. M. to 11 P. M. I work, work, work. I will write thee tomorrow or Sunday and detail to thee what I do each day. One thing is *done.* That's Tiger Lilies. I have corrected " The End."

A letter from Theodore F. Dwight, of Auburn, N. Y. asks, in very complimentary strain, for my Autograph. Who is Theodore F. Dwight? [117] Is Thine getting famous? I run up to Montgom'y this aft. hoping to meet Sissa: violating, so, a dozen engagements. Made a blazing speech last night to the debating club. Have 72 scholars, and good prospect of ninety in two weeks. Will write thee from Montg'y. Letters from everybody. Little insists on my coming to Oakland. Other people insist on many other things.

I am, Thou Darling, Thou Best-Beloved, Thine, who

Yearns for Thee.

[116] This is one of nine letters from Lanier to Mary Day written from Prattville during Oct.-Dec., 1867, which have been conjecturally dated from internal evidence, from surviving envelopes, and from partial datings on the letters themselves. The first of them—Oct. 10(?), 1867—has been omitted.

[117] The letter has not survived, and the writer has not been identified.

To Mary Day

[Prattville, Ala., Oct. 20, 1867]
Sunday Night.

My Darling:

I left Prattville late on Friday afternoon, and drove to Robinson Springs, on my way to Montg'y where I hoped to meet Sissa. Went to bed in splendid health, at Grandfather's, but, about 1 Oclock, was taken quite ill, and lay so all night, with severe cold which had settled, — well, where it hadn't oughter have " settled." I crawled out of bed and rode to Montg'y Saturday morning, but had to get into bed as soon as I arrived there. Found poor little pale Sissa there. This morning she and Auntie (Mrs Watt) and I rode over in carriage to Robinson Springs, where I spent day in bed. Have just come home: all of 'em protested against my leaving, but I hoped so to get to work again tomorrow that I couldn't stay.

Sissa looks well as one could expect. Is perfectly quiet: but her white calm is terrible and nigh broke my heart.

I suffer from overwhelming nausea, and other pains too numerous to mention. Will drop thee another line tommorrow. Hope to be well then. Thou wilt excuse this scrawl which, at any rate, bears thee the whole love of

Thy   Sidney.

Wrote on Friday last.

To Mary Day

[Prattville, Ala., Oct. 23, 1867]
Wednesday 23rd

My Darling Darling,   I am out of bed today and at work, tho' very weak and unergetic. How I long for thee, in these feeble moments of my poor physique! The days seem very slow, and malignantly drag themselves along, – the days which stand betwixt me and my wife.

I am just stolen away – leaving Williams in charge of the school while they write copies, – to lie down a minute and

scrawl thee my yearning, burning love, which illy waits till
I may be wholly and utterly

Thine

78 scholars today.

S.

To Mary Day

Prattville Ala
Oct. 24th 1867.

Sweet Wife-To-Be:

Tonight I violently laid hands upon and seized unto my
own behoof and use, three good hours of time the which hours
I had previously bargained, conveyed and covenanted unto the
Prattville Debating Society, – the same being the hours from
7 A. M. up to this present hour of half-past ten: and I have
been endeavoring with my most lightning-like scratching of the
pen, to empty a drawer-full of letters which have remained
unanswered for a month past: and have just succeeded. During
these hours I have been saying to myself, as I would finish each
letter, – *one* closer to my Darling: and so here am I, my Sweet,
gazing into thine eyes, and calling out to my soul which is gone
down into the gray loveliness as into the sea. And yet, I must
first talk to thee anent a wedding thou and I wot of. To-wit:
I would, My Darling, that thou wouldst write me down, in fair
black and white, good and true answers to these following
interrogatories, namely:

1. Precisely what day is this wedding hereinbefore alluded
to, – to come off?
2. Precisely what *hour* is this same wedding to be celebrated
and sanctioned by the priest?
3. Precisely who are to be the attendants, – the bottle-holders
and sponge-holders, as it were, – of this wedding?
4. Precisely at what time should the cards of this same wedding
be issued, and would My Lady Queen prefer the same to be
engraved in N. Y. or N. O?
5. Precisely whither is it my Liege's royal intention to order her
journey: her relays of carriages, how will they travel: her suites
of apartments, where: her ovations, her illuminations, her
rejoicings, – along what route of the land will these be?

Anent this last question, Dear Wife-I-yearn-for, let me say for thy consideration, and sole free decision: that of course the N. O. trip is *now* not feasible.[118] — As for any other place to which we might journey, I know none that offers enough pleasure to make it worth the fatigue of thy dainty limbs in getting there. Moreover, I have thought that what money we might spend in making any trip, would, if worked by thy brain and thy deft fingers, put many a sweet comfort in our home, and make it as nice a home for thine and my first year as thou or I could wish. Our dining-room and one of our bed-rooms want curtains and a carpet: and a thousand little orna-ments which would last us some years might be bought for that which would otherwise endure for only a few days. As for the *pleasure* of the trip, there *thou* must decide: I have no pleasure but in thee, with thee, *here.* I am happy as any king, and care for naught else of place or travel. My idea is, to bring thee immediately, or the morning after the wedding, to our loved ones in Montgomery, where thou and I will be petted and loved, by friends and kindred, until my work commences again. Thou lovest me too well not to speak me thy true mind: I have spoken thee mine: write: thou art my Queen.

Thou wilt like to know somewhat of household matters. Thou shalt know it. I have a Man-servant, the best I have ever seen: large, good-looking, respectful, smart, and quiet. I have no trouble whatever; he works all day long, at every thing he can find to do. Our cook is a woman of the severest dignity. Her habits of life are Spartan in their simplicity and stern self-denial. For instance, altho' it is well-known she has more good clo'es than any colored woman in the country, she yet dresses in a short homespun dress, — being set, by nature, upon "remarkable long and narrer" pedestals—, and disdains stockings averring that they are in de way anyhow. She pos-sesses, however, the loveliest traits of character: among which I may mention a son, 14 years of age, which I don't pay any hire for him, but which he knows all about a horse, and runs errands, and makes fires, and acts as my body-servant. To give you an idea of my cook's economical ideas: I had thought of putting out the washing, fearing it would be too much for her,

[118] Because of the yellow fever in New Orleans and because of the death of Mr. Shannon and Gertrude Lanier Shannon's departure from that city.

besides cooking: and had sent for a laundress to come and see me.

Enter Laundress, accompanied by Cook. My cook is a very sententious person. Laundress smiling; Cook severe.

" 'Oman come to see you, Mass Sid," says Cook.

" Yes, sir," says Laundress, all in a heap, " I'se splendid washer woman, bin livin' wid so and so five year, wash white, furnishes my own soap &c &c ad infinitum."

Cook listens, with thunder gathering on her brows. Laundress having finished, thunder peals.

" Mass Sid, you'se crazy. Let de 'oman go back home whar she cum fum!" and cook flounces out of the room, after ye manner of ye strong-minded.

I let de 'oman go back whar she cum fum, and find my washing well done.

We have War-fulls, beefsteak, butter, and good bread and coffee for breakfast: ham and salads (alias B. & G.),[119] okra, sweet potatoes, roast beef, butter-beans &c for dinner: tea, toast, cold round of beef, or broiled, with Worcester Sauce, for Supper. I am just importing some Buckwheat Cakes, Cheese, Mackerel, (I like 'em broiled, for breakfast) Codfish & Irish potatoes (fish-balls, you know) and maccaroni. My cow was to have been here yesterday, but ran away from her driver and got back home: will be over in a day or two. I have Cliff's horse, and will keep him until I start for Macon. We have the best garden-spot, so said, in the state: also a nice orchard of 3 or 4 acres, and stable-lot.

As for the neighbors: beyond kind greetings on the street, I have had no time to cultivate any of them. I prefer *not* to do so, even if I *had* time: since I wish to be alone with thee in all my spare moments.

I have five music-scholars, piano: teach them between school-hours. I am getting up a concert, proceeds to build a school-gymnasium. I play the cabinet-organ (Mason & Hamlin's) at Pres. church Sundays. Saturdays, run all over the country collecting monthly bills. Nights examine text-books, correct compositions, make out reports, post up books, reorganize school-exercises continually changed by new scholars & classes,

[119] Probably " Bacon and Greens."

speak at debating Society, play flute, piano, guitar & fiddle for visitors, attend to household business, and dream of thee, my Sweet, My Well-Beloved, My Blessing, My Rest, My

One.

78 Scholars today.

To Mary Day

Prattville Ala
Oct. 28th 1867.

My Darling May,

   Y'r letter, which contains only suffering, suffering, makes me so wretched that, what with other pressures, (OTHERS being only last straws in comparison with this) I am upon the point of giving up all, and rendering back to The Heavens what I have received from them, since it is more than any mortal soul can possibly endure. I find myself utterly unable to adopt the indurating policy which seems to be the refuge of all school-teachers. I *must* be interested, and discharge my conscience of the 80 souls that are waiting on me for instruction and example. These are a terrible weight upon me: I dream of them, I think of them in all lights, I study them, I anticipate for them, I labor for them, I suffer for the thousand brutalities and derelictions of their parents, which it requires all my patience, all my labor, all my ingenuity, all my art and culture and poetry and religion to withstand at all. I have had to *begin* everything: and this has doubled the labor. Amidst all this, – of which I can give you no conception at all – when I am attacked by the news of your illness and continued suffering, I become wild, I throw out my hands to the Heavens, and inquire piteously if *one* man is expected to do what I have to do when the one care of his heart, his vital life and being, his Love; is being all the time wounded by the shafts of sickness and weariness and desolation? – Shafts attacking *thee*, My one Rest?

 All of which murmur, wrung from my heart by the bitterness of life, no one has heard, not even God, – no one but

Thee.

To Mary Day

[Prattville, Ala., Nov. 1, 1867]

I have but just time to fall on my knees and humbly implore
forgiveness that I was for one moment so weak and so craven-
hearted as to allow even *thee* to hear from me a cry extorted
by the rack and torture-wheel of life. 'Twas a rare cowardly
thing: I despise myself for it more than thou wilt: I find no
excuse for it, save that a heart naturally weak and unmanly
was for the moment in such anguish of physical and mental
pain that it weakly thought it must cry out, and left silent
fortitude to some manlier time. I am then here on knees: I pray
thee, my fair Wife-to-be, forgive the folly and the shame and
the weakness of one who hath in him but a single thing that
is either strong or high or full or sweet or fair; and that is that
he loves
   Thee.

To Mary Day

Prattville
Sunday Nov. 3rd [1867]

My Darling May: I've been on the wing all the time since
Friday afternoon, and got back to my little home today at
eleven. Had intended to devote the afternoon to a long letter
of pretty things for thee, – when a miserable visitor came in,
dined with me, and stayed till sundown. I then dashed out for
a little walk amidst the brown November leaves, came back,
supped, (cold round of beef, cheese, tea, bread & butter), –
and here sit I, with six letters to write after I have finished
my little love-message to thee.
 Thou saidst the trunks from N. Y. were come. Thou art to
sit down immediately and write me of *everything,* in the housekeeping line, contained therein. Hast aught like window-cur-
tains? or towels? Hast silver; and *what* silver, – tea-service or
forks? Of course thou hast nothing like a carpet. I need *one:* –
it is for *our* – — Eden: I know not what they cost. Write me.

I have also written thee, a week ago, a long letter of inquiries anent a wedding whereof I desire to be posted: hast thou received the same?

'Tis settled, D. V. that Cliff. will be married on the morning of Nov. 12th prox. at daylight, and start immediately for N. Y. on a two weeks' trip.

I see by the papers that "Waterfalls 2 and 3, by Sidney Lanier" appear in Scott for September. Have not been able to see a copy.

Hear nothing from Hurd & Houghton about Tiger Lilies.

Thou writest me nothing of Thy Father, who is to be also mine. How, & where, is he? If with you, present to him my — love, an he will take it.

Thy Lover is hurried and is weary. Thou wilt pardon a short note from him whose love is long as life and death.

Enclose Note for Lilla. Thou mays't read it.

To Virginia Hankins

Prattville Ala.
Nov 3rd 1867.

My Darling, Darling Ginna, I would thy pure eyes had never seen the sight which thy pencil-letter, just received, intimates thou hast witnessed.[120] And having seen it, thou art to do as

[120] The earliest letter from Virginia Hankins to Lanier that has survived is dated Oct. 24, 1867. Since the passage here referred to seems to reflect, though indirectly, her sentiments concerning their own relationship, it is quoted here at length:

" Another Iphigenia! — and the drums beat, and the trumpets sound to drown the cries of the victim, while we unfurl our sails to take up our way again upon the uncertain Seas.— Just this, forces itself into my mind at the noise & laughter, the eating and dressing, the flirting & dancing incident to weddings. . . . Oh, I feel deeply that it is a fearful thing, to marry without love. It seems to me, that however much my reason may have persuaded me to a ' marriage de convenance,' when the last moment should have arrived and I saw behind me arrayed all the sweet usages of my childhood, and heard all the high-ideal-dreams of my youth-time moaning their farewell to me, I should no longer be able to resist my heart; I should no longer dare, by a false oath, to separate myself forever from the memory of my Mother; and I should even then, tear away the bridal-veil, & kneeling in my bridal robes, vow to love honor and obey only my heart's Love. Better by far to be always lonely & full of truth, than to hear the tones of an unloved voice, forever ringing in dull, monotonous changes to Duty, as if to a Sacrifice.—Yet how many such marriages in Vanity Fair, to one, when two royal

I do: – thou art to close thine eyes, and sigh, – and say to thyself, it is God's world, and He ruleth it, – and God is great!

If thou hadst but known how I wanted the sad-faced porcelain picture of thee! O, Ginna!

And I saw Joan [121] 'tother day, in Montgomery: Joan, – whose eyes, I daresay, had lately looked on thee, whose fingers had touched thee, aye, lips, maybe, had kissed thee. Happy eyes, thrice happy eyes, and finger, and lips, ——dear Ginna!

Thou must know that I have been elected Principal of the fine Academy at this place, that I have nearly ninety pupils, and fair prospect of one hundred, and am likely to do very well for the year, spite of the terrible depression of the country people.

Thou must know that I am probably the hardest worker in the whole world, since, what with legitimate school-duties, and the responsibility of so large a crowd, and the music-scholars between school-hours, and the book-making, and poetry and all, there's not a moment of the day or the night which is my own: and this, which I am giving thee, is stolen. Would God, all my thefts went to so sweet and holy purposes!

Thou must also know that Cliff marries at daylight on the 12th Nov. prox. and starts for New York on a flying trip of two weeks. I know not if he will have time to see thee. If so, he *will*.

Thou must further know that *to thee* there lives no such being as Professor Sidney Lanier.[122] O My Darling, I am one

Hearts meet, and ' Kiss, like crowned Kings.'— Pardon the moralizing which would come, inspite of me, & believe that I am not dealing in personalities, if you can give a woman credit for generalizing— Having just returned from a wedding I thought this, but I have looked deeply into many hearts, of late, and it makes me very full of pity,– and a little rebellious that what *is, must be.* — And after all, it may be I'm a little angry that the blind boy claps his wings, far above any reaching of mine— and so I *half* believe there is no blind boy at all, only a myth of the Ages far back, which repeats itself in each human heart, as a dream— nothing more."

[121] Virginia Hankins's cousin, Joan Douglas.

[122] In her letter of Oct. 24, 1867, Virginia Hankins had written: " What is this *audit*? ' Mamie Day is not married, Mr. A—— is badly treated.' I am sorry, (that is, if she is,) for I don't believe she treated any body badly— I also hear that Prof: Sidney Lanier, has at last resigned his hand & heart to– name unknown– as I am in profound awe of that gentleman I don't care what he does, but there's somebody by the same name, *without* the Prof: whom I don't want to get married;– not yet– Will you write me something about him– where he is– how he is and if he still thinks of his friend Ginna Hankins? "

who humbly falls on his knees when any words from thee come to him, who listens to all thou sayest with bended head and with child's-humility, and who has no rejoicing so great as when he hopes he has done something which might bring a smile of pride for him, or a flush of sympathy for him, to the face of Ginna Hankins. Little One, each letter of thine makes a Holy Day for me: — why dost thou not make more of my days sanctified? I do not beg thee to write me, as I would: I may not beg thee for anything: I fear to ask thee for aught that makes thy dainty tired fingers move, when I know in what loving labors thou hast wearied them and dost still weary them. But thou knowest, Child, Little Oue! And two or three of thy quiet words, thy holy, beautiful, serene words, are very sweet, — Ah me, — very sweet to me. When they come, send them to me addressed as above.

I am Thine humble, humble

S.

Is it our Reba that's gone playing Iphigenia? Great, gray-eyed Reba Alexander? [123] Himmel!

To Clifford A. Lanier

Prattville
Nov– 3rd 1867.

My Dear Cliff:

I left some reports to be printed at the " Mail " Office, price $5 for five hundred. They were to be ready on Monday. Please get 'em, as soon as you receive this, and roll 'em up and mail to me immediately so that they'll come down by Wednesday morning's mail –

Darling, Darling Clifford, my heart hovers about you so tenderly, so longingly, so wistfully. How cruel is this wretched necessity – to – work, which keeps me from thee whom I love best of all the world!

[123] Lanier's guess as tu the identity of " Iphigenia" (see note 120, above) was wrong. It was not their friend Rebecca Alexander (see Lanier's letter to her, Jan.(?), 1864), but apparently Lucy Douglas, a cousin of Virginia Hankins, whose marriage to a Mr. Johnson was later pronounced a success (see Virginia Hankins to Lanier, Apr. 13, 1869).

I have now-a-days but one prayer. It is: In prosperity or in Adversity, God bring thee and me together. Time, Time, get thee by, quickly, and let me be with whom I love!

I'm hurried.

I send thee all the change I have: tis $5, lacking a quarter, which I'll send other time.

Sid.

To Clifford A. Lanier

Prattville Nov 7, 1867

My Dear Brother Clifford:

There is no *saying* a word about it: be it *mine* to *feel* all that words would mock.[124]

Hast had time yet to rearrange thy plans? If so, write me *immediately,* putting letter in mail *Saturday,* that I may get it Monday, I would know, so that I may come to thee.

Poor, pale, sweet Will: — I would she might rest on my love which goes out to her so freely, so softly, so tenderly.

Canst not come with Salem? He spoke of coming over on Saturday.[125]

I am full of cares; which take away from thee only the pen, but not the heart of

Thy Brother.

To Mary Day

Prattville
Monday.   10th [Nov. 11?] "67

My Darling: I have only a bare moment in which to scratch off to thee that thy little note containing answer to question No. 3 [126] is received: and I hasten to reply that, while I *have*

[124] The reference is to the death of Wilhelmina Clopton's mother, which caused the postponement of Clifford Lanier's marriage from Nov. 12 until Nov. 26, 1867.

[125] Salem Dutcher had left New York on Oct. 31 and had arrived in Montgomery on Nov. 3 to report the convention of the Alabama legislature for the New York *World*. On Nov. 4 he wrote to say that he expected to visit Lanier in Prattville on Saturday, Nov. 9.

[126] Lanier's question, in his letter of Oct. 24, had referred to the attendants for their wedding. Conner and Ross, suggested in the next paragraph, were Macon friends.

some tall friends in Montg'y, yet I don't think any of 'em would *like* to leave just about that time since they (the tall men) are, I shrewdly suspect, *looking about for tall men to help* THEM out of a scrape just like mine. Voila a dilemma!

Wouldn't Toby Conner suit? Or Frank Ross? Do answer immediately: since it is time I were already writing those gentlemen.

Salem Dutcher is in Montg'y. Spent yesterday with him.[127] He's one of the editors of the N. Y. World. Will be at our Wedding.

Send me the *name* of the Episcopal Church in Macon. It must be on the card.

I'm wholly

Thine.

To Mary Day

Prattville Academy.
Prattville, Ala.
Nov 15th "/67

My Darling Wife-to-be:

Friday night brings me a host of unanswered letters instead of rest, and my head's in a muddle by reason of answering the same, and I write to beg thee keep me well bolstered up with all manner of minute instructions as to my duty in the premises, concerning this parlous wedding which is so soon to crown my life.[128]

---

[127] In a letter to his sister Annie Marie (Mamie) dated Montgomery, Nov. 13, 1867, Salem Dutcher wrote: " Among others my friend Sidney Lanier has been to see me, riding in 15 miles from the little country village where he now teaches. . . . The old fellow tarried with me from Saturday night last at about ten, for it was that hour before he got out of the deep mud of his journey, till near day on Monday morning of this week, when he turned his horses head towards his village and left me to battle with the beasts at Ephesus alone. He is soon to be married to a Mary Day, who lives in Macon Ga., and two romantic names there will be of them when they come to the altar, even more so than that of his brother, Clifford Lanier and *his* bride to be, Willie Clopton. Alas! my friends fall on all sides of me. . . . I wish you could hear Sidney and myself talk, and shall have the old fellows keen eyes and hawk-like beak, for he is far from ' pretty.' . . ."

[128] Lanier's letters of Nov. 13 and 18 to Mary Day, concerned with details of the wedding which were later changed or which are covered in other letters, are here omitted.

Thou art my one joy and my one hope and my one motive for endeavor. Already, here, they begin to jibe at me for prefacing so many of my fair projects with—" When my wife comes," or, " wait till May is here " and the like. Surely Child, when thou comest, the trees will burgeon through the frost, and the violets will smile i' the very grim face of the Winter and the hills will put on green as if Robin Hood were wedded, and the water will sing at his work!

An my arm were clasped about thy waist this moment, how could 'tother hand work on the page! Good My Ladye, here's a head needs the soft lightning of thy most tender strokes: needs this to put a fire into the cloudy happiness of its hard work. I have health, I have strength, I have courage, in myself: yonder sitteth God over the stars: what need I besides these, but thee, O my Sweet, Hymn of Love, Thee, My Music?

To Robert S. Lanier [129]

Prattville, Ala.   Nov. 15th "/67

My Dear Father:

'Tis Friday night, the hurry-scurry of the week is come to a momentary eddy, Nick Williams, (my assistant) has sallied out to a meeting of the " Prattville Debating Society," Clark is doing youthful devoirs at a school party in the neighborhood, and I — have been sitting before my cheerful fire, for the last five minutes, slippered, stretched comfortably, purring my cattish delight in the warm of the rug and the home-like-ness of the firelight. This same five minutes is the only five minutes I've had in a long time. It was *my* five minutes: and this idea brought a brother with it: for it has suddenly occurred to me that this house, these chairs, books, lamps, tables, – are mine, also, and that I am verily living after the similitude of men of substance. This is a marvellous pleasing thought: I would you might see the complacency of that patronizing smile which, in this happy moment, I cast as 'twere a king's largesse, upon the rocking-chair and the lounge,

[129] Excerpt previously published, Mims, p. 92. This letter and others written during the next eight months have PRATTVILLE ACADEMY on the letter-head.

whose polished veneerings, in the laughing fire-rays, seem to give a sleek return to my humor. Dear Papa, I'm the wraith, the double, the photograph animate, of *you!* So have I seen *you* smile: like this room, was *that* room: like these slippers, *your* slippers: the dear green old " Eclectic" lay *there,* as one lies here: and a wee bit pathos showed itself in the smile, by reason of a grim wrinkle alongside the nose, a wrinkle that *would* have smoothed itself if it *could,* a rare wound-like wrinkle, got i' the office. Such wrinkles – in my folly I have been wont to curse: but now, I know not if I do not half-way bless them, with that same affection wherewith Corporal Trim would cherish the scar of an old wound.[180]

—— And so you see that not even the wide-mouthed, villanous-nosed, tallow-faced drudgeries of my eighty-fold life can squeeze the sentiment out of me: and your immunity from sundry more pages of it, tonight, is only due to a pile of un-answered letters, that I must answer before bed-time. Apropos of bed-time, you'll be glad to hear that I'm turned model-man in that way: I go, on the stroke of ten: I rise at seven. By consequence, I'm in the most uproarious glow of health and appetite. I " do " my four biscuits and my right beef-steak – 6 x 6 inches in size, nightly: and as for six buckwheats and half a broiled mackerel at breakfast, – 'tis a mere anchovy to a Falstaff. I have, after due, though secretly-conducted, investigation, discovered that there is but one man in my school who could lick me, in a fair fight: whereat I rejoice and, by sundry arts have brought the aforesaid strong man into so infatuated a condition as that he thinks me at once a Sampson and a Solomon, and wouldn't dare strike me, if I were a pigmy, out of exceeding regard for my Solomon-ism.

I enclosed a letter received today from H & H,[181] that I may get you to attend to the copy-righting for me. I know not if my signature is required to anything: if so, you are hereby empowered to use it in any way.

Anything of Scott? Planters hold their cotton, and my collections come slowly. I ride all day tomorrow on a " tour."

---

[180] The allusion is to Laurence Sterne, *Tristram Shandy.*

[181] On Nov. 4, 1867, Hurd and Houghton had written Lanier that *Tiger-Lilies* would be out in a short time—the printing was complete, and only the binding remained to be done.

My best love and kisses to May & darling Sissa. Have written both.

Sid.

TO CLIFFORD A. LANIER

Prattville, Ala. Nov. 19th /67.

My Darling Cliff:

I wrote you by Miranda, and hoped to get answer by her. Do write me Thursday, (for Friday's mail) and let me know if your plans are definitely arranged for the wedding on Tuesday night next. If so, I propose to come up Monday morning and spend that day with you.

May writes me that my "Barnacles" has appeared in The Round Table,[132] and been highly applauded. Please get a copy, if you can, & send over by Friday's mail.

Nothing from Thorn-Fruit?

Very Hastily

Sid.

TO MARY DAY

Prattville, Ala. Nov. 27th 67.

My Darling:

I'm just back from Montg'y. Got there late on Monday night: met Salem, just off the stage from a big speech he made to the conservatives; he must needs take me to Pizzola's, where we drank Champagne ad lib. guzzled oysters, and crammed olives; sallied forth and discoursed learnedly, retired at 4, got up early, went to work, arrayed Cliff. in the pomp of war, and saw him married last night at 8 O'clock. He looked like a young God and his bride was beyond compare. They spoke of you tenderly. We feasted, drank, (being only a family party) and left them at nine. Salem and I then took Miss Mary Wyman in tow, broke into the Presbyterian Church by a back-

---

[132] "Barnacles" (I, 11), which had been composed the preceding summer, appeared in the *Round Table* of Nov. 9, 1867.

door, decoyed a small colored individual to blow the organ, and I took 'em both right up into skies and kept 'em there till 11. We held high converse, & went to bed very late. I arose at four, being sometime before light, jumped on my horse, and was back here in time for school, tho' I have taught the same all the morning in a marvellous sleepy fashion.

Y'r note, containing list, rec'd, and will send back with additions soon. I know and hear nothing of Tiger Lilies. Is it arrived? My best and most reverent love to Lady Clare & Lilla. We will go to Savannah.[133] Sweet Wife, I am Thy hurried

S.

Haven't a single envelope, and no time to get one before the mail – Hence! &c &c

To Clifford A. Lanier

Prattville, Ala. Nov. 28th 1867

My Darling Clifford, I will not sadden thee by recounting how, when I saw thee come in t'other night with sweet Will on thine arm, there did suddenly rush upon me all our past twin-ship, like a mighty wind; nor how this wind brought rain, – which thou sawest; nor what a dry and lonely heart I brought home with me. 'Twas very selfish, all; and it is past and gone, and I am very glad thou art happy, Brother Clifford.

If thou shouldst haply find any time when thou art not kissing Willie on thine own account, at such a time thou wilt edge in a brotherly kiss for me and tell her that she is received into my heart alongside of thee.

I have done a most terrible thing. A long list of names of people to be invited to my wedding, sent to me by Mamie with strict injunctions to return the same immediately, – I have left with Aunt Jane, forgetting to ask her for it. She was reading over the names. Do ask her about it, *immediately*: and send

---

[133] This part of the wedding trip was finally abandoned (see note 144, below).

it over to me *by next mail,* since I must make some additions
to it and send back quickly. Don't fail.

Love to all —

    Very hastily

           Bro Sid.

To Mary Day

              Prattville Academy.
              Prattville, Ala.
              Nov. 28th 1867.

Dearest Weibchen, Thinking to give thee a pleasant surprise,
I had, without telling thee, long ago arranged to employ
another person to teach in my place for a week before Christmas,[134] so that I might be with thee a day or two before the
wedding. Since, however, it will relieve thy heart of any anxiety
in regard to my prompt appearance, know that I will be in
Macon on the Sunday night preceding the eventful Thursday,
and will rush to find if thou art well.

Will send thy list with some emendations and additions next
week. Wrote thee yesterday. I'm still fearfully tired and sleepy.
My model habits here have rendered me wholly incapable of
any midnight debaucheries: and my red eyes have, I fear, been
the subject of unfeeling merriment on the part of sundry evil-
minded scholars of mine.

Hast received the letters to the Bottle-holders? And hast
heard from the cards? And *is* Tiger Lilies come? And DOST
thou love thy

        Lover?

To Mary Day

              Prattville, Ala.   Dec 9th "/67

My Darling:

        Y'r little note is just come. I sent Toby Conner's
letter through you, enclosed. You don't say whether it came.
Do let me know.

---

[134] Mrs. George L. Smith was the substitute teacher (see her letter to Mary
Day Lanier, Dec. 30, 1902).

My heart is too impatient. Poor Sissa ! Kiss her for me.
How does Tiger Lilies sell?[135] You don't write enthusiastically.
God help thee and

Thy Loving

S.

The enclosed was born while I rode eight miles this bitter
morning before breakfast.[136]

To MILTON H. NORTHRUP [137]

Macon, Ga. Dec. 16th 1867.

My Dear Milton:

Your answer to my Norfolk letter, of which
you advise me in y'r last, has never reached me: yet, if I had
had the remotest idea where to address you, I should have
exhibited the magnanimity which illuminates y'r conduct,—and
sh'd certainly have written you again.

It is charming that you should enter life at Washington under
such agreeable auspices, and I share y'r pleasure, believing that
you will extract the honey, and not be poisoned by the darker
juices,—of that Weed they call Society, there.[138]

Indeed, indeed, y'r trip-to-Europe invitation finds me all
thirsty to go with you: but alas, how little do you know of our
wretched poverties and distresses here, – that you ask me such
a thing! My Dear Boy, some members of my family, who used
to roll in wealth, are, every day, with their own hands,

[135] Mary Day's letter of Dec. 9, which crossed with this in the mails, reported:
" Sixty copies of Tiger Lilies sold at Havens & Brown on Saturday." On Dec. 11
Lanier wrote to his brother Clifford (letter omitted): " Letter from Pa says Tiger
Lilies is selling well in Macon. As soon as the lot arrives from N. Y. (ought to
be there [Montgomery] today) do take out a copy and present, with my compliments, to Ben Screws: also to any other persons you like." (Clifford Lanier had
already bought a copy in Montgomery on Dec. 3.)

[136] The poem was entitled " To M.," published as " In the Foam " in the
Round Table of Jan. 25, 1868 (I, 12).

[137] Previously published, *Lippincott's*, LXXV, 311 (Mar., 1905); excerpt reprinted, Mims, pp. 91-92. Lanier left Prattville for Montgomery at the close
of school, Friday, Dec. 13, and went to Macon the following morning (see his
letter to Clifford Lanier, Dec. 11, 1867, here omitted).

[138] Northrup had gone to Washington, D. C., as correspondent of the New
York *Express* (see vol. N, Obituary Notices, American History Room, Syracuse
Public Library).

ploughing the little patch of ground which the war has left them, while their wives do the cooking and washing. This, in itself, I confess I do not regret: being now a confirmed lunatic on the " dignity of labor " &c: yet it spoils our dreams of Germany, ruthlessly.[139] I've been presiding over eighty-six scholars, in a large Academy at Prattville, Ala., having two assistants under me: 'tis terrible work, and the labor difficulties, with the recent poor price of cotton, conspire to make the pay very slim. I think y'r people can have no idea of the slow terrors with which this winter has invested our life in the South. Some time I'm going to give you a few simple details, which you must publish in your paper.

Tiger Lilies is just out, and has succeeded finely in Macon. I have seen some highly complimentary criticisms in a few N. Y. papers on the book: tho' they mistake the whole plan of the book, and what was written in illustration of a very elaborate and deliberate theory of mine about plots of novels, has been mistaken for the " carelessness of a dreamy " (N. Y. Evening-Mail) writer. I would I knew some channel thro' which to put forth this same theory.

What a horribly jejune and altogether pointless affair is the " Southern Society," of Baltimore! My name was published as a contributor: but I shall certainly send nothing to such a set of asses.

Do write me what you think of Tiger Lilies. H & H. don't treat me well, and advertise very slimly: indeed, I have as yet seen *no* advertisement of *theirs*. The book would sell, if properly advertised: a firm took hold of it *here,* and have already disposed of a large number of copies. – Mine have not arrived: when they come, will send you one. – I have hope of getting you something to do, for " the Telegraph," of this place, one of the largest and heaviest papers of Georgia.

Write me. I have scratched off this, in a great haste, freezing in a hotel reading-room, where a big fire is snapping and (as is the Southern custom) all the doors and windows are open.

Yr Friend

Sidney Lanier.

A letter addressed here will always find me.

[139] At Oglethorpe, 1860-1861, Lanier and Northrup had planned to study at Heidelberg.

To Clifford A. Lanier

Macon, Ga. Dec. 16th 1867.

My Dear Clifford:

A continual heavy shower of compliments and congratulations has poured upon me ever since I came here, and the reputation of Tiger Lilies is fairly established at home. And not alone at home; for here come New York papers in which splendid compliments are paid the " Singular but eccentric power " of the new writer. About a hundred and twenty copies have been sold.

May promptly gives up the Sav. trip. We leave here on the night of Thursday 19th, stay one day at Atlánta, and reach Montg'y, D. V. Saturday night.

x   x   x   x   x   x   x 140

A parlous application comes for my biography, to be pub. in " The Home Journal " of Baltimore, by J. Wood Davidson.[141] Get from Whitfield, if you can, a copy of Macon " Journal & Messenger," of Dec. 15th: in which an editorial column is devoted to my book.[142]

[140] A brief paragraph is here omitted, being mutilated beyond restoration. It seems to refer to a musicale to be given by Mrs. Whittle in Lanier's honor on Dec. 17, and a reception by Augusta Lamar Ogden on Dec. 19, apparently after the wedding ceremony (see Mary Day to Lanier, Dec. 9, 1867).

[141] A biographical sketch of Lanier was published by J. W. Davidson in his *Living Writers of the South* (New York, 1869), pp. 319-324. A search of the files of the *Southern Home Journal* for 1867-1868 reveals no biographical sketch of Lanier. That this biographical sketch was not published in a periodical before its appearance in book form is indicated in a letter from Joel Chandler Harris on June 29, 1868, apparently in answer to a letter of inquiry by Lanier (not found): " The address of the S. H. Journal, is, John Y. Slater, 293 W. Baltimore St. Mr. D., however, does not publish his sketches any more. He is going to N. Y. about the 24th of July, when I daresay he will make arrangements for the publication of his book." Harris was at this time aiding Davidson in the preparation of his *Living Writers of the South* (see Julia Collier Harris, *Joel Chandler Harris*, Boston, 1918, p. 66).

[142] No file of the Macon *Journal and Messenger* for this year has been found, but an undated clipping survives (Charles D. Lanier Collection, Johns Hopkins University) apparently from the *Telegraph*, Dec. 17, 1867. It reads in part: " Mr. Lanier, our townsman and musical friend, has sprung before us, with all the active vigor of his versatile nature, full panoplied for a joust with the carping critics of his country. . . .

How I wish you and Will were here to share the cordial things that are done and said to me! God bless you both.

Telegraphed you today to send the black coat for Salem by Express. Hope it'll get here in time.

I enclose note for Aunt Jane.

> Very hastily
>
> Sid.

To Mary Day

> [Macon, Ga., Dec. 17? 1867]

My Darling Niñita, I've been up twice this morning to see you, but was told you were lying down, – and would not let them disturb you.

Have called on Clare & Mrs Whittle –

Enclose Salem's telegram. He is probably here now, and I must go down & see him two minutes, after which I dine with Mrs Sclater.[148]

> My love, my love! I am
>
> Thine

"'Tiger Lilies' is a book of genius and originality. In it we found romance—not a word of maudlin sentimentality—humor, that made an audible laugh startle us—word-painting, that made the printed page a canvas & his pen an appreciative eye—an *en passant* mention of unobjectionable metaphysics—frequent appeals for art, especially the art of music, and above all, and pervading all, a genuine love, a passionate appreciation, a reverential worship of Nature. . . .

"To the hyper critical who may say that 'Tiger Lilies' as a novel—a work of art—is a failure, we would say that the author intended it to be something of a sketch book—the vehicle for pleasant thought and sentiment, and for the delineation of character. The plot, however, without being very exciting, is agreeably sustained throughout. . . .

"A long life, a happy life, a useful life, to you S. L.!"

[148] Mrs. Sclater is mentioned in a letter from Harry Day to Lanier, Sept. 27, 1867: "Sclater's wife has arrived– I have seen her and think I shall like her." She may have been the wife of an official of the Macon & Brunswick Railroad, for which Harry Day had begun to work, and the same person as Mrs. Schlatter of Brunswick, Ga., who, in 1875, Lanier discovered was the sister of his new friend Gibson Peacock, editor of the Philadelphia *Bulletin*. Conjectural dating from the reference to Mrs. Whittle (see note 140, above).

To Mary Day

[Macon, Ga., December 19th 1867]

How fares our royal Spouse, this marriage-morn?
Hath our Queen aught of instruction to give the King?
Will our fair Queen, if the King (who is hurried) cannot
see her immediately, send the King a Prayer-book? [144]

The King.

To Clifford A. Lanier

My Darling Clifford: Prattville, Ala. Dec. 31st 1867.

It would be entirely impossible for me to tell you the sweet
cosiness of my sitting-room which May has adorned with all
sorts of beautiful things besides herself, as we sit here alone,

[144] Lanier's request for a prayer book was undoubtedly prompted by his lack
of familiarity with the ritual of the Episcopal Church, in which he was to be
married, and of which Mary Day was a devoted member throughout life.
  The weddiing took place at Christ Church, Macon, at 4 P. M. on Thursday,
Dec. 19, 1867, the Rev. Mr. Rees conducting the ceremony. An unidentified
clipping, obviously from a contemporary Macon newspaper (Charles D. Lanier
Collection, Johns Hopkins University), gives these facts and adds: " In the
lottery of life the gifted author of ' Tiger Lilies ' has drawn a brilliant prize. . . .
We beg that he will accept our heartiest congratulations and sincerest wishes for
a future that may never be shadowed by a passing cloud." From the evi-
dence of Mary Day's letters, Oct.-Dec., 1867, Lanier's groomsmen seem to have
been: C. E. Campbell, Harry Day, Salem Dutcher, Frank Ross, Granville (Toby)
Conner, Charles Taliaferro, and Robert Plant. Mary Day's attendants were:
Lilla Hazlehurst, Georgie Conner, Clare de Graffenried, Josie Wingfield, and
three others whose names have not been discovered.
  The wedding journey seems to have been to Atlanta on Dec. 20, and to
Montgomery a day or two later, to spend Christmas with Lanier's Alabama
relatives. Salem Dutcher either accompanied the Laniers to Atlanta or joined
them there. In a letter to Mrs. Cosby Smith, Apr. 2, 1868, Mary Day Lanier
says they enjoyed " private ' oyster suppers ' " in Atlanta with Dutcher. And in
some notes made for Henry W. Lanier in 1902 she says further of Dutcher: " He
was one of our attendants at our wedding, and went with us to Atlanta, and
companioned us closely for two days, until we left to visit all the Lanier kindred
in Montgomery, Ala." (Henry W. Lanier Collection, Johns Hopkins University.)
  R. S. Lanier apparently spent the holidays in Montgomery, where his daughter
Gertrude awaited her confinement, and made a brief visit to the Sidney Laniers
in Prattville between Christmas and New Year's Day.

tonight, busily engaged in the vain endeavor to write up the numerous letters we owe to kind friends. If you and sweet Will were here, Buddy!

– But I have only time to scrawl to you that the ten copies of Tiger-Lilies you sent here are sold and Maj. Smith thinks ten more *might* be: and to ask you if you will put up ten and give them to the mail-driver whom I will instruct to call for them at Exchange.

Also, – I'm getting up my biography for Davidson, and wish to send him " The Tournament " and " Barnacles " in print, so that he may embody them in it. If you have any copy of the Round Table containing either of these, please send it me and I'll endeavor to replace it in time, as I'm going to order several back numbers of the paper.

Maydie and I send a thousand kisses to you and Will, and beg you to write to your

Bro. & Sister.

[145] Kiss dear little Sissa for us, and tell them *all* – we love them *mightily!* – Dear Aunty must hurry to come to us – Tell her – the house *keeps me!*

---

[145] The postscript is in the handwriting of Mary Day Lanier.

1868

To Clifford A. Lanier

Prattville, Ala. Jany 7th 1868

My Darling Clifford:

Mac Smith bruited amongst ye righte pleasaunte news that perhaps you and sweet Will would come to us o' Saturday next: and I dash off a hasty scrawl to you to beg you will let us know if it be so by Friday's mail.

Got y'r consignment of Tiger Lilies & Thorn-Fruit and have placed ye same on sale, minus six copies of Tiger-Lilies which I despatched to various parties. Please send me *ten* more Tiger-Lilies by first chance; also some more Thorn-Fruit. Have not had time to read T. F.: Maydie saves it for us to enjoy together o' Friday night. Saw ye notice of youuuuuuuuuuuu in ye Mail.[1] Write me of any others. Love to Auntie & Sissa & Will from

Bro. Sid & Mamie.

---

[1] Clifford Lanier, in a note to his brother of Jan. 2, 1868, had said: "A pretty notice of Meeeeeeeeeeeeee appears in the [Montgomery] *Mail* of Monday [Dec. 30], I think."

His volume *Thorn-Fruit,* published as No. 3 of Blelock & Co.'s "Library of Select Novels by Southern Authors," had apparently been issued in December as a little paper-bound book selling at fifty cents. On Jan. 9, 1868, R. S. Lanier wrote to his son Sidney: "Haven [a Macon bookseller] told me he had sold out the first lot of Cliff's book & had ordered more & thought the sale would be good. But I have no heart in it, the poor thing was so badly printed. Cliff was sold, but I think he will survive it. . . . There is native ore in him & we have seen the crude but promising workings."

In a letter to J. A. Fisher many years later (Sept. 13, 1883), Clifford Lanier wrote: "My modest *novel* essay, 'Thorn-Fruit' seems to have bankrupted the publishers, Blelock & Co, for they failed immediately afterwards & I think assigned to Eydich, N. O. but I have not been able to obtain copies from the latter firm, although B. & Co. reported that not all of the 2,000 copies had been sold."

To Jane Lanier Watt

Prattville, Ala. Jan'y 12th 1868.

My Darling Auntie:

We half-way hoped that you would drop in on us yesterday, or today: we think you're very mean because you didn't, and we're going to punish you by writing to you.

Our little town was the scene of some excitement yesterday, – tho' we hope that the agitation is now entirely abated. The Radicals, in pursuance of their keeping-the-steam-up policy, must needs hold a meeting in the streets of the town, and make speeches to a crowd of foolish negroes who, as is their usual custom, were armed with all manner of muskets, shot-guns, pistols, bludgeons &c &c. During the speaking, one of the negroes became intoxicated with whiskey and patriotism and proceeded to vent his high-wrought soul by firing his pistol in the air and giving utterance to sundry threats against the white race in general. His conduct became so outrageous that a member of the town council, passing-by, ordered him to cease on penalty of arrest and lock-up. The refractory ward immediately presented his pistol at the Councilman and swore to shoot him if he advanced, while a large crowd of armed negroes gathered around to support their friend. The Councilman, (A brave fellow: Geo. Smith, of the Sash & Blind Factory, here) immediately walked up to him; the negro fired and missed; Smith, tho' armed with a pistol, did not fire but jumped on him and wrested his pistol away. By this time, however, a dozen negroes had rushed upon Smith and thrown him to the ground; several whites on the street joined in the attempt to relieve Smith; pistols, double-barrels, knives, brickbats & bludgeons came into play; and the scene was altogether a lively one, until by some miraculous means the infuriated crowd was quieted. I hear of five wounded, – four negroes and one white, besides Smith who wonderfully escaped with a few bruises. Was in my house eating dinner, and knew nothing of the fray until I heard the shots, when, thinking we must all fight for it, I valiantly seized my pistol, made Maydie don her bonnet, and sat me down to await the enemy's charge.

Which your pickles are surely the best pickles! And don't I
eat a whole one every day, bird-seeds and all? And don't we
bless you for 'em from the bottom of our – gastronomical
apparat*uses* ?

Sandy, the wagon-driver goes to town tomorrow: please tell
Cliff that he left the bundle of books at Watt & Beall's, and
ask him to see that Bob. [Watt] puts 'em aboard the wagon.
Sandy will call.

My school is smaller than last year. The people come to me
almost with tears in their eyes, and represent their fearful
impoverishment which prevents them from sending children to
school. I have so far only sixty-five scholars: and will have to
discharge one of my assistants.

Love to everybody. Receive a hundred kisses, Darling Auntie,
from

> Your loving
>
> Sid & Mamie.

To Virginia Hankins

> Prattville, Ala. Jany 14th 1868.

My Darling Ginna:
        There is one thing which my life does entirely desire.
It is, – that you should be here, in my house, where I may love
you. Is this impossible? Can you not come to visit Lucy Price,
or Joan? [2] Meeting Cliff in Montgomery, with what delight
would he drive you here in his buggy!

    Life is short, Little One: Why deny yours and mine and
May-Day's (my Wife's) this little Eternity which a few days,
we three being together, would expand into?

    In the Christmas-days, at many feasts, by many Yule-logs, in
many throngs of loving friends, I dreamed of you, and dreamed
again. The Night which is in your eyes and on your hair

---

[2] Lucy (Louise?) Price, a former schoolmate of Virginia Hankins in Richmond,
later married a Mr. Davidson and lived at Selma, Ala.; Joan Douglas was a
cousin of Virginia Hankins, living at this time in Montgomery.

To Clifford A. Lanier

Prattville, Ala.
Jan'y 21st 1868.

My Darling:

You mentioned sometime ago that there was much writing to be done in office of Clopton, Stone & Clanton, and that a considerable salary could be paid to a steady employee in that line. Will you enquire of Mr Clopton, if there would be any chance for me to obtain such a position, and what they could afford to give? It merely occurs to me that this would be a fine refuge in case we have to leave here: an event which, in view of the Stanton affair at Washington,[10] becomes a great probability. Tell 'em I'm a very rapid writer.

I am improving somewhat, and hope to resume school duties next week. May and I will probably visit Montg'y next Friday week, Jan. 31st.

Please make the inquiry of Mr Clopton immediately, and let me know by return mail, i. e. on Friday.

May sends love to Will and Sissa and Auntie & Sallie & Aunt Mollie & Tench & Lanier & Sterling & Russell & Bobolink & John & Alfred & Laura & Bell & Jim & Lulu & all my old sweethearts.[11]

So do
       I.

To Robert S. Lanier [12]

Prattville, Ala.
Jan'y 21st 1868.

My Dear Father:

Y'r kind letter announcing for^ding of H. & H.'s draft was rec^d, and I read with great pleasure y'r encouraging account of y'r business.

---

[10] The quarrel over Reconstruction policies between President Andrew Johnson and Congress came to a head over his attempt to remove Edward M. Stanton from his office as Secretary of War without consent of the Senate.

[11] "Auntie" was Mrs. Abram (Jane Lanier) Watt; "Sallie," Sallie Lanier, and "Tench" her husband, Tench Schley; "Aunt Mollie," Mary Russell, the widow of his uncle Sidney C. Lanier, and "Russell" her son. The others were unidentified Lanier relatives and Montgomery friends.

[12] Excerpt previously published, Mims, p. 94. The first three paragraphs of

A telegram from H. & H. dated Jan. 9th, but delayed in transit here, announced that one hundred & seventy two copies only of Tiger-Lilies remained on hand, and asked if they should issue a second edition. This is very cheering, and gives me some ground of hope that I may in time realize some small profit on the book. I did not reply to the telegram, as I had previously written them, (thro' you), inquiring terms upon which they would reprint.

The draft on J. F. D. L. was remainder of am't agreed upon between myself and him, sometime ago, and went towards the last payment due H & H, whom I still owe $200.

On Friday morning last I was attacked with a hemorrhage of the lungs, which lasted, tho' *not* copious, for fifteen or twenty minutes. I went up to school and taught till twelve, when, finding myself somewhat weakened, I returned home. Have not been to the schoolhouse since, (this is Tuesday!) finding much fatigue in using my voice, together with general weakness: but am improving daily, and will resume school duties, nothing interfering, by first of next week. Cannot at all account for the attack: had been in most vigorous health all the time previous; was suffering from slight cold when I retired night before: woke up at usual hour, and found my mouth full of blood. I have no pain, beyond a slight oppression about the chest: and no cough. Had not intended to tell you of it at all: but May, with her great eyes dilating serious, thought " it wouldn't be loving, not to tell you: " and so I yielded. I hope you will not be anxious: since I feel that I shall entirely recover.

I begin to entertain serious doubts of the safety of remaining out of the city. There are strong indications here of much bad feeling between whites and blacks, especially those engaged in the late row at this place: and I have fears, which are shared by Mr Pratt [18] and many citizens here, that some indiscretion of the more thoughtless among the whites may plunge us into bloodshed. The whites have no organization at all, and the

this letter were in answer to R. S. Lanier's inquiries in his letter of Jan. 9, 1868. In a letter of Jan. 14, Hurd & Houghton had acknowledged receipt of Lanier's letter of Jan. 2 (not found), inclosing check for $200.00. This letter Lanier had apparently submitted to his father for review before posting. (See also note 5, above.)

[18] Daniel Pratt, founder of Prattville (see note 70, 1867).

affair would be a mere butchery: in addition to the fact that it might come when we were unprepared for it. The Stanton imbroglio may precipitate matters. Give me y'r views.

Clifford & Willie spent last Saturday night and Sunday with us. We had a glorious reunion, and all wished for you. May sends many kisses. Love to Uncle C & fam.

Sid.

Don't forget to send the Eclectic you spoke of. I'm casting about for a plot. Cliff is at work on a very good thing, Have no criticisms of Thorn-Fruit appeared in Macon papers.[14]

To CLIFFORD A. LANIER [15]

Prattville
Jan'y 24th 1868.

This, Dear Clifford, was born O' Thursday.
" *Leser,* wie liebst du mir."

S. L.

To ROBERT S. LANIER

Prattville　Ala.
Jan'y 24th 1868

My Dear Father:
　　　　　　　I write a short note to let you know that I am improving still, and think to resume duties by the first of next week. I suffer from no acute pain whatever, and am almost

---

[14] In his reply of Jan. 26, R. S. Lanier wrote: " Sent Cliff to-day a pleasant notice of his book in [the Macon] ' Telegraph.' . . . I have sent you ' Southern Society's' criticism of ' Tigers.' . . .

" As to your second edition: I am thinking what to say about it. It strikes me as a hard bargain that a whole first edition should be exhausted & you get not a dollar for it. At all events I say if a second edition is to be published it must not be done *now* at your risk– & I say further, never hereafter put a line of yours in press where *you* have to *risk.*"

[15] With this letter Lanier sent a copy of " Spring and Tyranny " published under the shortened title " Tyranny " (I, 13) in the *Round Table*, Feb. 22, 1868. In his answer to this letter, on Jan. 28, 1868, Clifford Lanier wrote: " ' Spring and Tyranny ' . . . is the nearest approach you have made yet to the present feeling of the general heart." The poem dealt with the plight of the Southerner under the depression of Reconstruction.

entirely relieved of the slight soreness left by the hemorrhage. Want of exercise, – which the bad weather has rendered impossible, – is, I think, the main obstruction to entire recovery.

I wrote Havens & Brown several days ago, making some enquiries about their stock of Tiger-Lilies. No answer comes. Will you be kind enough to ask if they have rec^d my letter?

May sends love: she writes to Mr Day by this mail. Love to Uncle C.

Sid.

To Robert S. Lanier

Prattville Ala.
Feb'y 10th 1868.

My Dear Father:

I have only a few minutes in which to ask y'r advice in regard to a proposition which Harry [16] brings me, and which strikes me favorably.

McClellan wishes to leave Macon: but you must be very careful to say no word of it to any one, as it would materially injure both our prospects. He wishes me to take his school, and sends proposal to take the whole thing off his hands, by March 1st. The house will afford fine rooms for you, and SISTER and Harry Day, besides May & myself. Suppose we charged you and Harry $40.$\frac{00}{100}$ per month (y'r present rates) and Sister (*with Servant*) $60. A very low calculation of school-receipts (which are paid quarterly in advance) gives, by McC.'s estimate, over $3600 per year. Then the total receipts of my business, board &c would be

$$\$3600 + \$960 \text{ (you \& Hal)} + \$720 \text{ (Sissa)}$$
$$\underline{\begin{array}{r} 960 \\ 720 \end{array}}$$

= $5280. Out of this are Expenses of Rent, & of Assistant = $2400, leaving $2880 for household expenses, which would surely support us well. Hal will give you minuter details.

---

[16] Harry Day, who had come to Prattville on a visit. Jas. B. MacLellan, mentioned following, was a friend of the Days and the Laniers.

— The general reasons which incline me to accept the prop. are 1st It provides for my future, and gives me something established: 2nd It gives you and Sissa & me & May, *a home* which *might* become permanent: 3rd the house has a fine garden which *you* could cherish: 4th May and I *must* spend the summer in Macon *anyhow,* and it would be difficult to find a suitable place. To effect the arrangement I must buy about $600 of school & House furniture from McC., for which he will take notes at 6 and 12 months.

Do confer with Hal, who has a calculation of *both* schools, and after deliberation send me your advice by Telegraph,[17] doing *all* as soon as possible, since I shall have many arrangements & negotiations to make, in the short time allowed.

— Hurd & Houghton are to bring out a 2nd Edition of T. L. without any money advanced, and share profits equally with me. They " think a second Ed. can be sold, perhaps more." I take medicine. Am very well.

Very Hastily,

Sid.

[18] Brother will see you on Wednesday night – and give all particulars. Beg you will not until then, mention it to *any* one – – for until he has again seen Mr. McC. the proposition itself is uncertain.

To Mary Day Lanier [19]

Montgomery Ala.
Feb'y 14th 1868.

My Darling Darling:

I'm just here, have been duly kissed, exclaimed at, patted on the cheek, &c &c, and have heard a thousand " O, what a shame you didn't bring Mamie's," at each one of which

[17] R. S. Lanier's objections to MacLellan's proposition and to his son's plan, because of the uncertainty of his health, are detailed in a letter of Feb. 14 to Clifford Lanier. A letter of the same date to Sidney Lanier has not been found. No further evidence has been discovered to indicate why the scheme did not materialize.

[18] The postscript is by Mary Day Lanier.

[19] Seven brief undated notes from Lanier to his wife which seem to belong

I have cringed and felt the heart-wounds which will continue to scarify me as long as I am absent from your lonely heart.

We came by Reese's Ferry, and found it at once a pleasanter and shorter road, arriving here shortly after sundown. I've had a hot punch, and an oyster stew in Sissa's room, and feel more comfortable. Have not been in to see Salem yet. He's very ill with Diphtheria and is now asleep. Have to talk with Cliff, who goes up home at 9 oclock —; 'tis now after eight.

I send you a gallon of nice oysters, and only wish I could be with you while you enjoy them.

And now God take thee in His arms, O wife of mine. God fold thee, O Half-my soul, God lift thee high and free over the world, and float thee in His Love, My Love. God bear thee in His everlasting arms, full gently, full fatherly, full tenderly, Child. God keep thee in His bosom for the bosom of thine husband, whose heart, in this first moment of his absence from thee, is all gone out in an infinite yearning for his One, his May Lilian, his Next-to-God, his Christ's-Ambassadress, his Ministress of Heaven; his

Love.

I reopen to enclose letter from Hal this moment rec^d. We will talk it over when I get there.

To CLIFFORD A. LANIER

Prattville, Ala. March 3rd 1868

My Darling Clifford:

     I enclose a letter just rec'd from Mr Chandler Harris, of Forsyth Ga. from the first paragraph of which you will observe that Mr Davidson wishes to take your life.[20]

Forward it by all means, writing in as few words as possible. Was glad to see Spring and Tyranny in R. T.: sent him our

to the early part of 1868 have also survived, but they are here omitted since they are mere memoranda concerning domestic matters, apparently dispatched by Lanier from his schoolhouse to " Mrs. Sidney Lanier/ At Home."

[20] Harris's letter has not survived. Davidson had previously requested information for a biographical sketch of Sidney Lanier (see note 141, 1867). The sketches of the two brothers appeared in *Living Writers of the South* (New York, 1869), pp. 319-324.

Sea-shore Grave a week ago.[21] Y'r letter containing stamps and Bob's receipt duly rec^d.

We wait anxiously to hear from Sissa.

I've gotten off several little poems lately: [22] but have had so many little details and arrangements growing out of school affairs to think of, that I've found it almost impossible to do anything in the novel line. How come you on? [23]

[21] " A Sea-Shore Grave " (I, 214), by Sidney and Clifford Lanier, was a tribute to their mother. It was rejected by the *Round Table* and not published until 1871, when it appeared in the *Southern Magazine*.

[22] The poems here referred to cannot be identified with certainty, but they were probably a series of poems dealing with Reconstruction evils, dated drafts of which appear in Lanier's Ledger (Henry W. Lanier Collection, Johns Hopkins University) as follows: " Laughter in the Senate," Jan. 26, 1868 (published in the *Round Table*, Apr. 11) ; " Steel in Soft Hands," Feb. 7; " Burn the Stubble," Feb. 23; and " The Raven Days," Feb. 25 (published in *Scott's Monthly Magazine*, Dec., 1868, and reprinted in the *Banner of the South*, Jan. 30, 1869). The two bitterest of these, " Steel in Soft Hands " and " Burn the Stubble," were never published by Lanier (see I, 14-15, 169-170). A copy of " The Raven Days " was probably inclosed in this letter, as indicated in the last paragraph.

Another of the poems may have been " To Our Hills " (I, 166), which, though first written on July 14, 1867, had apparently been revised in the winter of 1867-1868 and sent to his father for criticism. For on Jan. 9, 1868, R. S. Lanier wrote in reply to a letter from his son Sidney (now lost): " I have not responded yet to ' Our Hills,' the poem you sent me. I will try & take it up tomorrow night; but may say now that I am satisfied you can greatly improve it. If I thought you had the genius of Byron I should say, take the pains of Pope. Elaborate. Elaborate. Work as the sculptor does. Demosthenes said eloquence lies in *action. I* say art lies in *pains,* pains in two senses."

[23] On Jan. 21, 1868, Lanier had written to his father: " I'm casting about for a plot. Cliff is at work on a very good thing." On the same date Clifford Lanier had written to his brother, in reply to a letter announcing his recent illness: " How I yearn constantly to clasp thee to my arms, and to say to thee, *work, my beloved, only with thy pen and thy heart, thy poetry and thy philosophy and thy novels made of both; I will feed thee and thine, till thy sure reward shall come in palpable greenbacks to pay me back!* . . . Work, work at the new novel; If in the end of spring we have two books for press, I believe I can have the means to send you and Mamie to New York to *press* them." These allusions are undoubtedly to the two Reconstruction novels begun by the Lanier brothers at about this time: Sidney Lanier's *John Lockwood's Mill* (V, 231), only four chapters of which were ever finished; and Clifford Lanier's posthumously published *Carpet-baggery: a Novel by Clifford Lanier . . . 1871* (Montgomery, Ala.: The Paragon Press, 1939).

It is possible that the genesis of these two books can be traced to a suggestion made by R. S. Lanier in his letter of Feb. 17, 1867, at the time when the Sherman Military Reconstruction Bill had just been passed: " I have just finished Butler's Hudibras— strange to say— for the first time. You know the author's object was to ridicule & show up the canting, whining Roundheads. I could not help noting how pat his wit & humor hit the vulgar Radical crew of our day. History so repeats itself that many parts of Hudibras could not have

Williams [24] left here for Greenville on Saturday last. I have about 50 scholars remaining. A sight of you and Will would be a rare blessing to these sore eyes of mine! Tell Pa to come over here, when he arrives in Montg'y.

I copy for you my last. Write if you like it. Love to Auntie & Will & Sissa from Mamie &

Sid.

To Clifford A. Lanier

Prattville Ala.
March 8th 1868.

My Darling Clifford:

Such a whistling and fluting and warble-chorussing of birds, such a flirtation of winds and flowers, such a tender smiling of the spring sky, – as we have had today! I have wandered about the yard and the porch all day in a tranquil dream which had in it but one regret: – that you could not be here with me.

My heart hovers about our darling Sissa with continual solicitude, and the moments drag, while I wait to hear of her safety and happiness. God grant this may find her out of danger and blessed with her great desire; and may convey to her my reverent kiss, – which I would I might deliver to the holy little woman on bent knee.

cudgeled the modern Yankee Puritans better if the licks had been aimed at them. But those hypocritical politicians and whining clerics do not read Hudibras & so are insensible to the lash. Will not another Butler arise to tear the mask from these fellows & laugh them out of decent men's conceit? What inviting materials are afforded for a poem that would expose canting ' loyalty ' & give fame to the author! Or, if not a poem then . . . a political novel– to work the same end. I think you have the genius for it; but you would have first to examine the whole field of the controversy & also find out much of the private & public life of many of the leaders, their party tricks &C. ere you could fairly take the bull by the horns. I have never read more pithy, full kernelled words than those of Hudibras.''

[24] Nick (N. M.) Williams, Lanier's assistant, had been dismissed because the falling off of attendance at the Prattville Academy had made it financially impossible for Lanier to employ him any longer. On Feb. 28 he was paid $350.00 '' on a/c services as assistant, Prattville Academy '' (receipt in the Charles D. Lanier Collection, Johns Hopkins University). In May, 1868, Clifford Lanier advanced $22.00 to pay on a note held by Williams.

"LITTLE ELLA," MUSICAL COMPOSITION BY LANIER

Published by R. W. Offutt & Co., Montgomery, Alabama, 1868

Do inquire of Offutt if the music is yet out, which he was to publish,[25] and ask him if he would like to buy other similar pieces.

If Father should be with you, present my love, and say that I have refrained from writing him, in the daily expectation of his arrival in Montg'y.

Love to Auntie and everybody. Your visit was like an Angel's to us. We discuss it, and caress it's memory, over and over again.

Hastily

Sid.

To Milton H. Northrup [26]

Prattville Ala.
March 8th 1868.

My Dear Northrop:

Your enclosing " Phot." is recd, and I have to thank you at once for your kindly expressions and your *eidolon.*

I'm glad to see you prospering on the [New York] Express, and to infer, from your hints at European trips and the like, that the world does not wag all unfavorably towards you. I know few thing I should like better than to go a-gadding about the great world over yonder with you: but, *eheu!* – from the present

[25] The reference is clearly to *Little Ella* (A Beautiful Ballad Dedicated to Ella S. Montgomery. By Her Friend S. C. Lanier. . . . Montgomery, Ala: R. W. Offutt & Co.). The front cover (see opposite) has a picture of Ella Montgomery and a vignette head of Lanier. This is the only one of Lanier's musical compositions published during his lifetime. A brief notice of this publication appeared in the New Orleans *Picayune*, Mar. 19, 1868. After referriing to Lanier's novel and poems, the reviewer said apropos of *Little Ella*: " But he is also a composer of no little merit, and a musician of rare skill, drawing from the flute— besides being master of other instruments—music of such brilliant power, airy warbling, and delicate, exquisite beauty, as none but an exceptional genius can give forth from that instrument. . . . By-the-by, though Sid. Lanier has not exactly the Byronic style of features, it strikes us he is, to say the least, a type or two less removed therefrom than the smudgy ' likeness ' that graces the cover of ' Little Ella.' " (Clipping in the Charles D. Lanier Collection, Johns Hopkins University.) Though dated on the cover 1866, it was apparently not published until 1868. For the words, see I, 9.

[26] Previously published, *Lippincott's*, LXXV, 312 (Mar., 1905); excerpt reprinted in Mims, p. 88.

complexion of affairs, private as well as political, it is like that I, who have loved Germany all my life, must after all die with only a dream of the child-land.

My book has been as well received as a young author could have expected on his first plunge, and I have seen few criticisms upon it which were not on the whole favorable. My publishers have just made me an offer to bring out a Second Ed. on very fair terms: from which I infer that the sale of the article is progressing.

Have rec^d. a paper marked " Compliments of Mrs Mary E. Tucker," – the same being a Syracuse Courier and Union, containing a very *sweet* notice of Tiger-Lilies.[27] Tell me something of the lady: – whom you doubtless know.

And pardon a scrawl from a man somewhat spent with the drudging struggle for daily bread, and utterly unfit, in his isolated country-life, to convey to you anything of greater interest than that he is

Your Friend
Sidney Lanier.

To Robert S. Lanier

Montgomery   Ala.
March 16th 1868.

My Dear Father:

I have refrained from writing you, in the daily expectation of hearing of y'r arrival at Montgomery in obedience to Sister's call. I had fully expected to see you on Friday: was disappointed: and again am disappointed, on learning that you were left by the train this morning. Hoping to meet you tonight, I had postponed my return to Prattville until daylight tomorrow morning: but will leave this afternoon at Four, since I have now no one to take charge of school in my absence.

Have just had the pleasure of saluting my young nephew and his Mother.[28]

[27] *Courier and Union*, Feb. 25, 1868.
[28] Edward Shannon was born on Mar. 16, 1868.

Shall remain in Prattville until the close of the school term, – about 7th July.

I suppose of course you will go to New Orleans, before returning to Macon. We shall also expect to see you at Prattville. Do write me on y'r arrival here. May sends love.

Very Hastily

Sid.

To Robert S. Lanier

Prattville, Ala.
April 7th 1868.

My Dear Father:

My Assistant, Mrs Morgan, has suddenly arrived at the conclusion to go North where she has friends, and, although I hold notes and accounts fully sufficient to meet my indebtedness to her, I fear I shall be unable to collect enough to settle with her, within the short time allowed. Can you arrange to loan me a hundred dollars, within the next week?

During the last six weeks I've paid out something over Five hundred dollars, and find myself pretty well drained.[29]

Will return you y'r hundred as soon as possible.

Maydie is well. We've both been hard at work all the week. I've written four somewhat elaborate pieces of music, which I send to New Orleans, for sale, tomorrow.[30]

Shall send you a poem for Reese in a few days.[31]

[29] By April, 1868, the Prattville Academy was in process of dissolution, and Lanier had faced the fact that he would do well to hold it together, and to collect tuition, for the rest of the term. In a letter of Apr. 2 to Mrs. Cosby Smith, Mary Day Lanier spoke of the "uncertain present" and of their approaching departure from Prattville. Of her husband she wrote: "He has not been as strong or cheerful since his sickness of two months ago; but few see that besides myself. . . . The school has decreased very greatly— for no one can spare the money or the children from home."

[30] None of these were published during Lanier's lifetime; but one of them may have been *Love That Hath Us in the Net* (to words by Tennyson), published by A. E. Blackmar & Co., New Orleans, 1884.

[31] Anderson Reese had apparently succeeded J. R. Sneed as editor of the Macon *Telegraph.* (In a letter of June 29, 1868 to Sidney Lanier, J. C. Harris said that

May sends you a very loving kiss, in which she is heartily joined by Yr loving

Sid.

TO VIRGINIA HANKINS

Prattville, Ala.
April 12th 1868.

My Little Ginna has been still, and has not sung me an out-of-the-world song in a long time. Why? Has she forgot how, long ago, she appointed herself to be a Brown Bird on the Eden tree, and sang to me " along the glare? " [32] And has she forgot that the old thunder-peal is still sounding among the rocks of the world, and the lion is still seizing his prey, and the serpents are still hissing, and Adam is still sad?

Ah, me; this wee trilling of the little Brown Bird was better and *is* better than the sound of a trumpet in the battle: for there are some men of us that like to move up into the fight to the sounds of " flutes, and the Dorian mood of soft recorders," and I swear that those same small treble notes of yours have been better ennerving to me than any clash of cymbal and clarion. It is five years now, Little One, and five years is a long way for these tiny bird-notes to be heard. Sing to me again.

How, in this spring, have I tenderly dwelt upon the out-shooting of buds and the flower-miracles that will go on about you there in the Old Castle, and the new smile that the Bay will wear, and the sweet wreaths of the mist that will float and curl and pray upward from the waters, and the long sweet days that will set your pure heart a-dreaming, and the warm sunsets and the silvery moon-rises that will glow and shimmer over your locust trees, and the fair grass that will play Sir Walter Raleigh for you and fling down his green cloak for your dainty

Sneed was going to establish a new newspaper in Savannah, Ga.) The poem may have been a contribution submitted to the *Telegraph* or a commemoration of the wedding of Reese and Viola Ross of Macon (see Harry Day to Lanier, June 1(?), 1868). It has not been identified, and possibly may not have been written.

[32] The allusion is to a poem Lanier had written to Virginia Hankins (see note 28, 1864). The quotation in the following paragraph is from Milton's *Paradise Lost* (inaccurately given).

foot to tread, and the fair green alleys of the woods that will sometimes rustle and shiver among all their leaves when you walk down among them!

Sing some more for

S. L.

To Robert S. Lanier

Prattville, Ala. May 20th 1868

My Dear Father:

Your last letter to me, recᵈ a month ago, stated that you would write again in a day or two, and I have been anxiously expecting to hear from you daily, the more especially as I had learned through Harry [Day] that you were quite ill. Since y'r last came I've written you twice, and fear, from your post-script to Sissa's letter, that my letter did not reach you.

I have not been so well as usual since the warm weather set in, and I think quite seriously of resigning my position at the end of this scholastic month, – which will be next week. I should, in that event remain here for six weeks longer; as I have already paid board for a part of that time, and, further, would be unable to find elsewhere a boarding-place which offered so many advantages of cheapness as well as of sur- roundings. We are delightfully situated; perched upon the side of a hill over looking the whole village, and befriended by the most magnificent oaks and luxuriant grasses. Our room is in a distant wing of the rambling house, and is very secluded: tho', in one sense, in the midst of company, since it opens into a finely-stocked classical library, collected by a son of our host, who is now at Heidelberg. I am anxious to write some things which have engaged my attention lately, in the form of essays: and could employ six weeks I hope, to some profit.[33]

---

[33] The metaphysical essays referred to here (and in his letter of May 28) are probably the same ones he had first started working on in the summer of 1867 in anticipation of a professorship of philosophy at the University of Alabama, and revived now in a renewal of this forlorn hope, drafts of which survive in his Ledger (V, xlix, note 95).

The rented house in which the Laniers had lived during the winter had been sold unexpectedly, and they had been compelled to move on May 1. He and his wife boarded in the home of a Dr. Smith for the rest of their stay in Prattville (see the following letter and also Mary Day Lanier's letter to Mrs. Cosby Smith, June 6, 1868, here omitted).

Mrs Fulton has written us that she was endeavoring to persuade you to buy the Troutman house, which, she adds, has been just repaired, newly fenced, and put in thorough order, and with, I think, forty acres of land, is offered for $8,000. Have you any idea of making a purchase? If so, I regard it in the highest degree advisable to make it *immediately*: for the favorable turn of impeachment [34] will attract democratic capitalists south, and the *un*favorable turn will, it would seem, attract *radical* emigrants: so that, either way, the present crisis is likely to result in an immediate enhancement of property-values.

I hold about Three hundred and fifty dollars of accounts which are good, but which will probably not be available, for the most part, until the next crop is realized upon — This amount would have paid off the small remainder of my debt to Mrs Morgan, my assistant,[35] and would have left enough for a month or two in Macon. As it is, I shall be compelled to borrow another hundred from you, if you can spare it: and would be glad to get it at an early date. It will suffice for all needs, for the next two or three months.

The plan of which you spoke when you were here, — of travelling during the summer — will be impossible for me, I fear. I shall be compelled to devote myself to hard work with the pen: or with whatever else may offer the prospect of making any money. I shall be glad if you will be on the look-out for any position available for the summer. Have just rec^d a very gentlemanly and kind letter from Mr Bonnell, inquiring if I would accept the place of Prof. of music in the College: but

[34] The impeachment trial of President Andrew Johnson, resulting in acquittal, lasted from Mar. 23 to May 26, 1868.

[35] In his letter of May 23, 1868, R. S. Lanier had advised that if it was imperative for his son to resign his position at the Prattville Academy, he should save all he could on unpaid accounts by getting notes or due bills from his debtors and discount them with Mr. Pratt or some other responsible citizen.

Lanier's financial status at the conclusion of the Prattville venture is not entirely clear. That he emerged in debt seems to be indicated by a letter of Dec. 30, 1868, from G. L. Smith of F. E. Smith & Co. (probably a Prattville banking firm), which said in part: "Your esteemed favor of the 24th inst is just at hand with enclosure of draft on N. Y. for fifty dollars which will be duly credited on your note. We further say that on receipt of the one hundred & ninety dollars which you propose to pay on the 4th January next, we will forward to you the note, and thus cancel all further claim of the Trustees." The letter concluded with a personal expression of sympathy for Lanier's plight.

there are several weighty reasons which will induce me to decline.[36] He had not mentioned this project to his colleagues: and probably does not wish it spoken of.

Maydie is very well, and sends a hundred kisses to you and dear Sissa & baby. She wrote you on Monday.

With great love,

Sid.

From Mary Day Lanier to Clifford and Wilhelmina Lanier

Prattville.
May 26th. 1868.

Dearest Cliffy! and sweet Willie,

I am watching my precious sweetheart while he sleeps – quite exhausted by the fatigue of going to the table for the first time since Friday – And, to *fill* the hour with treasures, I've come to talk to my blessèd brother and sister, of whom we daily talk and think. We say: " O, this lovely day! – this rare spot –, hidden among the old forest oaks, where we hear only Nature's voice all day! — it would be perfect, would'nt it? if just Cliffy and Willie were here – " – And then: " It would help to make you well and to rest you, my precious, if our darling " Tiffy " – could be with us? " – to which Sidney nods his head, with one of those *rare* sweet smiles which bloom on *his* face from weakness, pain, or self-sacrifice: bitter roots for heavenly fruit. Then, when I bring to his bedside an inviting little supper, and enjoy his appreciation of it – he pauses between two tastes, with: " Little Maydie, do you

---

[36] In his reply of May 23, 1868, R. S. Lanier urged acceptance of the offer, giving details of the terms: the program of teaching could be made flexible, from five to seven hours a day, with salary ranging from $1000 to $1400 annually; Lanier could use his spare time, including a three months' vacation, to improve himself in music and possibly to write a text-book on the subject; he and his wife could live with R. S. Lanier at a very reasonable board and have the use of his horse for exercise. He concluded that no other prospect of employment in Macon offered such favorable terms– " We all must work & no body who works industriously will lose *social position* or *reputation*." (For Lanier's answer see note 39, below.)

believe that Tiffy and Willie have such nice strawberries for
supper every evening? " And Maydie is afraid they *hav'nt!*

Sidney wrote you that he was tired and unwell – but his will
and energy deceived us both as to the degree of his feebleness.
He kept up one week too long, then failed utterly.[87] He has
been in bed three or four days without desire to rise, or
strength to sit up more than an hour, does not even try to read,
but lies there as calm and still and *sweet* and *good* as little
Eddie [Shannon] himself. He does not fret, as I have feared
he would at the forced inaction, – is so loving as to admit no
more than that it *would* be very irksome if he had not his happy
nurse. Indeed, to me they have been happy days – and the few
hours of doubt and anxiety last only long enough to endear
every privilege.

Dr. Smith has been kind in his attentions – and forbids him
all work of either hands or brain, under penalty of illness. It is
truly strange to see one so prostrated without any definite complaint. The Doctor says he must have wine, and promised to
inquire for some that is made here; that, with a tonic and
sedative now in use are the only remedies he considers necessary.

The latter has affected our patient very happily; you know he
is *hard to quiet!* I want him to spend a day with *you* – the
last of this week, or first of next – the change will do him so
much good. He feebly protests – and is half-crazy to go all
the time; but he longs to take me too – which is a luxury that
we *must* deny ourselves – it being simply *a luxury.* He thinks
he may possibly be able to go some day with the Doctor – who
is called there every two or three weeks. I know he will come
to you on Friday or Saturday if any mode of conveyance offers.
I want him to attend the concert of Friday night – it would
refresh him, mentally – but it is improbable that the chances
will be so gracious to my scheme. Can you imagine how
charming it was to hear from you, my Hermano? Since your
birthday we had not heard from father, Sissa – or anyone else
of the family. A short note came from Sissa last week – – but

---

[87] In a letter to Mrs. Cosby Smith on June 6, 1868, Mary Day Lanier wrote:
" My dear husband's health has suddenly failed again, without– however– any
symptoms of pulmonary weakness. He taught until– two weeks ago [*c.* May 23]–
he could neither walk nor stand up any longer, was confined to his bed for some
days from excessive prostration– and still continues a fine subject for *petting.*"

told us nothing except that she had been at home two or three weeks – and all were happy and our little nephew sweet as ever. Sidney was anxious for information of their plans, and has been disappointed by the long silence. I know Willie is *half* lost without dear Sissa and Baby! Auntie gone, too: how changed all must be at the scene of our former reunions –

Do you resent *crossed* letters – – when they are *not " cross " ?* Please, no ! – – but my little boy is waking and I will give ye our blessing and go to him. Cheer him by a letter: he wants one from you.

Du Schwester-Liebchen

To Robert S. Lanier [38]

Prattville, Ala. May 28th 1868.

My Dear Father:

We had no mail last Wednesday, and so your three letters arrived together today.

One of them contains check for One hundred Dollars, for which prompt assistance you have my very earnest thanks.

I have been in bed since last Friday, – a week today – and am only just able to get out today. I seem to have had a general break-down, physical and mental, from overwork, and am still suffering from intense feebleness in all faculties. I've been very deeply engaged in working out some metaphysical ideas, for some time, and I think the intense application of my mind to these things, – an application which goes on all the time, whether I sit at desk or walk the street, – has resulted in this protest of nature against all work and no play. I think it improbable that I shall be able to teach more this session, which is now within a month or so of expiration, and have no doubt that my plea of ill-health will be readily and cheerfully admitted by the parties interested in the school. Maydie and I have had many deliberate discussions on the matter, and it would seem, all things considered, that there is no resource for me, in order to get through the hot months now approaching, save to resign and devote myself to building up a little strength.

[38] Excerpt previously published, Mims, p. 96.

Before your letter reached me, I had written Mr Bonnell that purely on account of my attention having been so exclusively turned to other matters, I could not accept his proposition. I have not time now to detail all the reasons which influenced me in making this decision: but have no doubt you would recognize their validity.[39]

There is some prospect of my doing something in the matter of the Tuscaloosa prof-ship: tho' the Trustees, who are appointees of the state, are so hampered by the expected change of State government that nothing can be certainly predicted as to their action: the point under discussion with them being, whether in view of the possible immediate reversal of their proceedings, they had better act at all. A meeting of the Board is to be held June 10th at Montgomery, at which I hope to be present. In the event of their holding an election, I would not despair of getting a chair.

I close this hastily to catch the mail. Love to Sissa and Monsieur le President Shannon.

Sid.

To Hurd & Houghton

Prattville, Ala. May 28th 1868

Messrs. Hurd & Houghton:

Dr Sirs:

I write to ascertain if anything whatever has been done lately in the way of sales of "Tiger-Lilies" — and if there remains any prospect to justify the issue of a Second Edition, as contemplated in Y'r last letter.[40]

Very Truly Yrs,

Sidney Lanier

[39] No further statement has been discovered of Lanier's reasons for turning down the offer of a professorship of music at Wesleyan College. One suspects that the principal reason was his hope for the more important professorship of philosophy at the University of Alabama, mentioned in the next paragraph. But that did not materialize.

[40] In a letter of Feb. 27, 1868, Hurd & Houghton had stated that they would print a new edition as soon as 75 more copies were sold. On June 3 they wrote

To Robert S. Lanier [41]

Prattville, Ala. June 1st 1868.

My Dear Father:

Wrote you quite a letter last Friday, acknowledging receipt &c: and scratch a short note today, to say that Maydie has just received a letter from Mrs Fulton, announcing that she will be very glad to take us to board with her for the summer.[42] This is a very pleasant arrangement and I communicate it to you, in order that you may be at no trouble on our account, in the matter of looking out for places. I have now the prospect of being able to command funds sufficient to supply our wants until October, by which time I hope to make some business arrangements for the ensuing year.

Mrs F. writes us that she is very anxious to have you & Sissa for neighbors, I suppose she refers to the Troutman place, and should be very glad indeed to see you and Sissa snugly and permanently esconsed there.

My resignation was very pleasantly received by the President of the Board, who seemed to fully recognize the necessity for it, and was apparently very appreciative of all my motives in the business. It is probable that my old Assistant Williams will succeed me, here.

I shall go to work on my essays: and on a course of study in German and in the latin works of Lucretius, whom I have long desired to study. Maydie well.

Love to Sissa & You from

Sid.[43]

---

in answer to Lanier's letter that they would not print a new edition until the present one was exhausted, but that if the fall crop was good and the prospects were "flattering," a new edition should sell.

[41] Excerpt previously published, Mims, p. 96.

[42] In his letter of June 9 R. S. Lanier made the following objections to Lanier's plan to spend the summer at Mrs. Fulton's: "Her situation is so destitute that she cannot keep up a table such as I would wish . . . To live in that family is in a measure to become a part of it, to be affected with its trials, struggles & troubles. . . . The residence & grounds are so decayed that [you] could not sit down in the midst of them without great discomfort if not sadness."

[43] This is the last letter by Lanier from Prattville that has survived. But his movements for the next ten days can be pieced together out of evidence from

To a Publisher [44]

[Macon, Ga., Summer, 1868?]

Messrs. H. & H. of N. Y. recently published for me – the Author – a book entitled " T. L. A Novel by S. L.".

In spite of the facts that Messrs H & H had not sufficient interest in the book to authorize them in advertizing: that other avocations, prevented me from paying any attention to the matter: and that the entire book-trade was at that time experiencing an unprecedented dullness: – the First Ed. was almost immediately sold off.

collateral correspondence of the period. On June 6, 1868, Mary Day Lanier wrote from Prattville to Mrs. Cosby Smith: " He [Lanier] has been compelled to resign his post as Principal in the Academy, being overcome by any slight fatigue, so as to make any attempt to resume teaching an hazardous and foolish risk. We are, therefore, at liberty to move homeward when we will; – but there are sundry advantages combined in our present residence which dispose us to remain here until the opening of July– as first intended– not the least of which is economy."

These plans, however, were changed quite suddenly. For before receiving R. S. Lanier's letter of June 9 (see note 42, above)—in which his father expressed a wish to stop in Montgomery on his return from a trip to New Orleans, where he had gone to settle the estate of E. B. Shannon, in order to discuss his son's future plans—the Sidney Laniers were already on their way to Macon. By June 10 they were settled for the summer at Scott's Mills. (See Mary Day Lanier's letter of June 10, 1868, to Mrs. Cosby Smith, dated from " Mrs. Fulton's," expressing her chagrin that her pregnancy was a matter of common knowledge in Macon, and begging Mrs. Smith to come out to the plantation to see her.)

One piece of evidence exists which seems to indicate a later date for their departure for Macon. It is a surviving program in Lanier's handwriting (MS, Charles D. Lanier Collection, Johns Hopkins University) of a " Concert for the Orphans," Prattville Methodist Church, June 12, 1868. It is possible that the concert was not given or that Lanier stayed over for it and followed his wife to Macon a few days later. What is more interesting is that Lanier is listed as the performer of two of his own musical compositions, previously unknown— *Sounds from the Army* and *Sea-Spray* (both for the flute)—in addition to Strokoschi's *The Magic Bell*. Other performers listed are Lanier's old friend Mrs. Montgomery, Mrs. G. L. Smith of Prattville, and Mrs. Emily Wheat (sister of his music teacher at the Academy, Mrs. Hannah Williams).

[44] The MS indicates that this was a first draft, retained by Lanier. Whether the letter was finally sent, and to whom, and whether the sale materialized, are matters which have not been discovered. The conjectural dating has been arrived at from the fact of Hurd & Houghton's unsatisfactory report concerning a second edition of *Tiger-Lilies* on June 3 (see note 40, above) and the fact of Lanier's known financial straits at the beginning of the summer of 1868.

Other absorbing duties render it impossible for me to push the book, and I desire to sell the Copy-Right and Copper-plates. I offer both for five hundred Dollars.

The hearty commendations which T. L. rec^d from such Journals as the N– Y. Round Table, the N. Y. Ev'g Mail, the N. Y. Tribune, the Cincinnati Commercial, and many others of all shades of opinion would seem to indicate that the work might be a source of profit to an enterprising firm –

I send by this mail a copy of T. L. for your Examination.

An early reply to my proposition will greatly oblige

Your obdt Svt

Sidney Lanier

To Mary Day Lanier [45]

[Savannah, Ga? July 17, 1868?]
On Board " Lizzie Boker ".

Terrestrial Time – Friday Morning.

Time by My Account ⎱ NIGHT
Being absent from Thee ⎰

Young Eager-Soul is arrived and writeth to the Wifely Soul his husband's-greeting and his lover's-kiss and his great longing for the bosom whereon only his head findeth pillowage and for the gray eyes wherein only his heart findeth rest. And he sweareth that thou, O Viola, hast sung thyself and hummed thyself and played thyself through his brain all the night, until, here in the early breeze of the morn, there is no landward

[45] This and the following letter to Mary Day Lanier indicate that, after the failure of the Prattville Academy, Lanier contemplated a place for himself in the business world. Early in July he had accompanied his father to Brunswick, Ga., where Mr. Charles Day had extensive holdings in real estate (see Gertrude L. Shannon's letter of July 8 to Wilhelmina C. Lanier and Charles Day's letter to Lanier, Aug. 15, 1868). This second trip was made in connection with the same business.

A surviving program (Charles D. Lanier Collection, Johns Hopkins University) shows that Lanier participated in a concert of the Adelphian Society at Wesleyan on Monday, July 13, 1868. Hence the conjectural dating of this letter—July 17 being the first " Friday " thereafter (his second letter from Brunswick bearing the date July 20, 1868).

breath of the Sea which bringeth not *thee* in upon his wing,
even as Camarlzabod [46] went sailing on the Afrite's pinion:
and there is no vapor-wreath ascending from the water that
beareth not *thee* framed in its ring, till thou glitterest like the
nine diamonds of Guinevere, that Lancelot flung in the river
at Camelot: and here art thou rising and falling and swaying
in the lit sheen-spaces that the keen sun-rays have wrought
under the depths of the water: and yonder thou art bending
like Titania upon the top of a willow-tree fringing the bank;
and I, thy true husband, thank thee, my true wife, that distance
hath not power upon us nor time can be our king, since thou
art good enough to be and stay with me through all the
moments.

This, hurried, with my hand upon thy head and my lip upon
thy lip,

From

Thine.

To Mary Day Lanier

Brunswick Ga
July 20. 1868

My Darling Sweet Wife:

I thought that I had at least two hours in which to
write you, the regular hour for the return boat to leave here
being 12 M: but it has just been announced (now 10 O'clock)
that the steamer is approaching the wharf, and so my time is
cut down to a few minutes. I've been hard at work since I came
here: have made several little speeches to the City-Council, and
to a meeting of the citizens, and have had an immense deal of
outside palaver and pow-wow-ing to do. The talents which I
have developed as a pow-wow-ist utterly astound me, and I
begin to ask myself, am I after all sunk so low as to be able to
make a good politician! ? ! God forbid it: but I am fearful.

---

[46] The allusion is apparently to " The Amours of Prince Camaralzaman and
the Princess Badoura " in the *Arabian Nights' Entertainment.*

We found some unexpected opposition here, and it has taken some little trouble to remove it: but the citizen's meeting has just passed a set of resolutions (drawn up by me) instructing the City Council in the most unequivocal manner to comply with the proposition of the contracting parties, and in order to make these instructions final and binding, they are now balloting, as is required by City Ordinance. The result is not at all doubtful: since the opposition are confined entirely to a couple of members of the board of aldermen, who have rendered themselves very unpopular by their course in regard to the matter.

I have as yet been able to take but two rides with Maj. Dart over your land: and, although these have given me some of the features of the tract, I desire to remain, in order to make a thorough exploration of the tract, being loth to leave (since I am *here*) before possessing myself of every possible item of information which could hereafter make it desirable to send any one here. Have not been yet able to get out to the Clay tract: Maj. Dart was on the Committee of Council to whom the proposition was referred; and, although I went after him in the buggy yesterday afternoon, was unable, on that account, to accompany me.

The revenue cutter Nansemond is here, and will probably go up to Savannah next Wednesday or Thursday. Her officers are very polite, and offer to take me up, if I desire it. The regular boat will not leave here again until next Monday. It is therefore uncertain what time I shall return. I can only say, that I shall kiss you *anyhow* by Tuesday week (tomorrow-week), and *very probably* by next Friday night.

If you only knew, my darling, how rapidly this has been written, you wouldn't laugh at the horrible scrawling. Read it to our dear Father. Kiss Hal. I wrote you from Savannah.

I am, My Wife, thy true, true lover, thy faithful-hearted, thy longing

Sidney.

FROM PAUL H. HAYNE [47]

" Copse Hill," Ga R. R.
(18 *miles from Augusta*)
Sep 7th 1868:–

My Dear Mr. Lanier;

— Thanks for your *exceedingly* pleasant, &
entertaining letter. I like to receive such epistles. They warm
one's heart up, acting like a kind of spirit*ual* (not spirit*uous*
liquor), & producing as Holmes says, the " true, champaigny
old-particular, brandy, punchy feeling ! ".

You tell me, that I ought not to curse DESTINY, or to call
HER a " harridan" who has placed laurels upon my brow
&c!

My kind friend! I really am grateful for your compliment,
but alas! I know that *my* place is at the very *bottom* of *Parnassus,* & that in an age like ours, so fruitful of great thoughts
set to majestic harmonies, the music of MY poor little pipe is
not likely to survive a single year after the humble Minstrel
has departed. — — —

It surprised me beyond measure to hear that YOU are a
sufferer from *ill - health.* How a man with the insubordinate
" stomach " you describe, COULD have written *" Tiger Lillies,"*
is to me, the most puzzling of problems !!

---

[47] In an introduction to some letters of Sidney Lanier published in the *Critic,*
Feb. 13, 1886, Hayne said (VIII [o. s.], 77): " In the year 1867, if memory
serves me, a poem by him in one of the Southern periodicals attracted my notice,
It was a brief lyric, distinguished by a peculiar, and scarcely definable quality of
fancy, which affected the reader much as a loving observer of nature might be
affected by the strange, golden remoteness of an October horizon. I wrote to the
young poet, who was more than a decade my junior, some words of appreciation
touching these verses; and he replied in a manner so cordial that thenceforth a
correspondence was established between us, which, though with many interruptions, continued down to a period closely preceding his death." The poem of
Lanier's that attracted Hayne's attention has not been identified.

It is clear from a letter of Charles Day to Lanier, Aug. 15, 1868, that Hayne
had written to Lanier before that date, but hardly as early as 1867, as stated
above. The letter here printed is probably Hayne's second, in reply to Lanier's
first (now lost) to him. Hayne's use of x x x as a mark of punctuation has been
changed to — — —, since the former symbol is used in the present edition to
indicate *lacunae* in the MS. His whimsical underscorings have been strictly
followed: italics for one, small capitals for two.

Why, the animal life of that tale is superabundant. I pictured its author to myself as a young Giant –, hale, healthful, & happy! .

Certain I am that your constitution is sound at the CORE; & that these " megrims &c " will disappear like foul mists of morning. – – –

Apropos of the " R. Table " I fear we have *both* been a little unjust. With all its manifest faults, & shortcomings, this *weekly* is the only periodical of its class in America, which a thoughtful person can read with the certainty of being interested, often *instructed*.[48]

Disagreeing " *toto coelo* " with some of its *general* principles, & regarding not a few *indi[vid]ual* articles as equally impertinent & unjust, – I have nevertheless, come to estimate the " R T " as a sort of " *institution* ", the destruction of which would sincerely afflict me !. – – –

Have I seen *Bulwer Lytton's " New Poems "* ? – Yes, & perused many of them with great care. They show an immense versatility of fancy, multifarious scholarship, & an elaborate artistic conscientiousness, but the impulsive glow & fervour of *genius* are wanting. Compare him with Swinburne, for example. Truly as I detest the foul imagination of the *latter,* there can be no question as to the vast superiority of his *poetic genius*; = B. Lytton is, however, *a gentleman*: he deals with no " Petronian abominations," & would scorn to wallow like a hog among the atrocious conceptions of the *nastiest* beasts that ever breathed, I mean, the so-called Poets of the latter Roman Empire! – – –

As for WM MORRIS, I, – for one, consider him as beyond doubt, the *purest, sweetest, noblest* NARRATIVE poet, G. Britain has produced since CHAUCER! *This* may sound exaggerated, nevertheless 'tis simply TRUE !

By all means, procure his works, " Jason," & " The Earthly Paradise."

(By the way, let me remark, that " *Not Dead* ", was composed, in part, before I knew that such a *man as Morris existed!*

---

[48] Lanier's poem, " Life and Song " (I, 16), appeared in the *Round Table* of Sept. 5, 1868. It is not mentioned in any of his letters.

The stanza is an old *English stanza,* & the *refrain* of course, may be regarded as one of the most common of artistic points).

Please tell *your wife* how proud I am that any verses of mine, attracted her notice & praise. With best regards to HER, & hoping that you will write soon, I am as Always,

Faithfully yours,

Paul H. Hayne

To Clifford A. Lanier [49]

Macon, Ga.
Oct. 1st 1868.

My Darling Clifford:

I had a fearful trip back, being ill with dyspepsia insomuch that I was fain lie down all the way, and suffer grimly. Since I reached here, have been suffering with very bad sore-throat, and am only strong enough today to scratch you a line. I send the copies of the Golden Wedding,[50] with names worked on each. Please make the distribution accordingly.

Maydie & Boy well.[51] Love to everybody.

Hastily

Sid.

[49] No letters by Lanier between July 20 and Oct. 1, 1868, have survived (and only three more for the rest of this year). Presumably, with the exception of the short trips indicated, his residence for this period was in or near Macon, though just how much of the summer he and his wife spent at Mrs. Fulton's plantation has not been discovered.

In addition to Lanier's two business trips to Brunswick in July, he visited Montgomery for the celebration of the golden wedding anniversary of his grandparents, Sterling and Sarah Lanier, on Sept. 27. He had just returned to Macon at the time of writing this letter.

[50] " The Golden Wedding " (I, 17) was first published as a privately printed brochure.

[51] Lanier's first child, Charles Day Lanier, had been born on Sept. 12, 1868 (see Clifford Lanier's letter of congratulation dated Sept. 16). For this occasion they had apparently moved into the city, but it was another two months before they were permanently settled in a Macon home (see note 56, below).

To Clifford A. Lanier

Macon Ga.
Nov. 4th 1868.

My Dear Clifford:

I was glad to get your letter this morning, and, as I am in town today, reply immediately tho' life is so smooth and even here that I find no prominences whatever to tell you about.

I've been quite busy for the last two months, pushing some researches into the theory of Greek accents and Latin construction and German syntax. Have also finished and sent to Hurd & Houghton a small volume of Essays, which I shall try to sell to them — [52] Have not yet heard from them in relation to the matter, and as the essays are upon somewhat recondite matters I fear that the dullness in book-trade will not authorize H & H to buy.

Besides my regular studies, I have now another book on the stocks, which, if I could have but one week's access to Astor Library, I am certain I could make a great book. It is to be a novel in verse, with several lyric poems introduced by the action. The plot is founded on what was called " the Jacquerie," a very remarkable popular insurrection wh. happened in France about the year 1359, in the height of *Chivalry*. The subject is so beautiful and has taken so entire hold of me that I can scarcely think of aught else. But, unfortunately, I have only the very meagre account of the business given in Froissart, and am terribly crippled in my historical allusions by this fact. One week at Astor Library! and alas for poverty! I've already written a part of the book. I send you one of the *little* poems which

---

[52] One of these essays was probably " Retrospects and Prospects," a first draft of which had been written the previous year (see note 64, 1867), though it was not published until 1871; another, "Nature Metaphors," which was apparently written in the summer of 1868, though not published until 1872 (V, 280, 306). Still others may have been the metaphysical essays yet remaining in MS (see note 33, above). No letter from Hurd & Houghton relative to this prospective volumes of essays has been found. They were later submitted to several publishers, through the agency of the American Literary Bureau, with no success, and finally returned to Lanier in Dec., 1869 (see J. K. Medbery to Lanier, Feb. 9, 1870).

would occur in the course of the plot. It is to be full of rapid action.[53]

I enclose a letter wh. I've just received and wh. has amused us here mightily. The writer, Mrs Caroline C. R. Parker, is, I *believe,* connected with the Atlantic Monthly. I know I've seen her name in some such connection.[54]

I shall be glad if you will send me a copy of the Golden Wedding when published.[55] If you would send one *marked* to " The Telegraph " of Macon, and to " The Republican " of Savannah, it might be of assistance to me.

My boy grows apace, and his mother, tho' with occasional set-backs, improves. She sends a thousand kisses to *you three,* – you, and Willie, and – and soforth. What would I not give to have you in our grove, one of these splendid days! We won't get into the house for three weeks, yet.[56] It is not settled whether I shall go to Athens. The election comes off the latter part of November.[57] I would infinitely prefer leisure to write, during next year; but this is of course impossible.

Kiss Aunt Jane for me, and remember me very lovingly to Mr Clopton. I long to see Willie and you.

Very Hastily,

Your loving

Sid.

Please take care to *send the enclosed letter back* soon. It might be necessary, if any trouble should arise about the matter, tho' of course I do not apprehend any.

[53] This is the first mention in Lanier's letters of his plans for a long narrative poem, " The Jacquerie," on which he worked intermittently for the rest of his life, but never completed. The " little poem " inclosed was undoubtedly one of the three intercalary " Songs for ' The Jacquerie ' " (see notes, vol. I).

[54] See note 82, 1867, for an excerpt from this letter.

[55] Clifford Lanier had reprinted " The Golden Wedding " in a Montgomery newspaper of Nov. 2.

[56] In Sept., 1868, a house in suburban Vineville (formerly belonging to Abner Powers) had been bought by Gertrude Lanier Shannon as a home for her father, herself, and child. Sidney Lanier and his family made this their home also, through 1873. (See Deed Book T, 247, Bibb County, Ga. Information through courtesy of Mrs. Frank Jones, Lowther Hall, Clinton, Gray, Ga.)

[57] Lanier was hoping for an election to the faculty of the University of Georgia. But both this and a scheme to enter the hotel business with his brother fell through (see Clifford Lanier's letter of Nov. 1).

To Virginia Hankins [58]

Macon, Ga
Nov. 9' 1868.

Dear Friend whom I never forget for one moment, may I not hear from you, sometimes? Do you not get my letters? Where are you? *What* are you, i. e., are you still Little Ginna Hankins, and not Ginna somebody-else? Are the sweet fall-mists and fall-sunlights kind to you, as of old? Do they bring you out-world dreams, do the days shed meeknesses of Christ upon you from their wings as they fly, over, do the nights come and sit by you like veiled friends and tell you (as they tell *me* of *you*) of

Your Faithful

Sidney Lanier?

To Charles and Caroline Campbell [59]

[Macon, Ga., Dec. 2, 1868]

My dear Charlie and Carrie:

I was too unwell last night to be at your reception; but I love you both so well that I *must* send you some little word, however modest, in the hope that it may live like a wayside flower among the rosy recollections of these most beautiful days in your life.

Believe therefore, Two dear Friends, that however I may be separated from you by the dreadful necessities of that unceasing work to which life condemns me, I still never forget to desire very heartily that you may know, as fully as I have known, the wonder and the glory and the holiness and the passionate purity of being wholly *one* in works and loves and aspirations: and I entreat you to remember that I look forward to some happy

[58] Previously published, and in facsimile, *Southern Literary Messenger*, II, 6 (Jan., 1940).

[59] Charles E. Campbell, Lanier's early flute instructor and war-time comrade, was married on Dec. 1, 1868, to Caroline Amelia Weed, of Macon. Lanier is said to have played Mendelssohn's *Wedding March* at the services in the First Presbyterian Church of Macon.

moment, in the days to come, when I may *prove* myself, rather than only *sign* myself,

Your Faithful Friend,

Sidney Lanier.

Macon, December 2nd "/68 [60]

[60] No letters by Lanier between Dec. 2, 1868, and Feb.(?), 1869, have survived. At some time during this period he began the study of law in the office of his father and his uncle, Clifford Anderson, supporting himself meanwhile by performing clerical duties for the firm. Although he had been turned aside from literature as a profession, his devotion to it was sustained through these next five years during which he tried to cast himself in the mold of a lawyer. Not the least of the influences that kept the hope of authorship alive in him was the encouragement of Paul H. Hayne (1830-1886)—the most prominent Southern poet of the period—as is witnessed by Hayne's letter of Dec. 5, 1868, in reply to a lost letter by Lanier, which read in part:

" Did I answer your last kind letter, written during convalescence? . . . Have you been able to get back your strength, & health by this time? – I *hope* so, and I venture to hope further, that all your energies are being employed upon some new Tale, or work of fiction which may *fully* carry out, & *emphasise*– so to speak–, the brilliant talent– displayed in ' Tiger-Lilies.'

" We have here, at this unfortunate *South* so few men of *your* order of ability, & learning, that really you *must* do 'your devoirs' to the *uttermost*, & in elevating yourself, elevate your Section.

" I've been reading 'T. L' *again,* & my first favorable impression is *amply* confirmed.

" Every now & then, too, I see in the columns of ' *the* R. Table' some little quaint, original, *suggestive* poem of yours, which bears the stamp of a decided individuality, both in expression, & fancy.

" Your last piece, for example, about the *Earth,* is peculiarly quaint, & pleasing. Sometimes, I can't help envying you your singular command of language, & rhythm, especially the wealth of your *similes*, which recall forcibly to mind the style of the lyric Poets of the Elizabethan Age."

The reference is to Lanier's poem, " The Ship of Earth" (I, 15), which had appeared in the *Round Table,* Nov. 14. Another poem published in 1868— in the *Round Table* of Oct. 24—but not mentioned in any of Lanier's letters that have survived, was " Resurrection " (I, 16).